The A to Z of
Washington, D.C.

Robert Benedetto
Jane Donovan
Kathleen DuVall

The A to Z Guide Series, No. 12

The Scarecrow Press, Inc.
Lanham, Maryland • Toronto • Oxford
2005

SCARECROW PRESS, INC.

Published in the United States of America
by Scarecrow Press, Inc.
A wholly owned subsidiary of
The Rowman & Littlefield Publishing Group, Inc.
4501 Forbes Boulevard, Suite 200, Lanham, Maryland 20706
www.scarecrowpress.com

PO Box 317
Oxford
OX2 9RU, UK

The A to Z of Washington, D.C. is a revised paperback edition of the *Historical Dictionary of Washington, D.C.*, by Robert Benedetto, Jane Donovan, and Kathleen DuVall, published by Scarecrow Press in 2003.

British Library Cataloguing in Publication Information Available

Library of Congress Cataloging-in-Publication Data

Benedetto, Robert, 1950–
   Historical dictionary of Washington, D.C. / Robert Benedetto,
Jane Donovan, Kathleen DuVall.
     p. cm.—(Historical dictionaries of cities of the world ; no. 12)
   Includes bibliographical references.
    1. Washington (D.C.)–History–Dictionaries. I. Donovan, Jane, 1956–
II. DuVall, Kathleen, 1964– III. Title. IV. Series.
F192 .B46   2003
975.3′003–dc21   2002066894

   ISBN 0-8108-5509-7 (pbk. : alk. paper)

♾ ™ The paper used in this publication meets the minimum requirements of American National Standard for Information Sciences—Permanence of Paper for Printed Library Materials, ANSI/NISO Z39.48–1992.
Manufactured in the United States of America.

ES FROM RESS, INC.

1. *The A to Z of Buddhism* by Charles S. Prebish, 2001.
2. *The A to Z of Catholicism* by William J. Collinge, 2001.
3. *The A to Z of Hinduism* by Bruce M. Sullivan, 2001.
4. *The A to Z of Islam* by Ludwig W. Adamec, 2002.
5. *The A to Z of Slavery & Abolition* by Martin A. Klein, 2002.
6. *Terrorism: Assassins to Zealots* by Sean Kendall Anderson and Stephen Sloan, 2003.
7. *The A to Z of the Korean War* by Paul M. Edwards, 2005.
8. *The A to Z of the Cold War* by Joseph Smith and Simon Davis, 2005.
9. *The A to Z of the Vietnam War* by Edwin E. Moise, 2005.
10. *The A to Z of Science Fiction Literature* by Brian Stableford, 2005.
11. *The A to Z of the Holocaust* by Jack R. Fischel, 2005.
12. *The A to Z of Washington, D.C.* by Robert Benedetto, Jane Donovan, and Kathleen DuVall, 2005.

Capitol during the January 1993 inauguration of President Bill Clinton.
Courtesy of Prints and Photographs Division, Library of Congress.

Contents

Preface   vii

Acknowledgments   ix

Maps   x

Chronology   xiii

Introduction   1

THE DICTIONARY   15

Bibliography   249

Appendix 1: Washington, D.C., at a Glance   301

Appendix 2: Washington History Collections   304

Appendix 3: Calendar of Annual Events   305

Appendix 4: Mayors, Governors, and Founding Commissioners   309

About the Authors   313

Preface

Washington, D.C., is the capital of the United States and a vibrant and diverse city of more than half a million residents. Located along the Potomac River in the mid-Atlantic region, the 69 square mile (179 square kilometer) city is home to grand federal buildings and monuments, and is one of the richest cultural centers in the United States. This book is devoted to the history of Washington, along with the neighboring municipality of Georgetown, absorbed by the city in the late nineteenth century.

Washington is a complex city composed of federal and municipal governments. This book includes articles on the most important federal buildings, including the Capitol, White House, and Supreme Court, representing the three branches of government; the Federal Triangle, a complex of federal office buildings; the city's historic military fortifications and installations; and such federally operated cultural entities as the Library of Congress, the National Archives, and the Smithsonian Institution. Also included are the historic Old Brick Capitol, Old Patent Office, Old Post Office, and Pension Building. Other architecturally significant federal buildings are listed only in appendix 5. While this book recognizes the vital role played by the federal government in the political, economic, cultural, and social life of the city, it does not attempt to cover the massive federal presence, with its buildings, programs, and personalities.

There are more than 130 monuments and memorials located throughout the city in the form of honorary plaques, statues, busts, and buildings. The most-visited federal memorials honoring Presidents Washington, Jefferson, and Lincoln are included herein, as well as a selection of buildings and sites honoring several twentieth-century presidents, including Theodore Roosevelt, Woodrow Wilson, and Franklin D. Roosevelt. A small selection of war memorials is also included: two honoring African Americans, the Black Patriots Memorial and the African American Civil War Memorial, as well as two memorials for twentieth-century wars, the Korean War Veterans Memorial and the Vietnam Veterans Memorial. This selection of memorials is but a small fraction of the honorary sites that dot the city.

The book includes biographical sketches, representing a cross-section of persons, both living and dead, who have made an impact on Washington. Biographical articles have been prepared for architects and city planners, artists, bankers, civil rights leaders, educators, historians, journalists, mayors and administrators, musicians and composers, philanthropists, photographers, real estate developers, religious leaders, scientists, singers and entertainers, and writers and poets. Some of these figures are native sons and daughters who found success outside Washington, and others are persons who moved to the District of Columbia and made a mark on the city. Little biographical coverage is given to U.S. presidents, with the exception of Washington, Jefferson, and Taft, who were particularly important in the development of the city; other presidents found their way into the book because of events that took place in the city (Lincoln, Garfield, Truman, and Reagan).

Washington is a city defined by its many neighborhoods. The exact number of these neighborhoods depends on how they are identified and counted in light of political, geographical, cultural, ethnic, and historical considerations. For the purpose of general description, this book groups the major areas of the city into twenty-six neighborhoods. This book offers a brief history of each neighborhood, as well as cross-references to some of their variant and historic names. The suburbs of metropolitan Washington and the nearby cities of Alexandria and Arlington, Virginia, are beyond the scope of this book, as are sites, buildings, airports, cultural centers, and other entities and organizations that lie outside the city boundary.

There are several hundred churches, synagogues, mosques, and other houses of worship in Washington, some of which are historically or architecturally significant. This volume includes articles on many of the churches founded during the early history of the city, as well as other houses of worship, representing many religious traditions, that have played an important role in the local life and history.

Finally, the book includes articles on important events, cultural organizations, parks, cemeteries, educational institutions, and performing arts organizations. Many political, scientific, social, civic, and business groups make their home in Washington and exercise influence in the city by hosting conferences and national conventions. Most of these organizations are listed in standard city directories and guides and, with the exception of the business-oriented Greater Washington Board of Trade, the National Geographic Society, and a few other groups, are not included herein.

Acknowledgments

Several people have been particularly helpful to us in the preparation of this book. We wish to acknowledge the help provided by Gail Redmann of the Historical Society of Washington, D.C., who responded to numerous questions and provided suggestions and comments during the course of our research. Other librarians and curators assisted by supplying research materials and photographs, including Peggy Appleman of the Washingtoniana Division of the Martin Luther King, Jr., Memorial Library; Matthew Gilmore, formerly of the MLK Library, and now on the editorial board of *Washington History*; Virginia S. Wood of the Humanities and Social Sciences Division, Library of Congress; Lucinda Janke of the Kiplinger Collection; and Donna Wells of the Moorland-Spingarn Collection at Howard University. We would like also to thank our editor, Jon Woronoff, for his knowledgeable guidance of the project over several years.

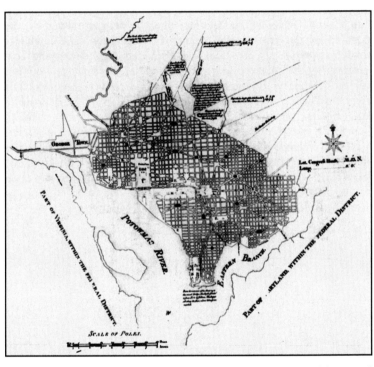

The 1790 L' Enfant Plan of Washington showing the size and layout of the future capital city.

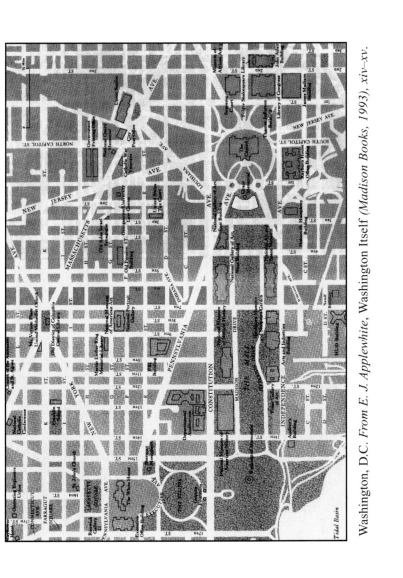

Washington, D.C. *From E. J. Applewhite, Washington Itself (Madison Books, 1993), xiv–xv.*

Chronology

The Colonial Era

1608   British Captain John Smith explores the Potomac River from the Jamestown settlement.

1634   Colonization of Maryland begins.

1662   First land patent granted on the future site of Washington, D.C.

1703   Ninian Beall acquires a 795-acre tract in the territory that would become Georgetown.

1712   St. Paul's Episcopal Church, Rock Creek Parish, is founded, the first house of worship in what would become the District of Columbia.

1715   Maryland land on which the federal city will be located is divided into the "Rock Creek Hundred."

1745   Tobacco inspection house is built at what is now the foot of Wisconsin Avenue in Georgetown.

1749   Town of Alexandria is created on the Potomac River in Virginia.

1751   Georgetown is chartered by the Maryland General Assembly on sixty acres of land on the Potomac River.

1752   Georgetown is surveyed into eighty lots.

1757   Robert Peter is elected to the Georgetown Board of Commissioners, eventually serving for more than three decades.

1765   Old Stone House is constructed in Georgetown.

1769   First racetrack is built in Georgetown.

1775   American Revolutionary War (–1783) fought for American independence.

1785   Construction of Patowmack Canal begins.

1787   U.S. Constitution is signed by the members of the Constitutional Convention.

1788   U.S. Constitution is ratified by the states: Article 1, Section 8, Clause 17 gives Congress exclusive legislative authority over the District of Columbia (not to exceed ten square miles) as the seat of the federal government. The states of Maryland and Virginia cede territory along the Potomac River for the site of the new federal city.

1789   George Washington becomes the first president of the United States. New York City is designated the first U.S. capital; the following year the capital is moved to Philadelphia. Georgetown is incorporated and local government is established by an act of the Maryland General Assembly. Georgetown University is founded.

1790   Permanent location of the U.S. capital city is born of a political compromise, whereby the northern states agree to place the capital in a central location in exchange for Southern support of federal assumption of all Revolutionary War debt incurred by the states. The Residence Act is passed by Congress, authorizing George Washington to choose a location for the national capital. A site is chosen on the east bank of the Potomac River between the mouth of the eastern branch Anacostia River and Conococheague Creek, seventy miles upstream, near Hagerstown, Maryland. The ten-mile square District of Columbia is drawn by the U.S. Congress and includes the existing towns of Georgetown and Alexandria. Robert Peter is elected Mayor of Georgetown and the following year surrenders half of his own land to the U.S. government for the national capital.

Construction of the National Capital

1791   George Washington appoints Thomas Johnson and Daniel Carroll of Rock Creek, representing Maryland, and David Stuart, representing Virginia, as commissioners for surveying the District of Columbia for a Federal City. Washington secures land for the federal city and hires French planner Pierre Charles L'Enfant to design the city. The Georgetown Council holds its first meeting. Stephen Bloomer Balch publishes two sermons, the first printing in the District of Columbia.

1792   Washington dismisses L'Enfant and hires Andrew Ellicott to map the federal city. Construction of the White House begins.

1793   Construction of the Capitol begins. The Bank of Columbia is chartered by the Maryland legislature and constructs its first building in Georgetown three years later.

1794   Stone masons walk off their jobs at the Capitol and White House, initiating the city's first strike.

1797   Georgetown-to-Frederick stagecoach line begins service.

1798   Racetrack is built at 17th Street and Pennsylvania Avenue NW.

1799   Rhodes Tavern is erected; it serves as city's first town hall. Navy Yard opens. Death of George Washington.

1800   U.S. capital is transferred from Philadelphia to Washington; President Adams moves into the unfinished White House and Congress meets in an unfinished Capitol. Three commissioners, appointed by the president, are given control of city government. Library of Congress is founded. *National Intelligencer* begins publication (–1869). The 1800 census reports the population of the new capital to be 10,006 whites, 793 free Negroes, and 3,244 slaves.

1801   Congress assumes jurisdiction over the District of Columbia and divides it into the counties of Washington and Alexandria.

1802   Washington City is incorporated by an act of Congress (amended 1804); its charter provides for a twelve-member elected city council and a mayor appointed by the president. Congress authorizes Thomas Law to build the Washington Canal. Robert Brent becomes Washington's first mayor.

1807   First public school for African Americans is established in Washington. Episcopalian Christ Church is completed on G Street SE.

1808   "Black code" laws are enacted by the city council, imposing restrictions on the lives of African Americans.

1810   Work on the Washington Canal begins along present-day
Constitution Avenue.

1811   Lancasterian School is founded in Georgetown.

The War of 1812 and
the Rebuilding of Washington

1812   War of 1812 begins (–1815). Congress amends the charter
of the City of Washington to provide for an eight-member
board of aldermen and a twelve-member common council,
with the aldermen and the common council to elect the
mayor. The city council adopts new restrictions on African
Americans, imposing, among other things, a 10 p.m. curfew.

1814   British forces raid and burn Washington, destroying the
White House, Capitol, and Library of Congress; rainstorms
save the city from complete destruction. President James
Madison moves to the Octagon. City banks offer $500,000
in loans to rebuild Washington. In Georgetown, African
American Methodists construct the city's first black
church, Mount Zion Church.

1815   U.S. Senate votes to keep the federal capital in Washington. The "Brick Capitol" building is constructed to temporarily house Congress until the Capitol can be rebuilt (–
1819). President Madison signs the Treaty of Ghent, ending the War of 1812. A large section of the Washington
Canal, running along the Mall, is completed.

1816   First publication of the District of Columbia law code.

1817   The White House is completed.

1819   The Capitol building and Decatur House are completed.

Growth of the City and
Municipal Government

1820   Washington receives a third charter of incorporation, which
provides for the election of a mayor by a vote of its citizens.

1821   Columbian College is founded; it is later renamed George Washington University.

1822   Patowmack Canal Company falls into bankruptcy. Washington Theater is destroyed by fire.

1824   Visit of Revolutionary War hero General Lafayette inspires the renaming of President's Square to Lafayette Square (–1825). Blair House is completed.

1827   New, more restrictive black code is enacted by city council.

1828   Construction of the Chesapeake and Ohio (C&O) Canal and the Baltimore and Ohio (B&O) Railroad begins.

1829   Influenza epidemic.

1830   Declining tobacco economy of Georgetown devastates the community (–1840). Jonathan Elliot publishes *Historical Sketches of the Ten Miles Square Forming the District of Columbia*.

1832   Cholera epidemic leaves 459 people dead.

1833   Washington Monument is authorized by Congress.

1835   Southard Report is submitted to Congress and recommends federal support for the city. B&O Railroad is extended to Washington. The "Snow Riots" occur, the first race riots in Washington. The bequest of James Smithson is received by the United States, leading to the creation of the Smithsonian Institution.

1836   William Corcoran opens a brokerage house in Georgetown that later becomes Riggs National Corporation, the oldest continuously operating bank in Washington.

1837   Economic panic sweeps through the national economy, but federal spending preserves Washington.

1838   Construction of the U.S. Treasury and Patent Office buildings begins.

1840   Mayor William Winston Seaton is elected to the first of five two-year terms (–1852).

1844   Samuel F. B. Morse transmits the first telegraph message, from the Supreme Court chambers in the Capitol to Baltimore, Maryland.

1846 Smithsonian Institution is established by an act of Congress. Street lamps are installed on Pennsylvania Avenue.

1847 County of Alexandria is ceded back to Virginia, reducing the size of the District of Columbia by a third, from 100 to 69 square miles.

1848 Congress adopts a fourth charter of incorporation for Washington, which abolishes a property qualification for voting in local elections and expands the number of elected offices to include a board of assessors, a surveyor, a collector, and a registrar. Seventy-six slaves attempt to escape from Washington on the sailing ship *Pearl*. Construction of the Washington Monument begins.

1849 Cholera epidemic.

1850 An act of Congress abolishes the slave trade, but not slavery, in the District of Columbia. The C&O Canal is completed from Georgetown to Cumberland, Maryland.

1851 Fire in the Capitol building destroys the Library of Congress.

1852 B&O Railroad opens a depot at New Jersey Avenue and C Street NE.

1853 Congress funds a water system for the city. Andrew Jackson equestrian statue is installed in Lafayette Square.

1855 Smithsonian Institution is completed. U.S. Naval Observatory begins publishing almanacs for astronomers and navigators.

1857 Know-Nothing riots. Congress authorizes a school for hearing- and sight-impaired children that later becomes Gallaudet University.

1860 Statue of George Washington is installed at Washington Circle. The city's first professional baseball team is organized.

The Civil War Era

1861 Civil War (–1865). Washington is at the center of war activities, with many public buildings temporarily converted to hospitals or army barracks. Forts are constructed around the perimeter of the city. A new police force under federal control is established in the city. Rose O'Neal Greenhow is arrested as a Confederate spy.

1862   Congress abolishes slavery in the federal district, freeing 3,100 slaves—the only compensated emancipation in the United States. First streetcars are used in Washington. Smallpox epidemic.

1863   President Abraham Lincoln issues the Emancipation Proclamation, freeing all slaves in the United States. Many former slaves move to the District of Columbia.

1864   An attack by Confederate forces under General Jubal Early is repulsed near Fort Stevens, saving the city. A fire department is established.

1865   Lincoln is assassinated in Ford's Theatre.

1867   Congress grants African American males the right to vote in local elections. Howard University is chartered by Congress.

1869   City council passes the city's first civil rights act.

1870   Georgetown's charter is repealed by Congress. The *New Era*, the city's first African American newspaper, edited by Frederick Douglass and Sella Martin, begins publication.

Federal Control of the City

1871   Congress passes the Territorial Act, ending municipal government in Washington and Georgetown (–1874). The act creates the District of Columbia, a combination of the governments of Georgetown, the City of Washington, and the County of Washington. The city is to be governed by a presidentially appointed governor and council; an elected, nonvoting delegate to Congress is also created. A seal and motto, "Justitia Omnibus" (Justice for All), is adopted. Alexander "Boss" Shepherd begins a public works program that transforms city services (–1874). Wormley Hotel is opened by African American businessman James Wormley.

1872   Smallpox epidemic. Two laws, later called the "lost laws," are passed that prohibit discrimination in public accommodations (–1873).

1873 Beginning of national economic depression (–1878); Washington's banks close, unemployment increases, and the city becomes bankrupt.

1874 City debt climbs to $19 million. Congress ends territorial government in the District of Columbia; the nonvoting delegate to Congress is abolished. President appoints three temporary commissioners and a subordinate military engineer to run Washington. Washington code, the Revised Statutes of the District of Columbia, codifies city laws enacted since 1801.

1876 Materials are shipped from the national centennial fair in Philadelphia for the Smithsonian Institution. Population of the District reaches 140,000.

1877 *Washington Post* is founded. Asaph Hall discovers the two moons of Mars from the U.S. Naval Observatory.

1878 Congress passes the Organic Act, which makes the commissioner system permanent. Two commissioners are to be civilians and a third is to be a member of the Army Corps of Engineers. Provision is made for a regular federal payment in lieu of taxes. This form of government lasts until August 1967. The Cosmos Club is organized.

1879 Clothing store is opened by Isadore Saks.

1881 Flood strikes the District, bringing major devastation to the city; six feet of flood waters cover the area between the Washington Monument and U.S. Capitol. President James Garfield is assassinated at the B&O Railway Station on the Mall. Clara Barton founds the American Red Cross.

1882 Filling of marshland is ordered and the Tidal Basin is constructed to control tide waters.

1884 Washington Monument is completed and dedicated (–1885).

1886 Four earthquakes strike the city.

1887 Catholic University of America is founded; its first class is admitted two years later.

1888 Great blizzard. Corcoran School of Art is founded. Gardiner Hubbard founds the National Geographic Society and becomes its first president. First electric streetcar. Washington Monument is opened to the public.

1889   Major flood in Georgetown begins its lengthy decline as an industrial center. Washington Board of Trade is organized. Gridiron Club is formed by Washington newspaper correspondents.

1890   Washington annexes the northern suburban communities of Mount Pleasant, Cleveland Park, and Woodley Park. Rock Creek Park is established. First cable cars run along 7th Street NW. Electric lights are installed in the White House. John Philip Sousa conducts a performance of his "*Washington Post* March" at the Smithsonian Institution.

1893   Economic depression (–1894). Cholera epidemic. Congress charters the National Cathedral Foundation, charged with building a national church in Washington.

1894   Coxey's "Army of the Unemployed" enters Washington. Historical Society of Washington is founded.

1895   An act of Congress incorporates Georgetown into the city of Washington, declares that the area should be known as "West Washington," and changes its street names to correspond with those in Washington.

1896   Potomac Electric Power Company is founded by O. T. Crosby. First automobile in the District.

1897   Tidal Basin is dredged by the Army Corps of Engineers to manage the Potomac River. Library of Congress moves from the Capitol into its own Jefferson Building. Corcoran Gallery of Art opens.

1898   Hubbard organizes the Washington Academy of Sciences.

Beautification of the City

1899   Congress passes the "Height of Buildings Act," which limits private construction to 14 stories. Great blizzard brings almost three feet of snow. Al Jolson makes his stage debut in Southwest Washington.

1900   Washington celebrates its centennial. The population reaches nearly 300,000, including 90,000 African Americans.

1901 President William McKinley establishes the McMillan Commission to develop a plan to beautify the city. New edition of the D.C. law code is published.

1902 McMillan Report to Congress recommends sweeping changes to the layout and beautification of the city.

1903 Carnegie Library is constructed on Mount Vernon Place and serves as the main public library of Washington until 1972.

1906 District Building at 14th Street and Pennsylvania Avenue NW becomes the official city hall. Train wreck at Terra Cotta Station.

1907 Board of Trade organizes the Washington Chamber of Commerce.

1908 Union Station is completed, at the time the largest train station in the world. Theodore Noyes becomes editor of the *Washington Star* (–1946).

1910 Congress creates the Fine Arts Commission and President William Howard Taft appoints Daniel Hudson Burnham chair of the commission. New building height restrictions allow a 20- to 50-foot increase over the 1899 law.

1912 Japan sends a gift of 3,000 cherry trees, which are planted around the Tidal Basin and other areas of the city. Washington branch of the National Association for the Advancement of Colored People is organized. Griffith Stadium is opened.

1913 John Whitelaw Lewis founds a building and loan association that later becomes the Industrial Bank of Washington, the only African American owned and operated commercial bank. African American YMCA is opened. Women's suffrage parade attracts 8,000 marchers on its Pennsylvania Avenue route.

1914 World War I begins (–1917). Congress passes the Alley Dwelling Act, which converts city alleys into streets or parks. Construction of the Lincoln Memorial begins.

1915   President Woodrow Wilson appoints Louis Brownlow to a five-year term on the D.C. Board of Commissioners.

1917   United States enters World War I. Temporary war buildings are constructed around the Mall. White House is picketed by women suffragists. Brownlow becomes president of the Board of Commissioners (–1920). The population of Washington reaches 400,000.

1918   Influenza epidemic; city manager Brownlow manages the crisis and institutes measures that save many lives. Wardman Park Hotel is constructed by Harry Wardman.

1919   General John Pershing returns from World War I, parading 25,000 troops along Pennsylvania Avenue before a crowd of about 400,000. Five days of summer race riots. John Whitelaw Lewis builds the African American Whitelaw Hotel. Hechinger Company is founded at 6th and C Streets SW.

1920   City manager Brownlow resigns to become city manager of Petersburg, Virginia.

1922   Lincoln Memorial is completed. Knickerbocker Theater collapses, killing 98 patrons.

1923   In collaboration with the American Institute of Architects, the Board of Trade revises the D.C. Building Code. The Public School Association is organized.

1924   Key Bridge is completed. J. Edgar Hoover becomes head of the Justice Department's Bureau of Investigation, which in 1935 becomes the FBI. Washington Senators baseball team wins World Series.

1925   Congress sets a $9 million dollar limit on the annual federal contribution to the District. Coolidge Auditorium and the Chamber of Commerce building are completed. More than 25,000 members of the Ku Klux Klan parade down Pennsylvania Avenue.

1926   Congress establishes the National Capital Park and Planning Commission for the improvement of the city. Public Buildings Act spurs construction of federal office buildings. Housing discrimination in Washington is upheld by the District Supreme Court, making it impossible for Afri-

can Americans to buy houses in white neighborhoods.
Carleton Hotel is constructed by Harry Wardman.

1927   Hay-Adams Hotel is constructed by Wardman. Brookings
Institution is established.

The Great Depression and World War II

1929   Stock market crashes and the Great Depression begins
(–1934). New edition of D.C. law code is published. Mellon Plan recommends consolidation of scattered federal
government offices into a unified symbol of national government. Constitution Hall opens.

1930   Construction of the Federal Triangle begins.

1931   Hunger march on Washington (–1932). Major public works
program is initiated in the city. National Symphony Orchestra is established.

1932   Economic depression hits Washington; salaries and jobs
are cut and banks close. "Bonus March" on Washington
leads to federal troops being called in response to the protests of World War I veterans who demand immediate payment of their war bonuses. Arlington Memorial Bridge begins operation. Constitution Avenue is named.

1933   President Franklin D. Roosevelt is inaugurated. Roosevelt
cuts 17,000 city residents from government pension rolls
as part of the Economy Act, but federal jobs in Washington
increase as a result of New Deal legislation. City banks
reopen. Folger Shakespeare Library opens. New Negro Alliance is established for equality in employment. Washington Senators win American League pennant.

1934   First Cherry Blossom Festival is held. Alley Dwelling Authority is created to clean up slums. Negro National
League is organized; Homestead Grays join league and
Griffith Stadium becomes one of their home fields (–
1949).

1935   Washington Transit System is established, merging all
streetcar and bus companies to a single system. National
Archives building is completed. Mary McLeod Bethune

founds the National Council of Negro Women.

1936 Congress passes the School Appropriation Act with a "Red Rider" clause that denies salary to any Washington teacher who teaches communism. City flood. Giant Food opens its first store, on Georgia Avenue NW.

1937 Department of Agriculture building, Supreme Court building, Federal Triangle, and Cannon House Office Building are completed. American University admits first African American students to its graduate school.

1939 Marian Anderson gives a concert for more than 75,000 people at the Lincoln Memorial, after being turned away from Constitution Hall because of her race. National Gallery of Art opens. Library of Congress Annex is completed and Archibald MacLeish is appointed Librarian of Congress.

1941 Pearl Harbor is bombed; United States enters World War II (–1945). National Gallery of Art opens. National Airport begins operation.

1942 Jefferson Memorial is dedicated.

1943 Washington Citizens' Committee on Race Relations is organized. Jefferson Memorial is completed.

1945 Congress passes the Redevelopment Act to rebuild the city's slum areas and construct new highways, parks, and public buildings. President Roosevelt's funeral procession makes its way to the White House.

The Civil Rights Movement
and the Cold War Era

1948 U.S. Senate's Strayer Report is highly critical of the city's public school system.

1950 Korean War (–1953). *District of Columbia v. Thompson Company* lawsuit results in desegregation of Washington's restaurants, theaters, and other public places. African American population of the city increases from 35 to 54 percent as new residents come from southern states. Planning Commission report proposes city improvements.

1951   Hecht Company begins serving African Americans; other stores and restaurants soon follow.

1952   Reorganization Plan transfers to three commissioners the functions of more than 50 district boards.

1953   D.C. Equal Services Act is upheld by the U.S. Supreme Court; enacted in the 1870s, it outlawed racial discrimination in restaurants and public places.

1954   Washington becomes the first U.S. city to introduce racial integration in the public school system.

1958   Washington Metropolitan Area Report studies the regional growth of the District of Columbia and makes recommendations to Congress. East front extension of the Capitol begins, adding a hundred new offices. Wesley Theological Seminary opens.

1959   Construction begins on the Capital Beltway around the city. Taft Memorial is dedicated. New Senate Office Building is completed.

1961   The 23rd Amendment to the Constitution gives District residents the right to vote in presidential elections. President John F. Kennedy plans renewal of Pennsylvania Avenue. Arena Stage theater opens. D.C. Stadium is completed (later renamed RFK Stadium). Woodrow Wilson Bridge and George Mason Bridge are constructed.

1962   Cuban Missile Crisis. Theodore Roosevelt Bridge constructed. Constance McLaughlin Green publishes Pulitzer Prize-winning book, *Washington: Village and Capital, 1800–1878*.

1963   U.S. military enters Vietnam War (–1973). During a civil rights march on Washington, Martin Luther King, Jr., delivers "I Have a Dream" speech to approximately 250,000 people gathered at the Lincoln Memorial.

1964   Washington citizens are able to vote in a presidential election for the first time since 1800.

1965   Washington Metropolitan Council of Governments is established. Rayburn House Office Building is completed.

1966   Washington Metropolitan Area Transit Authority is created through a compact among the District of Columbia, Maryland, and Virginia.

1967 President Lyndon Johnson's Reorganization Plan for Washington abolishes the three-member board of commissioners and provides for a presidentially appointed mayor, deputy mayor, and a nine-member council. Walter E. Washington is appointed mayor of Washington under the new plan. Federal City College is founded. Smithsonian Institution opens the Anacostia Neighborhood museum.

1968 Martin Luther King, Jr., delivers his last sermon at Washington National Cathedral. Following King's assassination in Memphis, Tennessee, Washington riots destroy parts of the old downtown and U Street NW. Poor People's March and Resurrection City encampment take place. City residents elect an 11-member Board of Education. D.C. Commission on the Arts and Humanities is founded. Anti-Vietnam War demonstrations take place on the Mall (–1973).

1969 Washington citizens are granted self-government and representation in the U.S. Senate and House of Representatives. Construction begins on the D.C. rapid transit system. More than 250,000 demonstrators urging the withdrawal of troops from Vietnam march down Pennsylvania Avenue.

1970 Washington gains an elected, nonvoting delegate to the U. S. House of Representatives. District courts are reorganized. Hugo J. Scott is the first African American to be appointed Superintendent of Schools for Washington, D.C. More than 100,000 people protest Vietnam War.

1971 Walter Fauntroy is elected the District's first representative to Congress in more than a century, but the seat carries no vote. Kennedy Center for the Performing Arts opens. C&O Canal is designated a national historic park.

1972 Bungled Republican break-in at the Democratic headquarters in the Watergate complex begins the Watergate scandal. The Martin Luther King, Jr., Memorial Library replaces the Carnegie Library as Washington's main public library.

Home Rule Returns

1973
Home Rule legislation, the District of Columbia Self-Government and Governmental Reorganization Act, passes Congress and establishes local government by an elected mayor and a 13-member city council.

1974
President Richard Nixon resigns as a result of Watergate scandal. Home Rule Charter is approved by D.C. voters and the first elections are held for mayor and city council.

1975
Washington voters elect a city council and a mayor, Walter Washington, for the first time in more than a century.

1976
U.S. bicentennial celebration takes place in Washington. First election for advisory neighborhood commissioners is held. Metrorail service begins.

1977
District Building is seized for three days by Hanafi Muslim terrorists.

1978
Congress passes a constitutional amendment allowing voting congressional representation for the District of Columbia, but approval by two-thirds of the states is never acquired, so the amendment dies. The first segment of the Metrorail Red Line opens.

1979
Mayor Marion Barry takes office for the first of four terms (–1991; 1994–98). U.S. farmers lead "tractorcade" to the Mall and stage protest.

1980
D.C. voters approved Statehood Initiative, which calls for convening a state constitutional convention.

1981
John Hinckley attempts to assassinate President Ronald Reagan outside the Washington Hilton Hotel.

1982
After a constitutional convention, a Constitution for the State of New Columbia is ratified by D.C. voters. Downtown Convention Center opens.

1984
District enters the municipal bond market. Old Post Office renovation is completed.

1986
Congress approves an amendment to the District of Columbia Stadium Act, which authorizes the transfer of Robert F. Kennedy Stadium from the federal government to the Dis-

trict of Columbia government.

1987   Metropolitan Washington Airport Authority is created to acquire National and Washington-Dulles International airports from the federal government. The authority begins operating the airports in June. St. Elizabeth's Hospital is transferred to the District of Columbia government.

1990   Washington National Cathedral is completed after seventy-three years of construction.

1991   Sharon Pratt Dixon becomes the first woman mayor of Washington.

1993   Bill proposing D.C. statehood is defeated in Congress. U.S. Holocaust Memorial Museum is dedicated.

1994   Marion Barry is elected to a fourth term as mayor.

1995   City reports $722 million debt; President Bill Clinton signs a law creating the presidentially appointed District of Columbia Financial Responsibility and Management Assistance Authority ("Financial Control Board") and a mayorally appointed Chief Financial Officer. Korean War Veterans Memorial is dedicated.

1996   Mayor Barry announces a plan to reduce the size of city government and increase its efficiency. Washington's population shrinks to 543,000.

1997   Financial Control Board given expanded authority over city government; reports budget surplus of $185 million. Reagan National Airport expansion is completed. MCI sports arena opens in downtown Washington.

1999   Agreement with Financial Control Board restores governmental power to mayor's office. Mayor Anthony Williams takes office.

2000   U.S. Census Bureau reports Washington's population at 572,000.

2001   September 11 Attacks destroy the southwest side of the Pentagon, killing 125 and 64 airline passengers; and anthrax-laced letters in the postal system disrupt mail service. The attacks lead to increased security in the capital.

2002   Beltway Sniper Attacks in the Washington metropolitan area take place over a three-week period in October; 10 people are killed and three are injured by spree killers.

2003   City Museum of Washington, D.C., opens in May.

Introduction

Washington is the capital of the United States, a national showplace of grand federal buildings, museums, and monuments and an international city of embassies and government offices. It is best known as the city of the U.S. Capitol, where Congress meets, and the White House, where the president lives. The buildings of the Smithsonian Institution, the government offices of the Federal Triangle, the Washington Monument, and the Mall are important city landmarks. Surrounding these public buildings and monuments are many historic neighborhoods, equally important in shaping the city's character, and home to an ethnically diverse population of approximately 572,000.

The city of Washington lies within a federal district, rather than a state. The District of Columbia was created from land donated by the states of Maryland and Virginia. The diamond-shaped tract was laid out in 1790 by surveyor Andrew Ellicott and mathematician Benjamin Banneker. In 1847 much of the southwest quadrant of the federal district was returned to Virginia so that the District no longer retains its original symmetry. It is now separated from Virginia by the Potomac River, and the state of Maryland lies along its northern and eastern borders. The city of Washington has grown to fill the entire federal district so that the municipality and the District of Columbia are now the same. While the city is confined to the District boundary of 69 square miles (179 square kilometers), a large metropolitan area extends beyond the city limits. Together with the city, the Washington metropolitan area is about 400 square miles (1,000 square kilometers) and has a population of about 5.4 million.

Pierre Charles L'Enfant planned Washington in four quadrants: Northwest, Northeast, Southeast, and Southwest, and these areas still designate the major sections of the city. These four quadrants radiate from the Capitol, one of the focal points of the city plan. Within the quadrants run wide, diagonal avenues named after states. Numbered streets run north and south, while lettered and named streets run east and west. The 13-story Capitol building symbolizes "the people" and, with the exception of the Washington Monument, District of Columbia law forbids the construction of buildings or other structures that rise above its height of 130 feet (40 meters). Architecturally, Washington is a mix of Federal-style office buildings, Baroque churches, Greco-Roman museums and memorials, Victorian-style townhouses, and Art Deco buildings and modern commercial centers. The McMillan Report (1902) resulted in the design and construction of several Beaux Arts buildings that inspire and delight tourists and residents. Many renowned architects have practiced in Washington, and in 1910 the city established a Commission of Fine Arts to oversee the development of the Washington skyline.

Government and Economy

The government of Washington is unique in that it functions as a state, county, and city. The executive branch of city government is the mayor's office, and the legislative branch is the Council of the District of Columbia. The council approves the city budget and financial plan; oversees various government agencies, commissions, committees, and boards; and issues reports and recommendations concerning the effectiveness of city government. Some of the duties performed by the Washington municipal government are normally state-level functions, including alcoholic beverage control, issuance of driver's licenses, food and drug inspection, maintenance of a state-level court system, and unemployment compensation. Interaction between the federal government and the Washington municipality has largely determined the growth, character, and fiscal health of the city from the time of its inception. Historically, the federal government has exhibited only periodic concern for the city, and modern Washington is a study in contrast between the grandeur of its federal buildings, museums, and monuments and the urban blight that troubles some areas of the city.

Congress granted self-government to Washington in December 1973, after 100 years of federal control. The district Home Rule Charter provided for an elected mayor, a city council composed of 13 members, and a nonvoting delegate to the U.S. House of Representatives. The local government is allowed to raise funds through taxation, but Congress retains control of the city budget and the power to overrule legislation enacted by the city. In 1975 Washington voters elected a city council, and Walter Washington became the first popularly elected mayor in more than a century. In 1993 a bill that would have granted statehood to the District of Columbia was defeated in Congress. In 1990 the city was embarrassed when Mayor Marion Barry was arrested and convicted for using drugs. Five years later the city reported a $722 million debt and Congress passed legislation that created a Financial Control Board to run the city government and reduce its debt. In 1997 the board was given expanded powers over the city and reported a budget surplus of $185 million. Power was restored to the mayor's office in 1999.

The federal government is by far the largest employer in the city, with more than 180,000 employees in Washington and many times this figure in the metropolitan area. Its presence has also attracted many business organizations, companies, trade unions, professional societies, and nonprofit organizations, which have established headquarters or offices in Washington to influence government legislation. These organizations bring with them many jobs that require professional skills and a highly educated workforce. Tourism is second in economic importance, with more than 20 million people visiting Washington each year. The city has developed new convention center facilities to support its growing popularity as a site of conferences and conventions. Education is the third largest employer, as Washington is an important center of higher education. The construction industry is also a major employer, as the needs of the federal government, private industry, and tourism demand offices, hotels, retail space, and residences in increasing numbers. Other important industries include banking, law, medical research, publishing, and telecommunications. The absence of large-scale manufacturing plants and heavy industry has helped to keep Washington a relatively clean city.

About two-thirds of Washington's workforce lives outside the city in suburban communities. The absence of this highly skilled workforce means a loss of potential tax revenue and a separation of the affluent suburbs from the more economically diverse city. The population of the city is predominantly African American (60 percent), with approximately 20 percent of city residents living below the poverty level. The city declined in population by 6 percent from 1990 to 2000, but the housing market remains strong as new Asian and Hispanic immigrants have moved to Washington and existing residents have formed new families. Some city neighborhoods have undergone a process of "gentrification," whereby existing apartments and single-family rental housing have been turned into condominiums and renovated dwellings, forcing out lower-income renters.

The city has a transportation network that utilizes all forms of public and private transportation. The metropolitan area is served by the Washington Metrorail System, a rapid transit system that covers more than 100 miles of tracks; a network of bridges and highways, including the 67-mile (108-km) Capitol Beltway that surrounds the city; and rail service from Virginia and Maryland by Amtrak and the Maryland Rail commuter rail services to Union Station, a centralized train terminal that grew out of the McMillan Plan of 1902 and was fully renovated and restored during the 1980s. The city is also served by the Metrobus system, with about 400 routes and 13,000 stops, and by more than 10,000 taxicabs. Those who must drive in Washington will find that parking is nearly impossible in many neighborhoods, including Adams Morgan, Dupont Circle, Georgetown, and areas near the Mall. The Washington area has three airports: Reagan National Airport which lies just across the Potomac River in Virginia; Dulles International Airport which is located 25 miles (40 km) west of the city, also in Virginia; and the Baltimore-Washington International Airport which is about the same distance northeast of Washington, in Maryland.

Cultural Life

Although the city of Washington had long aspired to be a national cultural center, prior to World War I it was largely an artistic backwater. The city lacked cultural facilities, art collections, and strong educational institutions. One of the most dramatic changes to the city in the latter part of the 20th century has been its meteoric rise as a cultural center. Famous for its jazz clubs on U Street during the early part of the century, the performing arts life of the city greatly expanded with the founding of Arena Stage (1950), the restoration of historic Ford's Theater (1968) where President Lincoln was shot, the construction of the John F. Kennedy Center for the Performing Arts (1971), and the organization of the Washington Ballet, the Washington Opera, and the National Symphony Orchestra. The city now boasts a wide range of artistic venues with first-class facilities.

During the 19th century, the cultural and artistic collections of Washington were limited to those of the Library of Congress, the Smithsonian Institution, and the Corcoran Gallery of Art (1871). However, largely through the generosity of private benefactors, the city of Washington is now home to more than 30 museums and galleries, including the privately owned Phillips Collection (1920s and 1930s), the Freer Gallery of Art (1923), the National Gallery of Art (1941), the National Portrait Gallery (1958), the Hirshhorn Museum and Sculpture Garden (1966), the National Museum of American Art (1968), the Arthur M. Sackler Gallery (1987), the National Museum of African Art (1987), and others. The city's Museum of Natural History, National Air and Space Museum, and other museums and galleries are among the world's finest. The social, cultural, and political history of the United States is commemorated in more than 130 monuments and memorials located throughout the city; among these are the Washington Monument, the Lincoln Memorial, and the Jefferson Memorial.

Washington's educational institutions have been greatly strengthened during the 20th century. The city now contains 18 institutions of higher learning, and the Washington workforce is one of the most educated in the United States. The District's six major institutions are American University, Catholic University of America, George Washington University, Georgetown University, Howard University, and the University of the District of Columbia. Together with Gallaudet University for the deaf, these schools are part of the Consortium of Universities, which offers a combined faculty and access to various undergraduate and graduate courses of study. In addition to these schools, the Department of Agriculture Graduate School offers a large curriculum to the public. These centers of learning are supported by their own expansive research libraries and by the world-renowned Library of Congress, the National Archives, and many specialized Washington libraries and research centers, such as the Folger Shakespeare Library, the Smithsonian Institution, the National Geographic Society Library, and the United States Chamber of Commerce business library. Washington has nearly 500 public and private libraries, making it one of the largest information centers in the world.

The city has a diverse religious life. The presence of Catholic University of America, Georgetown University, and the National Shrine of the Immaculate Conception (the largest Roman Catholic church in the United States) makes it a center of Roman Catholic faith and intellectual life. The city is also an important center of the Episcopal Church. The largest church in the city is the Episcopal Cathedral Church of St. Peter and St. Paul, known as the Washington National Cathedral. St. John's Episcopal Church, located near the White House, is one of the most historic churches in the city. Other historic churches are affiliated with Baptist, Lutheran, Methodist, and Presbyterian denominations. The city's Islamic Center is an important place of Muslim intellectual life and culture, and its first synagogue, Old Adas Israel Synagogue, contains the Lillian and Albert Small Jewish Museum, which documents Jewish life and history in Washington.

Parks and Recreation

With approximately 6,800 acres of federal parklands, Washington has become a city of parks and gardens as envisioned by L'Enfant. The premier park is the 2,800-acre Rock Creek Park, established in 1890. The park runs through the heart of the city, providing space for the National Zoo and about 15 miles (24 km) of hiking and riding trails. Other parks include Anacostia Park, the wooded paths of the Chesapeake and Ohio Canal, Constitution Gardens, the Mall, the National Arboretum, Potomac Park, and Theodore Roosevelt Island, a bird sanctuary. Washington also has many formal gardens, including the 10-acre Dumbarton Oaks garden, Enid Haupt Memorial Garden, the U.S. Botanic Gardens, the Kenilworth Aquatic Gardens, and other gardens and floral collections.

The city is home to several professional sports teams, including the Washington Redskins football team, the Washington Wizards basketball team, and the Washington Capitals ice hockey team. In the past, the city has been home to the Homestead Grays and Washington Senators baseball teams, and horse racing was a favorite pastime of its citizens until the last track was closed in 1908. Rowing is a popular sport on the Potomac River.

The Selection of the National Capital

The Washington area was explored by Captain John Smith, who sailed from Jamestown in 1608 and reported Nacostin Indian settlements along the banks of the Potomac. By mid-century the village of Nachotanke had become an important trading center. These same lands were granted to Scottish settlers by the early 1700s, and a half-century later the towns of Alexandria (1749) and George (1751) were founded; both grew into busy port cities, which prospered from the trade in tobacco.

After the Revolutionary War (1775–83), representatives of the newly independent American states drafted the Constitution (1787), which authorized the creation of a capital city, of not more than 10 miles square, to house the seat of government. The Constitution was ratified by all of the states, and George Washington became the first president of the country. In 1790 Congress passed the Residence Act, which gave President Washington the authority to select a site for the new capital city, "somewhere in the Potomac region." Northern and southern states equally coveted the federal capital, and a compromise was reached between Alexander Hamilton and Thomas Jefferson whereby the northern states would agree to place the capital in a central location if the southern states would support federal assumption of all Revolutionary War debt incurred by the states. The compromise worked, and Washington chose a site on the banks of the Potomac River, straddling the border between Maryland and Virginia.

In 1791 Washington hired French architect and planner Pierre Charles L'Enfant of the Continental Army staff to design the city and appointed three commissioners to run it. The commissioners named the capital Washington City. L'Enfant drew part of his inspiration from Paris, incorporating wide boulevards that intersect at park-filled circles, a vast expanse of rectangular open space from the Capitol to the Potomac River, a grand residence for the president, and monumental buildings and parks. Jefferson thought the plan, which envisioned a city of 800,000, was grandiose—and compared to his own smaller plan, it was. Congress was satisfied with the L'Enfant design, but not with the designer, who forged ahead with the plan, regardless of orders and budget considerations. When L'Enfant discovered that prominent landowner Daniel Carroll was building a house in the middle of one of his planned avenues, he quarreled with Carroll and had the foundation of the house demolished. The temperamental planner was dismissed by President Washington in 1792, but his masterful city plan went forward, beginning with the construction of the President's House and the Capitol in 1792 and 1793.

In 1800 Congress finally moved from Philadelphia to Washington, after sitting in several different cities during the first years of national life. Congressional representatives and the entire clerical staff of the federal government, which numbered only 137 employees, relocated to the small town. Two years later the city received its first charter. George Washington appointed its first mayor and a town council was publicly elected. The entire federal district had a population of only 8,000 and the city of Washington was popularly known as "Wilderness City," lacking paved streets, public amenities, and a cultural life befitting a national capital. Some of the land was marsh and the threat of malaria and cholera clouded the future of the city. The climate, too, was inhospitable, with hot, humid summers and cold, damp winters. Several attempts were made to relocate the unpromising capital to a more salubrious area.

The War of 1812 and the Growth of the City

Washington was attacked by British troops in August 1814. The troops burned Washington's few public buildings, including the President's House and the Capitol. When the fire-blackened walls of the President's House were painted white during reconstruction, its name was changed to the White House. The collection of books known as the Library of Congress was also lost in the flames. This devastation came as another blow to the struggling federal city, and there were renewed calls in Congress to move the capital. The city of Philadelphia tried to win over the legislators in a renewed bid for the seat of government. However, by the following year these attempts had failed and the repair and construction of federal buildings began. These public buildings were supported by an infrastructure of shops, taverns, and houses, built on the rural and floodplain lands of the federal city, often in a haphazard fashion that would have infuriated its original planners. The commercial centers of Georgetown and Alexandria helped to sustain the city. Washington continued to be governed by its town council, which from 1812 to 1820 appointed a mayor; thereafter city residents elected both the mayor and council.

Between 1820 and 1860 the federal city experienced a host of economic and social crises. In 1828 construction began on the Chesapeake and Ohio (C&O) Canal, which would eventually connect Georgetown with Cumberland, Maryland, but the cost of the 20-year project greatly accelerated public debt, and the canal never realized its economic promise as a means of transporting goods from the west to the port of Georgetown. The canal was eventually overtaken by the Baltimore and Ohio (B&O) Railroad, which opened a depot at New Jersey Avenue and C Street NE in 1852. During the 1830s the declining tobacco economy of Georgetown badly affected local economic conditions. The cholera epidemic of 1832 left more than 450 people dead, and another epidemic struck in 1849. In 1835 the city suffered its first race riot, called the "Snow Riots." Two years later an economic recession swept through the country, but federal spending in Washington managed to preserve the city. As a result of a declining economy and competition from the B&O Railroad, the port city of Alexandria desired its independence and was allowed to secede from the District of Columbia in 1847. The land south of the Potomac River originally donated by the state of Virginia was returned to that state, reducing the size of the 10-mile-square district by a third. Georgetown also tried to secede, but the state of Maryland refused to accept the municipality, and it was eventually annexed by Washington. In 1851 a fire in the Capitol building again destroyed the Library of Congress.

Amid these troubled times, a few successful enterprises were harbingers of better days to come. In 1835 a bequest of James Smithson was received by the U.S. government, and in 1846 Congress established the Smithsonian Institution; its first building was completed in 1855. In 1836 William Corcoran opened a brokerage house in Georgetown that later became Riggs National Bank, one of Washington's leading financial institutions. Construction of the U.S. Treasury and Patent Office buildings began in 1838. And in 1844 Samuel F. B. Morse transmitted the first telegraph message, from Washington to Baltimore, Maryland, bringing a new era of communications to the nation and its capital city.

The Civil War

During the late 1840s the questions of slavery and states' rights increased tensions between northern and southern states. The political Compromise of 1850 succeeded in abolishing the slave trade, but not slavery, in the city. This act of Congress only postponed the inevitable day of reckoning on the issue of slavery, and the strained relations between the northern and southern states were deeply felt in Washington. "Black codes" had been enacted by the Washington town council in 1808 and 1827 that restricted its African American population. Still, the city was more tolerant, and its African American population rapidly increased as it gained a reputation in the South for its more liberal views.

When Abraham Lincoln arrived in Washington for his first inaugural in 1861, there were rumors of an assassination plot and the president-elect was transported to the Willard Hotel in secret. Lincoln realized that Washington was compromised by its location in the South, and he quickly transformed the city into an armed camp, stationing thousands of Union troops there and ringing the city with a series of military fortifications. The population of Washington was suspect, and Lincoln established a new city police force under federal control. During the first year of the war Rose O'Neal Greenhow was arrested as a Confederate spy. Still, with the exception of sporadic raids on the C&O Canal and General Jubal Early's failed 1864 attack on Fort Stevens, the city was never seriously threatened. However the capture of Washington remained a goal of the Confederacy and periodic rumors of "Confederates at the city limits" took a psychological toll on the population.

A more serious psychological strain was the sight and sound of the wounded and the dead who were transported to the city from nearby battlegrounds in Virginia and Pennsylvania. The public buildings of the city, including the Capitol, became makeshift hospitals. Poet Walt Whitman and American Red Cross founder Clara Barton tended to the wounded in some of these hospitals. Lincoln himself would not be spared in the ordeal, later being assassinated by Confederate sympathizers at Ford's Theatre in 1865.

In 1862 Congress abolished slavery in the District of Columbia, freeing 3,100 slaves. The following year Lincoln delivered the Emancipation Proclamation, freeing all American slaves. Many of these newly freed slaves moved to Washington after the war. During the early 1870s Washington's African American population grew to approximately 35,000, triple its prewar size. The balance of the population also increased, so that after the war there was a serious housing shortage and an urgent need to upgrade the city's infrastructure and services. The city was in such poor condition that some members of Congress again urged that the capital be moved, this time to the Midwest.

Federal Control of the City

The squalid condition of Washington called for drastic measures. In 1871 Congress completely reorganized city government by passing the Territorial Act. This legislation created the Territory of Washington, with its own governor and legislature, a nonvoting delegate to the U.S. House of Representatives, and several oversight boards, including a health commission and a five-member Board of Public Works. Alexander "Boss" Shepherd became the head of the Board of Public Works and began a massive program to upgrade the city's infrastructure. Streets and sidewalks were paved and lighted. The open sewers that had been part of the Washington landscape for many years were finally upgraded with new sewer lines. About 100,000 trees were planted. And for the first time, the city of Washington enjoyed some of the amenities of 19th-century urban life.

President Ulysses S. Grant appointed Shepherd territorial governor in 1873. At first a hero who transformed Washington, it was soon revealed that the autocratic Shepherd had been a reckless manager, giving large parts of the municipal work to political and personal allies and running up a huge debt that the city could not repay. Shepherd himself was bankrupted and left town six years later to work in Mexico, where he died. Congress was forced to bail out the city, and in retribution the irritated legislators took away its status as an independent territory. In 1878 the District of Columbia became a municipal corporation run by three commissioners appointed by the president. The city would not be allowed to rule itself again until 1975.

The period of the 1870s to 1890s saw other changes in the city. New growth came through the annexation of Georgetown in congressional acts of 1871 and 1895 and through the absorption of Cleveland Park, Mount Pleasant, and other northern suburban communities in 1890. The flood of 1881 brought major devastation, as six feet of floodwaters covered the area between the Washington Monument and the Capitol. The following year the Army Corps of Engineers brought in landfill and created the Tidal Basin to control tide waters. Rock Creek Park was established in 1890, giving the city one of its premier open spaces. The Washington Monument was completed and dedicated in 1884–85, and the Potomac Electric Power Company was founded by O. T. Crosby in 1896.

Beautification of the City

The city had survived difficult economic times during the last quarter of the 19th century, including the Boss Shepherd fiasco and the economic depression of 1893–94 that prompted Coxey's "Army of the Unemployed" to march on Washington. By 1900 the population of the city had grown to 300,000, including 90,000 African Americans. With little housing left, the newcomers were crowded into the service alleys of the city, where they lived in unsanitary, makeshift housing. In 1901 Senator James McMillan of Michigan attempted to clean up Washington and transform the city. As chairman of the Senate's District Committee, McMillan was influenced by the "City Beautiful" movement that was sweeping the country. He assembled a distinguished commission, composed of architect Charles F. McKim, land-scape architect Frederick Law Olmsted, Jr., and sculptor Augustus Saint-Gaudens, to study the city plan and to make suggestions for beautifying Washington.

The McMillan Commission made a tour of several European cities and its Senate report of 1902 suggested sweeping changes, including a return to the original L'Enfant design as the basis of Washington's city plan. New memorials and parklands were to be constructed, the Mall was to function as a ceremonial place, Union Station was to be constructed as a major transportation center, and monumental federal office buildings were planned. In 1910 a permanent Fine Arts Commission was appointed by Congress. This commission has since become the arbiter of the McMillan Plan and the controlling architectural body of the city. Although not all of the proposed changes were implemented, the plan eventually succeeded in returning the city to the grandeur originally envisioned by L'Enfant.

The Great Depression and War Years

The coming of World War I interrupted the work of the Fine Arts Commission, as Washington was again militarized. The city hosted fewer soldiers than it did during the Civil War, but the employment of government workers and various kinds of support personnel soared. Washington grew into a city of policy makers, who sought to resolve world conflicts and problems. To meet the demands of the war effort, temporary buildings were constructed along the Mall and Pennsylvania Avenue, marring the landscape.

Washington's population increased during the 1930s, when hundreds of federal jobs were created through President Franklin Roosevelt's "New Deal" program to combat the economic depression that troubled the nation. World War II further accelerated urban growth in Washington. Office and living space in the city grew scarce and boarding houses sprang up overnight in many of Washington's row house neighborhoods. New agencies and programs were created, and the city was transformed by the influx of military personnel, federal employees, and offices and agencies involved in wartime planning and support. Between 1930 and 1950 the city grew from around 486,000 to 802,000, and the urban population of the city expanded beyond the boundaries of the District of Columbia into Maryland and Virginia. By the end of the 1950s African Americans constituted the majority of Washington's population, and the city represented 28 percent of the population of the Washington metropolitan area.

The Civil Rights Movement, Urban Problems, and Majestic Washington

During the 1960s and 1970s the civil rights struggle, the Vietnam War, and the effort to eliminate poverty in America inspired numerous marches and sit-ins in the nation's capital, with some of these events leading to violence and the arrest of participants. In 1963 Martin Luther King, Jr., delivered his famous "I Have a Dream" speech on the steps of the Lincoln Memorial to a crowd of 250,000. In 1968, he was assassinated in Tennessee and there was rioting in many American cities, including Washington. The four-day Washington riots badly damaged the Shaw neighborhood and businesses along the 14th Street corridor, and some of the devastation lasted for decades. Along with rapid urbanization have come poverty, illegal drugs, street crime, substandard housing, traffic congestion, and water pollution. Urban Washington has also experienced rapid population changes, and the city has worked to assimilate Asians, Hispanics, and other ethnic groups.

The many tourists who come to Washington to view its treasures now see a well-planned federal city, but the capital was very slow to take shape and many infrastructure and economic improvements came only during the last quarter of the 20th century. Major urban improvements such as the Capital Beltway around the city, the Washington Metro, the MCI Center and the renewal of the downtown commercial district, and the historic restoration of public and privately owned buildings have enhanced the quality of life in Washington. The city's growing telecommunications, service, and tourist industries and opportunities in higher education have provided new jobs for city residents. Washington has finally come to approximate the grandeur of its original design as envisioned by L'Enfant. The city's parks, tree-lined streets, wide avenues, majestic government buildings, and monuments and museums have come together in a way that makes the nation's capital a marvel of the 21st century.

The Dictionary

- A -

ADAMS, HENRY BROOKS (1838–1918). Historian and writer. The grandson and great-grandson of Presidents John Quincy Adams and John Adams, respectively, Henry Adams graduated from Harvard in 1858 and served as personal secretary to his father, Charles Francis Adams, Lincoln's ambassador to England during the **Civil War**. He later taught history at Harvard and coedited the *North American Review* with Henry Cabot Lodge. In 1872 Adams married photographer Marian "Clover" Hooper (1838–1885), and in 1877 moved to H Street NW in Washington, where they and neighbors Secretary of State John Hay and his wife Clara entertained the leading intellectuals of the time. The Hay and Adams houses were demolished in 1926 for construction of the **Hay-Adams Hotel**. Adams wrote a nine-volume *History of the United States during the Administrations of Thomas Jefferson and James Madison*; the political satire *Democracy*; biographies of **Thomas Jefferson**, Albert Gallatin, and John Randolph; and one of the classics of American literature, *The Education of Henry Adams*. When Clover Adams committed suicide in 1885, her husband commissioned a memorial to be placed at **Rock Creek Cemetery**. The statue, now popularly known as "Grief," was sculpted by Augustus Saint-Gaudens.

ADAMS BUILDING. *See* LIBRARY OF CONGRESS.

ADAMS MORGAN. Washington's most economically and culturally diverse neighborhood, located in the city's northwest quadrant. Adams Morgan is a vibrant enclave, with restaurants, shops, and nightlife that attract tourists despite parking problems, a housing shortage, and occasional street crime. The modern boundaries of Adams Morgan were established in the late 1950s. The area in-

---

Users of this volume should note that cross-references in each dictionary entry are printed in boldface type.

cludes portions of four late 19th-century neighborhoods: Meridian Hill, Lanier Heights, Washington Heights, and Kalorama Heights. These older neighborhoods, sitting on the hills above Boundary Street (now Florida Avenue), were some of Washington's earliest residential suburbs. **Mary Henderson** spent decades promoting 16th Street as the "Avenue of the Presidents" and built nearly a dozen ornate houses on Meridian Hill between 1888 and 1910, including her Victorian "Henderson Castle." In the early 20th century, several of the city's most expensive apartment buildings were erected in Adams Morgan, as were many row houses. By 1917, when the Knickerbocker Theater and the Avignon Freres catering company opened for business, the area was associated with wealth and social elitism.

During and after World War II, Washington experienced a dramatic housing shortage, and many Adams Morgan row houses were converted to boarding houses. Affluent residents migrated to the suburbs, and housing costs in the neighborhood fell dramatically, attracting working- and middle-class families. After public **school desegregation** in 1954, local citizens fought for control of the two elementary schools for which the neighborhood is named, the mostly white Adams School and the mostly black Morgan School. In 1958 the principals of the two schools helped organize the Adams Morgan Better Neighborhood Conference, an advocacy organization for civic improvements.

In the 1960s many of Washington's communes, collectives, and freedom houses were located in Adams Morgan, and a number of political activists took up residence there. The **riots of 1968** decimated the Adams Morgan commercial district, centered along 18th Street and Columbia Road, and many businesses were forced to close or relocate.

Many Spanish-speaking diplomats, international civil servants, and their employees had settled in Adams Morgan during the 1950s. From the 1960s to the 1980s hundreds of Central and South American immigrants also settled in Adams Morgan, and the neighborhood gradually became the home of Washington's Latino community. Small grocery stores, churches, and Carlos Rosario's Colony Theater became places of commercial activity, information, and community building. Rosario, who was born in Puerto Rico, came to the United States to work for the Department of Health, Education, and Welfare and subsequently established the city's first Latino theater program in 1962. Rosario was instrumental in convincing the D.C. government to establish an Office of Latino Affairs in 1969.

In the 1970s and 1980s Adams Morgan's population changed still more, as Africans, Asians, and young urban professionals settled there. In May 1991, the Cinco de Mayo riots in **Mount Pleasant**, protesting the police shooting of a Hispanic man during a routine arrest, spilled over into Adams Morgan. Community leaders formed the D.C. Latino Civil Rights Task Force to investigate the incident and to help find solutions to the community's economic and social problems. *See also* KNICKERBOCKER THEATER COLLAPSE.

ADAS ISRAEL. The first Jewish congregation to build its own synagogue in Washington, in 1876 on 5th Street NW. Adas Israel was founded by 35 families who left the **Washington Hebrew Congregation** in the late 1860s, when worship practices were liberalized there. After the Adas Israel congregation moved to a new building in 1908, the original structure became a Greek Orthodox church and then a restaurant. In 1969, rather than destroy the historic site, the D.C. government, which by then owned it, rented the building to the Jewish Historical Society of Greater Washington. It now houses the **Lillian and Albert Small Jewish Museum** and Archives. Adas Israel, a Conservative synagogue, is now located at Connecticut Avenue and Porter Street NW.

ADVISORY NEIGHBORHOOD COMMISSIONS. Neighborhood government advisory bodies. The Home Rule Act of 1973 authorized Washington's City Council to create 36 Advisory Neighborhood Commissions (ANCs) and 376 smaller single-member districts. Each serves about 2,000 residents. ANC meetings provide an opportunity for city residents to influence local policies and legislation, criticize the performance of city agencies and workers, and express views on everything from trash collection to police protection. The system has achieved varying degrees of success, being dependent upon the personalities of individual commissioners and the activism of local residents. The ANCs were intended to replace **Citizens' and Civic Associations**, although they have generally been less effective than the old volunteer organizations.

AFRICAN AMERICAN CIVIL WAR MEMORIAL. Monument to the more than 200,000 African Americans who served in the Union

Army during the **Civil War** and to the 7,000 white officers who led them. Dedicated in 1998, the memorial is located at U Street and Vermont Avenue NW, in the heart of the **Shaw** neighborhood, which is named for Robert Gould Shaw, commander of the legendary black 54th Massachusetts regiment. The memorial features a series of stainless steel panels bearing the names of the volunteer U.S. Colored Troops and their officers. A statue depicting a line of Civil War infantry and sailors and their waiting families is being added to the memorial by sculptor Ed Hamilton.

AFRICAN ART. *See* NATIONAL MUSEUM OF AFRICAN ART.

AFRICAN CONTINUUM THEATRE COMPANY. Washington's only African American-led theater company. The organization began in 1991 as the African Continuum Theatre Coalition (ACT), a service group established to develop black professional theater companies. Only one constituent group, the American Theatre Project in **Anacostia**, ever formed; it was artistically successful but not financially viable, and it closed in 1996. The coalition then became a company without a home theater, staging four productions between 1996 and 1999, including the **Helen Hayes** Award-winning "Torn from the Headlines," written by the company's artistic director, Jennifer Nelson. In early 2000, the African Continuum Theatre Company moved to the American Film Institute theater at the **John F. Kennedy Center for the Performing Arts.**

AIR AND SPACE MUSEUM. *See* NATIONAL AIR AND SPACE MUSEUM.

AIR FLORIDA PLANE CRASH. Airline disaster that occurred on January 13, 1982. Air Florida flight 90, a Boeing 737, took off from National Airport in a snowstorm and crashed into the 14th Street bridge, which was crowded with rush-hour traffic. The plane hit five cars and went nose-first into the frozen **Potomac River**. It punctured the ice and stuck there, with only the tail protruding. Rescue attempts were undertaken in the midst of hundreds of bystanders, and eight people were eventually rescued. In all, 78 people died, including five motorists who were crossing the bridge.

ALEXANDRIA. *See* RETROCESSION OF ALEXANDRIA.

ALL SOULS UNITARIAN UNIVERSALIST CHURCH. Unitarian congregation located at 16th and Harvard Streets NW. All Souls was founded in 1821 as First Unitarian Church at 6th and D Streets

NW. In 1877 the congregation moved to 14th and L Streets NW and adopted its current name. A new building, based on England's best known Baroque church, St. Martin-in-the-Fields, was designed by Henry Shepley and constructed in 1924. Many government leaders have worshiped at the church, including John C. Calhoun, Daniel Webster, Charles Sumner, and Presidents Millard Fillmore and **William Howard Taft**, whose funeral was conducted there. Pastors such as Ralph Waldo Emerson, Edward Everett Hale, and community activist David Eaton have maintained the church's tradition of social activism.

ALLEY DWELLINGS. Tenement buildings in the service alleys of Washington's residential neighborhoods. The alley dwelling problem came about because of the city plan of **Pierre Charles L'Enfant**, who drew Washington's streets and avenues with deep, wide building lots. Individual property owners found that they could profitably rent out the small section of their property that faced the service alleys. After the **Civil War**, an influx of freed slaves caused a housing shortage in Washington. Shacks of discarded materials were constructed in alleys throughout the city. In 1872 more than 25,000 people lived in alley dwellings without sanitation. The names of some of these alleys reflected their character: Louse Alley, Moonshine Alley, and Blood Alley. In 1914 Congress enacted the Alley Dwelling Act, which outlawed the building of residential structures in alleys. The act was later judged unconstitutional. The alley dwelling issue was addressed again in the 1930s when the **National Capital Park and Planning Commission** established the Alley Dwelling Authority, which relocated alley residents and cleaned up the alleys. The agency became the National Capital Housing Authority, which later oversaw the building of public housing in the city. By the 1950s the alley dwelling problem had been eradicated.

AMERICAN COLONIZATION SOCIETY. Private organization established in Washington in 1816 for the purpose of repatriating freed slaves to Africa. Presbyterian clergyman Robert Finley and **U.S. Supreme Court** clerk Elias B. Caldwell, inspired by British colonization in Sierra Leone, drew local and national officials into the Colonization Society, including Henry Clay, **Francis Scott Key**, and Andrew Jackson. Finley and Caldwell had a high purpose for the enterprise, including the eventual abolition of **slavery** in the

United States and religious evangelism in Africa by the settlers, but the organization fell under the control of slave-holding southerners, who wished to rid the country of free blacks. In 1822, with an appropriation of $100,000 from the U.S. government, the Colonization Society purchased 1,000 square miles of land on the West African coast and formed the colony of Liberia. The vast majority of African Americans opposed colonization; some families had been in America for two centuries by then, and few had any direct connection to Africa. By 1867 when the society dissolved, more than 18,000 Americans had been transported to Africa. The Colonization Society constructed a headquarters building at **Pennsylvania Avenue** and 4th Street NW in 1860; it was demolished in the 1930s when Constitution Avenue was extended from 6th Street to Pennsylvania Avenue.

AMERICAN INSTITUTE OF ARCHITECTS. *See* OCTAGON HOUSE.

AMERICAN NEGRO ACADEMY. African American learned society, composed of scholars, authors, and artists. Founded in 1897 in Washington, the society sought to strengthen the intellectual life of the African American community. The academy's founders included Alexander Crummell, **Paul Laurence Dunbar**, and **Kelly Miller**. Other African American intellectuals later joined, including W. E. B. DuBois, **Francis Grimké**, James Weldon Johnson, and Carter G. Woodson. The group met annually, mostly in Washington, and published 22 occasional papers. Membership declined in the 1920s, and the academy disbanded in 1928.

AMERICAN RED CROSS. *See* BARTON, CLARA; DREW, CHARLES R.; GLOVER, CHARLES CARROLL; GREEN, CONSTANCE McLAUGHLIN; SULGRAVE CLUB.

AMERICAN UNIVERSITY. University founded by Methodist Bishop John Fletcher Hurst and inspired by **George Washington**'s dream for a national university. In 1893 Hurst purchased 92 acres of land for the university, but students were not enrolled until 1914 because the Methodist General Conference refused to open the school until a $5 million endowment was raised. **Frederick Law Olmsted** designed the grounds and architects Van Brunt and Howe and Henry Ives Cobb designed the school's neoclassical buildings. The architects created an elegant, formal campus, intended as an extension of **Pierre Charles L'Enfant**'s city plan. In 1917 when the United States entered World War I, university trustees offered the campus to the U.S. Army, which set up Camp Leach, a training facility for more than 100,000 soldiers, and Camp American University, site of the nation's first chemical weapons laboratory. The university's ties to the United Methodist Church have diminished since its founding. The school enrolls more than 11,000 students from the United States and around the world and operates the Kogod College of Business, the School of International Service, and the Washington College of Law.

ANACOSTIA. A predominantly African American community located on the east side of the **Anacostia River**. In 1608 Captain **John Smith** sailed up the **Potomac River** and, turning into its eastern branch (the Anacostia River), found a well-established **Native American settlement**, Nacochtanke, which was rendered in English as "Anacostia." The riverside location soon attracted tobacco planters and merchants. When the District of Columbia was created in 1790, **Thomas Jefferson** insisted on including land east of the river for defensive purposes. During the British attack on Washington in August 1814, American troops retreated west from Anacostia toward the city center, burning the bridges across the Anacostia River.

In 1853, at the behest of reformer Dorothea Dix, the U.S government built in Anacostia the Government Hospital for the Insane, now known as **St. Elizabeths Hospital.** A year later, the Union Land Association purchased farmland nearby to develop housing for the workers at St. Elizabeths and the **Navy Yard.** The resulting tract was called Uniontown, the first suburban development in the District of Columbia. Restrictive housing covenants excluded all but native-born white citizens and prohibited commercial industries and pig ownership. Most lots were sold by 1860, but only a few houses were constructed. John Van Hook, a partner in the Land Association, built an elegant residence on Cedar Hill, overlooking Uniontown. When his company declared bankruptcy in the Panic of 1873, Van Hook was forced to sell Cedar Hill. The site was then purchased by **Frederick Douglass,** Washington's most prominent African American citizen.

During the **Civil War**, the U.S Army built 11 forts in Anacostia, which are now interconnected public parks. At the end of the war, the U.S. Bureau of Refugees, Freedmen, and Abandoned Lands (the Freedmen's Bureau) bought a 375-acre farm from James Barry. Located between Uniontown and St. Elizabeth's Hospital, the farm was used to house many of the freedmen who came to Washington during and after the war. For a price of $125 to $300 settlers received a one-acre lot and enough lumber to build a two-room house. By 1868 the community of 500 families had built a Baptist church and a school that enrolled 150 students. Further development stalled, however. The streetcar line reached Anacostia in 1875, 13 years after the rest of Washington. The **Pennsylvania Avenue** Bridge, which burned in 1845, was not replaced until 1890. Randle Highlands was built soon thereafter, at the end of the first streetcar line, and Congress Heights, at the end of Anacostia's second streetcar line, in the District's southernmost corner.

Until World War II, Uniontown, Barry's Farm, Randle Highlands, and Congress Heights were scattered small towns. Each of the four villages contained separate communities of blacks and whites, with separate schools and churches. The all-white Anacostia Citizens Association and the all-black Barry's Farm/ Hillsdale Civic Association both lobbied for services available elsewhere in Washington: water and sewer lines, electricity, and public transportation. During World War II, Washington's crowded conditions spurred the construction of hundreds of apartments in Anacostia. Public **school desegregation** in 1954 led to dramatic change in Anacostia's population. In 1950 more than 82 percent of the residents were white. By 1970 the neighborhood was 86 percent black, and in 1990 African Americans comprised more than 98 percent of Anacostia's population.

While education, income, and property values in Anacostia are among the city's lowest, civic activists have made important contributions to the community since the 1960s. Zoning changes have limited apartment construction. In 1967 the **Smithsonian Institution** opened the **Anacostia Museum,** which has since become an important community center. In 1972 Uniontown was given historic district designation to encourage local housing restoration. The **riots of 1968**, following the assassination of Martin Luther King, Jr., were a disaster for Anacostia's commercial district and so damaged the reputation of the neighborhood that planners of the **Washington Metrorail** subway system bypassed the area. However, Anacostia activists organized protests and the neighborhood eventually got a subway line, which has also become the focus of new commercial development.

ANACOSTIA MUSEUM AND CENTER FOR AFRICAN AMERICAN HISTORY AND CULTURE. A museum and cultural arts center in Fort Stanton Park that documents and interprets the African American experience in Washington, D.C., and surrounding communities. Founded in 1967 by the **Smithsonian Institution**, Anacostia Museum began as a small neighborhood museum. It was originally housed in an old movie theater in the predominantly African American **Anacostia** neighborhood. The museum has gradually expanded its programs to include art exhibitions, lectures, and performing arts events that explore local history and culture and examine the problems and prospects of African Americans in contemporary urban life.

ANACOSTIA PARK. A 1,200-acre park that lies along the eastern bank of the Anacostia River. Most of the park was created from reclaimed marshland that government engineers began to drain under the Reclamation Flats Act (1913–18). The dredging project, along with seawall construction that began in 1893, changed the winding course of the Anacostia River into a seawall-lined channel flanked by grassy slopes. The **Kenilworth Park and Aquatic Gardens** is a remnant of area's original wetlands.

Anacostia Park was placed under the jurisdiction of the National Park Service in 1922 and has been developed for recreational use by the addition of tennis and basketball courts, picnic areas, and grassy fields. The Anacostia Park Pavilion hosts special events within its 3,000 square feet of space. Water facilities include three marinas, a public boat launch that gives access to the Anacostia River, an Aquatic Education Center, and an indoor swimming pool. The park also has an ice-skating rink and the Langston Golf Course, opened in 1939 and named after John Mercer Langston, Virginia's first African American member of the U.S. House of Representatives.

ANACOSTIA RIVER. A river that originates in Maryland, flows through the District of Columbia, and empties into the **Potomac River**. The Anacostia River was explored by British Captain **John Smith** in 1608, and by the mid-17th century the surrounding land was the site of tobacco plantations worked by slaves. Some descendants of these plantation workers purchased land and settled in the **Anacostia** area of Washington. The riverfront area is also the site of two important naval fortifications, **Fort Lesley J. McNair** (1791) and the **Navy Yard** (1799). Several private organizations are working with the federal government to protect and restore the Anacostia River watershed.

ANDERSON HOUSE. *See* SOCIETY OF THE CINCINNATI.

ANTHONY BOWEN YMCA. The first YMCA (Young Men's Christian Association) for African Americans in the United States. The Anthony Bowen YMCA was founded in 1853 by former slave Anthony Bowen, an educator and religious leader. Contributions from the local African American community and from philanthropists John D. Rockefeller and Julius Rosenwald enabled the YMCA to construct a new building in 1908. Designed by Sidney Pittman, an African American architect, the five-story building on 12th Street NW, housing a swimming pool and gymnasium, opened in 1912. The YMCA sponsored many programs, including summer camps for African American youths and a traveler's aid service at **Union Station**. In 1972 the building was named in honor of Bowen. Ten years later it was declared unsafe and closed. A two-year renovation project was completed in 2000. The renovated structure is called the Thurgood Marshall Center for Service and Heritage and houses several local nonprofit organizations.

ARBORETUM. *See* U.S. NATIONAL ARBORETUM.

ARCHBOLD, ANNE. *See* GLOVER-ARCHBOLD PARK.

ARENA STAGE. Professional theater, founded in 1950 by Zelda Fichandler, Thomas C. Fichandler, and Edward Mangum after the **National Theatre**, then Washington's only legitimate theater, began showing second-run films rather than admit African American patrons. Arena's productions were performed in the old Hippodrome movie house and then in the abandoned **Heurich Brewing Company** building before its permanent home was built in 1961 at 6th Street and Maine Avenue SW. The building holds the 827-seat Fichandler Stage, the 514-seat Kreeger Theatre, and the Old Vat Room, a small, flexible performance space. Arena Stage is among America's most highly regarded regional theaters and helped develop the careers of several famous actors including Kevin Kline, Morgan Freeman, Kathleen Turner, and Robert Prosky. Its greatest success has been "The Great White Hope," starring James Earl

Jones and Jane Alexander; the production went from Arena to a lengthy Broadway run and was made into a motion picture.

ARMES, GEORGE AUGUSTUS. *See* CHEVY CHASE.

ARMORY. *See* D.C. ARMORY.

ART MUSEUM OF THE AMERICAS. Museum of Latin American art established by the Organization of American States (OAS) in 1976 in recognition of the U.S. bicentennial. The museum's Spanish Colonial building was designed in 1912 by Paul Cret and Albert Kelsey as the residence for secretaries-general of the OAS. Its gardens feature tilework in Inca and Aztec patterns. The museum's permanent collection, begun in 1957, specializes in 20th-century art of the Americas and the Caribbean. The museum also hosts temporary exhibitions, lectures, and seminars on Latin American art.

ARTHUR M. SACKLER GALLERY. **Smithsonian Institution** museum of Asian and Middle Eastern art. The Sackler Gallery was founded in 1982 when Arthur M. Sackler (1913–1987), a psychiatrist, researcher, and publisher from New York, gave about 1,000 pieces of Asian art to the Smithsonian, along with funds to construct a building for the collection. The building was opened to the public in 1987 and is part of the Quadrangle museum complex on the **Mall** designed by architect Jean Paul Carlhian. The Sackler Gallery is linked to the **Freer Gallery** by an underground exhibition space. The two museums are administrated by a shared director and staff. The Sackler Gallery collection features Chinese bronzes, jades, paintings, and lacquerware; ancient Near Eastern ceramics and metalware; sculpture from South and Southeast Asia; modern Japanese prints and porcelain; Indian and Korean paintings; arts of village India; and the Vever Collection of Islamic book art. The museum hosts changing exhibitions and public programs and houses a research library of more than 55,000 volumes.

ARTS AND INDUSTRIES BUILDING. Smithsonian Institution museum located on the **Mall**. Built in 1881, the Arts and Industries Building was the inspiration of Spencer Fullerton Baird, the second secretary of the Smithsonian. Baird lobbied Congress to build a national museum for art, science, and history exhibitions, and in 1879 Congress appropriated $250,000 for the project.

Originally known as the U.S National Museum, the red brick and sandstone Victorian building, designed by the architectural firm of **Adolph Cluss** and Paul Schulze with the help of **Montgomery Meigs**, had 80,000 square feet of exhibit space and was notably modern in its use of natural light. The building's first function, before any artifacts were exhibited, was to host the inaugural celebration of President James Garfield. When a new national museum was constructed, the old building was renamed the Arts and Industries Building.

Several Smithsonian Institution museums, including the Museum of Natural History, the Museum of American Art, the National Portrait Gallery, and the **National Air and Space Museum**, grew out of exhibits that originated in the Arts and Industries Building. The building has been renovated several times and was restored to its original appearance in 1976. In 1977 the Discovery Theater was added. The Arts and Industries Building is now home to two galleries of changing exhibitions.

ASSOCIATION OF THE OLDEST INHABITANTS OF THE DISTRICT OF COLUMBIA. Washington's oldest civic association, organized in 1865 to preserve the traditions of antebellum Washington society and encourage local historic preservation. For its first 115 years of existence, the society limited its membership to white males aged 50 years and older who had lived in the District of Columbia for at least 40 years. In 1980 the gender and race requirements were eliminated, and the residency and age requirements reduced. From 1909 until 1956, the association maintained its offices in the Union Engine Company building at 19th and H Streets NW, one of the city's oldest firehouses. When the building was razed in 1956 for construction of the International Monetary Fund headquarters, the Oldest Inhabitants donated part of their Washingtoniana collection to the **Historical Society of Washington** and the rest to the Smithsonian Institution, including an 1850 fire engine. The Oldest Inhabitants meet six times a year to hear historic and nostalgic presentations.

AVENUES. *See* STREETS AND AVENUES.

- B -

B&O RAILWAY STATION. *See* GARFIELD ASSASSINATION.

BACON, HENRY. *See* LINCOLN MEMORIAL.

BAILEY, GAMALIEL. *See NATIONAL ERA.*

BAILEY, PEARL (1918–1990). Singer and entertainer. Born in Newport News, Virginia, Bailey moved with her family to Washington, where she landed her first singing job in a U Street club at age 15. She moved to Philadelphia and made her stage debut in New York in 1946. After earlier marriages failed, Bailey married Louis Bellson, a drummer in **Duke Ellington**'s band. She won a Tony Award for her role in the Broadway musical *Hello Dolly* (1967–68) and made recordings for the Coral, Columbia, and Decca record companies. Her jazz-gospel style was influenced by her church upbringing and formative years in Washington, and after a long career as a singer, stage actress, and television and movie star, she returned to Washington to earn a degree in theology from **Georgetown University** (1985). Bailey was active on behalf of many charities and served as a special goodwill delegate to the United Nations.

BALCH, STEPHEN BLOOMER (1747–1833). Presbyterian minister and educator. Born in Harford County, Maryland, Balch was raised in North Carolina and educated (1773–74) at the College of New Jersey (now Princeton University). After graduating he became principal of Lower Marlborough Academy in Calvert County, Maryland. He was a captain during the Revolutionary War and served in several campaigns against the British (1775–77). Entering the ministry in 1778, he was licensed to preach and in 1780 became the first minister at the **Georgetown Presbyterian Church**, where he served until 1833. In 1791 two of Balch's sermons became the first publication printed in the District of Columbia. Balch continued to teach, becoming the founder and principal of the Columbian Academy (1794–1801) on N Street. Several Washington-area churches were begun with his assistance, and he is regarded as one of the founders of the Presbyterian Church in the mid-Atlantic region.

BALLET. *See* WASHINGTON BALLET; WASHINGTON SCHOOL OF BALLET.

BANK OF COLUMBIA. First bank in the District of Columbia. The Bank of Columbia was chartered by the Maryland legislature in 1793 and was capitalized at $1 million. In 1796 bank officials constructed a three-story brick structure on M Street NW in **George-**

town, where the institution remained for a decade before moving to a larger building across the street. The bank financed many municipal, federal, and private projects in the early days of the 19th century, but failed in 1826. Its failure was a great catastrophe for many local residents, who lost their life savings; for businesses, which lost working capital; and for the U.S. government, which lost the $469,000 it had on deposit with the bank. The original 1796 bank building still stands; at one time it housed the U.S. Bureau of Indian Trade (1806–22) and it later served as the Georgetown city hall (1823–71).

BANNEKER, BENJAMIN (1731–1806). African American author, surveyor, scientist, and social critic. Banneker was born in Baltimore County, Maryland, son of a freed slave. He was taught to read by his grandmother and attended Quaker school for a time, but was otherwise self-taught. As a young man Banneker took apart a clock and carved wooden replicas of each of its parts. His new clock, composed entirely of wood, kept perfect time for 40 years. In 1791 Banneker worked with **Andrew Ellicott** to survey and lay the **boundary stones** of the Federal Territory that became the District of Columbia. Banneker worked closely with **Pierre Charles L'Enfant**, the architect charged with designing the city of Washington. When the designer was fired by **George Washington**, Banneker was able to recreate L'Enfant's plans from memory, sparing the U.S. government the trouble of commissioning a new design. For 20 years, Banneker published an almanac, for which he did all the writing and calculation. Banneker is known for his correspondence with **Thomas Jefferson**, in which he argued fervently for the abolition of **slavery**.

BARLOW, JOEL. *See* KALORAMA.

BARNARD, JOHN GROSS (1815–1882). Engineer and author. Barnard graduated from West Point in 1833 and became a military engineer. He was responsible for the fortification of Washington during the **Civil War** and participated in several military campaigns. In addition to scientific studies, his publications include a memoir of Joseph Gilbert Trotten (1866), chief engineer of the U.S. Army. He also carried on a correspondence with Union general George B. McClellan (1826–1885).

BARNEY, ALICE PIKE (1857–1931). Artist, playwright, and theater director. Born in Cincinnati, Ohio, Barney studied art with Carolus Duran and Whistler in Paris. She exhibited portraits and other works in New York, London, Paris, and Washington. A strong advocate of the arts, she suggested the construction of an outdoor theater in Washington, which she named the **Sylvan Theatre**. She was the theater's original playwright, preparing scripts for the first six productions. In 1927 her play *The Lighthouse* won the Drama League of America contest. Barney's wealth allowed her to travel widely and maintain homes in Hollywood, California, and in Washington. Her Washington residence on Sheridan Circle was used as a studio and salon for entertaining prominent artists and politicians. Owned by the **Smithsonian Institution** from 1960 to 1999, the house is now used as a music school.

BARRY, MARION (b. 1936). Civil rights activist and four-time **mayor** of Washington. Born in rural Mississippi, Barry came to Washington in 1965 to work as a fundraiser for the Student Nonviolent Coordinating Committee (SNCC), a civil rights organization. He cofounded Pride, Inc., a jobs program for minority youth, with a grant from the U.S. Department of Labor. Barry was elected to the D.C. school board in 1971 and to the **City Council** in 1975. While serving on the council in 1977 he was shot and almost killed in the **Hanafi Muslim Siege**. Barry was elected mayor in 1978 and reelected to two more four-year terms. In 1990 he was arrested for drug possession, when an FBI sting produced a video of Barry using crack cocaine. He served a six-month federal jail term for this offense. Shortly after his release in 1992 Barry was elected again to the City Council, and in 1994 he ran for a fourth term as mayor and won. In 1995 in response to a growing financial crisis in the District government, Congress appointed a Financial Control Board (**District of Columbia Financial Responsibility and Management Assistance Authority**) to take financial control of the city. Barry was stripped of most of his mayoral power in 1997, but stayed on as mayor until the end of his term in 1998.

BARRY'S FARM. *See* ANACOSTIA.

BARTHOLDI PARK. *See* U.S. BOTANIC GARDEN.

BARTON, CLARA (1821–1912). **Civil War** battlefield nurse and founder of the American Red Cross. Born in Oxford, Massachusetts, Barton spent 18 years working as a schoolteacher in Massachusetts and New Jersey before moving to Washington in the 1850s. She was employed as a clerk in the U.S. Patent Office, where she became the first woman paid a salary equal to that of male government workers. In April 1861, Barton accompanied some friends to greet a regiment of Massachusetts soldiers injured during Baltimore riots. Moved by their suffering, she persuaded Union Army officials to allow her to deliver medical supplies to the war front, where she nursed Union casualties. Her compassion and courage during the Battles of Second Manassas, Sharpsburg, Warrenton, and Fredericksburg became legendary. After the war ended, she directed a government records department to help identify and locate missing Union soldiers. In 1869 while visiting Switzerland, the Franco-German War erupted and Barton became a volunteer with the International Committee of the Red Cross. She returned to Washington in 1873, and in 1877 she founded the American Association of the Red Cross. She directed the organization for more than two decades, resigning in 1904.

BEALL, GEORGE. *See* GEORGETOWN.

BEALL, NINIAN (1625–1717). First European settler in what became the District of Columbia. Royalist Beall fought against Cromwell's forces at the Battle of Dunbar, Scotland, where he was captured and transported to Maryland as a political prisoner and indentured servant. After his 1658 release and Charles II's Restoration, Beall became commander of colonial forces in Maryland and gradually accumulated 25,000 acres of land. In 1703 he acquired the first land patent in the territory that became **Georgetown**, a 795-acre tract he called Rock of Dunbarton. His son George deeded half the land that became Georgetown in 1751, and his descendants still play important roles in the political and civic life of District of Columbia and Maryland.

BELASCO THEATER. Historic theater. Lobbyist and civil engineer Uriah H. Painter commissioned Chicago architects Wood and Lovell to design the six-story building on Madison Place NW in 1894. Painter's **Lafayette Square** Opera House opened the following year with a production of *Tzigane*, starring Lillian Russell. By 1906 Painter had lost most of his investment and sold the building to New York entrepreneurs David Belasco and the Shubert Brothers, who renamed it. The 1,800-seat auditorium held three tiers of balconies and 32 boxes and hosted plays, opera, and ballet. The artists who performed there included Enrico Caruso, Sarah Bernhardt, **Al Jolson**, and Will Rogers. Washingtonian **Helen Hayes** made her stage debut at the Belasco. During the 1930s the Belasco was converted to a movie theater and then back to a stage, but it was never again profitable. The U.S. government bought the building in 1940 and in 1942 it became the Stage Door Canteen, where nearly 6,000 volunteers entertained more than two million servicemen during World War II. The theater was demolished in 1964 to make way for the U.S. Court of Claims building.

BELL, ALEXANDER GRAHAM (1847–1922). Teacher of the deaf, scientist, and inventor of the telephone. Bell was born in Edinburgh, Scotland, and largely educated by his father, Alexander Melville Bell, an authority in the fields of elocution and speech. The family moved to Canada in 1870, and in 1872 Bell opened a school for the deaf in Boston, where he taught a form of signing developed by his father. The following year he was appointed professor of vocal physiology at Boston University. Interested in the electrical transmission of sound, Bell's research led to the invention of the telephone in 1876. He received other patents for the phonograph, aerial vehicles, hydroairplanes, and the selenium cell. Bell moved to Washington in 1879 and with **Gardiner G. Hubbard** founded the journal *Science* (1883). In 1893 he constructed the Volta Bureau building for the education of the deaf. He succeeded Hubbard as president of the **National Geographic Society** (1896–1904) and with Gilbert Grosvenor turned the society's pamphlet into a national magazine that taught geography through photographs. From 1898 Bell served as a regent of the **Smithsonian Institution** and was a major contributor to its Astrophysical Observatory.

BELL, GEORGE. *See* CAPITOL HILL.

BELMONT, ALVA. *See* SEWALL-BELMONT HOUSE.

BELMONT HOUSE. *See* SEWALL-BELMONT HOUSE.

BELT, JOSEPH. *See* CHEVY CHASE.

BENJAMIN BANNEKER FOUNTAIN. *See* BANNEKER, BENJAMIN; L'ENFANT PLAZA.

BENNING HEIGHTS. A predominantly African American community located in far Southeast Washington, bounded by Benning and

Ridge Roads, East Capitol Street, and Alabama and Southern Avenues, sometimes referred to as Fort Dupont or Hillcrest Heights. In order to connect the plantations of Prince George's County, Maryland, to the Washington City markets, William Benning financed the construction of a wooden bridge across the **Anacostia River** in 1797, one of three Anacostia crossings built in the 1790s. During the Federalist period, this newly accessible land in Benning Heights lured rich and prominent Washingtonians to purchase thousands of acres. Some speculated that construction of the City Canal in 1815 would stimulate development along the shoreline. When profits did not materialize, the speculators sold the land for cultivation, but few people settled there until the 20th century.

Benning Heights is known for two prominent sites, which began to be developed during the 19th century: Fort Dupont Park and Woodlawn Cemetery. Fort Dupont Park is Washington's second largest park, built around one of the city's 68 **Civil War** forts. Fort Dupont was built on land commandeered from Michael Caton, a local farmer, and the park is named for Admiral Samuel F. Dupont, the same Civil War hero honored at Dupont Circle. After the war, the U.S. government returned the land to Caton, complete with several buildings, magazines, and stockyards added by the Union Army. The park later grew to include 400 acres. Woodlawn Cemetery was developed in 1895 after the closure of one of only three D.C. cemeteries that accepted African American interments. Many prominent local people are buried in the cemetery.

In 1927 the neighborhood was plotted and street names assigned, but the street layout did not conform to the grid plan of **Pierre Charles L'Enfant**, which was followed west of the Anacostia River. The development of Benning Heights was much more akin to that in suburban Maryland, with winding streets that follow hilly topography and cul-de-sacs and dead-end streets that limit the flow of traffic. Neighborhood development was halted during the Great Depression with only 50 houses constructed by 1936. However, a massive government expansion in post-World War II Washington led to a housing boom. Between 1948 and 1960 virtually all the housing stock of Benning Heights was built.

Nearly half the original residents of Benning Heights worked for the federal government, and nearly all were white, as stipulated in the community's original restrictive covenants. However, during the 1950s, residents of Benning Heights played a pivotal role in the social change that would soon envelop the nation. In 1950, 11 African American children attempted to enroll in the neighborhood's new, all-white Sousa Junior High School. When they were turned away, **Howard University** law professor James M. Nabrit, Jr., sued D.C. School Board president Melvin Sharpe on behalf of the students. That suit, *Bolling v. Sharpe*, eventually led to school integration in Benning Heights, and changed the ethnic character of the neighborhood.

BENNING RACETRACK. *See* HORSERACING; TEMPLE OF FREEDOM UNDER GOD, CHURCH OF GOD.

BETHUNE, MARY McLEOD (1875–1955). Educator and social activist. Born free into a large family of South Carolina sharecroppers, Bethune was educated at Scotia Seminary in North Carolina and spent one year at the Moody Bible Institute in Chicago. She returned to the South, and in 1904 opened the Daytona Normal and Industrial School for Negro Girls, where she taught five students on desks made from orange crates. In 1923 the school merged with Cookman Institute to form Bethune-Cookman College in Jacksonville, Florida. The merger secured the school's future and Bethune turned her attention to civil rights and social justice. In 1935 she founded the National Council of Negro Women as a forum to advocate anti-lynching laws, prison reform, and job training for black women. The following year she became the first African American woman to head a federal agency, when President Franklin Roosevelt appointed her director of Negro affairs in the National Youth Administration. As Roosevelt's advisor and leader of his "Black Cabinet," she was one of the most influential African Americans of the mid-20th century. In 1943 Bethune purchased a Victorian townhouse on Vermont Avenue NW, which served as her residence and the headquarters of the National Council for Negro Women; it is now a National Historic Site which houses the National Archives for Black Women's History, an extensive collection of manuscripts relating to African American women. A statue in **Lincoln Park** honors her work.

BIBLE WAY TEMPLE. An independent Protestant church. The Bible Way Church of Our Lord Jesus Christ was established by Smallwood E. Williams in 1927 in a storefront chapel. Beginning in 1931 the congregation held services in large tents, and in 1947 a 3,000-seat church was built on New Jersey Avenue NW. The church complex includes educational and recreational buildings and a bell tower with an 80-foot-high stainless steel cross adorned with the word "GOD." In 1973 the congregation built a 10-story low- and moderate-income housing complex, the Golden Rule Apartments, two blocks from the church. Williams staged Washington's first sit-in, protesting public school segregation in 1952, and served on the Board of Directors of the **National Association for the Advancement of Colored People.**

BIOGRAPH THEATRE. Counterculture movie house. Opened in 1966 on M Street NW in Georgetown, the Biograph was Washington's only independently owned, single-screen art cinema and the city's second repertory film presenter. The theater screened productions of the French *Cahiers du Cinema* school, Italian neorealists, German expressionists, and the work of avant-garde directors such as Ingmar Bergman, Akira Kurosawa, Rainer Werner Fassbinder, Wim Wenders, Todd Haynes, John Woo, and Alfred Hitchcock. The Biograph also featured animated programs, film festivals, retrospective tributes, pornographic movies, and on weekends, a midnight viewing of *The Rocky Horror Picture Show*. One critic called the theater's offerings "the eccentric and the marginal," and its audience gradually waned until it was forced to close in 1996.

BLACK CODES. Legal restrictions placed on free blacks and slaves. Washington City's first black code was enacted in 1808, imposing a 10:00 p.m. curfew, with a five-dollar fine for noncompliance. In response to fears that African Americans might cooperate with the British during the **War of 1812**, the code was strengthened; curfew violators were subject to a six-month jail term if free or 40 lashes if enslaved. Every free black was required to register with the city and to carry a certificate of freedom at all times, or face imprisonment and sale. Georgetown's first black code was enacted in 1831 in the wake of the Nat Turner Rebellion, and its punishable offenses included possession or circulation of insurrectionist or abolitionist literature. Washington City's rules grew harsher following the **Snow Riots** of 1835. Free blacks were required to post "peace bonds" of $1,000 and produce the signatures of five "reputable" white men to vouch for their character. Business activities were also restricted, but enforcement was lax and numerous black artisans openly worked at their crafts. With congressional passage of the Compromise of 1850, the peace bond was reduced to $50 and only one signature was required, but free blacks entering the city were forced to register at the mayor's office within five days or risk fines, jail terms, or expulsion. The Black Codes were repealed in the summer of 1862, a few weeks after Congress ordered the emancipation of all D.C. slaves. *See also* SLAVERY.

BLACK PATRIOTS MEMORIAL. Monument to more than 5,000 African Americans who fought in the American Revolution, including the first American casualty of the war, Crispus Attucks. Two curved, sloping walls designed by sculptor Ed Dwight and architect Marshall Purnell, are to be built in **Constitution Gardens.** The first wall will hold a 90-foot bronze sculpture with bas-relief figures representing the patriots and their families. The figures along the wall will appear increasingly distinct and will finally emerge as recognizable individuals, signifying their emancipation. A poem by Phyllis Wheatley, America's first black woman poet, will be inscribed on the second wall. The memorial's nearly $10 million construction costs are being raised by the Black Patriots Foundation, whose leaders hope to dedicate the memorial in 2005.

BLAIR HOUSE. Official guest house of the president of the United States. The wide Federal-style building was constructed in 1824 on **Pennsylvania Avenue** as the home of Joseph Lovell, who became the first U.S. surgeon general. Francis Preston Blair bought the house when Lovell died in 1836. Blair published the *Congressional Globe*, official newspaper of the Andrew Jackson administration and forerunner of the *Congressional Record*. He also served in Congress. The Blair family owned the house for several generations. In the 1860s an adjacent building, the Lee House, was built for Francis Preston Blair's daughter. His son, Montgomery Blair, served as postmaster general under Abraham Lincoln and offered the house for meetings. It was used for that purpose by John Calhoun, Henry Clay, Daniel Webster, and Jefferson Davis. In 1861 at a Blair House meeting, Robert E. Lee declined Lincoln's offer to command the Union Army. In 1942 the U.S. State Department bought the house from the Blair family and joined it to three neighboring houses (including the Lee House) to create a 112-room complex. The Blair House complex now serves as a residence for visiting diplomats and heads of state. *See also* TRUMAN ASSASSINATION ATTEMPT.

BLOCK, HERBERT LAWRENCE (1909–2001). *Washington Post* cartoonist. Born in Chicago, and known by his byname "Herblock," Block first drew cartoons for the *Chicago Daily News* in 1929. Four years later he became a syndicated cartoonist for the Newspaper Enterprise Association in Cleveland, and in 1946 he joined the staff of the *Washington Post*. He won Pulitzer Prizes in 1942, 1954, and 1979, and his work as been collected in several volumes, including *The Herblock Book* (1952), *Herblock's Here and Now* (1955), *The Herblock Gallery* (1968), and *Herblock on All Fronts* (1980). The liberal views and biting criticism of Block's cartoons have provoked strong reactions. In 1952, during the presidential campaign of Dwight D. Eisenhower and Adlai Stevenson, the *Post* endorsed Eisenhower, while Block supported Stevenson. His relentless criticism of Eisenhower undermined the *Post*'s editorial position and his cartoons were withheld near the end of the campaign, a move that embarrassed the newspaper. He was severely critical of President Richard Nixon during the **Watergate scandal** and had been an early critic of Senator Joseph McCarthy, first using the term "McCarthyism" on a drawing of a tar barrel.

BLODGETT'S HOTEL. Theater and federal office building. The hotel was designed by architect **James Hoban** and was constructed around 1796 by real estate developer Samuel Blodgett, Jr. Located on the corner of 8th and E Streets, the building was offered as prize in a lottery to promote the city, but Blodgett went bankrupt before the lottery was held. The hotel was used as the **United States Theatre** until 1810, when it was purchased by the federal government. A renovation carried out by **Charles Bulfinch** adapted the building for use as the U.S. Patent Office and Post Office. The hotel was also used as a temporary home of Congress in 1814 and 1815 and was destroyed by fire in 1836.

BLOOMINGDALE. *See* SHAW/U STREET.

B'NAI B'RITH KLUTZNICK NATIONAL JEWISH MUSEUM. A museum that chronicles Jewish contributions to American culture and history. Located on the ground floor of the B'nai B'rith International headquarters on Rhode Island Avenue NW, the museum is named for Philip Klutznick, a former president of B'nai B'rith. The museum was founded in 1957 and its collections have grown to represent aspects of worldwide Jewish history from antiquity to the present. A building expansion in 1976, designed by architects Croning, Moore, Elmore, Fisher, made room for a growing permanent collection and provided space for temporary exhibitions. The museum now comprises four galleries, a theater, and a bookstore.

BOARD OF PUBLIC WORKS. *See* SHEPHERD, ALEXANDER ROBEY "BOSS."

BOARD OF TRADE. *See* GREATER WASHINGTON BOARD OF TRADE.

BOLLING AIR FORCE BASE. Home of the 11th Wing, the largest fighter wing in the U.S. Air Force. Located in **Anacostia** between the I-95 highway and the **Potomac River**, the base is named after Raynal C. Bolling (1877–1918), one of the wing's organizers who was killed near Amiens, France, during World War I. Bolling's First Aero Company was organized in 1915, and in 1917 the U.S. government purchased land on the Anacostia flats for an airfield. The base moved to its present location during the 1930s and in 1941 it became the headquarters of the Army Air Forces. The flying mission of the base declined during the 1950s and flying operations ceased in 1962. The base was an administrative and support center until 1994, when the 11th Wing was returned to its historic home.

BONUS ARMY MARCH. A 1932 march on Washington by veterans of World War I who were due bonus payments for military service. A 1924 law permitted the U.S. government to delay payment of "war bonuses" until 1945, but during the Great Depression jobless veterans wanted their money. Tens of thousands of demonstrators from around the country gathered in Washington and set up camp. The city accommodated this "Bonus Army" for several months, but in July 1932 President Herbert Hoover, citing rumors that the protest had been organized by communists, ordered federal troops to drive the marchers out of the city. In the show of force that followed, one demonstrator was killed, dozens of others were injured, and the temporary dwellings of the Bonus Army were burned to the ground. The demonstrators fled the city and soldiers were posted at the bridges to make sure they could not return. Four years later Congress passed a law that provided immediate cash payments to the veterans.

BOOTH, JOHN WILKES. *See* FORD'S THEATRE; FORT LES-

LEY J. MCNAIR; LINCOLN ASSASSINATION; SURRATT, MARY ELIZABETH JENKINS.

BORGLUM, GUTZON. *See* ROCK CREEK CEMETERY; KALO-RAMA.

BOTANIC GARDEN. *See* U.S. BOTANIC GARDEN.

BOUNDARY STONES. Sandstone markers placed around the perimeter of the District of Columbia in 1791. After the District was laid out in the diamond shape envisioned by **Pierre Charles L'Enfant**, a group of surveyors and masons, led by **Andrew Ellicott** and **Benjamin Banneker**, placed 40 boundary stones around its perimeter, at one-mile intervals. The one-foot-square stones, with beveled tops, protrude about three feet from the ground. On one side they bear a date of placement; on the side facing Washington they are inscribed with the words "Jurisdiction of the United States," and on the opposite side is inscribed "Virginia" or "Maryland." In 1915 the **Daughters of the American Revolution** located and restored 30 of the boundary stones, including the four cornerstones, and had them covered with wrought-iron cages. Today most of the stones stand otherwise unprotected and in various states of disrepair. The south cornerstone is at Jones Point on the edge of the **Potomac River**, where water covers its base at high tide.

BOWEN, ANTHONY. *See* ANTHONY BOWEN YMCA; SLAVERY; SOUTHWEST.

BOWEN, SAYLES JENKS (1813–1896). **Mayor** of Washington. Born in Scipio, New York, Bowen was educated at the Aurora Academy. He moved to Washington in 1844, worked as a clerk in the U.S. Treasury Department (1845–48), and then became a private claims agent. As a reward for his work in the Republican party, Abraham Lincoln appointed him commissioner of police (1861) and city postmaster (1863–68). He was elected mayor of Washington in June 1868 and served a two-year term. Bowen came into the mayor's office with the pledge to secure federal money to help pay for badly needed city improvements. He began public works projects to employ former slaves and to modernize the city. Streets were paved, 15 miles of sidewalks were constructed, and the city installed four miles of sewers. However, by 1870 more than 200 miles of streets still lacked pavement and sewers. The optimism of the Bowen administration gradually faded when the mayor was unable to secure congressional support for his public works projects and as the city's debt increased by nearly one-third during his term. He also fell victim to opponents who disliked his progressive social policy and to charges of corruption in his public works projects. He was defeated in the election of 1870 and thereafter served as a trustee of the Public Schools for Colored Children in the District of Columbia.

BRADY, MATHEW B. (1823–1896). Photographer. Brady studied photography with **Samuel Morse** and opened a studio in New York City. Over the course of his life Brady photographed many prominent people, including Brigham Young, Edgar Allan Poe, Daniel Webster, and 19 U.S. presidents. In 1850 he published *Brady's Gallery of Illustrious Americans*, which received critical acclaim but was a commercial failure. Eight years later he opened a studio in Washington, on **Pennsylvania Avenue** at 7th Street NW; Abraham Lincoln had his first official portrait made there in 1861. When the **Civil War** broke out, Brady decided to document the conflict. Traveling with Union troops, Brady and his assistants carried photo equipment in darkroom wagons and took more than 3,500 pictures. He borrowed heavily for the project, confident that the government would purchase the photographs at war's end. However, the government declined to buy the collection and Brady went bankrupt. When his entire collection was sold at auction in 1871, the federal government finally bought the photographs. Although Congress later appropriated funds to compensate Brady for his contribution to the American historic record, he was already in financial ruin and died in a New York charity hospital. His body was returned to Washington and buried in **Congressional Cemetery**.

BRENT, ROBERT (1764–1819). The first **mayor** of Washington. Brent was born in Aquia, Virginia, where his family leased rock quarries that supplied stone for the colonial-era building industry. When the city of Washington was incorporated in 1802, President **Thomas Jefferson** appointed Brent mayor. Brent was reappointed for 10 consecutive terms until 1812, when the office of mayor became an elective office of the **City Council**. During Brent's tenure as mayor, Washington organized police and fire departments, established a school board and a university, carried out street repairs, and initiated other city services. In addition to his job as mayor, Brent served as a justice of the peace (1801–17), judge of the orphan's court (1806–14), and paymaster general of the army (1808–19). He also served on the school board and in 1814 was appointed a district commissioner. Brent built a house on the corner of 12th Street and Maryland Avenue SW and resided there until his death. *See also* CHARTER OF INCORPORATION.

BRIGHTWOOD. A predominantly African American community bordered by **Rock Creek Park**, Georgia Avenue, and Aspen and Kennedy Streets NW. Brightwood was virtually uninhabited until the 7th Street Turnpike was built between 1818 and 1822. Three small communities gradually emerged: one around the turnpike tollgate near the 1770s-era James White farm; Oak Grove, near the D.C. line; and an area around the Crystal Spring racetrack. There were only 31 households in 1855, mostly smallholder farms. Brightwood was named by local postmaster Lewis Burnett in 1861 and originally included a much larger section of the District, especially the lands of present-day **Shepherd Park** and **Petworth**.

The only **Civil War** battle fought in the District of Columbia took place in Brightwood. On July 11, 1864, troops under the command of Confederate General Jubal Early marched south on the 7th Street Turnpike toward Washington. The following day, they engaged Union troops at Fort Stevens, located at present-day 13th and Quackenbos Streets NW. Many Brightwood residents lost their houses, barns, and other structures when Union soldiers demolished buildings to ensure an unobstructed field of fire.

By 1880 Brightwood was occupied by only 146 households, 86 white and 60 black. As many as 85 percent of Brightwood's black residents were freedmen who arrived in Washington after Emancipation. African Americans settled mostly in Vinegar Hill, along Rock Creek Ford Road and Military Road, or along Brightwood Avenue and Piney Branch Road.

In 1887 the southern portion of Brightwood was subdivided, creating the community of Petworth. The new subdivision offered amenities designed to attract middle- and upper-income Washingtonians, especially modern public transportation up the 7th Street corridor provided by the Brightwood Railway Company. However, the railway was short-lived, failing in 1891. Residents then formed the Brightwood Avenue Citizens Association and demanded a functional streetcar system and other improvements such as paved streets, bridges, sanitation, and police protection.

Brightwood Park, another subdivision, was created in 1891, when a descendant of James White sold 82 acres and the land was divided into lots for 34 houses. By 1907 four additional subdivisions opened in Brightwood, completing the neighborhood's transition from rural to suburban. Real estate agent Louis P. Shoemaker led the Brightwood Avenue Citizens Association from 1900 to 1916. He was instrumental in persuading the U.S. Army to build Walter Reed Military Hospital near Brightwood and hoped for even more largesse by convincing his neighbors to change the name of Brightwood Avenue to Georgia Avenue. Unfortunately, the Georgia senator Shoemaker hoped to impress died soon thereafter.

Brightwood changed dramatically after the arrival of English businessman **Harry Wardman** in 1895. Known as "the man who overbuilt Washington," Wardman constructed more than 500 houses in Brightwood during the 1920s and 1930s. By the time he died in 1938, many of Brightwood's older single-family houses had been replaced by apartment buildings and row houses. Until the 1960s, Brightwood was a predominantly white neighborhood with a substantial Jewish community; by 1970 it had become an African American community.

BRIGHTWOOD DRIVING PARK. *See* HORSERACING.

BROOKE, EDWARD R. (b. 1919). Lawyer and U.S. Senator. Born in Washington, D.C., Brooke graduated from **Howard University** (1941) and earned two law degrees from Boston University (1948, 1950). He ran for the Massachusetts legislature in 1950 and 1952 and for Massachusetts secretary of state in 1960, but was defeated. In 1962 he was elected Massachusetts attorney general and was reelected in 1964. Brooke won a seat in the U.S. Senate in 1966, becoming the first African American to serve in the Senate since 1881. He was reelected in 1972, but lost in his 1978 attempt at a third term. Brooke's 12 years of Senate service as a Republican from Massachusetts were characterized by his liberal and moderate views. He supported school integration, affirmative action, public housing, mass transit, and the extension of the minimum wage laws. He criticized government policy in Southeast Asia during the era of the Vietnam War and was the first senator to call for the resignation of President Richard Nixon because of the **Watergate scandal**. After his Senate service he resumed private law practice in Washington.

BROOKLAND. A community bounded by Otis Street, the B&O Railroad tracks, Rhode Island Avenue, and 18th Street NE. Brookland traces its roots to the 1713 land patent of Richard Marsham. His descendant, Anne Queen, inherited part of his land in 1840. There, her husband, Colonel Jehiel Brooks, built a Greek Revival estate, known locally as the Brooks Mansion. Between 1887 and 1901, the Brooks farm was split into seven subdivisions. The modern street grid was established after 1889. By 1894 the settlement looked like a modern suburb, with paved streets, street lamps, a post office, and public transportation on the Eckington and Soldier's Home Railway.

The neighborhood also developed into a major center of the Roman Catholic Church. The community's "Little Rome" began with the founding of **Catholic University of America** in 1885. Within five years, the Marist Order inherited Brooks Mansion and established there a seminary and parish school, while the Order of St. Francis founded the **Franciscan Monastery** on Bunker Hill (now Mount St. Sepulchre). The Catholic complex was eventually expanded to include Trinity College, the Shrine of the Immaculate Conception, several parochial schools, and offices for the Archdiocese of Washington, as well as quarters for more than 50 religious orders.

The Brookland neighborhood developed into a middle-class suburb of federal government workers and professionals, tradesmen, and craftsmen, most of whom were white. Construction of the Brookland Courts Apartments in 1924 marked the neighborhood's transition from semirural to urban. During the 1920s, numerous ethnic groups, including Greeks, Italians, Irish, Jews, Germans, and Chinese moved into the area. The commercial districts on 12th Street and near the Michigan Avenue railroad station prospered. Despite the existence of restrictive housing covenants, African American academics and professionals bought houses in Brookland from the 1920s to the 1950s. Diplomat **Ralph Bunche**, Senator **Edward Brooke**, singer **Pearl Bailey**, and Housing and Urban Development Secretary Robert Weaver grew up in Brookland. The transition from a white to a black neighborhood was a gradual process, completed by the 1950s.

During the 1960s, regional transportation planners proposed construction of a North Central Freeway, which would have destroyed more than 200 Brookland residences. The D.C. government acquired title to 69 houses, but when it failed to relocate the residents appropriately, the community protested the freeway plan. The city withdrew the transit project in favor of creating a **Washington Metrorail** subway. The Brookland neighborhood has struggled with racial tension, high crime rates, and the exodus of its black middle class to the suburbs. With the cooperation of Catholic University, Brookland's Upper Northeast Coordinating Council built a community center and has led other revitalization efforts in recent years.

BROWN, GLENN (1854–1932). Architect and author. Brown attended Washington and Lee University and graduated from the Massachusetts Institute of Technology in 1876. He moved to Washington in 1880, where he began an architectural firm. Practicing architecture in Washington for the next 41 years, Brown designed the Egyptian embassy, Buffalo Bridge over **Rock Creek Park**, and Beale House on Massachusetts Avenue NW. He served as secretary of the American Institute of Architects and was an active supporter of the **Commission of Fine Arts**. A prolific author, Brown published small pamphlets, including "A Brief Description and History of the Octagon House" (1900) and "The Development of Washington with Special Reference to the Lincoln Memorial" (1911), and wrote a large two-volume *History of the United States Capitol* (1900–03).

BROWN, J[OHN] CARTER (1934–2002). Fine arts executive. Brown was probably more responsible for the appearance of modern Washington than any other individual. As chair of the **Commission of Fine Arts**, he wielded veto power over the design of every memorial, monument, statue, embassy, and public building in the city. Serving on the commission under six U.S. presidents, Brown expressed his strong views on architecture by arguing over designs for the **Franklin Delano Roosevelt Memorial, Pennsylvania Avenue** redevelopment, and renovation of the **Washington Monument**, among other projects. He was best known for his tenure as director of the **National Gallery of Art**. Under his leadership, the gallery's attendance increased fivefold, its physical plant doubled with construction of the East Wing, and its annual federal appropriation climbed from $3 million at Brown's appointment to $52 million in 1992 when he retired. Brown was also chair of Ovation television network, a fine arts programming channel delivered to 10 million American homes.

BROWN, LETITIA WOODS (1915–1976). Historian. Born in Tuskegee, Alabama, Brown was educated at Tuskegee Institute (1935), Ohio State University, Radcliffe College, and Harvard University (1966). She served as a professor at **George Washington University** and **Howard University** and was active in promoting Washington studies, historic preservation, and African American history. Brown was a member of the board of the **Historical Society of Washington**, vice chairman of the Joint Committee on Landmarks of the National Capital, and one of the organizers of the annual Washington, D.C., Historic Studies Conference. Her publications include *Free Negroes in the District of Columbia, 1790–1846* (1972).

BROWNLOW, LOUIS (1879–1963). Journalist and public administrator. Born in Buffalo, Missouri, Brownlow worked as a newspaper reporter and editor from 1902 to 1915, and for several years served as a Washington correspondent. In 1915 President Woodrow Wilson appointed Brownlow to a five-year term on the D.C. Board of Commissioners, and he served as president of the board from 1917 to 1920. During his term of service Brownlow proved to be an excellent administrator, improving the police department, coping with the **influenza epidemic of 1918**, and guiding the city during the military buildup of World War I. He also served as chair of the D.C. Public Utilities Commission (1917–20) and as a member of the Zoning Commission (1919–20). Brownlow became city manager of Petersburg, Virginia (1920–23), and of Knoxville, Tennessee (1924–26), and then director of the Public Administration Clearing House in Chicago (1931–45), before retiring to Washington in 1945. He wrote a two-volume autobiography, *A Passion for Anonymity* (1959).

BULFINCH, CHARLES (1763–1844). American architect of the Federal period; contributor to the design of the **U.S. Capitol**. Born in Boston, Bulfinch studied mathematics at Harvard, then traveled in Europe and studied architecture, where he was influenced by Scottish neoclassicist Robert Adam. Bulfinch returned to Boston, established an architecture firm, and served in the local government. He became a major figure in the development of Federal-style architecture, which characterizes many early American government buildings. He designed several Boston buildings, including the Massachusetts State House. When President James Monroe visited Boston, he was so impressed with Bulfinch's designs that he appointed him architect of the Capitol, successor to **Benjamin Henry Latrobe**. Bulfinch served in this position from 1818 to 1829. Bulfinch's contributions to the Capitol can be seen in the west portico and in the design of the Capitol grounds. Bulfinch died in Boston in 1844.

BUNCHE, RALPH JOHNSON (1904–1971). Educator and diplomat. Born in Detroit, Michigan, Bunche earned an undergraduate degree from the University of California at Los Angeles (1927) and graduate degrees in government and international relations from Harvard University (1928, 1934). In 1928 Bunche joined the faculty of **Howard University**, where he organized the department of political science and served as department chair. He did postdoctoral work in anthropology and colonial policy at Northwestern University (1936), the London School of Economics (1937), and the University of Cape Town, South Africa (1938). He was part of Gunnar Myrdal's research team that produced the monumental study on U.S. race relations *An American Dilemma* (1944). After serving in the State Department during World War II, Bunche helped to plan the United Nations and in 1947 joined the UN Secretariat in New York. He was a longtime troubleshooter for the UN secretary general, supervising the deployment of UN troops in the Suez Canal (1956), the Congo (1964), and Cyprus (1964). In 1950 he won the Nobel Peace Prize for negotiating an Arab-Israeli truce in the Middle East.

BUNKER HILL. *See* BRIGHTWOOD.

BURNES, DAVID (1739–1799). Landowner and county magistrate. Burnes enlisted in the Continental Army in 1778 and served as a second lieutenant with the First Maryland Brigades. He later served as a justice of the peace and overseer of highways in Prince George's County, Maryland, part of which was ceded for the District of Columbia. In 1774 Burnes secured title to large tracts of land originally settled by his father, James Burnes. These lands were located on the site that **George Washington** selected for the capital. The last landholder to agree to the city plan of **Pierre Charles L'Enfant**, Burnes was convinced to sell half of his land to the government only after several visits by Washington and "heated arguments." The sale of this land made Burnes wealthy, and he passed his fortune to his daughter, **Marcia Burnes Van Ness**. The **White House**, U.S. Treasury building, and a large portion of downtown Washington were built on land once owned by Burnes. The Burnes house near 17th Street and **Pennsylvania Avenue** NW was demolished in the 1890s.

BURNETT, FRANCES ELIZA HODGSON (1849–1924). Author and playwright. Born in Manchester, England, Hodgson came to Knoxville, Tennessee, with her family in 1865. She gained public attention in 1872 when one of her stories was published by *Scribner's Magazine*. The following year she married L. M. Burnett of Washington, D.C. She drew upon her impressions of Washington life to write *Through One Administration* (1883), a novel about corruption in the city. She is most famous for her novel and play *Little Lord Fauntleroy* (1886) and her children's book *The Secret Garden* (1909).

BURNHAM, DANIEL HUDSON (1846–1912). Architect and city planner. Born in Henderson, New York, Burnham moved with his family to Chicago when he was nine years old. After a high school education he became an apprentice at the architectural firm of Carter, Drake, and Wight. There he met John W. Root and in 1873 the two formed their own firm, Burnham & Root. With Burnham assuming the administrative responsibilities and Root handling most of the design work, the firm planned commercial buildings in Chicago. Their 16-story Monadnock Building (1891) was the tallest and last masonry skyscraper. The firm designed the grounds for the World's Columbian Exposition in Chicago (1893) and thereafter became deeply involved in city planning, developing plans for Cleveland; San Francisco; Baltimore; Manila, Philippines (1905); and Chicago (1907–09). As a result of the **McMillan Report** (1902), Burnham was directed to prepare plans for the city of Washington. In 1908 he completed the design and construction of **Union Station** and in 1910 President **William Howard Taft** appointed him chair of the **Commission of Fine Arts**. In his role as architect, organizer, and city planner, Burnham had a major impact on the city of Washington.

BURROUGHS, NANNIE HELEN (1883–1961). Educator. Burroughs was born in Orange, Virginia, and grew up in Washington. While employed by the National Baptist Convention in Louisville, Kentucky, she organized the Woman's Industrial Club to teach basic domestic skills to African American girls. In 1909 Burroughs returned to Washington and opened the National Training School for Women and Girls at 50th and Grant Streets NE. Bearing the motto "We specialize in the wholly impossible," the school taught gardening, domestic work, interior decoration, and other vocational skills. After Burroughs's death in 1961, the school closed and the building became the public Nannie Helen Burroughs Elementary School; it now houses a religious retreat center. Burroughs also founded the National Association of Wage Earners to address the concerns of black working women and was a strong advocate of the preservation of African American culture.

BURRVILLE SUBDIVISION. *See* DEANWOOD.

- C -

CAMP AMERICAN UNIVERSITY. *See* AMERICAN UNIVERSITY.

CAMP BARKER. *See* CONTRABANDS.

CAMP FRY. *See* FOGGY BOTTOM.

CAMP LEACH. *See* AMERICAN UNIVERSITY.

CANALS. *See* CHESAPEAKE AND OHIO CANAL NATIONAL HISTORIC PARK; PATOWMACK CANAL; WASHINGTON CANAL.

CAPITAL CRESCENT TRAIL. An 11-mile, C-shaped hiking trail that runs from **Georgetown** to Silver Spring, Maryland. The trail was constructed on the original Georgetown Branch railroad line that discontinued service in 1985. Several features of the public trail reveal its railroad origins, including a 300-foot long tunnel near the D.C. border and a steel trestle that extends over Arizona Avenue. The trail is paved with asphalt from Georgetown to Bethesda, Maryland, and has a gravel surface from Bethesda to Silver Spring. Access to the trail in Georgetown is via K Street.

CAPITAL SCHOOL OF PHOTOGRAPHY. *See* SCURLOCK, ROBERT.

CAPITALS. *See* WASHINGTON CAPITALS.

CAPITOL. *See* CAPITOL HILL; OLD CAPITOL; U.S. CAPITOL.

CAPITOL HILL. A vigorous neighborhood with a long tradition of social diversity that surrounds the **U.S. Capitol** and its cluster of congressional office buildings. When the District of Columbia was drawn onto the Maryland map in 1791, Capitol Hill—from the Capitol east to the **Anacostia River**—was farmland of the slave-holding Rozier, Young, and Carroll families. Washington planner **Pierre Charles L'Enfant** called the hill "a pedestal awaiting a monument" and located the Capitol there.

Construction of the city created a labor shortage. Marylanders and Virginians joined European immigrants, free blacks, and hired-out slaves as the neighborhood's first residents and employees. Most laborers lived in wooden barracks and shanties, some on the Capitol grounds; supervisors and master craftsmen fared better, in two-story frame or brick houses. In 1799 **George Washington** chose a site on the Eastern Branch (the Anacostia River) for the U.S. **Navy Yard**, which led to further neighborhood development. Strategically located to build warships and defend the Capitol, the Navy Yard also hired a multiethnic workforce. A third major employer was the U.S. Marine Barracks. Public schools for white children opened, followed in 1807 by a school for black children operated by George Bell, Moses Liverpool, and Nicholas Franklin. By 1810 Capitol Hill was flourishing.

The **War of 1812** brought Capitol Hill prosperity to an abrupt, if brief, halt. In August 1814 British troops invaded Washington, where they burned and looted the Capitol and the **White House**. The Navy Yard was burned by American troops to keep three ships still under construction out of enemy hands. Following the disaster, Congress threatened to abandon Washington for Philadelphia. At this critical time, 38 local citizens raised funds to build a large "Brick Capitol," located on the site where the **U.S. Supreme Court** now stands. The Congress met there until 1819, when the rebuilt Capitol was finally opened.

During the **Civil War**, the U.S. Army commandeered virtually every public building and constructed a military hospital on East Capitol Street. The **Old Capitol** imprisoned Southern soldiers, spies, and political prisoners. In the 1870s Eastern Market anchored new development between the Capitol and the Navy Yard. The government expanded dramatically, and with improved transportation, such as horse-drawn streetcars that appeared in 1862, employees no longer had to live near their jobs. Affluent citizens moved to neighborhoods in Northwest Washington; Capitol Hill increasingly became the domain of white, middle-income federal employees, especially after 1883, when civil service reform ended the political spoils system for federal government jobs, thereby stabilizing government employment.

In the 20th century, the neighborhood landscape changed when the **Library of Congress** and new congressional office buildings were constructed. After World War II, the 19th-century houses between the Capitol and **Lincoln Park** were gradually restored. The neighborhood experienced demographic changes as middle-income blacks and whites moved to outer D.C. neighborhoods and suburbs. In 1948, when the Supreme Court declared housing covenants unconstitutional, black families displaced by the Southwest Urban Renewal Project moved into the community's older residences and public housing projects. By 1960 the formerly integrated middle-class neighborhood was transformed into one of low-income blacks and upper-income whites. During the 1970s these new residents tried to maintain the character of the neighborhood by preventing the construction of a row of federal offices, a new freeway along East Capitol Street, and a 14-story office building planned for **Pennsylvania Avenue**. They integrated the public schools, revitalized Eastern Market and the police station, and in 1976 established Capitol Hill as one of the nation's largest historic districts. Capitol Hill remains one of America's most important symbols, but it also retains its character as one of Washington's most diverse neighborhoods.

CARNEGIE LIBRARY. Public library and city museum. The old Central Library—better known as the Carnegie Library—was constructed between 1898 and 1903. Steel magnate and philanthropist Andrew Carnegie donated $375,000 to construct the facility. An elegant Beaux-Arts building designed by New York architects Ackerman and Ross and located on Mount Vernon Square NW, the Carnegie Library served as the city's main public library until 1972, when the **Martin Luther King, Jr., Memorial Library** was opened. The Carnegie Library was then converted to classrooms for the University of the District of Columbia. In October 1998, the **Historical Society of Washington** entered into an agreement with the city government to transform the library into a city museum and visitors center, to open in 2003. Congress appropriated $2 million in support of the project, contingent upon the society raising matching funds.

CARROLL, DANIEL, of Duddington (1764–1849). Washington landowner, eldest son of Charles Carroll, and member of the large Carroll family of Maryland. In 1791 Carroll began to construct a brick house on **Capitol Hill.** During this same year, **Pierre Charles L'Enfant** was surveying Washington to lay out the capital city of the United States. Construction of the Carroll house infuriated L'Enfant because the house was placed on a site that he had reserved for a monument and fountain, and part of the house further interfered with L'Enfant's city plan by intruding into the planned New Jersey Avenue. L'Enfant demanded that the house be removed. When Carroll refused, L'Enfant instructed workers to demolish it. L'Enfant's action, along with Carroll's subsequent complaint to **George Washington,** was one of the incidents that led to the architect's dismissal.

CARROLL, JOHN. *See* GEORGETOWN UNIVERSITY; HOLY TRINITY ROMAN CATHOLIC CHURCH; ST. PATRICK'S ROMAN CATHOLIC CHURCH.

CARTER BARRON AMPHITHEATER. *See* ROCK CREEK PARK; SHAKESPEARE THEATRE.

CASTLE. *See* SMITHSONIAN INSTITUTION.

CATHEDRAL OF ST. PETER AND ST. PAUL. *See* WASHINGTON NATIONAL CATHEDRAL.

CATHOLIC UNIVERSITY OF AMERICA. A private institution affiliated with the Roman Catholic Church. Established in 1887 as a graduate school of theology for clergy, the school admitted its first class of students 1889 and by 1895 had opened schools of philosophy and social science. While retaining its character as a graduate school, the university offered its first undergraduate instruction in 1904. Enrollment greatly accelerated after World War II. The university now has 370 full-time faculty and enrolls about 6,000 students. It operates 10 schools on its 155-acre campus, including arts and sciences, architecture and planning, engineering, law, library and information science, music, nursing, philosophy, religious studies, and social service. Scholarly journals published by university faculty include the *Catholic Historical Review* (1915), *Anthropological Quarterly* (1928), *Catholic Biblical Quarterly* (1939), and the *Law Review* (1950).

CEDAR HILL. *See* DOUGLASS, FREDERICK; FREDERICK DOUGLASS NATIONAL HISTORIC SITE.

CEMETERIES. *See* CONGRESSIONAL CEMETERY; MOUNT ZION CEMETERY; OAK HILL CEMETERY; ROCK CREEK CEMETERY.

CENTER MARKET. *See* PUBLIC MARKETS; SEVENTH STREET.

CHARTER OF INCORPORATION (1802). An act of Congress that incorporated the city of Washington. The act was passed 12 years after the **Residence Act**, which had established the city. The charter provided for the governing of Washington by a **mayor**, annually appointed by the president, and by a **City Council** of 12 members elected by popular vote. The council was divided into two chambers. The first chamber consisted of seven members and the second of five members, "chosen from the whole number of councilors elected, by their joint ballot." In 1804 the charter was amended to expand the council to two nine-member chambers, to make both chambers popularly elected bodies, to give broader regulatory powers to the council, and to provide for **public education**.

CHASE, WILLIAM CALVIN. *See WASHINGTON BEE.*

CHERRY BLOSSOMS. Japanese cherry trees that bloom annually in the **Tidal Basin**, in East and West **Potomac Park**, and around the **Washington Monument**, attracting tourists and visitors to the spectacle. These 3,700 trees are the centerpiece of Washington's Cherry Blossom Festival, celebrated each spring since 1934. The festival begins with the lighting of a Japanese lantern located along the Tidal Basin near the spot where the first trees were planted. The celebration includes concerts, a parade, and other activities. The planting of cherry trees in Washington was the inspiration of Eliza Scidmore (1856–1928), a Washington travel writer who had visited Japan in 1885 and had marveled at the cherry blossoms she saw there. In 1890 when the **Potomac River** parks were created out of marshland, Scidmore pressed city officials to plant the trees to beautify the city. Her efforts were unsuccessful until she received the backing of first lady Helen Taft in 1909. Finally in 1912 almost 300 trees were planted, a gift of the city of Tokyo and Japanese chemist Jokichi Takamine. Today fewer than 200 trees remain from the original planting, but thousands of new trees have been added.

CHESAPEAKE AND OHIO CANAL NATIONAL HISTORIC PARK. A 185-mile canal that was to be a national transportation artery bringing natural resources and agricultural products from the American heartland to eastern markets. Chartered in 1824, the C&O Canal Company proposed to build a 360-mile canal along the **Potomac River** from Washington to the Ohio River. Incorporating the work of the **Patowmack Canal**, the project progressed in several stages, from **Georgetown** to Seneca (1831), to Harpers Ferry (1834), to Hancock (1839), and to Cumberland, Maryland (1850). The canal included 74 lift locks, seven dams, 11 stone aqueducts, culverts, bridges, and the 3,118-foot-long Paw Paw Tunnel that took the canal under a mountain. Competition from the Baltimore and Ohio Railroad prevented the C&O Canal Company from completing its proposed route, and a flood in 1889 left the company in financial distress. Purchased by the B&O Railroad, the canal was operated as a subsidiary from 1891 to 1924, when after another flood it fell into disuse. In 1938 the canal became the property of the U.S. government and in 1954 a plan to turn it into a highway was successfully opposed by Supreme Court Justice William O. Douglas, who publicized its historical, cultural, and botanical significance. In 1961 the canal was designated a national monument and 10 years later it became a national historic park. The canal's three-mile, tree-lined towpath from Georgetown to Fletcher's Boat House upriver is a favorite of joggers and cyclists.

CHEVY CHASE. The first major residential development northwest of Rock Creek, a picturesque neighborhood with tree-lined streets and a diverse architecture. A portion of the land that is now Chevy Chase was patented from Lord Baltimore to Joseph Belt in 1725 and sold to Assistant Postmaster General Abraham Bradley in 1815.

Between 1880 and 1890, Francis G. Newlands and his partner, Senator William M. Stewart of Nevada, purchased more than 1,700 acres of farmland extending from Boundary Street (now Florida Avenue) to Jones Bridge Road in Montgomery County, Maryland. The heart of this land acquisition was "Chevy Chase," a 305-acre parcel of land straddling the boundary between Maryland and the District. In 1890 the partners transferred these lands to the newly chartered Chevy Chase Land Company, formed with capital stock of $1 million, a third of which was held by William Sharon, another U.S. Senator from Nevada and father-in-law of Newlands (who was himself elected to Congress from Nevada in 1892). Another major partner in the company was George Augustus Armes, a retired army colonel.

Newlands was determined that Chevy Chase reflect the highest standards of Victorian America: There were to be no crowded alleys, row houses, industrial development, or unattractive commerce—only the finest residences, designed to the specifications of individual owners. Sharon and Newlands made a fortune representing the miners of Nevada who worked the Comstock Lode, and even after the Bank Panic of 1893 and the subsequent depression, they still had the financial resources to pursue their vision for Chevy Chase.

The Chevy Chase Land Company invested millions of dollars in the Connecticut Avenue corridor, building five miles of roads, two bridges, and a $1.5 million electric railway by 1892. By 1903 the six-mile trip from the U.S. Treasury Department to Chevy Chase took 35 minutes, with trains departing every 15 minutes. At the northern end of the line, two miles beyond the D.C. border, the company built a small lake and amusement park. Newlands arranged for coal, ice, and medicine deliveries for his neighbors. Throughout Chevy Chase, on both the D.C. and Maryland sides of the boundary, strict building covenants prevailed.

The first four houses in Chevy Chase were designed by architects Lindley Johnson of Philadelphia and Leon E. Dessez of Washington. Dessez became the first resident of the new development. Landscape architect Nathan Barrett planted the neighborhood's shade trees and ornamental shrubs. Despite early difficulties, the Chevy Chase neighborhood grew dramatically during Washington's World War I expansion. The D.C. portion of Chevy Chase was completely sold out by 1916. More than a century after development began, modern Chevy Chase retains the character envisioned by its founders. Most of the original residences still stand,

and the neighborhood features an eclectic residential architecture, a low-rise shopping strip south of Chevy Chase Circle, and a strong sense of community.

CHINATOWN. Two different downtown areas have been designated Chinatown. Although Washington has never had a large Chinese population, between 1880 and 1920 about 500 Chinese immigrants settled in the area around 4th Street and **Pennsylvania Avenue** NW. In 1935, when the U.S. government began acquiring their land for construction of the **Federal Triangle** office complex, virtually the entire Chinese community moved north to the area surrounding 7th and H Streets NW. Between 1950 and 1970, most residents of Chinatown moved to the suburbs, but the neighborhood's Chinese restaurants, grocery stores, and the self-help insurance society, the Chinese Consolidated Benevolent Association, remained in the community. When the D.C. government signed a sister-city accord with Beijing, China in 1986, a colorful Friendship Arch was constructed at 7th and H Streets NW. Although few Chinese people now live in the area, Chinatown has enjoyed an economic boom in recent years with the success of the nearby **MCI Center**. The Chinese New Year's Parade attracts about 10,000 spectators each year and features local high school marching bands, dragon dances, martial arts displays, and fireworks.

CHRIST CHURCH, GEORGETOWN. An Episcopal church at the corner of 31st and O Streets NW. Led by Thomas Corcoran and **Francis Scott Key**, a group from **St. John's Episcopal Church** in **Georgetown**, who were seeking a more evangelical worship experience, founded Christ Church in 1817. Consecrated in 1818, the building stood until 1886, when it was razed and the present structure built. During the **Civil War**, parishioners were predominantly Confederate in their sympathies, and the church lost nearly two-thirds of its membership, but recovered at war's end. Members of Christ Church were instrumental in the founding of Virginia Theological Seminary in Alexandria, and the church retains strong ties to the school.

CHRIST CHURCH, WASHINGTON PARISH. The oldest church within the original city boundaries of Washington. Christ Episcopal Church was organized on Christmas Eve in 1794 in a tobacco barn owned by **Daniel Carroll**. After occupying another temporary site on New Jersey Avenue, the congregation hired architect **Ben-**

jamin Henry Latrobe to design a permanent building. In 1807 Latrobe constructed a Gothic-style church building on G Street SE. The church became a focal point of religious life in Washington. Several early U.S. presidents worshiped at the church, including James Madison, **Thomas Jefferson**, and John Quincy Adams. Today the church has about 250 members.

CHURCH OF MOUNT ST. SEPULCHRE. *See* FRANCISCAN MONASTERY.

CHURCH OF THE EPIPHANY. *See* ST. MARY'S EPISCOPAL CHURCH.

CINCO DE MAYO RIOTS. *See* ADAMS MORGAN; MOUNT PLEASANT.

CIRCLE THEATRE. Historic movie theater built in 1911. Located at 21st Street and **Pennsylvania Avenue** NW, the Circle was remodeled in 1935 in Art Deco style. In 1957 the theater was purchased by Jim and Ted Pedas, who eventually acquired more than 70 movie theaters, an international film distribution company, and local real estate holdings. The Circle screened artistic films not shown elsewhere in the city, was the first theater to present films in repertory, and was popular for its one-dollar matinees and two-dollar evening shows. At the time of its closing in 1986, the Circle was thought to be the oldest continuously operating movie house in Washington. The **Foggy Bottom** Citizens Association and the **Advisory Neighborhood Commission** sought to have the theater declared a historic landmark, but it was demolished soon after closing.

CITIZENS' AND CIVIC ASSOCIATIONS. Voluntary neighborhood associations. When elected municipal government was abolished in the District of Columbia in 1873, D.C. residents formed Citizens' and Civic Associations as a substitute for political parties and partisan clubs. These groups worked to influence Congress and city commissioners who governed the city, and they provided some indirect representation for Washington residents. The associations were originally segregated, with groups organized by African Americans called Civic Associations and those organized by whites called Citizens' Associations. Many neighborhoods had both a Civic Association and a Citizens' Association. Two umbrella organizations, the Federation of Citizens' Associations and the Federation of Civic Associations, were formed to address city-wide concerns. Under the provisions of the 1973 Home Rule Act, **Advisory Neighborhood Commissions** were created to supplant the associations, but a few associations remain important political forces in the city, notably the **Georgetown** Citizens' Association.

CITIZENS' COMMITTEE ON RACE RELATIONS. Advocacy and research organization that monitored and publicized sources of racial tension during the World War II era. Devastating race riots in Detroit in June 1943 recalled Washington's **Red Summer of 1919**, leading to the formation of the Citizens' Committee on Race Relations. Led by an eclectic group of white clergymen, lawyers, educators, and lay members of the Catholic Interracial Council, as well as several prominent African Americans, the committee documented local segregationist practices that particularly enraged black Washingtonians, such as segregation of donated blood at the Red Cross and employment and housing restrictions. It played a valuable role as a relief valve for African American frustrations during the war years.

CITY COUNCIL. Legislative branch of elected city government. In 1802 the U.S. Congress granted a **charter of incorporation** to Washington City that included the establishment of an elected City Council. During its first two years of operation, council members chose five of their number to serve as an upper house. Charter revisions in 1804 provided for direct election of both chambers, and in 1812, further alterations created a 20-member council composed of two aldermen and three councilmen from each of the city's four wards. The powers of the City Council were limited to oversight of street repairs, bridge construction, health and nuisance abatement, license regulation, fire wards and street patrols, real estate taxes, and public schools. Those powers were expanded somewhat in 1820, and two additional wards were created.

    Georgetown, founded in 1751, had its own democratically elected city government, which included an 11-member Common Council. The community retained its independent municipal government until 1871, when Congress revoked the charters of both Georgetown and Washington City, and combined the two jurisdictions, along with Washington County, into a single jurisdiction administered by a presidentially appointed territorial governor and Board of Public Works. For 104 years the District had no popularly elected city council.

When **Home Rule** was established in 1975, the District gained a 13-member City Council, which had the power to levy taxes, regulate financial institutions, and reorganize city government. Legislation passed by the City Council is subject to veto by the U.S. Congress. Home Rule was temporarily withdrawn by Congress in 1995 because of a fiscal crisis, and most of the City Council's power was vested in a presidentially appointed financial control board, officially called **District of Columbia Financial Responsibility and Management Assistance Authority.** Power was restored to the council and **mayor**'s office in 2001.

CITY HALL. Washington's original municipal office building. Located at 5th Street and Indiana Avenue NW, the building was designed by George Hadfield and is considered one of the city's finest examples of Greek Revival architecture. The central section of City Hall was built in 1820, but financial problems delayed completion of the building. A public lottery was held to raise construction money, but the lottery manager embezzled the funds. An 1823 congressional appropriation of $10,000 added an east wing to house the U.S. Circuit Court, and additional federal funding completed the west wing in 1849. In 1873 the federal government purchased City Hall from the D.C. Territorial Government for $75,000 to house federal courts. The proceeds of the sale were designated for the construction of new District government offices, but the city's Board of Public Works spent 70,000 dollars of the money on street improvements, and city officials were relegated to a small office on 4th Street NW. In 1908 a new District Building, now known as the **John A. Wilson Building**, was finally completed. Between 1910 and 1939, four public buildings were constructed around City Hall: the Court of Appeals Building designed by Elliot Woods, and the Juvenile Court, Municipal Court, and Police Court buildings, all designed by Nathan C. Wyeth.

CITY HISTORY MUSEUM. *See* HISTORICAL SOCIETY OF WASHINGTON.

CIVIC ASSOCIATIONS. *See* CITIZENS' AND CIVIC ASSOCIATIONS.

CIVIL WAR. Armed conflict from 1861 to 1865 between the U.S. government and 11 southern states, which formed a Confederacy and tried to secede from the Union. With Washington located only 100 miles north of Richmond, the Confederate capital, and just across the **Potomac River** from secessionist Virginia, Union support in the city was far from unanimous; many residents, in fact, supported the South. Several local militia companies were deemed untrustworthy, and one, the National Rifles, joined the Confederacy's First Virginia Infantry. The elected municipal governments and police forces of Washington and **Georgetown** were put under a military governor. All local officials, and later all voters, were required to take an oath of loyalty to the Union. Washington Mayor James G. Berret was arrested and briefly imprisoned for treason when he refused the oath.

During the early months of the war, 200,000 soldiers of the Army of the Potomac camped in and around Washington, and as many as 50,000 troops were stationed in the capital at other times. The District of Columbia was transformed into a vast camp and supply center for the Union Army. The **U.S. Capitol** building held barracks, a hospital, and a massive bakery that produced 60,000 loaves of bread a day. The **Washington Monument** grounds became a cattle pen and slaughterhouse, producing army rations. While residents suffered from high inflation, some local businessmen profited from supplying the war effort, thus laying the foundation of several banking and commercial fortunes.

The Union Army's sick and wounded poured into the city from nearby Virginia battlefields. At least 56 separate structures became medical facilities. Virtually every public building in Georgetown, plus many others in Washington City, were commandeered for army hospitals: churches, hotels, schools and colleges, **City Hall**, the U.S. Patent Office, country estates of several wealthy citizens, and even the Capitol building. The largest was Lincoln Hospital on East Capitol Street with 2,575 beds; some of the churches and schools held fewer than 100 beds. Many northerners visited or ministered to the wounded, including poet **Walt Whitman**, author Louisa May Alcott, doctor Oliver Wendell Holmes, and battlefield nurse **Clara Barton**.

The defense of the federal capital was vastly improved after the First Battle of Manassas in July 1861. Colonel **John Gross Barnard** supervised construction of a 37-mile ring of 68 small forts, armed with more than 800 heavy fortress cannon, connected by 20 miles of trenches. Between the forts were 93 field artillery positions. More than 20 of the forts were built in Northern Virginia. Following the Second Battle of Bull Run, about 70,000 troops were stationed in the forts, but by the summer of 1864 only 10,000 soldiers occupied these fortifications. Remains of 32 of the forts are still visible, although most are now in neighborhood parks.

The city was attacked only once, on July 11, 1864, when 20,000 Confederate soldiers led by Jubal Early defeated Union forces at the Battle of Monocacy, south of Frederick, Maryland, and marched down what are now Rockville Pike, Viers Mill Road, and Georgia Avenue to Fort Stevens. While Early paused to organize his troops, Union general Ulysses S. Grant sent two experienced units from the siege of Petersburg, Virginia, to the fort and Union defenses held. Forty U.S. soldiers killed in the Battle of Fort Stevens are buried at nearby Battleground Cemetery, one of the country's smallest military burial grounds. A memorial for 17 unknown Confederate battle casualties stands at Georgia Avenue and Grace Church Road.

The District's population more than tripled during the four-year war, from 63,000 to 200,000. Included in this number were about 10,000 African Americans, mostly escaped slaves, who fled to Washington between 1861 and 1862, and another 30,000 former slaves who came to Washington in 1863, after President Abraham Lincoln issued the Emancipation Proclamation. No national welfare system or resettlement plan was in place, and many ended up in squalid living conditions. Just before the war's end, the federal Freedmen's Bureau was organized to assist the former slaves. In 1863 two locally recruited companies of black troops trained on Analostan (now **Theodore Roosevelt**) Island and took part in the battles of Port Hudson and Vicksburg.

The Confederacy surrendered on April 14, 1865, and five days later Lincoln was assassinated by John Wilkes Booth during a performance at **Ford's Theatre** in downtown Washington. His successor, President Andrew Johnson, reviewed more than 200,000 combat veterans in the Union Victory Parade on May 24, 1865; the site of his reviewing stand on **Pennsylvania Avenue** NW is where modern presidents view their inaugural parades. *See also* LINCOLN ASSASSINATION.

CLEVELAND PARK. A community located in Northwest Washington, between Wisconsin and Connecticut Avenues, north of

Georgetown and south of **Chevy Chase**. In the early 1790s Uriah Forrest, a former Georgetown mayor and general during the American Revolutionary War, accumulated 1,282 acres on the hills above Washington, where he built a farmhouse. During the first half of the 19th century, his holdings were gradually divided among some of Washington's wealthier residents, who built country estates on the land. In 1885 President Grover Cleveland purchased 23 acres from a Forrest descendant and converted an 1869 stone farmhouse to a fanciful Victorian mansion, complete with turret. The mansion served as Cleveland's summer White House and was sold after his electoral defeat.

Infrastructure improvements undertaken by Senator Francis Newlands and the Chevy Chase Land Company opened Cleveland Park to development. In 1894 Thomas Waggaman and John Sherman established the Cleveland Park Company and began building houses. The residences were designed by some of America's leading architects, including Paul Pelz, Waddy Wood, Frederick Bennett Pyle, and Robert Thompson Head. Sherman's wife, Ella Bennett Sherman, an artist, also designed several residences. The Cleveland Park Company added a community center, stables, a firehouse, and a police station.

Neighborhood development was spurred by new job opportunities. Between 1890 and 1900 the National Bureau of Standards, the geophysical laboratory of the Carnegie Institute, and the U.S. Geological Survey and **U.S. Naval Observatory** located nearby. One of America's first shopping centers was built in Cleveland Park in 1931 at Connecticut Avenue and Ordway Street NW. The Park and Shop introduced the revolutionary concept of "one-stop shopping," with every consumer need from groceries to automotive care under one roof. Construction of the Art Deco Uptown Theater in 1936, post office in 1940, library in 1952, and subway stop in 1981 attracted numerous small businesses to the Connecticut Avenue corridor.

A tradition of diverse, professional architecture has continued in Cleveland Park into the 20th century, with new residences designed by I. M. Pei, Appleton P. Clark, and Marsh and Peter. In the late 1950s and early 1960s, the neighborhood was discovered by a new generation of politicians, journalists, and academics. These professionals joined with long-time residents to prevent further commercial development. Since then, two major building projects have enriched the community, the University of the District of Columbia campus at Connecticut Avenue and Van Ness Street, and several embassies and chanceries on International Drive.

CLUSS, ADOLPH (1825–1905). Architect. Born in Heilbronn, Germany, Cluss came to Washington in 1848. He worked as a draftsman in several government offices and was put in charge of the design and construction of public buildings in Washington. In 1859 he also began a 10-year private practice with Joseph Wildrech von Kammerhueber. Between 1862 and 1878 Cluss designed eight schools, most notably the Wallach School (1862; demolished), the Franklin School (1869), and the **Sumner School** (1872). He designed several churches, including Calvary Baptist Church (1866), the Eastern Market building on **Capitol Hill** (1871), and some of Washington's fashionable row houses. His public buildings include an expansion of the fire-damaged **Smithsonian Institution** (1865), the Department of Agriculture (1869; demolished), and the Smithsonian's **Arts and Industries Building** (1881). His buildings are characterized by the use of pressed brickwork and colored tiles. In 1872 President Ulysses S. Grant appointed Cluss to the Board of Public Works and, following his retirement in 1890, he served for five years as inspector of public buildings of the United States.

COLONIAL DAMES. *See* NATIONAL SOCIETY OF THE COLONIAL DAMES OF AMERICA.

COLONIAL VILLAGE. *See* SHEPHERD PARK.

COLORED AMERICAN OPERA COMPANY. First professional opera company in Washington. John Esputa of the U.S. Marine Corps Band founded the company in 1872, a decade before New York's Metropolitan Opera first took the stage. The singers were African American, and the leading voice belonged to Henry Fleet Grant, a native Washingtonian. Although the company maintained an excellent reputation, it remained in business only a few years. Several of Washington's most important musicians were connected with the opera company, including **John Philip Sousa**, who studied violin with Esputa, and **Duke Ellington**, who studied with Grant's son.

COLUMBIA FOUNDRY. *See* FOXALL, HENRY.

COLUMBIA HEIGHTS. A community located between Florida

Avenue, Spring Road, and 15th and 7th Streets NW. In 1840 retired engraver William James Stone built "Mount Pleasant," a country estate located at present-day Florida Avenue and Columbia Road NW. Stone leased his residence to the U.S. Army as a military hospital during the **Civil War**. A war- and postwar-related housing shortage made the area a prime target for real estate development.

In 1868 Amzi Lorenzo Barber moved to Washington and became chair of the Education Department at newly established **Howard University**. Within four years he abandoned teaching and embarked on the construction of **LeDroit Park**, an elegant residential neighborhood located near the Howard campus. Following this successful endeavor, he subdivided a portion of the 122-acre Stone estate, which he named Columbia Heights after nearby Columbian College (now **George Washington University**). Barber resided in "Belmont," a "Richardsonian eclectic" mansion he constructed at present 13th and Clifton Streets NW. In 1882 he abandoned real estate development for asphalt paving, an even more lucrative field. The second parcel of Stone's estate was developed by Ohio Senator John Sherman in 1881. One year before his death Sherman moved into Stone's mansion and renamed it "Calumet Place." Neither of the two grand houses associated with Columbia Heights have survived. Barber's Belmont was demolished in 1915; three major apartment complexes, three smaller apartment houses, and several dozen row houses were constructed in its place. Calumet Place was razed in 1925 for construction of the Highview Apartments. After the 14th Street bus and trolley lines were built, Columbia Heights saw an influx of federal government employees, who were drawn to the neighborhood's moderately priced townhouses and apartments.

During the **riots of 1968** more than 300 Columbia Heights businesses were looted or demolished. After property owners abandoned the neighborhood, the existing housing gradually became ill-maintained rental properties. The 14th Street corridor deteriorated into one of the city's most desolate urban areas, with numerous boarded-up, graffiti-covered buildings. In the last three decades, Columbia Heights has housed African Americans and recently arrived Hispanics from Central America. Despite the availability of its desirable older housing, the neighborhood's high crime rates have kept demand and prices low.

It took transit officials nearly 20 years to reach agreement with local activists on a subway route and subway stop in the neighborhood. The opening of the stop in 1999 attracted new real estate developers, who bid $135 million to renovate and reconstruct the area around 14th Street and Park Road, the heart of the Columbia Heights commercial district. This development promises to bring much-needed revitalization to the neighborhood.

COLUMBIA HISTORICAL SOCIETY. *See* HISTORICAL SOCIETY OF WASHINGTON.

COLUMBIAN ACADEMY. *See* BALCH, STEPHEN BLOOMER.

COLUMBIAN COLLEGE. *See* GEORGE WASHINGTON UNIVERSITY.

COMBAT ART GALLERY. *See* NAVY YARD.

COMMISSION OF FINE ARTS. A seven-member body that reviews, advises, and approves construction projects, art commissions, monuments, memorials, parks, and other architectural and artistic features of Washington. First located in the Lemon Building on New York Avenue NW, commission offices are now housed in the old Pension Building. The commission was founded in 1910 to assist the federal government in the orderly planning of the city. Its work grew out of the City Beautiful movement, the **Washington centennial** of 1900, the **McMillan Report** of 1902, and the work of the Public Art League of Washington, all of which encouraged the beautification and orderly development of the capital. The commission operates in accord with the basic principles of the 1791 city plan of **Pierre Charles L'Enfant**. Initially, the commission's work was limited to artistic and architectural matters, but subsequent acts of Congress and presidential executive orders have broadened its authority to include the review of all public buildings and other construction projects. The Commission of Fine Arts has had a major role in the development of Washington, influencing the design of such projects as the **Lincoln Memorial**, the **Mall** area, city parks, the **Federal Triangle**, the **National Gallery of Art**, the **Jefferson Memorial**, the **John F. Kennedy Center for the Performing Arts**, the **Washington Metrorail System**, the **Franklin Delano Roosevelt Memorial** and many others.

COMMUNITY FOR CREATIVE NONVIOLENCE. Social justice organization that held a series of protests against homelessness in

Washington in the 1970s and 1980s. Founded by Mitch Snyder in 1970, the group began as a commune opposing the Vietnam War. Snyder led the CCNV in high-profile protests that included occupying part of **Union Station** as a homeless shelter. In the 1980s the CCNV built a tent city in **Lafayette Park**, occupied an abandoned federal building, and publicized a hunger strike by Snyder. Public attention drawn to the plight of the city's poor resulted in the funding of the Federal City Shelter, authorized in 1984 by President Ronald Reagan. Several local and federal initiatives providing aid to the homeless were subsequently enacted, partly due to the group's efforts. Today with the help of thousands of volunteers and donations of food from restaurants and food distributors, the Federal City Shelter and the D.C. Central Kitchen provide help for thousands of poor and homeless people in Washington. They also provide free legal and medical services, literacy training, and employment counseling.

COMPENSATED EMANCIPATION (1862). Federal purchase and emancipation of slaves owned by residents of the District of Columbia. Nearly nine months before he issued the Emancipation Proclamation, President Abraham Lincoln signed legislation authorizing $1 million to fund the only compensated emancipation in U.S. history. Eligible slave owners were required to demonstrate legal title and swear a loyalty oath to the United States; 100 slave owners declined to file, based on their unwillingness to meet the latter requirement. The slaves had to appear in person and be examined and assessed by an experienced Baltimore slave dealer. Three commissioners administered the program, which paid 966 petitioners an average of less than $300 for each of 3,128 slaves.

COMPROMISE OF 1850. *See* BLACK CODES; SLAVERY.

CONGRESS HEIGHTS. *See* ANACOSTIA.

CONGRESSIONAL CEMETERY. A private, 32-acre cemetery owned by the Episcopal Church and administered by the Association for the Preservation of Historic Congressional Cemetery. Located on the north bank of the **Anacostia River** in Southeast Washington, the cemetery was founded in 1807 by members of Christ Episcopal Church on Capitol Hill. Congressional Cemetery has no official connection to the federal government, although before World War I Congress occasionally provided small appropriations for improvements. The property has two distinctive features: the cenotaphs and the chapel. Six rows of sandstone cenotaphs designed by **Benjamin Latrobe** honor members of Congress who died in office, some of whom are buried there. The stucco chapel was constructed in 1903. Among the 70,000 interments are 19 U.S. Senators; 68 U.S. Representatives; Vice President Elbridge Gerry; photographer **Mathew Brady**; composer **John Philip Sousa**; FBI Director **J. Edgar Hoover**; architects **William Thornton**, who designed the **U.S. Capitol**, and **Robert Mills**, who designed the **Washington Monument**, and Thomas Blount, a signer of the Declaration of Independence.

CONGRESSIONAL RACETRACK. *See* HORSERACING.

CONGRESSIONAL UNION FOR WOMAN SUFFRAGE. *See* WOMEN'S SUFFRAGE PARADE.

CONSTITUTION GARDENS. A 45-acre park that features walking paths, landscaped grounds, and a small artificial lake. Located west of the **Mall** between 17th Street and Bacon Drive NW, the park was placed on land dredged from the **Potomac River**. The project was the result of the **McMillan Report** of 1902, which sought to restore the city plan of **Pierre Charles L'Enfant** by extending park-like open space from the Mall to the Potomac River. The development of this open space was delayed by World War I and World War II, which saw the construction of temporary navy office buildings on the site. These "tempos" were finally demolished in 1971 and President Richard Nixon had the land developed into a park. In 1976 the park was dedicated as part of the U.S. bicentennial. Six years later a memorial to the Signers of the Declaration of Independence was created on a small island in the lake. Accessible by footbridge, the memorial consists of a low semicircular wall of 56 granite blocks, each carved with the signature of one of the signers of the Declaration. In 1986 President Ronald Reagan named the park Constitution Gardens in honor of the bicentennial of the U.S. Constitution.

CONSTITUTION HALL. *See* DAUGHTERS OF THE AMERICAN REVOLUTION, NATIONAL SOCIETY; GLOVER, CHARLES CARROLL; NATIONAL SYMPHONY ORCHESTRA; POPE, JOHN RUSSELL.

CONTINENTAL HALL. *See* DAUGHTERS OF THE AMERICAN

REVOLUTION, NATIONAL SOCIETY.

CONTRABANDS. Slaves from southern states who escaped into the Union Army lines during the **Civil War.** Washington became an important destination for many contrabands. By early 1862, about 400 contrabands and other fugitives lived in Duff Green's Row on East Capitol Street, now the site of the **Folger Shakespeare Library.** Within six months, that number grew to 4,200 and the Freedmen's Relief Association was organized to furnish clothing, temporary housing, employment, and education. In June 1862 the military governor of Washington created the "contraband department," headquartered in a military barracks at 12th and O Streets NW. Contrabands registered at the office and were granted passes that ensured protection by the military. Many were employed as day laborers in military hospitals, for army transport, and on road repair crews. When Duff Green's was converted to a military prison, the contraband settlement moved to Camp Barker, adjacent to the Contraband Department offices. By war's end, there were more than 40,000 African American refugees in Washington. Most lived in crowded, unsanitary huts located in a few small settlements around Camp Barker, in southern **Anacostia** around Forts Carroll and Greble, and in Murder Bay (site of the present **Federal Triangle** development). *See also* SLAVERY.

CONTROL BOARD. *See* DISTRICT OF COLUMBIA FINANCIAL RESPONSIBILITY AND MANAGEMENT ASSISTANCE AUTHORITY.

CONVENTION CENTER. *See* WASHINGTON CONVENTION CENTER.

COOK, JOHN FRANCIS (1810–1855). Presbyterian minister and educator. In 1834 Cook became the principal of a small, private school in Washington, which he reorganized and called Union Seminary. The school provided a basic education for African American students. In 1841 he became the founding minister of the all-black **Fifteenth Street Presbyterian Church,** where he remained for the rest of his life. A critic of **slavery** and the **American Colonization Society** that tried to return blacks to Africa, Cook founded the Young Men's Moral and Literary Society and was a prominent leader in the city's African American community.

COOK, WILL MARION (1869–1944). Composer, conductor, and

musician. Born in Washington, Cook was educated at the Oberlin Conservatory of Music (1884–88). He studied violin in Berlin for three years and then enrolled at the National Conservatory of Music in New York (1894–95). With limited opportunities for African Americans in classical composition, Cook began to prepare popular compositions for African American audiences. With the help of **Paul Laurence Dunbar**, Cook composed the music for *Clorindy: The Origin of the Cake-Walk* (1898). The musical comedy opened at the Casino Theatre Roof Garden in New York and played for several months. Other musicals featuring George Walker and Bert Williams followed, including *Dahomey* (1903), *Abyssinia* (1906), and *Bandana Land* (1908). Cook help to organize the Memphis Students in 1906, a band that toured the United States and Europe. He also conducted the New York Syncopated Orchestra, which helped to introduce jazz to European audiences on its 1919 tour. Cook's hit songs include "Red, Red Rose," "That's How the Cake-Walk's Done," and "A Little Bit of Heaven Called Home." He influenced the work of **Duke Ellington** and other musicians.

COOKE, JACK KENT (1912–1997). Diversified company executive, multimillionaire, and one-time owner of several sports franchises, including the **Washington Redskins** professional football team. Born in Hamilton, Ontario, Canada, Cooke was a partner of Thomson Cooke Newspapers (1937–52), president of the Toronto Maple Leafs baseball team (1951–64), and chairman of Cooke Properties (1966–97) and Cooke Media Group (1985–97). Cooke acquired the Redskins in 1960. Under his ownership the team won six Eastern Division championships and three Super Bowls. In 1987 Cooke announced plans to build a new stadium to replace the aging **RFK Memorial Stadium**. It took a decade and contentious negotiations with the District of Columbia, Maryland, and Virginia before Cooke found a home for his stadium in Landover, Maryland. Cooke spent $175 million to construct the 80,000-seat stadium and died five months before it was completed.

COOPER, ANNA J. (1858–1964). Educator. Born in Raleigh, North Carolina, Cooper was educated at St. Augustine's Normal School and graduated from Oberlin College (1885). After serving as a professor of modern languages at Wilberforce University, she became a teacher and high school principal at M Street High School in Washington. Except for a brief tenure at Lincoln University

(1906–10), she served in the Washington schools from 1887 to 1929. At the age of 66 she earned a doctorate in French language from the Sorbonne in Paris and from 1929 to 1941 served as president of Frelinghuysen University (founded 1906), which operated out of her home on T Street NW. She published *A Voice from the South* (1892) and participated with Booker T. Washington in the Hampton Conference (1892) and in the Pan-African Conference in London (1900).

CORCORAN, WILLIAM WILSON (1798–1888). Banker, art collector, and philanthropist. William W. Corcoran's 1840 partnership with George W. Riggs led to the organization of the Corcoran and Riggs Bank, which still operates as **Riggs National Bank,** one of Washington's leading commercial institutions. Corcoran sold bonds in Europe to help finance the Mexican War (1846–48) and arranged the transfer of federal funds for the Alaska Purchase (1867). When his art collection outgrew his private residence, he commissioned the **Corcoran Gallery of Art.** During the **Civil War**, Corcoran, a southern sympathizer, went to Paris after his country estate and art gallery were commandeered by the U.S. Army. After the war, he returned to Washington and became one of the city's most generous benefactors. In addition to the Corcoran Gallery of Art, he also established **Oak Hill Cemetery** and the Louise Home, a residence for destitute "gentlewomen."

CORCORAN GALLERY OF ART. Privately funded museum of American and European art. The Corcoran Gallery was founded by **William Wilson Corcoran,** who began by exhibiting his collection of American art in his own home, open to visitors two days a week. In 1869 Corcoran commissioned **James Renwick** to design a museum building at 17th Street and **Pennsylvania Avenue** (now the home of the **Renwick Gallery**). Because of the **Civil War**, the museum did not open until 1875. The collection quickly outgrew Renwick's building, and Ernest Flagg won an architectural competition to design a new building two blocks away. Flagg's Beaux-Arts-style building opened in 1897. A wing designed by Charles Platt was added in 1925; architect Frank O. Gehry has been commissioned to design a second and final wing. The collection now contains 11,000 works. Corcoran originally intended for the museum to specialize in American art, but after his death the museum received several large donations of European masterworks. The gallery building also houses a Salon Doré, a gilded room exhibit of 18th-century French interior design. In 1998 the gallery acquired the core of the Evans-Tibbs collection of African American art. When Corcoran founded the museum, he also endowed a school, which now exists as the only school of design in Washington, the Corcoran College of Art and Design.

COSMOS CLUB. A private social club for scientists and leading intellectuals in Washington. Founded in 1878 by John Wesley Powell, an explorer and director of the U.S. Geological Survey, the club rented space in the downtown Corcoran building from 1879 to 1882. It moved to **Lafayette Square** and in 1886 bought the Dolley Madison House, which served as its headquarters until 1952. The club then bought the Massachusetts Avenue Townsend Mansion on **Embassy Row** and carried out an extensive expansion and renovation that turned it into a social club. The club employs a staff of 150 and has 25 committees that carry out its administrative, cultural, and social affairs. Published since 1991, its annual *Cosmos Journal* contains articles on timely issues. The club was the birthplace of the **National Geographic Society** and was a gathering place for scientists from the Manhattan Project.

COUNCIL OF GOVERNMENTS. *See* METROPOLITAN WASHINGTON COUNCIL OF GOVERNMENTS.

COURTS. *See* DISTRICT OF COLUMBIA COURTS.

COX, JOHN (1775–1845). **Mayor** of **Georgetown**. Orphaned as a child, Cox was raised by an uncle in Baltimore. He lived in Philadelphia and then moved to Georgetown, where he became a wealthy merchant and landowner. He served as a colonel in the **War of 1812**. Cox became a leader in the civic affairs of Georgetown and, by a vote of the city council, became mayor in 1823. The following year Cox was an official host during **Lafayette's tour of Washington**. The French war hero stayed in a Georgetown row house that Cox had built on First Street, near Cox's home, and was given a grand banquet there. In 1830 the governance of Georgetown was changed so that the mayor was elected by popular vote. Cox, who had served as mayor since 1823, was the first person to be popularly elected to the mayor's office. He continued to be reelected every two years until 1845—serving as mayor for 22 consecutive years.

COXEY'S ARMY. An 1894 gathering of several thousand men who marched to Washington to protest high unemployment and the absence of federal relief programs. In the wake of the Bank Panic of 1893 and the subsequent worldwide depression, American unemployment skyrocketed. Gangs of destitute men roamed the country, creating fears of large-scale domestic violence and even revolution. General Jacob S. Coxey of Massillon, Ohio, proposed a half-billion-dollar federal program to employ men at $1.50 per day to build roads and to work on other locally managed public works projects. Coxey then led 300 Ohioans in a march to Washington, and several other "armies" from around the United States joined them in makeshift camps around the city. When Coxey's Army attempted to hold a peaceful protest on the **U.S. Capitol** grounds, mounted police used their horses to trample parts of the crowd and other demonstrators were beaten with billy clubs. Coxey and several "lieutenants" were arrested and incarcerated for 20 days for stepping on the Capitol lawn. The encamped protesters were fed by Frank Hume, Washington's leading wholesale grocer, who also made arrangements with District commissioners to have the men sent home by railroad.

CRANDALL, HARRY M. (1877–1937). Theater builder and operator. Crandall owned and operated more than 12 vaudeville and movie theaters in Washington, including the Metropolitan Theater on F Street NW and the **Knickerbocker Theater** on Columbia Road at 18th Street NW. The Knickerbocker was the site of one of Washington's greatest disasters, when its snow-laden roof collapsed in 1922, killing 98 people. Although an inquiry implicated the theater's contractor for shoddy construction practices, Crandall, who was not involved in the construction of the theater, was attacked in the press. The Great Depression led to Crandall's retirement and sale of his chain of theaters in Washington, Maryland, Pennsylvania, and West Virginia to Warner Brothers. His successful, 21-year career was marred by the Knickerbocker tragedy, which weighed heavily upon him and led to his eventual suicide.

CRUMMELL, ALEXANDER. *See* AMERICAN NEGRO ACADEMY; ST. LUKE'S EPISCOPAL CHURCH.

CRYSTAL SPRING RACETRACK. *See* BRIGHTWOOD; HORSE-RACING.

CULTURAL ALLIANCE OF GREATER WASHINGTON. A non-profit regional arts organization. Founded in 1978, the Cultural Alliance is a membership organization composed of actors, artists, arts administrators, dancers, musicians, writers, and arts organizations and schools, including art schools, community theaters, dance companies, museums, symphony orchestras, and other groups. The programs of the alliance include arts management workshops, job listings, group buying plans, and group health insurance. By working closely with the Washington business community, the alliance seeks to provide its members with leadership, marketing, and financial expertise to help in the business side of their work. The alliance publishes an events calendar, the *Cultural Alliance Directory*, and *Arts Washington*, an arts trade newspaper issued 10 times a year.

- D -

DANCE PLACE. Dance theater and training center. Dance Place grew from a performing company established in 1978 by dancer-choreographer Carla Perlo and musician-composer Steve Bloom. In 1980 they opened a studio in **Adams Morgan**, but in 1986 a dramatic rent increase led the company to purchase and renovate a building on 8th Street NE, becoming one of very few dance organizations in the United States to hold its own property. Dance Place is the city's leading presenter of contemporary and culturally specific dance concerts, including the annual DanceAfrica festival. Theater, music, and performance art programs are also hosted in a year-round performing season. Dance Place received the 1986 Mayor's Arts Award for Service to the Arts.

DAUGHTERS OF THE AMERICAN REVOLUTION, NATIONAL SOCIETY. An organization formed in 1890 for the purposes of historic preservation and patriotism education. The 180,000 female members of the Daughters of the American Revolution (DAR) trace their genealogy back to participants in the American Revolution. The DAR's national headquarters complex, located on D Street NW and occupying a full city block, is the largest group of buildings in the world owned and operated by women. It includes three structures: Memorial Continental Hall, which features a research library and museum of decorative and fine arts; an administration building; and Constitution Hall, a 4,000-seat auditorium designed by **John Russell Pope** in 1929. Constitution Hall was the city's premiere cultural center until 1939, when the DAR refused permission for African American contralto Marian Anderson to perform there. First Lady Eleanor Roosevelt resigned her DAR membership in protest, and Anderson sang instead at the **Lincoln Memorial** to an audience of 75,000 on Easter Sunday. The Anderson affair was a major turning point in the American civil rights struggle. Although Anderson was invited to perform at the hall in 1943, and its white-performers-only policy was discontinued in 1952, Constitution Hall never recovered its prominence.

DAY, MARY. *See* WASHINGTON BALLET; WASHINGTON SCHOOL OF BALLET.

D.C. ARMORY. An arena at the foot of East Capitol Street on the bank of the **Anacostia River**. Designed by Nathan C. Wyeth, the armory was built in 1941 as a headquarters and military staging grounds for the D.C. National Guard and local militia. The building features limestone walls and a 90-foot arched roof and has a seating capacity of 10,000. The armory is the site of conventions, sporting events, inaugural balls, and other large events.

D.C. STADIUM. *See* RFK MEMORIAL STADIUM.

DEANWOOD. One of Washington's oldest African American communities, bounded by Eastern and Kenilworth Avenues and East Capitol Street in Northeast Washington. Until the **Civil War**, the Deanwood area was agricultural. Most of the land was owned by Levi Sheriff and James H. Fowler, and slaves worked on the area's mixed-crop farms. With the outbreak of the Civil War, the Union Army set up checkpoints at the Benning and Navy Yard bridges, and everyone who entered or left the District of Columbia was stopped and searched. Union troops cleared dozens of acres of woodlands, felling the original growth forest to create unobstructed sight lines for military guards. The farms never recovered from the war's depredations.

During the late 1800s, the Southern Maryland Railroad laid tracks along the old Bladensburg-Piscataway Road (now Minnesota Avenue), and the Sheriff heirs created three subdivisions: Whittingham, Lincoln, and Burrville. However, the isolated community attracted little interest during the **Boss Shepherd** era, when Washington City was in the throes of major public works projects. By 1873 only two lots had sold, and the Sheriff daughters traded the undeveloped portions of Whittingham for two downtown lots. The new owner of Whittingham, John H. W. Burley, national secretary of the African Methodist Episcopal Church, renamed the development Burley's Subdivision and planned to establish a black community there. However, residential development remained slow. In 1888 Julian Dean, Levi Sheriff's grandson, renamed the community "Deanwood." He built about 20 houses on the remaining holdings of his family, but a bad investment led to bankruptcy, and he was forced to sell his real estate holdings at public auction.

By the turn of the century, new residents were joining the old farm families of Deanwood. Many residents worked for the railroads, at the **Navy Yard**, or in the building trades. Although Deanwood was developed as a black neighborhood, for many years the community's housing market was largely controlled by white investors who bought and subdivided the land and then held the mortgages of black residents.

In 1909 two schools opened in Deanwood: George Washington Carver Elementary, which also enrolled black students from nearby Maryland, and the National Trade and Professional School for Women and Girls, directed by innovative educator **Nannie Helen Burroughs**. The community also attracted the Suburban Gardens Amusement Park, a major recreational center for African Americans, which opened in 1921. It featured a swimming pool, carousel, rollercoaster, and entertainment by such entertainers as Cab Calloway and **Duke Ellington**. Deanwood remained semirural until World War II, with few city services such as paved streets, sewers, or sidewalks.

During the late 1970s, Deanwood was threatened by street crime and drug traffic, but residents worked hard to reclaim the community. Deanwood is now a family-oriented, middle-class enclave with many third- and fourth-generation residents.

DECATUR HOUSE. A large Federal-style red brick residence. Built in 1818 near the **White House** on "President's Park," which later became **Lafayette Park**, Decatur House was designed by **Benjamin Latrobe**, who had a short time earlier been dismissed as architect of the **U.S. Capitol**. It was to become the home of Stephen

Decatur, an American naval hero, who lived in the house for only 14 months before he was killed in a duel. His widow, Susan Wheeler Decatur, moved out and rented the house to a succession of prominent politicians and diplomats, including Henry Clay and Martin Van Buren, until she lost the property to creditors in 1836. During the **Civil War** the house was used by the Union army for administrative offices. In 1872 it was sold by the federal government to the Beale family from California. A member of this family later bequeathed the house to the National Trust for Historic Preservation, which now operates a museum there. The first-floor furnishings represent Stephen Decatur's era (1818) and the second floor displays the house as it looked in the late 1930s.

DEPARTMENT STORES. Six stores founded during the 19th and early 20th centuries have shaped the retail life of Washington, providing jobs and distributing goods and services to the city. Some of these **7th Street** NW stores served the local market exclusively, while others branched out regionally and nationally. The earliest was the Lansburgh Department Store, founded as a dry goods store by Gustave Lansburgh in 1860. The Lansburgh Department Store was opened on 7th Street in 1916 and closed in 1970. Saks and Company began in 1867 as a clothing store operated by two brothers, Isidore and Andrew Saks of Baltimore. In 1887 the brothers built a large store on 7th Street. Saks, which also opened a chain of stores in other cities, sold its Washington building to Kann's in 1932 and became more widely known as a New York company. Kann's Department Store was opened in 1875 and grew to occupy four buildings on Market Space, between 7th and 8th Streets. Owned by Solomon Kann of Baltimore, the discount retailer closed in 1975. Garfinckel's was founded by Julius Garfinckel on F Street NW in 1905. The store closed its operations during the economic recession of 1989. The Hecht Company was founded by two brothers, Moses and Alexander Hecht of Baltimore, on 7th Street in 1896. Hecht stores merged with the May department store chain in 1959 and has been operated as a division of the parent company. Woodward and Lothrop began as a small store dry goods store on 7th Street at **Pennsylvania Avenue** NW in 1880. The store, which eventually closed in the mid-1990s, moved to F Street, which became Washington's main shopping district.

DESEGREGATION. *See* SCHOOL DESEGREGATION.

DISTRICT BUILDING. *See* CITY HALL; JOHN A. WILSON BUILDING.

DISTRICT OF COLUMBIA ARMORY. *See* D.C. ARMORY.

DISTRICT OF COLUMBIA COMMISSION ON THE ARTS AND HUMANITIES. The official cultural arts agency of the District of Columbia. Founded in 1968, the agency is operated by a 12-member staff and governed by 18 commissioners appointed by the **mayor** and approved by the **City Council.** The commission dispenses grants to organizations and individuals involved in a variety of artistic expressions, including crafts, dance, literature, music, theater, performance art, and visual arts. The commission initiates and funds programming in its Arts Education Projects Program and its City Arts Projects Program. These programs provide training and exposure to the arts for children and youth in schools, churches, and community centers, and they reach out to urban residents through concerts, festivals, public readings, and displays of visual art. The commission sponsors public art competitions and purchases artworks related to the city of Washington that become part of its Art Bank, a growing body of work that is loaned to agencies and offices for temporary display.

DISTRICT OF COLUMBIA COURTS. Judicial branch of the D.C. government. The U.S. Constitution grants Congress the power to establish the D.C. judiciary. All judges are appointed by the president and confirmed by the Senate.

Congress established the first local court system in 1801, which included the Justice of the Peace Court, renamed the Municipal Court in 1909, and the Orphans Court, abolished in 1870. The only court of general jurisdiction was the Circuit Court of the District of Columbia, comprising three judges who were authorized to hold a U.S. District Court with the same powers and jurisdiction as other U.S. District Courts, thus functioning as both a federal and local court. The Circuit Court was abolished in 1863 when Judge William M. Merrick, a suspected Confederate sympathizer, issued a writ of habeas corpus permitting release of an underage Union soldier. President Abraham Lincoln suspended the writ, placed Merrick under house arrest, and convinced Congress to abolish the court, all in direct violation of the Constitution's provisions on separation of powers and the tenure of federal judges.

Congress then created the nine-member Supreme Court of the

District of Columbia. It was not only the District's court of first instance but also served as the appellate court, hearing appeals from the rulings of its individual judges. The Supreme Court took over the functions of the D.C. Criminal Court (established in 1838) and, like its predecessor, served as a U.S. District Court. The court's five-to-four decision in 1865 not to execute **Mary Surratt**, one of the conspirators in the **Lincoln assassination**, was overridden by President Andrew Johnson, in violation of the Constitution.

In 1893, the appellate function of the D.C. Supreme Court was transferred to the newly created Court of Appeals of the District of Columbia, renamed in 1934 the U.S. Court of Appeals for the District of Columbia Circuit. The D.C. Supreme Court in 1936 was renamed the District Court of the United States for the District of Columbia. Only the Justice of the Peace Court, by then known as Municipal Court, was a local judiciary. Everything else was under the control of federal courts.

The Court Reform and Criminal Procedure Act of 1970 mandated a major reorganization of the D.C. judicial system. The Court of General Sessions (formerly the Municipal Court) was consolidated with the Juvenile and Tax Courts to form the Superior Court of the District of Columbia. Its 44 judges administer all criminal cases and all nonfederal civil matters. The legislation also created the D.C. Court of Appeals. Its nine judges hear all appeals from Superior Court and review decisions of the **mayor**, **City Council**, and city agencies. The Appeals Court is comparable to state supreme courts; its decisions may be appealed only to the U.S. Supreme Court.

The **Home Rule** Act of 1973 created the Judicial Nomination Commission to advise the president on appointments to the Superior Court and Court of Appeals, an attempt to remove partisan politics from the selection process, although appointees are still subject to Senate approval. Judges serve 15-year terms and may be removed by the District Commission on Judicial Disabilities and Tenure. *See also* DISTRICT OF COLUMBIA LAW CODE.

DISTRICT OF COLUMBIA FINANCIAL RESPONSIBILITY AND MANAGEMENT ASSISTANCE AUTHORITY. The interim body responsible for overseeing the government and finances of the District of Columbia from 1995 to 2001. The **Home Rule** Act of 1973, which brought self-government to Washington, also left the city government with many problems, including a bloated bureaucracy and financial problems consisting of a declining tax base, an unfunded pension liability of $1.8 billion for city employees, and financial obligations for services provided to the federal government. These problems, accompanied by several years of financial mismanagement, led to a deterioration in city services and a $722 million city debt in 1995. In response, Congress created a five-member "Financial Control Board" to return the city to fiscal health. Board members appointed by the president and approved by Congress were charged with balancing the city budget for four consecutive fiscal years. The board was given the power to approve budgets, hire and fire city personnel, make contracts, hold hearings, and restructure city government. In 1997 Congress increased the board's authority over city life, severely reducing the power of the **City Council** and **mayor**. By reducing the size of city government, replacing key city administrators, and restructuring various city offices and departments, the board reported a $185 million surplus in 1997. An agreement between the board and mayor-elect Anthony A. Williams returned power to the mayor's office in 1999.

DISTRICT OF COLUMBIA LAW CODE. A 15-volume compilation of laws relating to the District of Columbia. The D.C. law code is complicated by the early history of the District of Columbia. Because it was created from a portion of Virginia and Maryland, the District of Columbia is governed by a code that includes common law and British statutes in effect in 1776, laws enacted by the legislatures and state governments of Virginia and Maryland up to 1800, and acts of Congress and local laws passed thereafter. The D.C. law code has gone through more than 15 editions from its first publication in 1816. In 1895 the D.C. Board of Trade requested the preparation of a new code, which was passed by Congress in 1901. Between 1901 and 1977 the code was revised by various congressional committees and offices, including the Congressional Committee on Revision of Laws, the Judiciary Committee of the House of Representatives, and the Office of the Law Revision Counsel of the House of Representatives. Since 1977, editions have been published under the supervision of the **City Council** of the District of Columbia. *See also* GREATER WASHINGTON BOARD OF TRADE.

DISTRICT OF COLUMBIA SELF-GOVERNMENT AND RE-ORGANIZATION ACT (1973). The **Home Rule** Act that delegated legislative power from the federal government to the District; it essentially restored self-government to Washington. Under the act, Congress retains legislative power with respect to the **District of Columbia court** system and reserves the right to "enact, amend, or repeal any law" made by the District. The act provides for an elected **mayor, City Council, Advisory Neighborhood Commissioners**, and a Board of Education. The council is empowered to enact laws, review and approve the mayor's budget, write tax legislation, establish and organize municipal government, and appoint a D.C. auditor. The mayor proposes and vetoes legislation, makes appointments, prepares the budget, recommends federal payments, proposes bond issues, and writes a comprehensive city plan.

DISTRICT OF COLUMBIA v. THOMPSON COMPANY. Lawsuit that resulted in the desegregation of Washington restaurants, theaters, and other public places. In 1950 the Coordinating Committee for the Enforcement of the D.C. Anti-Discrimination Laws, led by octogenarian civil rights pioneer **Mary Church Terrell**, sued the John R. Thompson Company after Terrell and three others were denied service by Thompson's Restaurant on 14th Street NW. The committee argued that two laws prohibiting discrimination in public accommodations, passed in 1872 and 1873—the "Lost Laws"—had never been repealed and were still valid. The laws were arbitrarily omitted from the **District of Columbia Law Code** in 1901. When the D.C. Municipal Court dismissed the suit in July 1950, citizens' groups picketed segregated lunch counters at several downtown **department stores**. The Hecht Company began serving African Americans in 1951 and other stores soon followed. The **U.S. Supreme Court** unanimously ruled in 1953 that the Lost Laws were valid and still enforceable, ending decades of racial discrimination in a major sector of city commerce.

DISTRICT TERRITORIAL ACT (1871). An act passed by Congress that ended municipal government in the District of Columbia. The act vested authority in the governor, "who shall be appointed by the president, by and with the advice and consent of the Senate." The governor was appointed to a four-year term of office. The act also created a legislative assembly consisting of a council and house of delegates. While the 11-member council was appointed by the president, the 22-member house of delegates was an elected body that provided "District representation in the ratio of its population."

DOUGLAS, WILLIAM O. *See* CHESAPEAKE AND OHIO CANAL NATIONAL HISTORIC PARK.

DOUGLASS, FREDERICK [AUGUSTUS WASHINGTON BAILEY] (1817–1895). Writer, abolitionist, ambassador to Haiti, and advisor to President Abraham Lincoln. Born a slave in Maryland, Bailey escaped in 1838 to New York City and then to New Bedford, Massachusetts, using the alias Frederick Douglass. In 1841 he spoke at an antislavery convention in Nantucket, Massachusetts, and afterward became an agent of the Massachusetts Anti-Slavery Society. Douglass wrote an autobiography in 1845 that he revised and published as *The Life and Times of Frederick Douglass* (1882). During a two-year speaking tour in the United Kingdom, British sympathizers contributed funds to purchase Douglass's freedom (1846) and he began an abolitionist newspaper, the *North Star*. Douglass published the newspaper, later called "Frederick Douglass's Paper," from 1847 to 1860 in Rochester, New York. During the **Civil War**, Douglass advised President Lincoln to legally end **slavery**, and he recruited African American troops for the Union Army. During Reconstruction (1865–77) Douglass went to Washington, where he lived in a row house on **Capitol Hill**. In 1877 he moved to his Cedar Hill estate. Douglass served as assistant secretary of the Santo Domingo Commission (1871), marshal (1877–81), and recorder of deeds (1881–86) in the District of Columbia and as U.S. ambassador to Haiti (1889–91). *See also* FREDERICK DOUGLASS NATIONAL HISTORIC SITE.

DOWNING, ANDREW JACKSON (1815–1852). Landscape architect. Born in Newburgh, New York, Downing attended Montgomery Academy and began working in his father's nursery at an early age. His ideas on landscape design were published in *A Treatise on the Theory and Practice of Landscape Gardening* (1841) and other works. In 1846, he became editor of a new periodical, *The Horticulturist*, and designed houses and gardens in the Hudson Valley with partner Calvert Vaux. His reputation and interest in the design of large urban parks led to a commission to design the Washington **Mall** area in 1850. His design of gardens and paths for the Mall was a departure from the open space envisioned by **Pierre Charles L'Enfant**. The virtue of his plan was the attempt to unify the Mall area under a single design concept. Downing's plans were never carried out because of his premature death in a steamship fire in New York harbor. However, his work influenced later planners.

DREW, CHARLES R. (1904–1950). Physician and biomedical researcher who developed the blood bank. A native of Washington and a graduate of Dunbar High School, Drew attended Amherst College and completed a medical degree at Canada's McGill University. He began landmark research on blood preservation during postdoctoral training at Columbia University, earning the first Doctor of Science degree granted to an African American. In 1940, as medical director of the first American Red Cross blood bank, Drew developed blood collection programs used throughout the United States. After he left the Red Cross, the organization began to collect blood from white donors only. When the **National Association for the Advancement of Colored People** and National Medical Association protested, the Red Cross began accepting African American donations, but stored and labeled them separately. Drew argued, to no avail, that the only scientific basis for separating blood is type, not race. From 1941 until his death in a North Carolina car accident, he was chair of surgery at **Howard University** Medical School and chief surgeon at Freedmen's Hospital. A persistent myth falsely claims that Drew bled to death after being refused treatment at a whites-only hospital, but he actually died of his injuries. Drew is a hero to many, and numerous schools, hospitals, bridges, highways, and scholarships are named for him.

DUFF GREEN'S ROW. *See* CONTRABANDS.

DUMBARTON HOUSE. *See* NATIONAL SOCIETY OF THE COLONIAL DAMES OF AMERICA.

DUMBARTON OAKS. Historic mansion and gardens in **Georgetown**. In the 1600s **Ninian Beall**, a Maryland colonist, acquired the tract of land where Dumbarton Oaks now stands. He named it the Rock of Dunbarton, a pun on the Battle of Dunbar and the Rock of Dumbarton in his native Scotland. In 1800 a subsequent owner, William Hammond Dorsey, built a Federal-style house there. Other 19th-century owners expanded, renovated, and renamed the house; one called his estate "The Oaks," after the white oak trees on the grounds. John C. Calhoun lived there for several years, including during his stint as vice president. In 1920 the property was bought by Mildred and Robert Woods Bliss, who gave it the name Dumbarton Oaks. They hired landscape gardener Beatrix Farrand to create gardens on the steeply sloping land around the house, and architect Frederick H. Brook to rework the building's irregular renovations into a unified design. The Blisses lived abroad during most of their 20 years as owners of Dumbarton Oaks and during their travels amassed a large collection of art and artifacts. In 1940 they gave the building, its grounds, and their collections to Harvard University, to be used as a study center for Byzantine art, pre-Columbian Native American art, and landscape gardening. In 1944 Dumbarton Oaks was used for an international conference that led to the founding of the United Nations.

DUMBARTON UNITED METHODIST CHURCH. The city's oldest Methodist congregation. Dumbarton grew from the first Methodist sermon preached in **Georgetown** in October 1772. The congregation built its first church on Montgomery (now 28th) Street by 1795 and its current home on Dumbarton Street in 1850. The church was commandeered by the U.S. Army as a hospital during the **Civil War,** and President Abraham Lincoln worshiped at its reconsecration in March 1863. The Romanesque Revival facade and art glass windows were installed in 1898. Since the mid-1960s Dumbarton has maintained an active social justice ministry.

DUNBAR, PAUL LAURENCE (1872–1906). Poet and novelist. Born in Dayton, Ohio, Dunbar's mother encouraged him to write poetry from an early age. After graduating from high school in 1891, Dunbar supported himself by working as an elevator operator. In 1893 he published *Oak and Ivory*, and at the invitation of **Frederick Douglass,** he recited at the World's Columbian Exposition in Chicago. Dunbar's growing notoriety led to the publication of *Majors and Minors* (1895) and *Lyrics of a Lowly Life* (1896), a work that reprinted the best material from his previous books. After a trip to England, Dunbar settled in Washington, where he lived on the campus of **Howard University** and then in **LeDroit Park** on U Street NW. Between 1898 and 1899 he worked as an assistant to **Daniel Murray** in the reading room of the **Library of Congress.** Dunbar married Alice Moore in 1898, and the couple became part of the social and intellectual life of the black community. Dunbar presided at the well-known Bachelor-Benedict Club. The breakup of his marriage in 1902 and declining health from tuberculosis and alcohol dependency led to his return to Ohio in 1904. Dunbar wrote 12 books of poetry, a play, four books of short stories, and five novels, including *The Sport of the Gods* (1902).

DUNBAR HIGH SCHOOL. *See* DREW, CHARLES R.; DUNBAR, PAUL LAURENCE; FAUNTROY, WALTER EDWARD; FIFTEENTH STREET PRESBYTERIAN CHURCH; NORTON, ELEANOR HOLMES; PUBLIC EDUCATION; SCURLOCK, ROBERT; SHAW/U STREET.

DUNCAN, TODD (1903–1998). Educator, singer, and actor. Born in Kentucky, Duncan was educated at Butler University and Columbia University, and in 1930 he joined the faculty of **Howard University**. For more than 40 years Duncan directed Howard's Public School Music Department, training hundreds of music teachers. A classically trained baritone, he also established a distinguished performing career, making his New York stage debut in an all-black production of *Cavalleria Rusticana* in 1934. He was personally selected by composer George Gershwin to create the role of Porgy in the opera *Porgy and Bess*. He also appeared in the Broadway production of *Cabin in the Sky*, the film *Syncopation*, and more than 1,500 concerts, including the inaugural festivities for President Lyndon Johnson. Duncan served as the first chairman of the Washington Performing Arts Society, one of the country's earliest nonprofit fine arts presenters.

DUPONT CIRCLE. An area around the intersection of Massachusetts, Connecticut, and New Hampshire Avenues and 19th and P Streets NW. Although a circle with surrounding streets was featured on **Pierre Charles L'Enfant**'s original plan for Washington, little more than a creek and a few shacks existed on the site until the post-**Civil War** period. The area was called "The Slashes," after the Slash Run tributary and surrounding marshland that fed Rock Creek. During the 1870s, this marshland was transformed by **Alexander "Boss" Shepherd**, head of the city's Board of Public Works. In 1873 Shepherd built three elegant stone houses on Connecticut Avenue; one was his personal residence, and the other two were rental properties. Soon streets were graded and paved, a metal truss bridge was built across Rock Creek to **Georgetown**, railroad tracks were laid along Connecticut Avenue, and a circular federal park was established at the heart of the neighborhood, then known as Pacific Circle.

Civic improvements attracted noted real estate developers Curtis Hillyer, Thomas Sunderland, and William Stewart, a U.S. Senator from Nevada. These developers were all western mining magnates and the group came to be known as the California Syndicate. In 1873 Stewart built an extravagant Second Empire mansion on the circle. The mansion was known as "Stewart's Folly" and "Stewart's Castle." A year later, the British Legation constructed an ornate companion structure. By the end of the 1870s the neighborhood also included the modest brick and frame houses of tradesmen, servants, and laborers, as well as undeveloped lots. In 1884 a bronze statue of Civil War hero Admiral Samuel Francis Dupont was erected in Pacific Circle. The circular park was landscaped with more than 850 ornamental plantings, and neighborhood residents took advantage of the park's 56 cast-iron benches. In 1920 the Dupont statue was replaced by a memorial fountain sculpted by Daniel Chester French.

At the beginning of the 20th century, Dupont Circle was one of Washington's most fashionable addresses. The perimeter of the circle was formed by elegant mansions, and brick or stone row houses were constructed on the side streets. On the eve of World War I, many of the city's black elite moved into the northeast section of the neighborhood, especially around 17th and U Streets NW, an area that became known as the "Strivers' Section." A row of Second Empire townhouses was built on 17th Street for **Frederick Douglass**; the property remained in the Douglass family until 1965. Other notable residents included **Mary Church Terrell, Todd Duncan**, and Elder Lightfoot Solomon Michaux.

By World War II, Dupont Circle had undergone extensive change. Most of the mansions had been razed or converted to foreign embassies or offices. In 1947 the city constructed a streetcar underpass and tunnels under Dupont Circle, leaving the park a muddy mess for more than three years. Eleven years after the underpass was completed, streetcars became obsolete. Dupont Circle was enlivened by the presence of the American counterculture during the 1960s and 1970s. The park filled with hippies, black power advocates, and **Vietnam War protestors.** Many of the row houses were used for experiments in group living. The neighborhood's longtime residents urged police action to clear the park of those who loitered and encamped there. In 1978 the neighborhood, with the exception of the Strivers' Section, was declared a historic district; two years later the Strivers' area was also included. Modern Dupont Circle is an eclectic mix of coffeehouses, bookstores, residential brownstones, modern office buildings, gay bars, restaurants, nightclubs, and high-end retailers.

- E -

EARLE THEATRE. *See* WARNER THEATRE.

EARLY, JUBAL. *See* CIVIL WAR.

EAST POTOMAC PARK. *See* POTOMAC PARK.

EASTERN MARKET. *See* PUBLIC MARKETS.

ECKSTINE, BILLY. *See* SHAW/U STREET.

EDSON, JOHN JOY (1846–1935). Banker and civic leader. An executive with the Washington Loan and Trust Company, Edson participated in every significant civic project in the District of Columbia for more than 30 years. He was a leader in the city's "Social Betterment" movement of the 1880s and 1890s and worked to improve living conditions and economic opportunities for the city's poor. As chair of the Penal Commission of 1908, Edson introduced rehabilitation for first offenders and those convicted of misdemeanors. These offenders were held in minimum custody and employed in farming and brickmaking. His reforms led to the opening of Lorton Reformatory in 1916. An early advocate for congressional representation for District residents, Edson led the District Board of Charities and served on the Board of Public Welfare and Joint Committee on National Representation for the District of Columbia.

ELECTRIC COMPANY. *See* POTOMAC ELECTRIC POWER COMPANY.

ELLICOTT, ANDREW (1754–1820). Surveyor who established the original boundaries of Washington, D.C. Ellicott was born in Pennsylvania to a prominent Quaker family and educated in the sciences. He learned surveying as a profession and was commissioned by the state of Virginia to survey its northern border. In 1791 **George Washington** appointed Ellicott to survey the boundaries of the new capital city, which was to be built on land ceded to the federal government by Virginia and Maryland. With the help of **Benjamin Banneker**, Ellicott mapped the 10-mile square capital city and laid its **boundary stones**. Banneker and Ellicott were then asked to reconstruct and complete the city plan begun and abandoned by **Pierre Charles L'Enfant**. Later, on congressional commission, Ellicott mapped out the United States' southern and western borders with the territory held by Spain. When he retired from government service, Ellicott taught mathematics at West Point.

ELLINGTON, [DUKE] EDWARD KENNEDY (1899–1974). Jazz pianist, composer, and bandleader. Ellington was born on 22nd Street NW; his father was a butler at the **White House** and later worked at the **Navy Yard**. The young Ellington studied piano at age seven and began his professional career at age 17. During the 1910s he worked with various jazz bands in Washington, first appearing under the name "Duke's Serenaders" at True Reformers Hall, a dance club on U Street. In 1923 Ellington moved to New York with his Washington band: Sonny Greer (drums), Toby Hardwicke (bass and saxophone), Elmer Snowden (banjo), and Arthur Whetsol (trumpet); this group played at the Kentucky Club on Broadway until 1927. Between 1927 and 1932 Ellington was featured at the Cotton Club in Harlem, where the band grew into a small orchestra. During this period, Ellington's complex arrangements revolutionized the concept of jazz. By the 1940s the band had grown to 19 musicians, and Ellington's work, through hundreds of recordings and tours in the United States and abroad, received international acclaim. He is credited with more than 1,000 compositions, including "Black, Brown, and Beige" (1943), a musical history of the African American experience. In 1969, on his 70th birthday, Ellington received the Presidential Medal of Freedom at a White House ceremony. In 1974 Western High School in **Georgetown** was renamed Duke Ellington School of the Arts. A bridge on Calvert Street is also named after Ellington.

ELLIOT, JONATHAN (1784–1846). Author, editor, and publisher. Born near Carlisle, England, Elliot came to New York in 1802 and worked as a printer. He settled in Washington in 1813 and the following year he began printing the *Washington City Gazette*, the city's first daily newspaper. Suspended during the summer of 1814 when the city was under British attack, the paper resumed publication in November 1815 as the *Washington City Weekly Gazette*. By 1817 the *Gazette* was a daily newspaper and in 1926 Elliot sold the business. He then turned his attention to historical editing and writing. He compiled important documents relating to the founding of the nation, including *Debates, Resolutions, and Other Proceedings in Convention on the Adoption of the Federal Constitution* (5 vols.; 1827–34), and a book of U.S. international treaties titled *The Diplomatic Code of the United States of America* (1827; 2d ed. 1934). He also wrote a popular guidebook, *Historical Sketches of the Ten Miles Square Forming the District of Columbia* (1830), and *A Large Study of the Funding System of the United States and of Great Britain* (1845).

ELLIPSE. A 36-acre expanse of land between the **White House** and the **Washington Monument**. The open space is used as a ceremonial area for the White House, for public gatherings and demonstrations, and for recreational events including ball games and the annual White House Easter Egg Roll. A marker on its north side is the zero milestone from which all distances in Washington are measured. Originally marshland, the area was used as a military livestock enclosure during the **Civil War**. Reclaimed during the late 19th century, the Ellipse contains two gatehouses designed in 1828 by **U.S. Capitol** architect **Charles Bulfinch**. The gatehouses were moved from the Capitol grounds to their present sites in 1874. The Ellipse also contains several memorials, including two fountains and stone memorials to Civil War general William Tecumseh Sherman and to the Boy Scouts. A blue spruce tree growing on the northern edge of the property serves as the site for the national Christmas tree.

EMANCIPATION. *See* COMPENSATED EMANCIPATION; SLAVERY.

EMANCIPATION STATUE. *See* LINCOLN PARK.

EMBASSY ROW. An area on Massachusetts Avenue NW between **Dupont Circle** and Wisconsin Avenue. This tree-lined street is home to many foreign embassies and chanceries, although others are located in several areas of Northwest Washington. A number of the embassies near Dupont Circle are housed in Victorian mansions constructed during the 1880s and 1890s. Noted Massachusetts Avenue landmarks include the **Islamic Center**, the statue of Winston Churchill on the grounds of the British Embassy, Khalil Gibran Park, and the **U.S. Naval Observatory**, where the vice president resides.

ENID A. HAUPT GARDEN. A 4.2-acre Victorian garden located between the **Smithsonian Institution** Castle and Independence Avenue. Named after its donor, a journalist, horticulturist, and philanthropist, the street-level garden features lawns, shrubbery, and flowerbeds laid out in a geometric design of diamonds and squares. The $3 million garden lies above two underground museums, the **Arthur M. Sackler Gallery** and the **National Museum of African Art**. Seasonal plantings include tulips in spring and red begonias in summer. The garden includes Moorish- and Asian-inspired plantings, a fountain, and a children's carousel.

EPIPHANY CATHOLIC CHURCH. *See* HOLY TRINITY ROMAN CATHOLIC CHURCH.

EXECUTIVE BRANCH. *See* MAYOR.

- F -

F STREET PRESBYTERIAN CHURCH. *See* NEW YORK AVENUE PRESBYTERIAN CHURCH.

FARMERS AND MECHANICS BANK OF GEORGETOWN. *See* RIGGS NATIONAL BANK.

FARRAGUT SQUARE. A square honoring **Civil War** hero David Glasgow Farragut (1801–1870), who led the Union naval forces at the Battle of New Orleans (1862). Farragut's victory, achieved in 10 days, led to his promotion to vice admiral, and in 1866 he became the Navy's first four-star admiral. Located on 17th Street NW, the square features a statue of Farragut by Vinnie Ream Hoxie (1814–1914), a noted sculptor who lived across from the square. Hoxie cast the statue from the propeller of Farragut's ship, the USS *Hartford*, and it was dedicated in 1881.

FAUNTROY, WALTER EDWARD (b. 1933). Civil rights activist and political leader. A native of Washington, Fauntroy graduated from Dunbar High School and earned degrees at Virginia Union University and Yale Divinity School. He worked in the civil rights movement in the 1960s. In Washington Fauntroy founded an urban renewal planning agency, Model Inner City Community Organization (MICCO), for the revitalization of the **Shaw** neighborhood. His first political position was that of vice-chair of the District of Columbia Council (1967–69). In 1971 Fauntroy became the first elected congressional representative of Washington, D.C., in more than a century. In Congress he worked on **home rule** legislation for the District, and in 1973 the **District of Columbia Self-Government and Reorganization Act** became law. Fauntroy has served as pastor of the New Bethel Baptist Church since the 1960s.

FEDERAL CITY SHELTER. *See* COMMUNITY FOR CREATIVE NONVIOLENCE.

FEDERAL TRIANGLE. The largest complex of federal office buildings in Washington, bounded by Constitution and **Pennsylvania Avenue**s and 6th and 15th Streets. The federal triangle was determined by the placement of the **Mall** and Pennsylvania Avenue in the original city plan of **Pierre Charles L'Enfant**. The location and design of federal office buildings within the triangle is a result of the **McMillan Report** (1902) and the Mellon Plan (1929), which recommended the consolidation of scattered government offices into a unified symbol of national government. The federal buildings of the triangle are monumental in scale and classical in design, with prominent colonnades on their facades. These buildings set an architectural standard for later federal construction between the **Washington Monument** and the **U.S. Capitol**. Three buildings—the District Building, the National Archives, and the **Old Post Office Pavilion and Clock Tower**—are listed on the National Register of Historic Places. *See also* PERSHING PARK.

FEMALE UNION BAND SOCIETY. *See* MOUNT ZION CEMETERY.

FICHANDLER, ZELDA. *See* ARENA STAGE.

FIFTEENTH STREET PRESBYTERIAN CHURCH. An African American congregation located on 15th Street NW. The church was organized in 1841 with 18 members. **John F. Cook** served as the first pastor until his death in 1855. In 1866 the church lobbied Congress to extend suffrage to African Americans, and in 1870 it organized the Preparatory High School of Negro Youth in its basement. The small school evolved into the M Street High School, now Dunbar High School. By 1873 the congregation had grown to 214 members, and in 1878 **Francis J. Grimké** began a 46-year ministry at the church (1878–85; 1889–1928). Grimké established himself as a leader in Washington's African American community and his presence at the church brought notoriety to the congregation. He was active in the national life of the Presbyterian Church, where he allied himself with other black ministers and spoke out against racism in the Christian churches. During the 1920s **Rosina Tucker** joined the church and later became an important union organizer and civil rights leader. The church constructed a new building in 1979 and today it has about 300 members.

FINANCIAL CONTROL BOARD. *See* DISTRICT OF COLUMBIA FINANCIAL RESPONSIBILITY AND MANAGEMENT ASSISTANCE AUTHORITY.

FIRST BAPTIST CHURCH. *See* FORD'S THEATRE.

FIRST PRESBYTERIAN CHURCH. *See* SUNDERLAND, BYRON.

FIRST UNITARIAN CHURCH. *See* ALL SOULS UNITARIAN UNIVERSALIST CHURCH.

FLEET, JAMES H. (ca. 1810–ca. 1870). Educator and civic leader. Fleet, a free black, grew up in **Georgetown** and attended the **Lancasterian School**. The **American Colonization Society** paid for his medical education at Columbian College (now **George Washington University**), intending that he emigrate to Liberia, but Fleet refused to go. Instead, he practiced medicine in Georgetown and in 1836 opened a school for black students, which was destroyed by arson. His second school, located at 23rd and N Streets NW was successful. Fleet was elected vice president of the Convention of the Free People of Color and was an leader in the national Colored Convention Movement.

FLETCHER'S BOAT HOUSE. *See* CHESAPEAKE AND OHIO CANAL NATIONAL HISTORIC PARK.

FLOOD OF 1881. See TIDAL BASIN.

FOGGY BOTTOM. An area bounded by Rock Creek, 19th Street, H Street, and the **Potomac River** in northwest Washington. In 1765 German immigrant Jacob Funk divided a 130-acre parcel of marshy, frog-infested bottomland along the Potomac River into 234 lots and named his settlement "Hamburgh." The few who moved there before 1791 referred to the area as "Funkstown." In 1792 the U.S. military constructed battlements near modern Washington Circle in the heart of Foggy Bottom.

By 1800 the neighborhood was home to carpenters and architects, pump borers, and the British ambassador. Newly arrived German artisans established a Bohemian glassworks and two breweries. American troops encamped in Foggy Bottom during the **War of 1812**, and in 1828 the community's Irish laborers helped to construct the **Chesapeake and Ohio Canal** in neighboring **Georgetown**. The following year, William Easby founded a shipyard and became the most prominent businessman in the village. The area's largest employers included a wood yard, three lime kilns, an icehouse, and a factory that produced plaster, ammonia, and fertilizer. In 1844 the first **U.S. Naval Observatory** was built there, and in 1856 Washington's new Gas Light Company built a gas storage facility at Virginia and New Hampshire Avenues; the unsightly structure dominated the landscape for nearly a century.

During the **Civil War**, military horse corrals were built on 21st and 22nd Streets near the Potomac River. Camp Fry, home to invalid soldiers and volunteers who guarded federal buildings, was located along 23rd Street. After the war, Irish and German enclaves maintained separate Catholic parishes and commercial establishments. The Irish mostly worked for the gas company and the Germans were employed at the breweries. African American residents established **St. Mary's Episcopal Church** in 1867, and in 1886 they moved into a **James Renwick**-designed church on 23rd Street. After brick row houses filled the neighborhood, hundreds of families crowded into narrow, unsanitary **alley dwellings**. By the time Congress banned such construction in 1892, more than 1,500 people lived in Foggy Bottom alleyways.

The neighborhood underwent dramatic changes during the 20th century. Rail transport displaced the C&O Canal, and when the trains bypassed Foggy Bottom, numerous businesses were forced to move or close. The breweries were decimated by **Prohibition**. Gentrification came to the neighborhood in 1947, when the U.S. Department of State moved to 23rd and D Streets and its employees bought and renovated neglected historic row houses. The unsightly Washington Gas Light storage tanks were removed in the late 1940s and early 1950s. A 1958 zoning decision that permitted high-rise development, along with construction of the Theodore

Roosevelt Bridge, the **John F. Kennedy Center for the Performing Arts**, and several government and professional office buildings, led to rapidly rising rents and housing prices. By 1960 poorer African American residents were forced out, and Foggy Bottom became a middle- to upper middle-class white neighborhood. **George Washington University**, which occupied the area around 20th and G Streets in 1912, continued to expand its land holdings throughout the century. Construction of luxury apartments and hotels such as Columbia Plaza and the **Watergate** complex, completed the transformation of Foggy Bottom.

FOLGER SHAKESPEARE LIBRARY. Private research library housing the world's largest collection of Shakespeare's printed works. Begun as the Shakespeareana collection of Standard Oil magnate Henry Clay Folger (1857–1930) and his wife, Emily Jordan Folger (1858–1936), the library now contains about 280,000 books and manuscripts, including a set of First Folios, which are the original text-source for more than half of Shakespeare's plays. The collection also includes many works of literature and history that were available to Shakespeare. Dedicated in 1932, the marble library building on East Capitol Street features a garden with nine bas-relief sculptures depicting scenes from Shakespearean drama. The interior of the building houses a reading room, a Great Hall for special events and exhibitions, and the Elizabethan Theatre, which is designed to replicate the atmosphere of an innyard theatre of Shakespeare's time. The Folger Shakespeare Library is administered by the trustees of Amherst College in Massachusetts. *See also* SHAKESPEARE THEATRE.

FORD'S THEATRE. The site of President Abraham **Lincoln's assassination**. Impresario John T. Ford converted Washington's First Baptist Church into a music hall in 1861, only to see it burn a few months later. He rebuilt the theater and reopened it in August 1863. On April 14, 1865, during the third act of *Our American Cousin*, actor John Wilkes Booth shot Lincoln, who was attending the performance with his wife and two friends. After receiving numerous threats, Ford closed the theater and sold it to the federal government, which used the building as office and warehouse space for 90 years. Congress passed legislation in 1954 to restore the playhouse, but 10 years passed before reconstruction began. Ford's Theatre reopened in 1968 with the Lincoln-era play

John Brown's Body. Under the leadership of artistic director Frankie Hewitt, the theater presents national touring companies of Broadway and other American musicals and plays. The building also houses a museum dedicated to the last days of President Lincoln.

FORREST, URIAH. *See* CLEVELAND PARK.

FORT CARROLL. *See* CONTRABANDS.

FORT GREBLE. *See* CONTRABANDS.

FORT LESLEY J. McNAIR. U.S. army fort constructed for the defense of Washington. Established in 1791 on 28 acres of land at the confluence of the Washington Channel and the **Anacostia River**, the site was originally a military reservation and arsenal, to which defenses were added in 1794. During the **War of 1812**, the arsenal was captured by the invading British (1814) and later rebuilt. The fort contained a federal penitentiary (1826), where in 1865 John Wilkes Booth and his co-conspirators were imprisoned, tried, and hanged for the **Lincoln assassination**; a **Civil War** era hospital (1857–81); and a general hospital (1898–1909), where Walter Reed helped to discover the cause of yellow fever. Now consisting of 98 acres, the fort is the home of National Defense University (1976), which consists of a consortium of independent schools: the army's National War College (1901), the Industrial College of the Armed Forces (1924), the Information Resources Management College at Fort McNair (1990), and the Armed Forces Staff College in Norfolk, Virginia. The fort also hosts the Inter-American Defense College (1962), a school for military leaders in the Americas. In 1948 the fort was named in honor of Lieutenant General Lesley J. McNair, a Word War II army commander, headquartered at the fort, who was killed in Normandy, France, in 1944.

FORT RENO. *See* TENLEYTOWN.

FORT STANTON PARK. *See* ANACOSTIA MUSEUM AND CENTER FOR AFRICAN AMERICAN HISTORY AND CULTURE.

FORT STEVENS. *See* BRIGHTWOOD; CIVIL WAR; PETWORTH.

FOUNDRIES. *See* FOXALL, HENRY.

FOXALL, HENRY (1758–1823). Defense contractor, **Georgetown mayor**, and Methodist preacher. Born in Wales, Foxall learned iron manufacture from Henry Cort, an important figure in Britain's Industrial Revolution. Foxall immigrated to Philadelphia in 1795, where he established the Eagle Works in partnership with Robert Morris, Jr., and began manufacturing cannon for the U.S. military. When the federal government relocated to Washington in 1800, Foxall, armed with thousands of dollars in Navy weaponry contracts, moved to Georgetown and built the Columbia Foundry, which became D.C.'s leading manufacturing concern. Foxall's products were of superior quality and he introduced several technological innovations into U.S. manufacturing. He earned a substantial fortune supplying Navy cannon during the **War of 1812** and in local real estate speculation. In 1816, he sold his foundry to John Mason and focused on civic affairs, serving two terms as mayor of Georgetown. Foxall was a highly regarded preacher and donated large sums to various Methodist causes in the United States and Britain.

FOXALL CRESCENT. *See* GLOVER-ARCHBOLD PARK.

FRANCISCAN MONASTERY. American headquarters of the Roman Catholic Order of St. Francis, the mendicant brotherhood founded by St. Francis of Assisi. The 42-acre property on Quincy Street NE includes the 500-seat Church of Mount St. Sepulchre, built in the shape of a Byzantine cross and dedicated in 1899, and spacious gardens. The Franciscan Order was charged with protecting the Christian shrines in the Middle East and the grounds of the monastery contain life-size replicas of several of these Holy Land shrines, including Ascension Chapel on Mount Olivet, the Lourdes Grotto, the Bethlehem site where Jesus was born, and the Holy Sepulcher, Jesus' tomb. Reproductions of the Catacombs of Rome are found below ground. Interest in these replicas peaked in the 1950s, when 120,000 pilgrims visited each year. In 1998 about half as many callers were received.

FRANKLIN, NICHOLAS. *See* CAPITOL HILL.

FRANKLIN DELANO ROOSEVELT MEMORIAL. A 7.5-acre memorial to the 32nd president of the United States. Dedicated in 1997, the memorial is located in West **Potomac Park** near the **Tidal Basin.** The outdoor site contains walkways, waterfalls and pools, and thousands of plants, shrubs, and trees. The memorial is divided into four galleries or rooms, connected by granite passageways. Each room depicts one term of Roosevelt's four-term presidency (1933–45). Room one, introducing Roosevelt's presidency, features Tom Hardy's bas-relief sculptures of the Great Seal of the President and FDR waving from an open car at his first inaugural. Room two, depicting the Great Depression, contains three sculptural groups by George Segal: a bread line (Hunger), a rural couple (Despair), and a man listening to one of Roosevelt's "fireside chats" on a radio (Hope). A large bas-relief sculpture by Robert Graham depicts Roosevelt's New Deal legislation. Room three, devoted to World War II, features a nine-foot sculpture by Neil Estern of FDR in his wheelchair. Room four, devoted to Roosevelt's life and legacy, contains a 30-foot sculptural relief of Roosevelt's funeral cortege by Leonard Baskin, a statue of Eleanor Roosevelt by Neil Estern, and a timeline of important events that occurred during Roosevelt's life. The red granite passageways that connect the rooms are engraved with some of Roosevelt's most inspiring words, including, "The only thing we have to fear is fear itself."

FREDERICK DOUGLASS NATIONAL HISTORIC SITE. The restored home of **Frederick Douglass** (1817–1895), called Cedar Hill. The white Victorian house was built in the 1850s by John Van Hook, a local developer. Cedar Hill was constructed on the highest point of **Anacostia**, overlooking the **Anacostia River** and the capital beyond. Douglass lived at Cedar Hill from 1877 until his death in 1895. Many of the furnishings now displayed in the house belonged to Douglass. The main floor of the two-story house contains a portrait of Douglass by Sarah James Eddy, Douglass's 1,000-volume library, and the desk at which Harriet Beecher Stowe wrote *Uncle Tom's Cabin* (1852). The historic site includes a visitor's center, exhibits, and an audiovisual program.

FREEDMEN'S HOSPITAL. *See* DREW, CHARLES R.; GRIFFING, JOSEPHINE SOPHIE WHITE.

FREER GALLERY. The first **Smithsonian Institution** museum dedicated to fine art. The gallery's founder, Detroit businessman Charles Lang Freer (1854–1919), made his fortune in the manufacture of railroad cars. Freer's bequest to the Smithsonian included a large art collection and funds to construct a building to house it. Both the art and the money came with the stipulation that pieces of the collection not be lent to other museums. Architect Charles Platt designed an Italian Renaissance building of granite and marble, constructing it on the **Mall** in 1923. The Freer Gallery houses a National Museum of Asian Art; this collection spans 6,000 years of art and treasure and comprises works from China, Japan, Korea, Southeast Asia, and the Near East. It includes Japanese folding screens, Indian and Persian manuscripts, and Buddhist sculpture. The Freer Gallery also holds a large collection of modern American paintings, including many artworks by James McNeill Whistler, a friend of Freer. Particularly noteworthy is the lavish blue and gold Peacock Room, decorated by Whistler in 1876. Once part of an English townhouse, the Peacock Room was moved from London and installed as a permanent exhibit.

FRELINGHUYSEN UNIVERSITY. *See* COOPER, ANNA J.

FRENCH, DANIEL CHESTER. *See* DUPONT CIRCLE; GALLAUDET UNIVERSITY; LINCOLN MEMORIAL.

FRIENDS MEETINGHOUSE. Society of Friends (Quaker) house of worship, located on Florida Avenue NW. Although a Quaker meetinghouse was constructed in Washington City in 1808, by the early 20th century, the sect had a reduced presence in the town. Upon the election of the nation's first Quaker president, Herbert Hoover, an unnamed Rhode Island Quaker paid for construction of the Florida Avenue Meetinghouse, in a then-fashionable neighborhood where it was surrounded by embassies, chanceries, and distinguished private residences. First Lady Lou Henry Hoover laid the meetinghouse cornerstone; she and President Hoover attended the first service in the structure in 1931 and were regular worshipers thereafter. A ground floor room of the meetinghouse contains a beamed timber ceiling removed from the **White House** after the British attack in 1814. Noted landscape architect Rose Greeley designed the extensive grounds, which feature a sundial inscribed with the names of Quaker leaders George Fox, William Penn, and John Woolman, above the inscription, "I mind the Light, dost Thou?" In 1970 the congregation acquired an adjacent property at Decatur Place NW for educational and community events.

FRIENDSHIP ARCH. *See* CHINATOWN.

FUNKSTOWN. *See* FOGGY BOTTOM.

- G -

GALA HISPANIC THEATRE. Washington's only professional Hispanic arts organization. Located on Park Road NW in **Adams Morgan**, GALA Theatre was founded in 1976 to preserve and promote Hispanic culture. GALA's more than 100 productions of classical and contemporary drama, poetry, music, and dance have been presented with simultaneous English interpretation through audiophones, making performances accessible to both the Spanish- and English-speaking public. Several of the company's productions have toured Latin America, performing at the International Theater Festival of San Jose for Peace in Costa Rica and at the International Theatre Festival of Central America in El Salvador. The company also provides performance space for theatrical groups and individual artists from Latin America. GALA has won several local, national, and international public service and artistic awards.

GALLAUDET UNIVERSITY. Liberal arts college for the deaf and hearing-impaired. The school was founded by U.S. Postmaster General Amos Kendall on his Northeast Washington farm in 1857, and later chartered by Congress as the Columbia Institution for the Instruction of the Deaf and Blind, which began as an elementary school directed by Edward Miner Gallaudet. A college degree program was added in 1864, and programs for the blind were discontinued. In 1894 the institution was renamed Gallaudet College and in 1986 it became a university. A model secondary school for the deaf was added in 1969. Gallaudet University also houses the National Information Center on Deafness, the Gallaudet Research Institute, and the International Center on Deafness. Two-thirds of all deaf college graduates in the United States are educated at Gallaudet. The original grounds were designed by **Frederick Law Olmsted** and the school is listed on the National Register of Historic Places. A statue of Gallaudet's father, Thomas Hopkins Gallaudet, who organized the first school for the deaf in the United States, is found on the grounds of the campus. Sculpted by Daniel Chester French in 1889, the statue depicts Gallaudet with his first student, Alice Cogswell. Gallaudet's football team invented the huddle in the 1890s, to keep opposing teams from seeing their hand signals.

GARFIELD ASSASSINATION. The murder of President James A.

Garfield on July 2, 1881, at the B&O Railway station. Garfield had been in office only six months when he was shot in the back as he prepared to board a train out of Washington to escape the summer heat. His assassin, Charles J. Guiteau, was a deranged federal office-seeker who had hoped to be appointed U.S. ambassador to France. Garfield survived two months after the shooting; it is thought that inadequate medical care contributed greatly to his death. Guiteau was convicted and hanged for the crime, and Chester A. Arthur succeeded to the presidency.

GARFINCKEL'S. *See* DEPARTMENT STORES.

GAYE, MARVIN (1939–1984). Singer. Born in Washington and educated at Cardozo High School, Gaye was one of the leading rhythm-and-blues singers of the mid- to late 20th century. While still a teenager, Gaye formed his first singing group, the D.C. Tones, later known as the Marquees. The group had only one nationally successful record in 1958, and by 1962 Gaye embarked on a solo career. Gaye achieved stardom as a solo artist, recording some of the most popular songs of the 1960s through the 1980s, including "I Heard It Through the Grapevine," "What's Going On?" and "Sexual Healing." One critic called Gaye "one of the great voices of the last half-century, a master of both erotic ballads and social commentary." Gaye was shot to death in a fight with his father.

GEORGE WASHINGTON UNIVERSITY. Private university serving 17,000 students. President **George Washington** wanted to establish a national university in the capital city and in 1795 donated 50 shares of stock in the Potomac Company for this purpose. However, the Potomac Company went bankrupt and Washington's university was never constructed. A second attempt to fulfill Washington's dream was made in 1821 with the founding of Columbian College by the Baptist Church. Initially located on College Hill in **Mount Pleasant**, a 1904 charter changed its name to George Washington University and removed the institution from Baptist patronage. In 1912 the school moved to G Street NW in **Foggy Bottom**, where it has grown into a major university. Its 74 buildings on 23 city blocks make it the largest nonfederal landowner in the neighborhood. The university is staffed by 10,000 employees and has 1,100 faculty members. Academic programs include the National Law Center, opened in 1865; School of Government, built with a $1 million grant from the Scottish Rite Masons; and the School of Medicine and Health Sciences, established in 1824. The George Washington University Hospital treats more than 250,000 patients each year. In 1998 the university purchased the campus of **Mount Vernon College** on Foxhall Road NW.

GEORGETOWN. A historic seaport town. A trading center of Native Americans, this rough-and-tumble tobacco port and its inspection station were established in 1745 and chartered by the Maryland General Assembly in 1751. George Town was built on 60 acres purchased by the colonial government of George II from George Beall and George Gordon. By the late 18th century, it was one of America's largest tobacco ports. It was included in the District of Columbia in 1791 and thereafter served as a bedroom community and commercial hub for the new capital. By the early 19th century, tobacco had destroyed the local soils and the crop was replaced by wheat. By 1810 Georgetown housed a vigorous African American community, which comprised about 35 percent of the population; by 1860 the black population fell to 22 percent, about one-third of whom were enslaved.

When the **Civil War** broke out in 1861, the secessionist-leaning town was occupied by Federal troops. The **Chesapeake and Ohio Canal** was a constant target of Confederate raiders, and the flour mills that processed much of the locally grown wheat found their entire production required by the U.S. Army. In 1862 **Georgetown University**, three churches, a school, and a hotel were commandeered as military hospitals. Toward the end of the war, emancipated slaves poured into the town, and many settled near the university.

In 1870 Congress revoked the town's charter and created a single municipal government for the District of Columbia. Despite unhappiness at losing their autonomy, Georgetowners kept their sense of identity and the town prospered. During the golden age of the C&O Canal, coal, limestone, wheat, and other raw materials were shipped from western Maryland to the manufacturers and traders of Georgetown. However, the devastating flood of 1889 ushered in a lengthy period of decline. The Georgetown-based canal lost its race with the Baltimore and Ohio Railroad to reach western Maryland, and after it declared bankruptcy it came under control of the railroad. Thereafter, the Port of Baltimore became a more important shipping center. As the shipping industry declined, numerous Georgetown families moved to the newer suburbs and the town became a center for meat rendering and power production.

The revitalization of Georgetown began after World War I. Many government officials and business leaders, including Newton Baker, Woodrow Wilson's secretary of war, purchased the town's older residences and renovated them into the elegant townhouses of today. By 1930 property values were rising and the Georgetown Citizens Association was organized to work for strict zoning regulations. In 1950 Congress approved the **Old Georgetown Act**, which requires that all exterior changes, demolition, and construction be approved by a panel of architects selected by the **Commission of Fine Arts**.

Beginning with **Perle Mesta** in the 1950s, high-society figures such as Katharine Graham and Pamela Harriman have entertained the Washington elite in their Georgetown mansions. The gentrification of Georgetown had the effect of reducing the African American population from 22 percent in 1940 to 3 percent by 1960. During the 1970s, many of Georgetown's early waterfront commercial properties were converted into offices, shops, boutiques, and restaurants. Ambivalence about subway construction left the neighborhood without a **Washington Metrorail** stop and severe traffic problems persist. The community has been the site of spontaneous parties to celebrate the victories of the **Washington Redskins**, and Halloween in Georgetown is the city's equivalent of Mardi Gras, as streets fill with costumed revelers. *See also* BEALL, NINIAN; GEORGETOWN ACT.

GEORGETOWN ACT (1895). An act passed by Congress by which the city of **Georgetown** was incorporated into Washington, D.C. The act repealed all of the laws of Georgetown and directed the commissioners of the District of Columbia to "cause the nomenclature of the **streets and avenues** of Georgetown to conform to those of Washington so far as practicable."

GEORGETOWN CITIZENS' ASSOCIATION. *See* CITIZENS' AND CIVIC ASSOCIATIONS.

GEORGETOWN LUTHERAN CHURCH. Oldest Lutheran congregation in the District of Columbia. In 1766 Charles Beatty, one of the founders of **Georgetown**, donated a lot at High and 4th Streets (now Wisconsin Avenue and Volta Place NW) to a group of German settlers on the condition that they build a church on the property. Over the years, the congregation has constructed four different church buildings on the site. The original church was a log cabin erected in 1769. This building was replaced by a frame structure in 1835, by a stone church in 1867, and by a larger stone church dedicated in 1914. Until 1869, when the congregation hired its first full-time pastor, the church was served by Lutheran itinerants. The congregation is affiliated with the Evangelical Lutheran Church of America.

GEORGETOWN MARKET. *See* PUBLIC MARKETS.

GEORGETOWN PRESBYTERIAN CHURCH. One of Washington's most historic churches, organized in 1780 by **Stephen Bloomer Balch**. The first building was a 30-foot-square brick structure constructed in 1782 on the corner of 30th and M Streets. Enlarged several times, the building served the community until it was replaced by a Federal-style church erected on the same site in 1821. In 1874 a new building and adjacent Cissel Chapel and manse were constructed on P Street NW and dedicated in 1879. The church was renovated during the 1950s. The congregation has increased from 15 members in 1780 to about 650 members today.

GEORGETOWN UNIVERSITY. The oldest Catholic university in the United States. Founded in 1789 by Archbishop John Carroll, Georgetown University is composed of four undergraduate schools and several graduate schools, including a law school, medical school and cancer research center, School of Foreign Service, and School of Languages and Linguistics. Although operated by the Society of Jesus since 1805, the university has always had a substantial number of non-Catholic students.

From 1789 until 1919 when Georgetown Preparatory School became an independent institution, boys were admitted from the age of eight, and provided primary through college education. Women began matriculating at the Nursing School in 1902, but were not accepted into other programs until 1969. Georgetown University built the third astronomical observatory in the United States in 1841, where the latitude and longitude of the District were first calculated in 1844. Because of a high degree of southern sympathy among its faculty and students, the college was occupied by Union troops early in the **Civil War**, and campus buildings were commandeered for use as a military hospital in 1862. After the war, Father Patrick Healy, son of a freed slave, was appointed Georgetown's president. He raised scholastic standards, beginning the school's development into a leading academic and research institution. The 104-acre campus has 61 buildings and a 407-bed teaching hospital. Of architectural interest are Old North Hall, constructed in 1795, and Dahlgren Chapel, dedicated in 1893 and renovated in 1976.

GIANT FOOD. Washington's first supermarket and the area's leading grocery chain, with nearly half of local retail sales. The first Giant Food store was opened on Georgia Avenue NW in 1936 by Nehemiah M. Cohen. His son, Israel (Izzy), became president of the company in 1977. The company maintained an emphasis on public service, consumer education, and fair selling and hiring practices. Giant supplied 1.5 million meals to residents of Resurrection City, a civil rights protest encampment of the **Poor People's Campaign** during the summer of 1968. In 1970 the firm established an innovative consumer affairs program. Giant was the first grocery chain to introduce computer-assisted checkout scanning equipment, in 1979. After Israel Cohen's death, the company was bought by Dutch grocery conglomerate Royal Ahold. At the time of the sale in 1998, Giant Food had 177 stores from New Jersey to Virginia, annual sales of $4.2 billion, and 28,000 employees.

GILBERT, BENJAMIN FRANKLIN. *See* TAKOMA PARK.

GLOVER, CHARLES CARROLL (1846–1936). Banker and civic leader. Born on a farm near Asheville, North Carolina, Glover's father died in 1850 and four years later the young boy was sent to live with his grandmother in Washington. He was educated at Rittenhouse Academy and worked as a bookstore clerk before joining Riggs Bank in 1865. By age 26 he worked his way up from clerk to become a partner in the bank. Glover's innovative business practices helped the bank to more than double its deposits. When the bank was reorganized from a private partnership to **Riggs National Bank** in 1896, he was appointed president and served for 25 years before resigning in 1921 at the age of 73. Glover was very active in Washington's civic life and was instrumental in the creation of East and West **Potomac Park**, **Rock Creek Park**, and **Glover-**

Archbold Park. He also served as president of the **Corcoran Gallery of Art** for 27 years, was the primary fundraiser for the **Washington National Cathedral** in the early 1900s, and oversaw much of the latter project during his lifetime. He helped to select sites for the **Lincoln Memorial,** Constitution Hall, the American Red Cross building, and other structures that have made an impact on the life of the city.

GLOVER-ARCHBOLD PARK. A heavily forested neck of land that crosses several Washington neighborhoods, including **Georgetown**, Wesley Heights, and Foxall Crescent. The park was created in 1924 and 1925 when Congress received gifts of land from **Charles Carroll Glover** and Anne Archbold. Originally 105 acres, the park expanded through subsequent additions, including Whitehaven Parkway. Plans for a long-proposed highway that would have cut across the park were dropped by the District in 1962, when they were opposed by city residents, the National Park Service, and the families who donated the land. The 183-acre park contains groves of beech trees, black walnuts, elms, hickories, maples, oaks, sycamores, and tulip poplars. A 3.1-mile nature trail that begins on Van Ness Street, near Wisconsin Avenue, runs the length of the park. Several connecting trails lead to **Rock Creek Park**.

GONZAGA HIGH SCHOOL. *See* ST. PATRICK'S ROMAN CATHOLIC CHURCH.

GORDON, GEORGE. *See* GEORGETOWN.

GRAHAM, KATHARINE. *See* *WASHINGTON POST*; WATERGATE SCANDAL.

GRAND HOTEL. *See* HOBAN, JAMES.

GRANT, HENRY FLEET. *See* COLORED AMERICAN OPERA COMPANY.

GREATER WASHINGTON BOARD OF TRADE. The primary organization that represents the business interests of Washington and the surrounding communities. The Board of Trade was founded by *Washington Post* publisher Beriah Wilkins in 1889, when he invited 34 executives to form a business organization to help the city. Over the years, the Board of Trade has played an important part in the life of Washington by recommending candidates to serve on the District Commission, by lobbying for congressional support of various economic development plans and local business ventures, and by working to improve local government. It advocated a new subway system for Washington (1912), urged the construction of regional airports (National 1928; Dulles 1952) and a new convention center (1937), and undertook the construction of 490 units of low-income housing (1969). The board has published studies and reports that assess the economic and social needs of the community and has been a major promoter of the city as a place of business.

GREEN, CONSTANCE McLAUGHLIN (1897–1975). Historian. Born in Ann Arbor, Michigan, Green was educated at Mount Holyoke College and Yale University. After the death of her husband in World War II, Green moved to the Washington area, where she lived in **Georgetown**, Alexandria, and **Capitol Hill**. She worked on a history of the American Red Cross and then served as chief historian on a project to write the history of the Army Ordnance Department (1948–51). In 1954, while working as a research associate at **American University**, Green began writing a two-volume history of Washington. The publication of volume 1, *Washington: Village and Capital, 1800–1878* (1962), earned her the 1964 Pulitzer Prize in history. She also published *The Secret City: A History of Race Relations in the Nation's Capital* (1967), which documents the history of Washington's African American community and laments the missed opportunities for achieving racial integration. In addition, Green wrote a history of one of Washington's oldest churches, *The Church on Lafayette Square: A History of St. John's Church, 1815–1970* (1970) about **St. John's Episcopal Church.**

GREENHOW, ROSE O'NEAL (ca. 1818–1864). Confederate spy. Greenhow was a leading Washington socialite and hostess, the widow of historian and linguist Robert Greenhow. After the **Civil War** broke out, Greenhow used her great charm and persuasion to obtain military and government secrets from her indiscreet guests, which she then passed to Confederate general Pierre Beauregard. Greenhow's most noted contribution was a map of the Union Army's route to the First Battle of Manassas, along with information on the timing of the Union attack. This information contributed to a major Confederate military victory. She was arrested in August 1861 and held under guard in her **Lafayette Square** residence, dubbed "Fort Greenhow," where she was joined by other female prisoners of war. In January 1862 the house was closed and Greenhow and her eight-year-old daughter were transferred to the Old Capitol Prison; three months later they were released and escorted to Richmond, Virginia. Greenhow told her story in a book, *My Imprisonment*, and in August 1864 she sailed in a blockade runner to Wilmington, North Carolina, where she drowned, weighted down by a bag of gold coins tied around her waist.

GREENLEAF'S POINT. *See* SOUTHWEST.

GRIFFING, JOSEPHINE SOPHIE WHITE (1814–1872). Antislavery and women's suffrage advocate. Born in Hebron, Connecticut, Griffing moved to Ohio in 1842, where she became active in the antislavery movement. Her house was a station on the Underground Railroad. In 1863 she moved to Washington and became an agent of the newly organized National Freedman's Relief Association of the District of Columbia. She lobbied Congress for federal support for freed slaves in the form of educational opportunities, economic aid, and other assistance. She urged the establishment of a Freedman's Bureau to direct these efforts and when it was established in 1865, she became an assistant commissioner. Griffing had been a strong supporter of woman's suffrage since 1848, and she continued her efforts by helping to organize the Universal Franchise Association of the District of Columbia in 1867 and by serving as the organization's first president.

GRIFFITH STADIUM. The home of baseball's **Washington Senators** from 1903 to 1961, and during the 1930s and 1940s one of the home fields of the **Homestead Grays** of the Negro National League. Located in Northwest Washington, the stadium was opened in 1891 and rebuilt after a fire in 1911. In 1920 the park was named Griffith Stadium after Clark Griffith, who had worked for the Senators and eventually became the team's owner. The stadium held more than 27,000 people in 1961 and was noted for its center field wall, built around five houses and a tree, which jutted into the playing field. It was also famous for its baseline from home plate to first base that was graded downhill as an aid to the slow-footed Senators. In 1965, following construction of D.C. Stadium (later renamed **RFK Stadium**), Griffith Stadium was demolished.

GRIMKÉ, ARCHIBALD HENRY (1849–1930). Civil rights leader. Born in South Carolina, Grimké graduated from Harvard Law School in 1874. He was cofounder of the **American Negro Academy**, an important intellectual organization, and served as its president from 1903 to 1919. He became editor of the *Boston Hub* (1884–86), a Republican newspaper, published biographies of William Lloyd Garrison and Charles Sumner, and served as consul to the Dominican Republic (1894–98). Grimké moved to Washington in 1905 and addressed questions of racial discrimination and segregation in his publications and speeches in the African American community. In 1913 he became president of the 1,164-member Washington chapter of the **National Association for the Advancement of Colored People** (NAACP). In this position he challenged the legal basis of the racial policies of President Woodrow Wilson. *See also* GRIMKÉ, FRANCIS JAMES.

GRIMKÉ, FRANCIS JAMES (1850–1937). Presbyterian minister. Born in South Carolina, Grimké was the brother of **Archibald Henry Grimké**. He was educated at Lincoln University in Pennsylvania (1866–70), **Howard University** (1874), and Princeton Theological Seminary (1875–78). Ordained in the Presbyterian Church, Grimké served the **Fifteenth Street Presbyterian Church** in Washington for most of his career (1878–85; 1889–1928). He helped to organize the Afro-Presbyterian Council and supported the work of the **National Association for the Advancement of Colored People**. He was especially troubled by the racist policies of Christian organizations and churches, and in his 1923 convocation address at Howard University, he questioned these policies in his speech, "What Is the Trouble with Christianity Today?" Along with his brother, Grimké was an early leader of the civil rights movement and helped to make Washington one of the movement's intellectual centers.

GROCERY STORES. *See* GIANT FOOD.

GUDE, WILLIAM F. (1868–1940). Florist and civic leader. Born in Lynchburg, Virginia, Gude grew up on a farm in Prince George's County, Maryland. Along with his brother, Adolphus Gude, he founded a floral business, A. Gude and Brother, in 1889. The retail business was located on F Street and the brothers maintained greenhouses in **Anacostia**. The Gude family pioneered the floral business in the United States, and Gude was a charter member of the Society of American Florists in 1888 and served on its board of directors. He was also active in government and civic affairs, serving on several presidential inaugural committees and appointed rent commissioner by President Warren G. Harding. He was a member of the **Greater Washington Board of Trade** and a three-time president of the Washington Chamber of Commerce. One of Gude's children, [Frederick] Granville Gude (b. 1903), became president of the company in 1940 and also served as president of the Board of Trade (1943) and the Society of American Florists (1946).

GUERIN, JULES. *See* LINCOLN MEMORIAL.

- H -

HAMBURGH. *See* FOGGY BOTTOM.

HANAFI MUSLIM SIEGE. Three-day terrorist incident in March 1977 in three Washington buildings. The District Building, B'nai B'rith International headquarters, and the **Islamic Center** were simultaneously seized by a group of Hanafi Muslim terrorists brandishing shotguns and machetes. They killed a reporter, wounded several other people, including city councilman **Marion Barry**, and took 149 hostages inside the three buildings. The group was led by Hamaas Abdul Khaalis, who sought revenge for the murders in D.C. of members of his family by Black Muslims. The terrorists made an unsuccessful attempt to trade three hostages for Mayor **Walter Washington**. Eventually police working with negotiators from Iran, Egypt, and Pakistan won the release of the hostages, and the hostage-takers were imprisoned. *See also* B'NAI B'RITH KLUTZNICK NATIONAL JEWISH MUSEUM; JOHN A. WILSON BUILDING.

HANSEN, CARL. *See* HOBSON v. HANSEN.

HARRIS, BILL (ca. 1930–1988). Jazz guitarist and vocalist. The classically trained Harris was an important figure in the development of jazz and one of the originators of the "doo wop" style of singing. As a member of the Clovers, one of the city's most successful vocal groups, he collaborated on more than 20 "top-twenty" recordings between 1951 and 1956. After leaving the group, he recorded the music industry's first solo jazz guitar album and became the first African American student at Washington's Columbia School of Music. During the 1970s, Harris opened a nightclub in Northeast Washington and operated the Bill Harris Guitar Studios.

HAUPT GARDEN. *See* ENID A. HAUPT GARDEN.

HAY-ADAMS HOTEL. Hotel on **Lafayette Square** across from the **White House**. On the site where the hotel now stands was the home of **Rose O'Neal Greenhow**, a Confederate spy. The hotel is named for John Milton Hay, secretary of state in the McKinley and Theodore Roosevelt administrations, and **Henry Brooks Adams**. In 1884 Hay and Adams bought adjoining lots facing Lafayette Square and had architect Henry Hobson Richardson design two adjoining Romanesque houses. With visitors like Teddy Roosevelt, Calvin Coolidge, and Henry James, the Hay and Adams houses were a hub of Washington social life and culture for many years. In 1927 the houses were purchased by developer **Harry Wardman**, who built a hotel on the site. Designed by Turkish-born Armenian architect Mirhan Mesrobian, the 143-room hotel with an Italian Renaissance exterior is modeled after the Farnese Palace in Rome. In 1928 the hotel opened with lavish accommodations: hand-carved ceilings in the lobby, marble baths, and rooms for servants. In the 1980s the Hay-Adams Hotel was the setting for several meetings in which Oliver North raised more than $2 million for the Iran-Contra scheme.

HAYES, HELEN (1900–1993). Actress. Born in Washington, Hayes worked on the Broadway stage, in radio, on television, and in motion pictures. She received Academy Awards for her roles in the films *The Sin of Madelon Claudet* (1931) and *Airport* (1969), but she is best remembered as a Broadway stage actress who became widely known following her appearance in the play *Dear Brutus* (1918). Hayes worked in many New York productions, including George Bernard Shaw's *Caesar and Cleopatra* (1925), Tennessee Williams's *The Glass Menagerie* (1956), and Jean Anouilh's *Time Remembered* (1957), for which she won a Tony Award. She wrote three autobiographical works: *A Gift of Joy* (1965), *On Reflection* (1968), and *My Life in Three Acts* (1990). The annual Washington theater awards are named for Hayes.

HAYES, PATRICK (1909–1998). Arts advocate. A New York native and Harvard University graduate, Hayes became manager of the **National Symphony Orchestra** in 1941. His creative leadership strengthened the orchestra's fundraising, and he defied segregationist practices by arranging for singer Paul Robeson to appear with the orchestra on a barge on the **Potomac River**. After forming the Hayes Concert Bureau in 1946, he became Washington's most important impresario, bringing leading artists, including Leontyne Price, Arturo Toscanini, Marian Anderson, Rudolf Nureyev, Margot Fonteyn, and Van Cliburn, to local audiences. In 1965 Hayes founded the Washington Performing Arts Society, one of the country's first nonprofit presenting organizations, and recruited African American baritone **Todd Duncan** to lead the organization. Hayes was also a founding director of the **Cultural Alliance of Greater Washington**.

HECHINGER COMPANY. The first major home improvement retail chain in the United States. Founded in 1919 by building salvage salesman Sidney Hechinger at 6th and C Streets SW, by 1980 Hechinger Company had 27 stores in the Washington metropolitan area and began extending its reach into the Midwest and Southeast. At the height of the chain's prosperity in the mid-1980s, the average Hechinger store served 500,000 customers each year. During the 1990s, competition from Home Depot, Lowe's Company, and other retailers cut into the Hechinger market share and in 1997 the family sold the company to Los Angeles investor Leonard Green. The company was merged with Kmart's Builders Square division and the HQ-Home Quarters Warehouse Outlets, creating the nation's third-largest hardware chain, with 206 stores. In 1999 Hechinger Company filed for bankruptcy and all its stores were closed. The Hechinger family has a long history of community service. John W. Hechinger, son of the chain's founder, was chairman of the first presidentially appointed D.C. Council and a strong advocate for **home rule**; other family members have had distinguished careers in charitable endeavors and community development.

HECHT COMPANY. *See* DEPARTMENT STORES.

HENDERSON, MARY (1841–1931). Washington sophisticate who promoted 16th Street NW as a place for Washington's wealthy and power elite. Henderson was married to Missouri Senator John Brooks Henderson. After the senator lost his 1872 bid for reelection, the Hendersons settled on 16th Street in Meridian Hill and built "Boundary Castle," an elaborate residence with turrets and a medieval gated entrance. Completed in 1888, the house offered a commanding view of the **White House** and the city of Washington. Desiring to make her neighborhood the most exclusive in Washington, she lobbied Congress to move the White House to a nearby 12-acre site. Congress refused, but they eventually paid her $490,000 for the land and developed it into the park she desired, naming it **Meridian Hill Park**. With architect George Oakley Totten, she designed and built about 15 mansions in a real estate development scheme she hoped would house embassies. Although her vision for 16th Street never came to fruition and her "castle" was eventually replaced by Beekman Place condominiums, she did succeed in shaping the 16th Street neighborhood.

HEURICH BREWING COMPANY. A brewery founded in 1873 by German immigrant Christian Heurich, who arrived in the United States in 1866 with $24 in his pocket. After the original building on 20th Street NW was destroyed by fire in 1892, Heurich built a four-story brewery on the banks of the **Potomac River**. He directed the company until his death at the age of 102. Christian Heurich, Jr., led the company from 1945 until 1956, when the brewery closed. The **Arena Stage** occupied the building in the late 1950s, and in 1965 the Heurich family donated the site for the **John F. Kennedy Center for the Performing Arts**. In 1956 the Christian Heurich mansion near **Dupont Circle** was given to the **Historical Society of Washington** for its headquarters. Gary Heurich, the founder's grandson, reestablished the family business in 1986.

HILLCREST CHILDREN'S CENTER. *See* VAN NESS, MARCIA BURNES.

HILLWOOD MUSEUM. Private art museum overlooking **Rock Creek Park** in Northwest Washington. The red brick Georgian mansion, originally called "Arbremont," was designed in 1926 by John Deibert. The property was bought in 1955 by Marjorie Merriweather Post (1887–1973), heir to the Post cereal fortune, who renamed it "Hillwood." Post commissioned architect Alexander McIlvaine to redesign the building to be both a residence, where she lived the last 16 years of her life, and museum, which she left to the public when she died. In 1958 Post hired art historian Marvin Ross to assemble a collection of 18th- and 19th-century

Russian and French decorative art. Post began collecting Russian art in 1937, when she lived in Moscow with her husband, Ambassador Joseph Davies. The Soviet government under Joseph Stalin approved the selling of Russian imperial art treasures, and Post managed to acquire what is now the largest collection of such works outside Russia. Hillwood's Russian collection includes Fabergé eggs, religious icons in gold and silver, official portraits of tsars, and decorative porcelain tableware used by Catherine the Great. The French collection includes Beauvais tapestries and a chair that belonged to Marie Antoinette.

HIRSHHORN MUSEUM AND SCULPTURE GARDEN. Smithsonian Institution museum of modern art. The Hirshhorn collection comprises about 12,000 pieces, including one of the world's most extensive collections of modern sculpture. The museum was founded in 1966 when Joseph Hirshhorn (1899–1981), a Latvian-born millionaire industrialist and financier, gave his collection of modern art to the United States. Congress appropriated funds for a national museum building on the **Mall** to house the collection. A design by Gordon Bunshaft (1909–1990) was chosen by juried competition. Opened to the public in 1974, the building is an elevated cylinder resting on four piers. It is surrounded by four acres of green space for the exhibition of sculpture. The museum gardens have been twice redesigned, in 1981 and 1993. In addition to art exhibitions, the Hirshhorn sponsors research, publications, and community outreach programs.

HISTORICAL SOCIETY OF WASHINGTON. A society organized in 1894 to gather and preserve the history of Washington. The society began as the Columbia Historical Society and its members held monthly meetings where they presented research papers on aspects of Washington's history. These papers were published from 1895 to 1988 as *Records of the Columbia Historical Society.* For 60 years the society and its research collection lived a peripatetic life. In 1955, Amelia Keyser Heurich, widow of brewer Christian Heurich, donated the family's Victorian mansion on New Hampshire Avenue NW, which became the society's permanent headquarters. During the past 30 years, the society has worked to broaden its scope and appeal, changing its name to the Historical Society of Washington in 1989. The society's publication became *Washington History,* now a scholarly journal. In 1998 the Historical Society secured a $2 million congressional appropriation to convert the **Carnegie Library** at Mount Vernon Square NW to a city history museum, scheduled to open in 2003. The new museum will also house the historical society.

HOBAN, JAMES (ca. 1762–1831). Architect. Born in Callan, Ireland, Hoban studied architecture in Dublin and immigrated to the United States after the American Revolution. He first settled in Philadelphia and then moved to South Carolina, where he designed houses in Charleston and in 1791 the capital building at Columbia, which burned during the **Civil War**. In 1792 he won a competition to design the **White House**. He supervised its construction between 1792 and 1801, as well as its reconstruction between 1814 and 1818, after it was burned by the British during the **War of 1812**. He was one of the superintendents in charge of constructing the **U.S. Capitol** (1793–1802) and designed the Grand Hotel (1793–95), the Little Hotel (1795), and the U.S. State and War Offices (1918). Hoban was also a leading citizen of Washington, becoming a captain in the Washington artillery, serving on the **City Council**, and taking the city's first census.

HOBSON v. HANSEN. A 1966 lawsuit alleging racial and economic discrimination in the resource allocations of the D.C. public schools. Civil rights activist Julius Hobson sued Superintendent of Schools Carl Hansen, asking the school system to equalize per-pupil expenditures in the city's elementary schools. The U.S. District Court found in Hobson's favor, ordering an end to academic tracking; directing the school system to provide buses for African American students from overcrowded schools who wished to attend underutilized, predominantly white schools west of **Rock Creek Park**; and discontinuing optional attendance zones, which allowed parents to bypass neighborhood schools and enroll their children elsewhere in the city. In 1971, when Hobson petitioned for further enforcement, the court ruled that per-pupil expenditures at every school could not deviate more than five percent from the system's mean. Between 1971 and 1975, more than 600 D.C. teachers were transferred under the "equalization" ruling, causing enormous disruptions and a 1972 teachers' strike. In 1975, the court modified its ruling to use teacher-pupil ratios instead of actual salary dollars.

HOLLERITH, HERMAN (1860–1929). Inventor of the tabulating machine. Born in Buffalo, New York, Hollerith graduated from the Columbia School of Mines (1879). Along with his teacher, William P. Trowbridge, he helped to compile the U.S. census of 1880 and later worked at the Patent Office in Washington. He became interested in automating the census work and his idea for a tabulating machine was born after watching a train conductor punch tickets. Hollerith invented a punch card system to record the statistics of the 1890 census, saving the government about $5 million and two years' time. His work led to the founding of the Tabulating Machine Company in 1896. The company became the Computer Tabulating Recording Company and in 1924 changed its name to IBM, the International Business Machines Corporation.

HOLOCAUST MUSEUM. *See* U.S. HOLOCAUST MEMORIAL MUSEUM.

HOLY TRINITY ROMAN CATHOLIC CHURCH. The oldest Roman Catholic church in the District, consecrated in 1793. Known as Trinity Church until 1845, it was founded by John Carroll, who later became the first Catholic bishop in the United States. The 1793 building is the oldest church in continuous use in Washington, although it has served as the Parish Center since the 1850s, when the current church was constructed on N Street NW. The earliest parishioners were an ethnically and socioeconomically diverse group, including descendants of Maryland's first English Catholic settlers, Irish laborers who built the **Chesapeake and Ohio Canal** and federal government buildings, and French refugees from Haiti's 1793 slave revolt. The congregation was about 30 percent African American until 1925, when black communicants established Epiphany Catholic Church in eastern **Georgetown.** Holy Trinity maintains close relationships with **Georgetown University** and Georgetown Visitation Convent.

HOME RULE. Control over local municipal government by D.C. voters. A cryptic passage in the U.S. Constitution granted legislative authority over the District of Columbia to Congress. Scholars have disputed the meaning of the passage for two centuries, during which time Washington has remained under the exclusive control of the U.S. Congress.

Pre-federal residents were citizens of Maryland or Virginia, with full voting and civic rights in those jurisdictions, which they retained for a decade after the District was established. In 1802,

Congress granted Washington City a municipal **charter of incorporation**, which permitted voters to elect a local legislature, but retained for the U.S. president the right to appoint the city's **mayor**. A subsequent 1871 city charter eliminated most home rule, and the **Organic Act** of 1878 took away the citizens' influence over their local government. A succession of weak and uninterested presidentially appointed District commissioners provoked a coalition of 271 civic organizations to sponsor a 1938 plebiscite on home rule, local suffrage in presidential elections, and D.C. representation in Congress, which passed overwhelmingly. Despite six subsequent Senate-passed bills providing for some form of home rule, the House of Representatives Committee on the District of Columbia prevented any reform until the mid-1960s.

In 1965 the **Greater Washington Board of Trade**, an organization of city business leaders, urged newspapers across the United States to oppose D.C. government reform. This infuriated local activists who, led by **Marion Barry**, organized the Free D.C. Movement, threatening boycotts and pickets of city businesses that did not display Free D.C. emblems in their windows. The Free D.C. Movement was criticized by many home rule supporters, but did convince some Board of Trade members to withdraw their opposition to reform.

After home rule legislation failed to pass Congress again in 1966, President Lyndon Johnson reorganized the District government by executive order. Johnson established a presidentially appointed mayor, deputy mayor, and nine-member **City Council** and installed **Walter Washington** as mayor. Washington's calm leadership gained him strong support and gave further impetus to the home rule movement.

In 1972, U.S. Representative John L. McMillan of South Carolina, the chair of the House District Committee and self-proclaimed roadblock to D.C. government reform, was defeated for reelection. The chairmanship passed to Charles Diggs of Michigan, who wrote the **District of Columbia Self-Government and Reorganization Act** of 1973, which created a limited home rule for the District. The bill was signed by President Richard Nixon in 1973 and approved by D.C. voters in 1974. It called for election of the mayor and **City Council**, permitted legislation passed by the council and signed by the mayor to become law unless vetoed by both Houses of Congress, and created the city's unique **Advisory**

Neighborhood Commissions. With the failure of the D.C. statehood movement, no further progress on achieving complete home rule has occurred.

During Washington's 1995 financial crisis, Congress seized control of the District government, and delegated authority to run the city to the **District of Columbia Financial Responsibility and Management Assistance Authority**, whose members were appointed by President Bill Clinton. Operational authority was restored to the mayor in January 1999, and power was restored to the City Council in 2001.

HOMESTEAD GRAYS. A professional baseball team of the Negro National League. Organized in 1910 in Pittsburgh, Pennsylvania, the Grays were made up of steelworkers from Homestead, Pennsylvania. The team played around the Pittsburgh area and traveled to other cities. The club was independent from 1912 to 1928 and joined the American Negro League for its only season (1929). With the collapse of that league, the team again became independent. When the Negro National League was organized in 1934, the Grays joined, and during the 1930s and 1940s **Griffith Stadium** in Washington served as one of their home fields. Led by Hall of Fame players Walter F. ("Buck") Leonard and Josh Gibson, the Grays were the league's dominant team. During its 40-year history, the club won 10 pennants (1937–45, 1948) and three World Series (1943–44, 1948). Racial integration of major league baseball resulted in the disbanding of the team in 1950.

HOOVER, J. EDGAR (1895–1972). Director of the Federal Bureau of Investigation (1924–72). Born in Washington, Hoover graduated from **George Washington University** Law School. In 1917 he was employed by the U.S. Justice Department and in 1924 he was selected to head the Justice Department's Bureau of Investigation, which in 1935 became the FBI. Hoover was a respected figure who built and professionalized the FBI. He was also a tough, controversial director who set paternalistic codes of behavior within the agency and abused his power by harassing civil rights leader Martin Luther King, Jr., and others whom he considered subversive. A longtime member of the Masonic Brothers, Hoover joined Washington's Federal Lodge No. 1 in 1920. He was also a man of habit; he lunched daily at the **Mayflower Hotel** for more than 20 years.

HORSERACING. A favorite spectator sport of early Washingtonians. The first racetrack was built in **Georgetown** in 1769. With the growth of Washington, a track was constructed in 1798 at 17th Street and **Pennsylvania Avenue** NW. The track extended toward 25th Street and the judges' stand was located at 19th and F streets. Here races took place between the horses of Ben Ogle Tayloe of Washington and Governor Charles G. Ridgely of Maryland. Early racetracks were built on the south end of the Jenkins farm, between 4th and 6th Streets and K and N Streets, and in 1802 on the Holmead farm, between 10th and 16th Streets. The Holmead track was popularly known as the "Congressional Race Track" because Congress often adjourned to take in the races. Other tracks were constructed during the 19th century, including Crystal Springs (1860s), later called the Brightwood Driving Park; Piney Branch (1860s–70s); and Ivy City Race Course (1870), located between Brentwood Road and Mt. Olivet Cemetery. The premier track was the Benning Race Course. The Benning track dates back to 1876, when it was developed as a private venture known as Hill's Racetrack. In 1890 the Washington City Jockey Club assumed control of the track and reopened it with great fanfare. The track was a successful venture, but congressional antigambling legislation forced its closure in 1908; attempts to renovate and reopen the track in 1934 and 1936 failed.

HOTEL WASHINGTON. A 344-room hotel located at **Pennsylvania Avenue** and 15th Street NW, near the **White House**. Designed in Italian Renaissance style by John Carrere and Thomas Hastings, architects of the New York Public Library, the nine-story building opened in 1918 on a site previously occupied by the Corcoran federal office building. The hotel is well known for its Sky Terrace, an open-air, rooftop restaurant with a panoramic view of the **Washington Monument** and the grounds of the White House. The hotel underwent a major restoration in 1988.

HOWARD THEATRE. The first theater in the segregated United States to be built for an African American audience. Constructed in 1910, the 1,500-seat Italianate hall epitomized Washington's glamorous black society for half a century. During an era of racial segregation, the theater presented a glittering array of performers, from **Duke Ellington** and **Marvin**

Gaye to Ella Fitzgerald and Diana Ross. The theater remained a performing venue except for a brief period between 1929 and 1931, when Elder Lightfoot Solomon Michaux leased it for evangelical revivals. In 1931 Philadelphia businessman Sam Steifel bought the Howard, hired promoter Shep Allen, and reopened it as a place of entertainment. When looters decimated the surrounding **Shaw** neighborhood during the **riots of 1968**, the Howard Theatre was left untouched. However, the theater was unable to sustain itself after desegregation and the advent of television, and it closed in 1970. The building was added to the National Register of Historic Places in 1973. The theater was reopened briefly in 1974, and between 1977 and 1984 it hosted plays and musical shows sponsored by the nonprofit Howard Theatre Foundation. The property was purchased by the city in 1986, but remains closed pending restoration.

HOWARD UNIVERSITY. A predominantly African American university located in Northwest Washington. Established in 1867 as a school for freed men and women, the university is a private institution named for one of its founders, Oliver O. Howard, a **Civil War** general and commissioner of the Freedmen's Bureau. The school began with a college of arts and sciences (1867), and within four years added medicine and pharmacy (1868), law (1869), and divinity (1870). Over the next 100 years it added 10 additional colleges: dentistry, engineering, architecture and planning, social work, fine arts, nursing, business, education, communications, and health sciences. The university was supported by the Freedmen's Bureau, by a special appropriation of Congress in 1879, and by an annual federal appropriation since 1928. The school enrolls more than 11,000 students and operates several research centers and institutes, including the African American Resource Center, the Center for Disability and Socioeconomic Policy Studies, and the Computational Science and Engineering Research Center. Its School of Law made an important contribution to the civil rights movement of the 1960s. Howard graduates include physician **Charles R. Drew** and Supreme Court Justice Thurgood Marshall.

HOWARDTOWN. *See* LEDROIT PARK.

HOXIE, VINNIE REAM. *See* FARRAGUT SQUARE.

HUBBARD, GARDINER GREENE (1822–1897). Lawyer, civic

leader, and founder of the **National Geographic Society**. Born in Boston, Hubbard graduated from Dartmouth College (1841) and studied law at Harvard University. He worked at a law firm in Cambridge, Massachusetts, and was active in the community, serving on the Boston and Massachusetts school boards. Hubbard met **Alexander Graham Bell** in 1871 and became the principal financial backer of Bell's telephone, which he developed commercially after it received a patent in 1876. The following year Bell married Hubbard's daughter, Mabel, and when the Bells moved to Washington in 1879 Hubbard followed. Hubbard's scientific interests led him to found with Bell the magazine *Science* (1883), now the journal of the American Association for the Advancement of Science, and he was an active member of the Joint Commission of the Scientific Societies of Washington. He also founded the National Geographic Society (1888) and served as its first president. Other institutions that benefited from Hubbard's leadership and philanthropy include **George Washington University**, where he served as a trustee for 12 years; the **Smithsonian Institution**, where he was a regent; and the **Historical Society of Washington**.

- I -

IBM. *See* HOLLERITH, HERMAN.

INDUSTRIAL BANK OF WASHINGTON. The only African American-owned and -operated commercial bank in Washington. Located on 11th Street NW, in the **Shaw/U Street** area, the bank traces its roots to the building and loan association founded by John Whitelaw Lewis among local black laborers in 1913. After Lewis died in 1925, Jesse H. Mitchell, proprietor of a local realty and investment company, became head of the bank. Industrial Bank nearly collapsed during the Great Depression. In 1933 a national, presidentially ordered bank closing shut down the bank, and it appeared that it would not be able to reopen. Evangelist Elder Lightfoot Solomon Michaux saved the bank by negotiating a settlement that paid depositors 35 cents on the dollar, and the bank reopened in August 1934 with $200,000 in assets and five employees. During the days of segregation, white-owned banks refused to give loans to African American depositors, so the services of Industrial Bank were crucial to the development of Washington's black community. Still owned by the Mitchell family, the bank today has eight branch locations and more than $225 million in assets.

INFLUENZA EPIDEMIC OF 1918. Deadly outbreak of "Spanish flu," part of a worldwide epidemic. During the months of October and November 1918, a dangerous strain of influenza struck more than 35,000 people in the Washington area, resulting in more than 3,500 deaths. Commissioner **Louis Brownlow** managed the citywide crisis by closing nonessential offices and businesses and setting up makeshift hospitals, ambulance services, and morgues. These efforts helped to contain the epidemic in the Washington area, and it gradually subsided.

INTERNATIONAL BUSINESS MACHINES. *See* HOLLERITH, HERMAN.

ISLAMIC CENTER. Mosque and cultural center, which serves Washington's Muslims, including the Islamic diplomatic community. The building was constructed on **Embassy Row** between 1949 and 1957 by Egypt's Ministry of Works. The mosque is set at an angle to the street so that it faces Mecca, the holy city of Islam toward which all Muslims pray. Its focal point is a 168-foot minaret and its interior features decorative details associated with Islamic architecture, including horseshoe arches, corbeling, sculpted crenellations, and a blue-and-gold mosaic created by the John Joseph Earley Studio in 1953. The center maintains an extensive library of Islamic culture and is an important place of learning for American Muslims. In March 1977, the Islamic Center was occupied during the **Hanafi Muslim siege**, but all hostages held there were released without injury.

- J -

JACOBSEN, HUGH NEWELL (b. 1929). Architect. Born in Grand Rapids, Michigan, Jacobsen moved to Washington after World War II. He received degrees from the University of Maryland (1951) and Yale University (1955), where he was influenced by modernist Louis I. Kahn. In 1958 Jacobsen opened a **Georgetown** office, and during a 40-year career he blended modern architectural style with historical sensitivity. His work includes a redesigned row house on Q Street NW (1961), the redesign of the interiors of the **Renwick Gallery** (1972) and the Smithsonian's **Arts and Industries Building** (1976), and the office additions under the west terrace of the **U.S. Capitol** (1993). Jacobsen's architectural style, featuring geometric forms and clean lines, may be best seen in his design of the **Georgetown University** Alumni Square student dormitory (1983). He edited *A Guide to the Architecture of Washington, D.C.* (1965).

JEFFERSON, THOMAS (1743–1826). As a member of the Continental Congress (1783–84), secretary of state (1789–94), vice president (1797–1801), and president (1801–09), Jefferson had more influence on the early development of Washington than any other president or public official. His interest in Greek and Roman architecture, the fine arts, and natural history found expression in the public buildings, intellectual life, and landscaping of the capital. Jefferson drew a 1791 plan of Washington that placed Congress, the **White House**, and the **Mall** on approximately the same sites they occupy today. He worked with **Benjamin Latrobe** to develop the architectural style of Washington's public buildings, suggested the tree-lined approach from **Pennsylvania Avenue** to **Capitol Hill**, and issued a decree that forbade construction of buildings under three stories, lest the capital city look inconsequential. Less successful was Jefferson's proposed city plan of some 300 acres, in contrast to **Pierre Charles L'Enfant's** grand city of 6,111 acres, and his proposed design of the White House, which was rejected. Aspects of his White House design, which featured the round, columned style of classical architecture, have survived in his own **Jefferson Memorial**, which lies on the south side of the **Tidal Basin**.

JEFFERSON BUILDING. *See* LIBRARY OF CONGRESS.

JEFFERSON MEMORIAL. Memorial to **Thomas Jefferson**, third president of the United States. In 1934 Congress authorized creation of the Thomas Jefferson Memorial Commission. In 1937 this commission chose a location overlooking the **Tidal Basin** for the memorial. Project architects were **John Russell Pope**, Otto R. Eggers, and Daniel P. Higgins. Pope, who died before construction began, based the design on the Roman Pantheon, incorporating Jefferson's architectural tastes. The **Commission of Fine Arts** tried to prevent construction of Pope's Roman building, with its interior statue of Jefferson, because of its similarity to the **Lincoln Memo-**

rial. However, President Franklin Roosevelt approved the design and construction began in 1938 under the auspices of the National Park Service. The memorial was completed in 1943 and Roosevelt presided over the dedication ceremony. Above the entrance to the marble building is a sculpture depicting the committee of the Declaration of Independence. The interior walls contain excerpts from Jefferson's writings and a 19-foot tall, five-ton bronze statue of the president. Sculptor Rudolph Evans's Jefferson holds a document that depicts him as the author of American political thought.

JEWISH HISTORICAL SOCIETY OF GREATER WASHINGTON. *See* ADAS ISRAEL; LILLIAN AND ALBERT SMALL JEWISH MUSEUM; WASHINGTON HEBREW CONGREGATION.

JOHN A. WILSON BUILDING. City Hall. When the federal government purchased Washington's original **City Hall** from the D.C. Territorial Government in 1873, the $75,000 purchase price was designated for construction of new city offices. However, the city's Board of Public Works spent all but $5,000 of the funds on street improvements, and deposited $80,000 in sewer certificates in trust to replace the federal funds. The certificates were invalidated by Congress in 1874, and the remaining $5,000 later paid for only a small excavation at 14th and E Streets NW, on the site of the former Washington and Georgetown Railway, which was destroyed in an 1897 fire. In 1908 a Beaux-Arts structure was finally erected on the property. Designed by Cope and Stewardson of Philadelphia and known as the District Building, the structure was renamed in 1993 in memory of city councilman **John A. Wilson**. A statue of **Alexander "Boss" Shepherd**, the city's first outdoor statuary honoring a native Washingtonian, proved to be as controversial as the man it honored, and it was removed by Mayor **Marion Barry** in 1980; it remains in storage.

JOHN ADAMS BUILDING. *See* LIBRARY OF CONGRESS.

JOHN F. KENNEDY CENTER FOR THE PERFORMING ARTS. A national cultural center that occupies eight acres along the Potomac waterfront. Despite passage of the National Cultural Center Act in 1958, disputes about fundraising and the design and location of the 10-story facility delayed its opening until September 1971. President John F. Kennedy took an interest in the project, appointing **Roger L. Stevens** to chair the center's trustees. Stevens, a noted theatrical producer and real estate magnate, later became executive director of the Kennedy Center and led the theater to national prominence during his 30-year tenure. Designed by Edward Durrell Stone, the center is constructed of 3,700 tons of Carrara marble donated by Italy. Three foyers lead patrons into the performance areas: the Grand Foyer, which holds a 3,000-pound bust of President Kennedy sculpted by Robert Berks, is the site of daily "Millennium Stage" performances; the Hall of States, featuring flags of all 50 states, the District of Columbia, and the five U.S. territories; and the Hall of Nations, which displays flags of all countries maintaining diplomatic relations with the United States. The center holds three major theaters: the Concert Hall is home to the **National Symphony Orchestra**; the Eisenhower Theater generally houses dramatic productions; and the Opera House is the home of the Washington Opera, and also presents dance and musical theater performances. The smaller Terrace Theater hosts experimental productions. Since 1978 the center has been the site of the annual Kennedy Center Honors, the American equivalent of a British knighthood or a French Legion of Honor. Five American artists from various disciplines are celebrated each year in a nationally televised show. Honorees represent a wide range of American performance, from George Balanchine and Leonard Bernstein to Shirley Temple and Bill Cosby.

JOHN WESLEY AFRICAN METHODIST EPISCOPAL ZION CHURCH. National church of the African Methodist Episcopal Zion denomination. John Wesley Church was founded in 1847 by the Little Society of Nine, a group of free blacks. Although pressed by financial difficulties, the congregation operated a school for African Americans from 1855 until 1868. The church has been located in four different buildings in the area around 18th Street and Connecticut Avenue NW. Financial help received from the Philadelphia and Baltimore AME Zion conferences in 1914 enabled the congregation to purchase and renovate the former St. Andrew's Episcopal Church at 14th and Corcoran Streets NW as the national center of the AME Zion Church. John Wesley Church has been an important force in Washington's cultural and civic life, sponsoring the work of Marcus Garvey, Paul Robeson, Roland Hayes, and jazz legend **Duke Ellington**. Assistant pastor John Kinard helped to develop the **Anacostia Museum**, now part of the **Smithsonian Institution**. In 1984 artist Ron Anderson's magnificent "Victory Skylight," a 12,000-piece stained-glass representation of the struggles and triumphs of African Americans, was installed in the church sanctuary.

JOHNSON, VIRGINIA (b. 1950). First African American prima ballerina. Born and raised in Washington, Johnson received her early dance training with Mary Day at the **Washington School of Ballet** and briefly attended New York University on a performing arts scholarship. In 1969 she joined Dance Theatre of Harlem, rising to the rank of principal dancer. Johnson graced stages around the world, appearing in the works of leading choreographers such as George Balanchine and Agnes deMille. In 1984 Valerie Bettis created Johnson's most notable role, the title character in a Creole version of "Giselle." Lauded for her lyricism, musicality, and intensity, Johnson retired from performing in 1997.

JOLSON, AL (1886–1950). Singer and actor. Born near St. Petersburg, Russia, Jolson was brought to the United States at age seven and raised in Southwest Washington, where he made his stage debut in 1899. He played to audiences in vaudeville and had many successful performances in New York, appearing in the musicals *La Belle Paree* (1911), *Honeymoon Express* (1913), *Sinbad* (1918), *Bombo* (1921), and *Big Boy* (1925). His movie credits include *The Jazz Singer* (1927), *The Singing Fool* (1928), and *Say It with Songs* (1929). He wrote many hit songs, including "Swanee," "California Here I Come," "April Showers," and "Me and My Shadow." Performing in blackface, Jolson was one of the premier entertainers of his era.

JONES, LOIS MAILOU (1905–1998). Painter, designer, and professor of art at **Howard University**. Jones was born in Boston and studied art at Boston's Museum of Fine Arts. She went on to study in Paris and Rome, and in 1930 settled in Washington, where she taught at Howard University for 47 years. Jones's early work was primarily Postimpressionist watercolor; she later developed an interest in African art, and in 1938 painted "Les Fetiches," an oil painting of African masks considered one of her masterpieces. The painting now belongs to the National Museum of American Art. In 1953 Jones married Haitian graphic artist Louis Vergniaud Pierre-Noel, and she began making frequent trips to Haiti. During this period, her work reflects a fascination with Haiti and its culture. In the 1970s her travels in Africa brought new influences to her work derived from African art. Jones's work is exhibited by the **Hirshhorn Museum**, the **Corcoran Gallery of Art**, and the **Phillips Collection**.

JUDICIAL BRANCH. *See* DISTRICT OF COLUMBIA COURTS.

JUNGLE INN. *See* MORTON, JELLY ROLL.

- K -

KALORAMA. An area bounded by Rock Creek, Florida Avenue, Kalorama Circle, and 18th Street in Northwest Washington. In 1668 Charles II of England granted a 600-acre parcel called the Widow's Mite to John Langworth of St. Mary's County, Maryland. Belair, a 30-acre portion of this land was purchased in 1807 by Joel Barlow, a Revolutionary War veteran, shipping magnate, and diplomat. Barlow renamed the estate "Kalorama," which is the Greek word for "beautiful view." Barlow's Kalorama was mostly virgin woodlands that rose from Rock Creek to a height of 200 feet and overlooked the new capital city. Barlow cut roads, built stables, planted orchards, and dammed Rock Creek to create a small lake for the steamboat experiments of Robert Fulton. In 1822 Colonel George Bomford purchased Kalorama from Barlow's heirs, and he gradually added to the property until he held 90 acres. His attempt to develop commercial grist and cotton mills failed, and in 1846 he was forced to sell the property to Thomas Lovett of Philadelphia. During the **Civil War**, Lovett's mansion was commandeered by the U.S. Army as a hospital for smallpox patients; the house was damaged by fire in 1865. After the war, Lovett's family sold a 30-acre parcel to the Freedmen's Savings and Trust Company.

In 1887 the area north of Boundary Street (now Florida Avenue), including Kalorama, was ripe for development. The Freedmen's Trust land that had been purchased for $15,000 sold for $300,000. Later that year, the Lovett heirs finally succumbed to the inevitable and sold their remaining 60 acres to real estate developers for $354,000. The sale was the largest financial transaction beyond the original city boundaries to that time. The Barlow mansion was demolished, Kalorama was subdivided, and housing construction began. However, in 1893 development was halted by congressional legislation that mandated that **Pierre Charles L'Enfant**'s street design for Washington City be extended to all of the District. It took five years to amend the law to exempt pre-1893 subdivisions, including Kalorama.

Construction then proceeded at a furious pace. Two distinct areas quickly developed: Kalorama Triangle and Sheridan-Kalorama. Kalorama Triangle developed working- and middle-class housing near the streetcar lines on 18th Street, Calvert Street, and Columbia Road. Although several large private residences were built, Triangle development comprised mostly row houses and apartments, several of which are architecturally significant. Nearly 50 apartment buildings were constructed in Kalorama Triangle between 1903 and 1930. These dwellings housed government employees and other white-collar workers. Sheridan-Kalorama, the neighborhood's western side, attracted the wealthy and powerful. Some of Washington's most influential citizens built elegant Beaux-Arts mansions along Massachusetts Avenue near Sheridan Circle. Neighborhood residents have included business executives, cabinet secretaries, and five U.S. presidents during their pre- or post-**White House** lives: Herbert Hoover, Franklin D. Roosevelt, Warren G. Harding, **William Howard Taft**, and Woodrow Wilson. Since 1963 the **Woodrow Wilson House** on S Street has been operated as a museum by the National Trust for Historic Preservation.

Sheridan Circle is named for and features a statue of **Civil War** general Philip Sheridan astride his famous horse, Winchester, sculpted by Gutzon Borglum, who also created the figures on Mount Rushmore. Sheridan's son posed for Borglum, and the general's widow loved the results so much that she built a residence overlooking the statue. Sheridan Circle has remained virtually unchanged since 1920. During the mid-20th century, many of the Kalorama mansions were sold to foreign governments for use as embassies and chanceries. Kalorama remains one of Washington's most beautiful and exclusive neighborhoods, an unexpected enclave in what is now the inner city.

KALORAMA HEIGHTS. *See* ADAMS MORGAN.

KANN'S. *See* DEPARTMENT STORES.

KEIM, DE BENNEVILLE RANDOLPH (1841–1914). Journalist

and author. Born in Reading, Pennsylvania, Keim attended Beloit College in Wisconsin and served as a captain in the National Guard in Harrisburg, Pennsylvania (1860–61). He then embarked on a career in journalism and became a correspondent for the *New York Herald*. Keim covered several military battles and in 1870, as an agent of President Ulysses S. Grant, he traveled abroad to inspect U.S. consulates. He became the *Herald*'s Washington correspondent during the 1880s and subsequently wrote for many newspapers and magazines. Keim prepared a Washington handbook, *Washington and Its Environs: A Descriptive and Historical Handbook of the Capital* (1881), which went through many editions. His other publications include *A Guide to the Potomac River* (1881); *Society in Washington: Its Noted Men, Accomplished Women, Established Customs, and Notable Events* (1887); and *Handbook of Official and Social Etiquette and Public Ceremonials at Washington* (1889). He wrote a five-act drama on the life of General Lafayette and books on General William Tecumseh Sherman, President Grant, Alexander Hamilton, and Alaska.

KENILWORTH PARK AND AQUATIC GARDENS. A 12-acre aquatic garden along the eastern bank of the **Anacostia River**, opposite the **U.S. National Arboretum** The gardens were begun in the early 1880s by Walter B. Shaw, a government clerk who planted water lilies at his home on the Anacostia River. Shaw's gardens flourished and became a local attraction. In 1938 the gardens were purchased by the U.S. Department of the Interior to be preserved for public enjoyment. Now administered by the National Park Service, the gardens feature many specimens of water plants and they provide a habitat for a variety of wetland animals. *See also* ANACOSTIA PARK.

KENNEDY CENTER. *See* JOHN F. KENNEDY CENTER FOR THE PERFORMING ARTS.

KEY, FRANCIS SCOTT (1780–1843). Lawyer, poet, and civic leader. Key was appointed U.S. district attorney for the District of Columbia by President James Madison and moved to **Georgetown** in 1809. During his 22-year residence there, he was active in religious and civic affairs. When British troops marched on Washington in August 1814, they captured Key's friend, physician William Beanes. Key traveled to Baltimore to negotiate Beanes's release and was himself imprisoned. When the siege of Baltimore ended and the American flag still flew over Fort McHenry, Key wrote the poem "The Star Spangled Banner" on the back of an envelope. Local tavern patrons sang Key's poem to the old tune "To Anacreon in Heaven." It became the U.S. national anthem in 1931. Key's house on M Street NW, built in 1802, served as an American flag factory during World War I and was demolished in 1949 for construction of the Whitehurst Freeway. In 1993 a memorial park was opened on the site of Key's home. Adjacent to the park is the Francis Scott Key Memorial Bridge, connecting Georgetown to Rosslyn, Virginia.

KHALIL GIBRAN PARK. *See* EMBASSY ROW.

KING, CHARLES BIRD (1785–1862). Artist. Born in Newport, Rhode Island, King traveled to London in 1806 to study with American expatriate Benjamin West, then president of the Royal Academy. He returned to the United States when the **War of 1812** broke out and itinerated along the East Coast. Settling in Washington in 1818, he built a large house on 12th Street NW that included a 160-painting public exhibit gallery. King painted the portraits of many leaders of Federalist and Antebellum Washington. Between 1821 and 1842 he accepted 143 commissions from the U.S. Department of War to paint Native American leaders who came to Washington to negotiate treaties and conduct business with the government. The portraits, which included likenesses of Sequoyah, the Prophet, and John Ridge, were exhibited at the War Department to public delight. Artist Henry Inman made lithograph copies of King's Indian portraits, 120 of which were printed in *The Indian Tribes of North America* (3 vols., 1837–44) by Thomas L. McKenney and James Hall, the first major work on the American Indian. In 1858 King's portraits were transferred to the **Smithsonian Institution**'s art collection, but in 1865 nearly all were destroyed in a fire.

KING, MARTIN LUTHER, JR. *See* ANACOSTIA; HOOVER, J. EDGAR; LINCOLN MEMORIAL; MARCH ON WASHINGTON FOR JOBS AND FREEDOM; MARTIN LUTHER KING, JR., MEMORIAL LIBRARY; POOR PEOPLE'S CAMPAIGN; RIOTS OF 1968; WILLARD HOTEL.

KING, WILLIAM (1771–1854). A furniture maker of the Potomac Valley School of cabinet making. A native of Ireland, King emigrated to the United States as a child and moved to **Georgetown** in 1795. He served in the U.S. Army during the **War of 1812** and was wounded in the Battle of Bladensburg. After the British burned the **White House,** President James Madison ordered two dozen chairs from King to replace furniture destroyed; one chair remains in the White House collection today. King trained several generations of local artisans during a career of almost 60 years.

KIROV BALLET ACADEMY. *See* UNIFICATION CHURCH.

KNICKERBOCKER THEATER COLLAPSE. One of the worst disasters in Washington history took place at the Knickerbocker Theater on the southeast corner of 18th Street and Columbia Road NW. On Saturday, January 28, 1922, the five-year-old Knickerbocker had just begun the evening's second showing of George M. Cohan's light comedy "Get Rich Quick Wallingford," when plaster began falling from the ceiling. A massive rupture occurred and the theater collapsed under the weight of 26 inches of snow. The collapse sent its balcony into the orchestra pit and of the theater's 300 movie patrons, 98 were killed and 133 injured. Both owner Harry Crandall and the architect of the building later committed suicide.

KNOW-NOTHING RIOTS (1857). Anti-immigrant violence by the "Know-Nothings" against Irish and German Catholic citizens of Washington. The Know-Nothing movement began as a secret society, grew in prominence, and succeeded in electing several anti-immigration candidates to political office, including Washington **mayor** John Towers in 1854. The movement developed in response to a large influx of immigrants to the eastern United States because of famine in Ireland. Local economies could not accommodate the swelling labor force and many immigrants took menial jobs and lived in violent, poverty-stricken neighborhoods like **Swampoodle.** Throughout the 1850s the Know-Nothings engaged in street violence against these immigrants. In June 1857 groups of Know-Nothings began to attack Irish voters in Washington. The president called in the Marines to subdue the rioting, which left eight people dead and 21 wounded. Dismayed by the violence, many Know-Nothings withdrew their support from the movement, and by 1859 it had collapsed.

KOREAN WAR VETERANS MEMORIAL. A memorial to the veterans of the Korean War (1950–53). Located across from the **Lin-**

coln Memorial and dedicated in 1995, the Korean War Veterans Memorial consists of a column of 19 life-size soldiers marching up an incline toward an American flag. The soldiers are silhouetted against a 180-foot-long granite wall etched with war scenes. The soldiers were designed by sculptor Frank Gaylord and the wall mural by Louis Nelson. A reflecting pool symbolizes those who died during the conflict. The memorial was designed by a team of architects from Pennsylvania State University and revised by Kent Cooper.

KREEGER MUSEUM. A private, nonprofit art museum, featuring works collected over a 15-year period by David Kreeger, an insurance magnate, and his wife Carmen. The museum is housed in a postmodern mansion on five and a half acres of land in Northwest Washington. Designed by architects Philip Johnson and Richard Foster and constructed in 1967, the building was intended to serve as both a residence and an art gallery and concert hall. Opened to the public in 1994, the museum features a permanent art collection of 19th- and 20th-century European and American painting and sculpture, as well as examples of traditional African, Indian, and Pre-Columbian art.

KU KLUX KLAN DEMONSTRATION (1925). An August 1925 march on Washington by more than 25,000 members of the Ku Klux Klan (KKK) and their families. Since its founding in the 19th century, the all-white Klan has had a history of violence against racial, ethnic, and religious minorities in the United States. In the 1920s the KKK's membership peaked at around four million, including 15,000 members in Washington. KKK leader Hiram Wesley Evans moved the group's national office from Atlanta to Washington, hoping to influence national elections. In the summer of 1925, demonstrators camped throughout Washington were directed from temporary KKK headquarters at the **Willard Hotel**. After the march, the group burned an 80-foot cross at Arlington Cemetery.

- L -

LAFAYETTE SQUARE. A public park named in honor of the Marquis de Lafayette (1757–1834), the French nobleman who came to America to fight in the Revolutionary War. Located across from the **White House**, the area was originally designed as a private "president's park" by city planner **Pierre Charles L'Enfant**, but **Thomas Jefferson** gave the park to the public. It served as a campsite for soldiers during the **War of 1812** and the **Civil War**, and later as a center of Washington social life. It now serves as a place for public demonstrations and for picnicking and recreation in the heart of Washington. The center of the park contains an equestrian statue of Andrew Jackson dedicated in 1853. The statue is made of brass from guns captured by Jackson at the Battle of Pensacola in 1812. The four guns at the base of the monument were captured at the Battle of New Orleans. Four statues at the corners of the park honor foreign-born soldiers who were also heroes in the war: the Frenchmen Lafayette at the Battle of Brandywine and Comte de Rochambeau at Yorktown; the Prussian Baron von Steuben, who was the drillmaster of **George Washington**'s troops; and Thaddeus Kosciusko, whose engineering fortifications led to victory at the Battle of Saratoga.

LAFAYETTE SQUARE OPERA HOUSE. *See* BELASCO THEATER.

LAFAYETTE'S TOUR OF WASHINGTON (1824). Anniversary tour of the United States by a French hero of the American Revolutionary War. Born in Chavaniac, France, the young Marquis de Lafayette (1757–1834) inherited a fortune from his grandfather. Desiring to aid the American colonies in their struggle for independence, in 1777 Lafayette purchased a ship and sailed it to America with other French officers. He was given command of several Virginia divisions and took part in the major battles of the war, including Yorktown. He became one of **George Washington**'s advisors and helped to secure funds and military aid from the king of France. In 1824 the city government invited Lafayette to Washington as part of the country's 50th anniversary celebration of the war of independence. While Lafayette was honored throughout the 24 states of the union, in Washington he was welcomed at the rotunda of the **U.S. Capitol**, where he was greeted by Washington mayor Roger C. Weightman. When Lafayette entered the House chamber, all of the members removed their hats, rose, and remained standing. Lafayette was lodged at Franklin House, and the city spent $2,700 on the Lafayette visit, the largest appropriation of the year. Lafayette's personal secretary, Auguste Levasseur, published an account of his American tour titled *Lafayette in America in 1824 and 1825; or, Journal of a Voyage to the United States* (1829).

LANCASTERIAN SCHOOL. A school founded in 1811 in **Georgetown** on educational principles developed by English educator Joseph Lancaster (1778–1838). The school was one of the earliest attempts at publicly subsidized education in the District of Columbia. Lancaster's London school introduced original methods to teach writing and mathematics and borrowed from Andrew Bell the system of promoting advanced students to the status of subordinate teachers. A group of about 100 Georgetowners recruited one of Lancaster's instructors in 1811; beginning in 1816, the Georgetown Council annually appropriated $1,000 for the school on the condition that it enroll destitute children. The Lancasterian Schoolhouse still stands on O Street NW. It has long since been converted to a private residence.

LANGSTON, JOHN MERCER (1829–1897). Lawyer, educator, and civil servant. Born in Louisa, Virginia, Langston was sent to Ohio in 1834 after the death of his parents. He graduated from Oberlin College (B.A., 1849; M.A., 1852) and studied law with Philemon Bliss in Elyria, Ohio. He was admitted to the Ohio bar in 1854, was elected clerk of Brownhelm Township in 1855, and served on the Oberlin, Ohio, board of education (1860) and city council (1865–67). He was an advocate of suffrage and equal rights for African Americans and in 1867 became inspector general of the U.S. Freedman's Bureau. In Washington he organized the law department of **Howard University** and served as its dean (1868–77). He also served as vice president (1872–76) and acting president (1874–75) of the university. In 1877 President Rutherford B. Hayes appointed him resident minister to Haiti and chargé d'affaires in Santo Domingo. After serving as president of Virginia Normal and Collegiate Institute in Petersburg (1885–87), Langston was elected to the House of Representatives from Virginia's 4th congressional district. However, the 1888 election was marred by racially motivated voter fraud and he was denied a seat in the house until 1890. He declined to run for reelection in 1891 and wrote an autobiography, *From the Virginia Plantation to the National Capital* (1894).

LANGSTON GOLF COURSE. *See* ANACOSTIA PARK.

LANIER HEIGHTS. *See* ADAMS MORGAN.

LANSBURGH BUILDING. *See* SHAKESPEARE THEATRE.

LANSBURGH DEPARTMENT STORE. *See* DEPARTMENT STORES.

LATROBE, BENJAMIN HENRY BONEVAL (1764–1820). Architect of the **U.S. Capitol**. Latrobe was born near Leeds, England, and studied architecture and civil engineering in Germany. He emigrated to the United States in 1796 and established himself as an architect in the Greek Revival style, which was favored by **Thomas Jefferson**. In 1803 Jefferson appointed Latrobe to the position of surveyor of public buildings, a job that included the completion of the Capitol. Latrobe modified the original design of **William Thornton**, strengthening the interior structure of the north and south wings, which had been poorly constructed. After the Capitol was burned by the British in 1814, Latrobe was charged with rebuilding it. Other Washington buildings designed by Latrobe include **St. John's Church** and **Decatur House**; he also worked in Philadelphia, Pittsburgh, Baltimore, and New Orleans. Latrobe died of malaria while traveling to New Orleans.

LAW CODE. *See* DISTRICT OF COLUMBIA LAW CODE.

LAYMAN, CHRISTOPHER. *See* OLD STONE HOUSE.

LeDROIT PARK. An area just south of **Howard University**, bounded by Florida Avenue and 2nd and 7th Streets in Northwest Washington. In 1873 acting Howard University president Amzi L. Barber and his brother-in-law, Andrew Langdon, purchased a 55-acre tract from the university, just north of the city boundary. They named the tract after Langdon's father, real estate agent LeDroit Langdon. Contractor and architect James H. McGill built 41 residences in four years, and during the following decade, he built another 23 residences in the neighborhood. The McGill houses were in the "picturesque" architectural styles pioneered by Andrew Jackson Downing: Eastlake, Second Empire, Gothic Revival, and Italianate. The white, upper-middle-class development was encircled by a cast-iron and wood fence, and no through traffic was permitted.

A nearly decade-long controversy arose when residents of Howardtown, an all-black development that simultaneously grew up on the north side of Howard University, began to take shortcuts through LeDroit Park to their places of work. A "fence war" began in 1886, when LeDroit Park banned "intruders." In response, Howardtown developers dismantled the LeDroit Park fence and tore down a barbed wire fence that was subsequently erected by the LeDroit Park Citizens Association. The controversy continued until 1891, when the LeDroit Park Association finally succumbed to the Howardtown residents.

In 1893 Octavius A. Williams became the first African American homeowner in LeDroit Park. A barber at the **U.S. Capitol**, Williams and his family purchased one of the McGill houses and suffered much harassment, including a gunshot fired through their window. A year later, they were joined by a second black family, Robert and **Mary Church Terrell**, then a young couple just beginning their careers in education, women's suffrage, and civil rights. After white homeowners refused to sell to the Terrells, a white real estate agent purchased a house and sold it to them. During the next two decades, the neighborhood gradually changed from white to black, becoming part of a larger black area in Northwest Washington, where African American businesses, social clubs, and cultural institutions were located. Some of Washington's most important African American literary figures and civic leaders resided in LeDroit Park, including poets **Paul Laurence Dunbar** and Langston Hughes; Oscar dePriest, the first black Congressman since Reconstruction; Senator **Edward Brooke**; and educators **Kelly Miller, Anna J. Cooper**, and Garnet Wilkinson.

Demographic and social changes continued in the neighborhood during the 20th century. Public housing was erected on the edge of LeDroit Park during the Great Depression. Post-World War II urban renewal and desegregation caused many LeDroit Park families to leave the neighborhood. By 1970 the area was in physical decline, with overcrowding and street crime becoming serious neighborhood problems. The LeDroit Park Civic Association, led by Bennetta and **Walter Washington**, worked for greater police protection, improved government services, and expanded youth programs. The association also persuaded Howard University to take a greater interest in neighborhood affairs. In 1974 LeDroit Park was designated a historic district, and since then nearly two-thirds of the McGill houses have been restored, making the neighborhood an important part of Washington's historic inner city.

L'ENFANT, PIERRE CHARLES (1754–1833). Architect of the city plan of Washington. Born in France, L'Enfant studied engineering at the Royal Academy in Paris and came to America in 1777 to fight in the Revolutionary War. He joined **George Washington**'s army as an engineer, spent his first winter at Valley Forge, Pennsylvania, and went on to survive injury and imprisonment by the British. After the war, L'Enfant redesigned the City Hall in New York City for the meeting of the first U.S. Congress, and in 1791 George Washington appointed him to design the new capital city. Inspired by Versailles, L'Enfant planned the city around a grand avenue (the **Mall**), from which other large avenues radiate outward, to represent power radiating from a central source. L'Enfant quarreled with city commissioners, who were unhappy that he overspent, worked slowly, and released only sketchy plans. In response to these complaints, President Washington fired L'Enfant. When L'Enfant departed, he took his plans with him, and his design was reconstructed and modified by **Andrew Ellicott** and **Benjamin Banneker**. L'Enfant refused the payment later offered for his design of the capital city and died in poverty in Maryland.

L'ENFANT PLAZA. A 1966 urban development designed by architect I. M. Pei. Located at Frontage Road and D Street SW, the plaza is a mix of office buildings, a hotel, the underground 10th Street Mall, a **Washington metrorail** station, and pedestrian walkways. The development is named after city planner **Pierre Charles L'Enfant** and includes the **Benjamin Banneker** Fountain.

LETELIER-MOFFITT ASSASSINATION. The murder of Chilean politician Orlando Letelier and American human rights activist Ronni Karpen Moffitt on September 21, 1976. The two died when a bomb exploded under the Chilean's car as they traversed Sheridan Circle NW during morning rush hour. Letelier served as Chile's ambassador to the United States and later as defense and foreign minister in the democratically elected government of Salvador Allende. He fled to the United States when Allende was overthrown by a junta led by General Augusto Pinochet. General Pinochet's rule was notorious for its disregard of human rights and for the murder of political opponents in Chile, Argentina, Italy, and elsewhere. Former Chilean secret police chief Manuel Contreras, convicted of the crime in 1993, testified in 1998 that Letelier's murder was ordered by Pinochet. At the request of the

Spanish government, Pinochet was arrested in London in 1998 to be tried for crimes against humanity. However, a British court deemed the elderly prisoner unfit for trial and he was returned to Chile. Letelier and Moffitt were employed by the Institute for Policy Studies, which has since awarded an annual Letelier-Moffitt prize to persons or organizations notable in the struggle for human rights.

LEWIS, JOHN WHITELAW. *See* WHITELAW HOTEL.

LIBRARIES. *See* CARNEGIE LIBRARY; LIBRARY OF CONGRESS; MARTIN LUTHER KING, JR., MEMORIAL LIBRARY.

LIBRARY OF CONGRESS. The research library of Congress and the national library of the United States. The library was established by Congress in 1800 and located in the **U.S. Capitol**. When the invading British burned the Capitol in 1814, the library was destroyed. The following year Congress purchased the 6,487-volume library of **Thomas Jefferson**, which became the heart of a new national library. The modern library was developed by Ainsworth Rand Spofford, who served as librarian of Congress from 1864 to 1897. During his tenure a copyright law was passed that led to a great expansion of library collections, and the library's first building was constructed. Located at 1st and Independent Avenues SE, the library now consists of three buildings: the Thomas Jefferson Building (1897), the John Adams Building (1938), and the James Madison Memorial Building (1965). These three buildings contain numerous reading and exhibit rooms and house a staggering amount of material: 27 million books and pamphlets; 40 million manuscripts; four million maps; seven million pieces of music; 13 million photographs, drawings, and posters; 750,000 films and videotapes; three million sound recordings; and 75,000 current periodicals. The Jefferson Building contains the library's main reading room and a Great Hall decorated with marble flooring, mosaics, stained glass, and a 75-foot-high domed ceiling.

LILLIAN AND ALBERT SMALL JEWISH MUSEUM. Museum of the Washington Jewish community. The museum is housed in the oldest synagogue in the city, the former **Adas Israel**, built in 1876. The congregation moved to a new home in 1908, and the synagogue became a Greek Orthodox church and then a restaurant. By 1969, the building was owned by the D.C. government, which intended to demolish it. The Jewish Historical Society of Greater Washington negotiated a 99-year lease for the synagogue and moved it three blocks to its current location at 3rd and G Streets NW. The museum includes changing exhibits on local Jewish history, an archival collection, the restored 19th-century sanctuary, and the offices of the Jewish Historical Society. The society sponsors a variety of public and educational programs and publishes an annual journal, *The Record*.

LINCOLN, ABRAHAM. *See* CIVIL WAR; COMPENSATED EMANCIPATION; FORD'S THEATRE; LINCOLN ASSASSINATION; LINCOLN MEMORIAL; SLAVERY.

LINCOLN ASSASSINATION. The murder of President Abraham Lincoln on April 14, 1865, at **Ford's Theatre** in Washington. After several failed attempts to kidnap and kill the president, John Wilkes Booth, an actor, led a group of conspirators in plotting to kill the three top U.S. officials: president, vice president, and secretary of state. The conspirators wanted to avenge the **Civil War** defeat of the Confederacy and hoped that the assassinations would send the U.S. government into chaos. While the president was attending a play, Booth entered the presidential box and shot Lincoln in the head. Simultaneously, conspirator Lewis Payne attacked and almost killed Secretary of State William Seward at his home on **Lafayette Square**. A third conspirator failed to follow through on the plan to kill Vice President Andrew Johnson the same night. Lincoln was carried across 10th Street to Petersen House, but he never regained consciousness and died the next morning.

After shooting Lincoln, Booth jumped to the stage and broke his leg, crossed the stage in front of the audience, and went out a back door, escaping on horseback over the Navy Yard Bridge into Maryland. With an accomplice, Booth went to the home of Samuel Mudd, a doctor, who set Booth's broken leg. The assassins then fled south to Virginia. Twelve days after the assassination, military police trapped Booth in a burning tobacco barn and shot him to death when he refused to give himself up. Other conspirators were arrested, tried, and convicted in June 1865. Four were hanged at the Old Penitentiary at **Fort Lesley J. McNair**, and others were imprisoned. Lincoln's body was taken from Washington to Illinois for burial. Andrew Johnson succeeded to the presidency.

LINCOLN COLONNADE. *See* LINCOLN THEATER.

LINCOLN HOSPITAL. *See* CIVIL WAR.

LINCOLN MEMORIAL. A memorial honoring President Abraham Lincoln, who preserved the Union in the **Civil War.** Although a congressional commission was established in 1865 to plan the memorial, its design and location on drained marshland became a controversial issue and the monument was not completed until 1922. Designed by Henry Bacon and built in **Potomac Park** at the west end of the **Mall,** the memorial resembles the Parthenon in Athens. The 36 Doric columns that ring the building represent the 36 states of the Union at the time of Lincoln's death. The interior contains an eight-ton, 19-foot statue of a seated Lincoln, carved from white marble by Daniel Chester French. Lincoln's Gettysburg Address (1863) is inscribed on the left interior wall and his second inaugural address appears on the right wall. The walls also feature murals by Jules Guerdon on the freeing of the slaves and the unity of the North and South. Directly behind the statue are the words, "In this temple as in the hearts of the people for whom he saved the Union the memory of Abraham Lincoln is enshrined forever." The memorial was the site of the 1963 **March on Washington for Jobs and Freedom** and the "I Have a Dream" speech of Martin Luther King, Jr., delivered from its steps to a crowd of 200,000 people.

LINCOLN PARK. A small park located on East Capitol Street, between 11th and 13th Streets. The park's Emancipation statue, designed by Thomas Ball and dedicated in 1876, was the city's only monument to Abraham Lincoln before the **Lincoln Memorial** was completed in 1922. Made possible by the contributions of freed slaves, the statue depicts Abraham Lincoln as the Great Emancipator, holding the Emancipation Proclamation in one hand, while extending the other hand to an unshackled slave at his feet, bidding him to rise to freedom. The park also contains a 17-foot bronze statue that honors the African American educator **Mary McLeod Bethune.** Designed by Robert Berk, the statue depicts Bethune handing a scroll, which represents her legacy of education, to two children.

LINCOLN SUBDIVISION. *See* DEANWOOD.

LINCOLN THEATER. Historic movie palace. Located in the **Shaw/U Street** neighborhood, the theater was opened by **Harry Cran-**

dall in 1922. U Street NW was known as Washington's "Black Broadway," and the Lincoln Theater was an importance presence, hosting vaudeville shows and first-run movies. Its 1,600-seat auditorium featured a superb Manuel Mohler organ, played by musician Louis N. Brown during the silent film era. Adjoining the theater was the Lincoln Colonnade, a popular dance hall entered through a tunnel from U Street. The Lincoln Theater was the site of one of Washington's earliest civil rights protests, when **Ralph Bunche** and Sterling Brown led a group of **Howard University** students in the picketing of the 1939 movie *Gone with the Wind*. By 1984 the neighborhood had declined and the Lincoln Theater closed its doors. Historic preservationists fought to prevent its demolition, and during the 1980s the D.C. government spent more than $9 million to restore the theater to its former grandeur. Since its 1994 reopening, the building has served as an African American cultural center, hosting live performances, film festivals, charity benefits, and the annual Mayor's Arts Awards. *See also* SHAW/U STREET.

LITTLE HOTEL. *See* HOBAN, JAMES.

LITTLE SOCIETY OF NINE. *See* JOHN WESLEY AFRICAN METHODIST EPISCOPAL ZION CHURCH.

LIVERPOOL, MOSES. *See* CAPITOL HILL.

LOCKWOOD, BELVA ANN (1830–1917). Lawyer and activist for women's rights; the first woman to practice law before the **U.S. Supreme Court**. Lockwood (née Bennett) began working as a schoolteacher when she was 14 years old; she was married at 19 and widowed a short time later. Left with an infant, she nevertheless continued her education and graduated with honors from Genesee College in 1857. She moved to Washington, married Ezekiel Lockwood, and earned a law degree at the National University Law School. Lockwood was admitted to the D.C. bar, but as a woman was unable to practice before the Supreme Court. She successfully lobbied members of Congress to change the discriminatory law and went on to win several prominent cases, including a large settlement from the U.S. government on behalf of the Cherokee nation. One of the most effective advocates for women's rights of her time, Lockwood was also the first woman to run for president, in 1884 and 1888.

LOGAN CIRCLE. *See* SHAW/U STREET.

LONGWORTH, ALICE ROOSEVELT (1884–1980). Grande dame
of Washington society. The eldest child of President Theodore
Roosevelt, 17-year old "Princess Alice" was subjected to intense
media and public scrutiny when her father entered the **White
House**. She was a favorite subject of photographers and two popular songs were written about her, "Alice, Where Art Thou?" and
"Alice Blue Gown." Millions of American women dressed in the
color "Alice Blue," named for her blue eyes. Outspoken, unpre-
dictable, uninhibited, and mischievous, she married Ohio Congressman, later Speaker of the House, Nicholas Longworth (d.
1931) in a 1906 White House ceremony. After his death, Alice
Longworth wrote a best-selling memoir and a widely syndicated
newspaper column and entertained Washington's elite in her Massachusetts Avenue mansion. She referred to herself as "a combination of Scarlett O'Hara and Whistler's Mother" and became known
for her stinging one-liners, most notably, "If you can't say any-
thing nice about anyone, come sit here by me."

LOST LAWS. *See* DISTRICT OF COLUMBIA v. THOMPSON
COMPANY.

LOUISE HOME. *See* CORCORAN, WILLIAM WILSON.

- M -

MADISON BUILDING. *See* LIBRARY OF CONGRESS.

MALCOLM X PARK. *See* MERIDIAN HILL PARK.

MALL. A "grand avenue" of open space, 400 feet wide and almost a
mile long, that begins at the **U.S. Capitol** and ends at the **Lincoln
Memorial**. The area surrounding the Mall is occupied by nine of
the **Smithsonian Institution**'s 14 museums and by the Department
of Agriculture. The Mall between the Capitol and the **Washington
Monument** site was envisioned by **Pierre Charles L'Enfant** in
his city plan of 1791, but remained undeveloped until 1850 when
Andrew Jackson Downing designed the first gardens and paths
for the area. However, by the late 19th century the Mall had become an unsightly area. The **McMillan Report** (1902) led to its
gradual beautification: a railroad station and train tracks were relocated, sheds were torn down, a canal was filled, and open space

was extended from the Washington Monument to the Lincoln Memorial. Temporary buildings used during World War I and World War II were removed during the 1960s and 1970s. These improvements led to the restoration of the Mall as a grand avenue. The Mall now serves as a staging area for concerts, public forums, and political demonstrations, and it is the site of the annual Festival of American Folk Life, Washington's Birthday celebration, and Independence Day celebration.

MAMOUT, YARROW (ca. 1715–ca. 1823). Businessman. Mamout was born in Africa; as a child he was kidnapped, enslaved, and transported to **Georgetown**. Industrious and popular, within a few years he purchased his freedom, acquired a small cart, and established a successful hauling business. By 1800 he had purchased a house on what is now Dent Place NW. He was an early investor in the **Bank of Columbia**. An abstemious and devout Muslim, Mamout is best known as the subject of a portrait executed by Charles Willson Peale in 1819, now owned by the Historical Society of Pennsylvania. An 1822 portrait of Mamout by James Alexander Simpson hangs in the Peabody Collection of the Georgetown Public Library.

MARCH ON WASHINGTON FOR JOBS AND FREEDOM (1963). Historic civil rights demonstration in Washington on August 28, 1963. The nonviolent march began on the **Mall** at the **Washington Monument** and ended at the **Lincoln Memorial**. Led by union leader A. Philip Randolph, the march was organized by Bayard Rustin. The multiethnic, multiracial crowd of 250,000 attracted extensive media coverage. Unemployment among people of color was at the time double that of whites, and income roughly half. The leaders hoped to show widespread support for the Civil Rights Act, which would be passed the following year. President John F. Kennedy at first opposed plans for the demonstration, worried that violence would break out, but later gave his open support. Martin Luther King, Jr., gave his famous "I Have a Dream" speech as the closing address.

MARINE CORPS MUSEUM. *See* NAVY YARD.

MARKETS. *See* PUBLIC MARKETS.

MARSH MARKET. *See* PUBLIC MARKETS.

MARSHALL, HARRIET GIBBS (1869–1941). Music educator.

Marshall graduated from Oberlin Conservatory in 1889, the first African American woman to receive a music diploma there. She also studied in Boston, Chicago, and Paris and then began a teaching career at a small college in Kentucky. After moving to Washington at the turn of the century, she taught in the D.C. public schools and then established the Washington Conservatory of Music in 1903. Her school provided conservatory-level training for black students and was the site of many performances by African American artists.

MARSHALL, PETER (1902–1949). Presbyterian minister and chaplain of the U.S. Senate. Born in Coatbridge, Scotland, Marshall emigrated to the United States, arriving at Ellis Island in 1927. He worked for a year in New Jersey, traveled to Birmingham, Alabama, and attended Columbia Theological Seminary in Decatur, Georgia (1928–31). He served as pastor of a small church in Covington, Georgia (1931–33), and of the Westminster Presbyterian Church in Atlanta (1933–37). Marshall's success at the Westminster church attracted the attention of the **New York Avenue Presbyterian Church** in Washington, and he became the pastor there in 1937, serving for 11 years. He was appointed Senate chaplain in 1947 and reappointed in 1949. His prayers before the Senate were reprinted in the *New Yorker* and other publications, and a popular biography, *A Man Called Peter* (1951), was written by his wife, Catherine Wood Marshall.

MARTIN LUTHER KING, JR., MEMORIAL LIBRARY. The main building and administrative headquarters of the D.C. Public Library System. The MLK Memorial Library is the only building in Washington designed by noted architect Ludwig Mies van der Rohe. The building was constructed between 1968 and 1972 at a cost of $18 million. Located on G Street NW, the library's 400,000 square feet of floor space, meeting rooms, and exhibition space greatly exceed the 1903-built **Carnegie Library** that it replaced. The library entrance features a dramatic mural by Jamaican-American artist Don Miller that portrays King and the impact of the civil rights movement of the 1960s. The library's third floor contains the Washingtoniana Division, a local history collection containing 20,000 volumes, 8,000 reels of microfilm, and more than one million photographs.

MASONIC TEMPLE. *See* SCOTTISH RITE TEMPLE.

MAYFAIR MANSION. *See* TEMPLE OF FREEDOM UNDER GOD, CHURCH OF GOD.

MAYFLOWER HOTEL. A 600-room hotel located on Connecticut Avenue NW four blocks from the **White House**. Designed by Warren and Wetmore, the New York architectural firm that designed Grand Central Station, the hotel opened in 1924. Its official opening came the following year, when it hosted more than 1,000 people at the inaugural ball of President Calvin Coolidge. Designed in the Beaux-Arts tradition, the 10-floor hotel featured more gold leaf than any American building except the **Library of Congress** and a spectacular 475-foot-long interior lobby that joins Connecticut Avenue and 17th Street. Renovations completed in 1992 uncovered a 25-foot skylight blacked out during World War II and saw the installation of 56 miles of millwork in crown moldings and 46,000 square feet of Italian marble in baths. Guests of the hotel have included presidents and foreign dignitaries, and for more than 20 years it was the daily lunch spot of FBI director **J. Edgar Hoover**.

MAYOR. Chief of the executive branch of government. At the establishment of the District of Columbia in 1790, Congress empowered the U.S. president to appoint commissioners to govern the federal district. In 1802, Washington City's new municipal charter allowed election of a **City Council**, but the mayor was appointed by the president. In 1820, another city charter was issued, and the mayoralty became an elected office. **Georgetown** had existed as a separate political jurisdiction since 1751, predating the District of Columbia, and Georgetown's city government, established in 1789, included a popularly elected mayor.

In 1871, Congress revoked the charters of Washington City, Georgetown, and Washington County and combined the three jurisdictions into one entity, the Territory of the District of Columbia, managed by a territorial governor appointed by the U.S. president. Three years later, Congress abolished the territorial government and created a panel of three presidentially appointed commissioners who exercised virtually absolute control over District matters. Nearly a century later, President Lyndon Johnson convinced Congress to replace the commission government with a single mayor-commissioner, whom he appointed: **Walter Washington**. Washington took office in November 1967; five months later, the city was devastated by the **riots of 1968** following the death of Martin

Luther King, Jr. Washington's strong, calm performance in office gained him respect both in Congress and across the city and he was credited with hastening the return of limited **home rule** in 1974, when he became the city's first elected mayor in 103 years.

Walter Washington was succeeded in 1978 by civil rights activist **Marion Barry**, who served three terms before leaving office under conviction for possession of illegal drugs. Barry was once again elected mayor in 1994, of a city facing a half-billion-dollar budget deficit. Congress stripped Barry of nearly all the job's powers and established a **District of Columbia Financial Responsibility and Management Assistance Authority** to run the city. Most functions were returned to the mayor's office following the election of Anthony Williams in 1999.

MCI CENTER. A five-acre sports facility that hosts professional sporting events, concerts, and conventions. Located in downtown Washington, the 20,600-seat MCI Center is the home of the **Washington Capitals** hockey team, the Washington Wizards basketball team, and the **Georgetown University** Hoyas. The center was completed in 1997 and includes retail shops; the MCI National Sports Gallery, which commemorates great moments in American sports history; and the American Sportscasters Hall of Fame and Museum.

McKIM, CHARLES F. *See* McMILLAN REPORT; WHITE HOUSE.

McLEAN, EDWARD BEALE "NED" (1885–1941). Newspaper publisher. Born in Washington, McLean was raised in a wealthy family. His grandfather was a founder and owner of the *Cincinnati Enquirer* and McLean's father, John R. McLean, added the *Washington Post* to the family businesses. When McLean's father died in 1916, his fortune was put in a trust. The young McLean challenged the will and was given ownership of the two newspapers as part of a settlement. He changed the editorial position of the *Post* from independent to Republican, but otherwise neglected the newspaper. He and his wife, **Evalyn Walsh McLean**, busied themselves in the affairs of Washington's high society. In 1923 he was implicated in the Teapot Dome scandal. The scandal destroyed his reputation and compromised the *Post*, which after a downward spiral was sold at auction to Eugene Meyer in 1933. McLean suffered an emotional breakdown and was institutionalized in Towson, Maryland.

McLEAN, EVALYN WALSH (1886–1947). Wealthy socialite and the last private owner of the Hope Diamond. Evalyn's marriage to **Edward "Ned" McLean** united two of America's great fortunes. Evalyn was the daughter of Colorado Senator Thomas F. Walsh, owner of the famous Camp Bird Silver Mine. Her husband inherited a vast steamboat and newspaper fortune. In addition to three in-town mansions, the McLeans owned "Friendship," a 70-acre estate on upper Wisconsin Avenue, where they lived and entertained in lavish style, allegedly running through more than $100 million. McLean was known for her quirky philanthropy, purchasing more than 1,000 sandwiches for **Bonus Army** protesters and installing a public water fountain at a **Georgetown** bus stop. She owned some of the world's most famous diamonds, including the Star of the East, the Star of the South, the McLean Diamond, and the Hope Diamond. After McLean's death, New York jeweler Harry Winston bought her collection, and in 1958 donated the Hope Diamond to the **Smithsonian Institution**. In 1942 McLean sold Friendship to the Defense Homes Corporation, which built apartments on the site during the city's war-related housing shortage. Now converted to condominiums, the complex is known as McLean Gardens.

McMILLAN REPORT (1902). The 171-page report of the Senate Park Commission in which Republican Senator James McMillan from Michigan proposed significant changes to the city plan of Washington. The study was undertaken as part of the **Washington Centennial** celebration marking the city's 100th anniversary as the federal capital. The McMillan Report, with considerable input from the American Institute of Architects, directed **Daniel H. Burnham** and Frederick Law Olmsted, Jr., to prepare plans for the beautification of the city. Charles F. McKim, Augustus Saint-Gaudens, and McMillan's assistant Charles Moore also became heavily involved. This group of architects, planners, and artists proposed to revive **Pierre Charles L'Enfant**'s original plan for the city, making it a place of parks and monumental buildings. It restored to prominence the triad of the **U.S. Capitol**, the **White House**, and the **Washington Monument**. Its recommendations led to the beautification of the **Mall** area, the extension of the Mall to the **Potomac River**, development of the site for the **Lincoln Memorial**, construction of **Union Station**, and the development of parks and public drives along the Potomac and **Anacostia River**s. Nearly half of the report was implemented, making it of primary importance in shaping the features of today's city.

MEIGS, MONTGOMERY C. (1816–1892). Engineer and architect. Born in Philadelphia, Meigs spent a year at the University of Pennsylvania before receiving an appointment to the U.S. Military Academy at West Point. After graduation, he joined the Army Corps of Engineers and spent several years employed in public works projects. In 1849 Meigs moved to Washington and served as assistant to the Army's chief engineer, General Joseph C. Totten. When Congress authorized a study of the D.C. water supply in 1852, Totten nominated Meigs to direct the project. Meigs supervised construction of the city's first municipal water system, a $2 million network that daily brought 68 million gallons of water into Washington. The network included aqueduct bridges (most notably the Cabin John Bridge, then the longest masonry arch in the world), a nine-foot-diameter conduit from Great Falls to Washington, and two large reservoirs, one of which, the Dalecarlia, is still in use. Meigs revised architect Thomas U. Walter's design for the 1851 extension of the **U.S. Capitol** building and directed its construction. In the 1880s, Meigs designed and built the massive Italian Renaissance-style Pension Building to house the 1,500 government clerks who processed the pension applications of **Civil War** veterans. The structure now houses the **National Building Museum**.

MELLON, PAUL (1907–1999). Philanthropist. As the son of banker and U.S. treasury secretary Andrew Mellon, billionaire Paul Mellon was heir to one of America's great fortunes and he played an enormous role in Washington's cultural life. When his father provided funds to build the National Gallery of Art's West Building in 1941, Mellon supervised its construction. He served in the U.S. Army during World War II and upon returning to the United States in 1945, he established the Bollingen Foundation, which awarded the prestigious Bollingen Prize for Poetry. Mellon was president and chief executive of the **Smithsonian Institution**'s National Gallery of Art from 1979 to 1985 and donated more than 900 paintings to that institution, including works by Monet, Renoir, Degas, Picasso, and Van Gogh. He paid for construction of the $100 million East Wing in 1978 and left the gallery another $75 million and 100 artworks in his will. Mellon also endowed Yale University's Center for British Art and British Studies, provided funds for the National Park Service to purchase the land that became Cape Hatteras National Seashore, and supported numerous nature preservation and cultural organizations. Mellon's racehorses, bred at his Upperville, Virginia, farm, won the Kentucky Derby, Belmont Stakes, and Britain's Epsom Derby.

MELLON PLAN. *See* FEDERAL TRIANGLE.

MEMORIAL CONTINENTAL HALL. *See* DAUGHTERS OF THE AMERICAN REVOLUTION, NATIONAL SOCIETY.

MERIDIAN HILL. *See* ADAMS MORGAN.

MERIDIAN HILL PARK. A 12-acre hillside park located about one mile north of the **White House**. The park was originally surveyed in 1816 and is on one of the oldest north-south meridian lines of the city. The land was acquired by the federal government in 1910 and between 1912 and 1914 the park was designed in neoclassical style, with an upper grassy mall and a lower section that was finally completed in 1936. Created by George Burnap and landscape architect Horace Peaslee, the park incorporates elements of several European parks Peaslee had visited in 1917. Some of these elements include a water cascade, plantings, terraces of French and Italian design, and a reflecting pool modeled after a pool in Zurich, Switzerland. The park used a considerable amount of exposed aggregate concrete in its stairs, walks, retaining walls, and fountains. The exposed polished stones of the aggregate concrete come from the **Potomac River**. The park also features statues of President James Buchanan, the Italian poet Dante, and Joan of Arc. During the 1970s the Washington **City Council** renamed the park "Malcolm X Park," after the African American activist who once spoke here. However, the official name of the federally owned park was never changed. Neglected for many years, in 1994 the park was designated a national historic landmark and the National Park Service plans long-needed repairs and restoration.

MERIDIAN INTERNATIONAL CENTER. Nonprofit educational and cultural institution that serves as a hospitality house for diplomats and foreign visitors and as a center for international affairs. Meridian International Center is housed in two historic buildings on three acres of gardens that occupy a full city block on Meridian

Hill. Meridian House is a decorated limestone reconstruction of an 18th-century French townhouse, designed by architect **John Russell Pope** and constructed in 1921 for American diplomat Irwin Laughlin. White-Meyer House is a Georgian mansion, also designed by Pope, built in 1911 for American diplomat Henry White. Meridian International Center sponsors a program of international cultural exchange, lectures, briefings, seminars, conferences, school outreach programs, and art exhibitions.

MESTA, PERLE (1891–1975). Ambassador, political fundraiser, and society hostess. Born in Newport, Rhode Island, Mesta became interested in politics in the 1930s and was active in the National Woman's Party. In the mid-1940s, she moved to Washington and plunged into fundraising for the presidential campaign of Harry S. Truman, who rewarded her with appointment as ambassador to Luxembourg (1949–1953). Upon her return to Washington, she became known for her glamorous dinner parties. When asked how she attracted the elite to her Tilden Street NW home, she tartly replied, "Just hang a pork chop in the window." Known as "the hostess with the mostest," Mesta inspired the successful Broadway musical and subsequent film, *Call Me Madam*, starring Ethel Merman.

METHODIST BURYING GROUNDS. *See* MOUNT ZION CEMETERY.

METRO. *See* WASHINGTON METRORAIL SYSTEM.

METROPOLITAN AFRICAN METHODIST EPISCOPAL CHURCH. Historic African American congregation, which serves as the national headquarters of the African Methodist Episcopal denomination. The church was founded in 1854 by a merger of Israel Bethel and Union Bethel AME churches. Located on M Street NW, the current building is the result of a major renovation and expansion completed in 1886 with hand-washed bricks taken from the razed Bethel Hall, headquarters of the Bethel Literary and Historical Association, an early black cultural and political club. Metropolitan AME Church is one of Washington's most important African American institutions, a site of community events, town meetings, literary societies, and the graduation ceremonies of M Street (Dunbar) High School and **Howard University**. A famous gathering took place at the church in 1913, when outraged citizens expressed their shock and anger over President Woodrow Wilson's declaration that segregation "benefited" African Americans. The church has had many prominent members, including poet **Paul Laurence Dunbar**, civic leader Julia West Hamilton, U.S. Senator Blanche Kelso Bruce, and statesman **Frederick Douglass**. Douglass's 1882 speech "The Self-Made Man" was given from the pulpit of Metropolitan Church. Presidents William McKinley, **William Howard Taft**, and Theodore Roosevelt and First Lady Eleanor Roosevelt have also addressed church audiences.

METROPOLITAN THEATRE. *See* CRANDALL, HARRY M.

METROPOLITAN WASHINGTON COUNCIL OF GOVERN-MENTS. Organization of local governments and the official planning organization for the Washington metropolitan region. Founded in 1957, the council serves as a forum for solving regional problems, especially in the areas of transportation, public safety, the environment, and housing. Council members include the Maryland and Virginia legislatures, D.C. municipal government, U.S. House of Representatives, U.S. Senate, three counties in Maryland, four counties in Virginia, and nine of the area's larger incorporated cities—all comprising 3,011 square miles and serving a population of more than four million. The council is supported by contributions from the participating jurisdictions and by grants and private donations.

MEYER, EUGENE. *See* McLEAN, EDWARD BEALE "NED"; PATTERSON, ELEANOR M.; *WASHINGTON POST.*

MICHAUX, ELDER LIGHTFOOT SOLOMON. *See* DUPONT CIRCLE; HOWARD THEATRE; INDUSTRIAL BANK OF WASHINGTON; TEMPLE OF FREEDOM UNDER GOD, CHURCH OF GOD.

MILLER, KELLY (1863–1939). Educator. Born in Winnsboro, South Carolina, Miller worked in the Pension Office in Washington and was educated at **Howard University** (1880–86). He studied mathematics, physics, and astronomy with Simon Newcomb at the **U.S. Naval Observatory** and for two years at Johns Hopkins University (1887–89). After returning to Washington, he taught high school mathematics (1889) and then college mathematics at Howard. Miller served as dean of the College of Arts and Sciences (1907–18) at Howard and then turned his attention to sociology, which he introduced into the university curriculum. Miller's switch to sociology allowed him to address many of the racial issues that affected American society in general, and the African American community in particular. He helped W. E. B. DuBois edit the journal *Crisis*, but was more optimistic than DuBois that discrimination based on race would eventually disappear. He believed that higher education was the key to social advancement for African Americans. His views were expressed in several publications, including *Race Adjustment* (1903), *Out of the House of Bondage* (1914), *The Everlasting Stain* (1924), and *An Appeal to Conscience* (1918).

MILLS, ROBERT (1781–1855). Architect. Born in Charleston, South Carolina, Mills was educated at the College of Charleston and worked under **James Hoban** and **Benjamin Latrobe**. He spent two years in Philadelphia (1810–12) and resided in Baltimore (1812–20) and Charleston (1820–30) before returning to Washington. As Architect of Public Buildings, Mills was largely responsible for three of the four public buildings erected in Washington between 1836 and 1851: the Treasury Department; the Patent Office, now **Smithsonian Institution** museums; and the Post Office, which now houses the International Trade Commission. He also won a design competition for the **Washington Monument**, although it was not completed according to his original plans, which called for a Greco-Roman rotunda designed to hold the graves of Revolutionary War heroes. In these structures Mills tried to adapt ancient architectural forms—Greek Ionic, Greek Corinthian, and Egyptian—to the needs of a new nation in search of an architectural identity. He also worked on the **U.S. Capitol** and published *A Guide to the Capital of the U.S., 1832* (1834).

MINER, MYRTILLA (1815–1864). Educator who established the first U.S. school for training black female teachers. Shocked by the brutality and injustice of **slavery**, and despite local opposition and a lukewarm reception from abolitionists who feared for her safety, Miner opened a School for Colored Girls at 11th Street and New York Avenue NW in 1851. With the aid of Philadelphia Quaker businessmen and a portion of Harriet Beecher Stowe's profits from the serialization of *Uncle Tom's Cabin*, Miner purchased a house for her school at 20th Street and New Hampshire Avenue NW in 1853. In 1856 she tried to expand her facilities and curriculum, but a newspaper editorial by former Washington mayor Walter Lenox killed all hopes for local fundraising, and the school closed in 1860. Miner moved to California, where she supported herself as a clairvoyant and "magnetic healer" until she died from injuries sustained in a horse and buggy accident. Miner's school was reopened in 1871 by **Howard University**, was later absorbed by the D.C. Colored School System, and in 1930 became known as Miner Teachers' College. In 1955 the school participated in the merger that created D.C. Teachers' College, which in 1977 became part of the University of the District of Columbia.

MITCHELL, JESSE H. *See* INDUSTRIAL BANK OF WASHINGTON.

MOFFITT, RONNI KARPEN. *See* LETELIER-MOFFITT ASSASSINATION.

MONTROSE PARK. A grassy 16-acre park in the heart of **Georgetown**. Located between 30th and 31st Streets NW, the park links Dumbarton Oaks Park and **Rock Creek Park**. The land was originally known as Parrott's Woods, after owner Richard Parrott. The land came up for sale and in 1902 Georgetown resident Sarah Louisa Rittenhouse (d. 1947) urged local officials and Congress to buy the Montrose property in order to save it from commercial development. Her idea of creating a Georgetown park was realized in 1911 when Congress appropriated $110,000 to buy the land and to build a bridge, completed in 1915, to connect the park with Washington. In 1956 a bronze sphere, dedicated to Rittenhouse, was placed at the park's entrance.

MOORE, ARTHUR COTTON (b. 1935). Architect. Born in Washington, Moore was educated at Princeton University (1954–60), worked for the Washington architectural firm of Cloethiel Woodward Smith and Associates (1961–65), and subsequently operated his own firm, Arthur Cotton Moore Associates of Washington. He was a contributing editor on "Urban Affairs" to *Washingtonian* magazine (1965–78) and has written articles on urban planning and related subjects for the *Washington Post*. Of the many Moore-designed projects in Washington, the best known are Canal Square in **Georgetown** (1969), where a 19th-century warehouse was joined to a 75,000-square-foot complex housing shops and offices grouped around courtyards; the **Old Post Office Pavilion and Clock Tower** development and restoration (1980, 1983), **Dupont**

Circle Shopping Center (1980), the **Library of Congress** restoration (1980), the Duke Ellington School for the Performing Arts (1981), and the Washington Harbor Complex (1985). Moore's work has combined historic preservation with modern urban design, and his buildings are known for their "juxtaposition of dissimilar elements."

MOORE, CHARLES. *See* McMILLAN REPORT.

MORSE, SAMUEL FINLEY BREESE (1791–1872). Artist and inventor. Born in Charlestown, Massachusetts, Morse graduated from Yale University (1810), studied art in England (1811–15), worked as an artist in Boston and New York, and founded the National Academy of Design (1826). After three years of study and travel in Europe (1829–32), he returned to New York, where he painted and taught art at what is now New York University. In 1838 he invented the telegraph, an electrical device used to transmit information long distances over wires. His telegraph and Morse Code, which translates letters and numbers into dots and dashes, are still used today. The invention attracted little public interest until 1843, when Congress appropriated $30,000 to run a telegraph line from Washington to Baltimore. In 1844 Morse sat in the **U.S. Supreme Court** chamber in the **U.S. Capitol** and sent the first telegraphic message, "What hath God wrought!" Although he had other scientific interests and later in life became an important philanthropist, he is best remembered for his invention and the drama that took place in the chamber of the Supreme Court.

MORTON, JELLY ROLL [Ferdinand Joseph LaMenthe] (1885–1941). Pianist and composer. Morton was born Ferdinand Joseph LaMenthe in New Orleans and at age 17 began playing at clubs in the fabled Storyville District. He traveled and performed throughout North America, most notably at the 1904 St. Louis World's Fair. Morton is considered the first true jazz composer; he wrote many of the genre's classics, several of which were influenced by his early roots in ragtime and blues. His best known works include "Kansas City Stomp," "Frog-I-More Rag," "The Naked Dance," and "Wolverine Blues." He was the first to produce jazz arrangements in written musical notation, and his "Original Jelly Roll Blues" (1915) was the first jazz arrangement ever published. Morton moved to Washington in the 1930s, where he managed and performed at the Jungle Inn, a nightclub on 9th Street NW. Between

May and July 1938, Morton recorded his version of the history of jazz at the **Library of Congress**, a remarkable spoken narrative illustrated with piano solos. The project included 52 records and more than 100 songs. It is one of the most important documentary records in the history of American music.

MOUNT PLEASANT. An area bordered by **Rock Creek Park**, 16th Street, Columbia Road, and Piney Branch Parkway in Northwest Washington. Mount Pleasant takes its name from Pleasant Plains, an enormous 18th-century estate owned by **Georgetown** mayor **Robert Peter**. In the 1800s, the Washington Jockey Club racetrack and several country estates were built on its gently rolling hills. By mid-century, the mansion of U.S. treasurer William Seldon dominated the landscape. When Seldon, a Southern sympathizer, left Washington at the outbreak of the **Civil War**, his property passed into the hands of Samuel Brown, a former army contractor. Brown became president of the Metropolitan Railway and was appointed to the city's Board of Public Works. He took advantage of war-depressed real estate prices to acquire land near his house, which he laid out in one-acre lots. Although he sold only a few lots in 1865, during the next five years demand for the land increased and prices rose dramatically.

After the Civil War, a group of New Englanders moved to Washington and found employment with the rapidly expanding federal government. These newcomers pooled their money to buy a tract of land and laid out Mount Pleasant's first streets: Newton (formerly Howard), Meridian, Brown, and Oak. Early Mount Pleasant was so homogeneous that New England village traditions developed there, and the area was known as "Clerksville," because of the neighborhood's numerous government clerks.

At the turn of the 20th century, **Mary Henderson** undertook a campaign to transform 16th Street into the "avenue of the Presidents." The street was widened and straightened to the Maryland line, and electric streetcar service was extended to Park Road. Classically influenced single-family residences and row houses were built on the west side of Mount Pleasant, between 16th Street and Rock Creek Park, giving the area a unified architectural style. The older, eastern section of Mount Pleasant developed a commercial district, and the **Columbia Heights** neighborhood grew up east of 16th Street.

During the housing crisis of World War II, many elegant row houses were subdivided into apartments and group homes. After the war, a substantial number of white families moved to Washington's newly built suburbs, and African Americans moved into the neighborhood. The **riots of 1968** dramatically accelerated "white flight," and Mount Pleasant became an ethnically diverse neighborhood, with newer residents coming from Central America and Asia. The neighborhood was included in the National Register of Historic Places, and historic preservation of elegant turn-of-the-century residences was gradually undertaken without displacing lower-income residents. Economic recession, high crime rates, and poor community relations led to the 1991 Cinco de Mayo Riots. The three days of violence were triggered by the shooting of a Hispanic resident by a white police officer. During the ensuing decade city government officials have improved community relations and an economic upturn has returned stability to the neighborhood.

MOUNT VERNON COLLEGE. Private women's college in operation from 1875 until 1998. Elizabeth J. Somers founded the Mount Vernon Seminary in downtown Washington as a six-year program that included four years of high school and two years of college instruction. In 1916 the school moved to Nebraska Avenue NW, but that site was commandeered by the U.S. Navy during World War II. Mount Vernon temporarily relocated on the second floor of a nearby department store, then purchased the 26-acre Palisades Dairy Farm on Foxhall Road NW in 1946. The college discontinued high school programs in 1969 and began granting Bachelor of Arts degrees in 1973. During the 1980s and 1990s, popular concert series and continuing education programs were offered to the public. **George Washington University** purchased Mount Vernon College in 1998 and added a dormitory and athletic facilities. The university may use the property as a satellite campus or as a self-contained honors college.

MOUNT ZION CEMETERY. Historic burial ground that incorporates the Old Methodist Burying Grounds and the Female Union Band Society Cemetery. In 1808 the Montgomery Street Methodist Church (now **Dumbarton United Methodist Church**) bought 1.5 acres on the heights of **Georgetown** to use as a cemetery. In the years before the **Civil War**, the cemetery was probably a hiding place for African Americans escaping slavery on the Underground

Railroad. In 1842 the Female Union Band Society, a free black burial society, purchased 1.5 acres adjacent to the Methodist property. In 1879 the Methodist property was leased to **Mount Zion United Methodist Church**. Most Band Society members also belonged to Mount Zion Church, and when Mount Zion took over the Methodist cemetery, distinctions between the two properties blurred. Burials stopped in 1950 and a decade later real estate developers tried to buy the property. A series of lawsuits ensued, and in 1975 a U.S. District Court ordered the cemeteries held in trust as a historic property. They are now listed on the National Register of Historic Places and are under consideration for inclusion in an Underground Railroad National Park.

MOUNT ZION UNITED METHODIST CHURCH. The oldest African American congregation in the District of Columbia. In January 1813, trustees of Montgomery Street Methodist Church (now **Dumbarton United Methodist Church**) in **Georgetown** purchased a lot at 27th and P Streets "for the use and benefit" of the congregation's African American members, about half of whom were enslaved. Within three years, 125 blacks had built a meetinghouse, known as "The Ark," and formed their own congregation. Renamed Mount Zion in 1844, the church provided important leaders for Georgetown's black community, including Joseph Cartwright, the first African American ordained Methodist elder in the region. The congregation opened a school for blacks in 1823, and the church served as a station on the Underground Railroad. In 1880 the church burned, probably from arson, and the current structure on 29th Street NW was constructed. Mount Zion members helped found several other congregations, including the earliest African Methodist Episcopal and African Methodist Episcopal Zion churches in the District. In recent years, Mount Zion has been recognized for its History and Records Center, housed in the last remaining example of English cottage architecture in Georgetown. *See also* MOUNT ZION CEMETERY.

MUNICIPAL CENTER. *See* REEVES MUNICIPAL CENTER.

MURDER BAY. *See* CONTRABANDS; OLD POST OFFICE PAVILION AND CLOCK TOWER; PENNSYLVANIA AVENUE; SWAMPOODLE.

MURRAY, DANIEL ALEXANDER PAYNE (1852–1925). Librar-

ian and civic leader. Born in Baltimore, Maryland, Murray moved
to Washington at age nine. In 1871, at the age of 18, he joined the
12-member staff of the **Library of Congress**, serving as personal
assistant to Librarian Ainsworth Rand Spofford. In 1881 he was
named assistant librarian, a position he held for more than 40
years. Murray developed an expertise in African American publications and in 1900 compiled a bibliography of more than 1,000
titles. He had a deep interest in African American history and
wrote articles in *The Voice of the Negro* and other journals. His
dream was to compile *A Historical and Biographical Encyclopedia
of the Colored Race*, but the project was never completed. Active
in the social life of Washington, Murray was the first African
American to serve on the **Greater Washington Board of Trade**
and was a two-time delegate to the Republican National Convention.

- N -

**NATIONAL AIR AND SPACE MUSEUM. Smithsonian Institu-
tion** museum dedicated to the history of human flight. The Smithsonian began its collection of flight artifacts in 1876 with a group
of Chinese kites, but it wasn't until 1946 that Congress passed a
law founding the National Air Museum to chronicle the history of
aviation. Congress amended the law in 1966, changing the museum's name to the National Air and Space Museum and authorizing the construction of a new building on the **Mall**. Designed by
Gyo Obata, the building was constructed of pink Tennessee marble. In 1976 it was opened to the public with a dramatic ceremony
in which the ribbon cutting was done by a robot arm, initiated by a
signal from the Mars-bound Viking Lander. The museum's 23 exhibition galleries hold artifacts that span the entire history of human flight, including the Wright brothers' airplane, the Spirit of
St. Louis, and the Apollo 11 spacecraft. The Air and Space Museum is visited by more people than any other museum in the
world.

NATIONAL ARBORETUM. *See* U.S. NATIONAL ARBORETUM.

NATIONAL ARCHIVES AND RECORDS ADMINISTRATION.
The official repository of the United States, housing papers and
records of the executive, legislative, and judicial branches of gov-

ernment. Located on Constitution Avenue between 7th and 9th Streets NW, the National Archives building was designed by **John Russell Pope** and completed in 1937. The rectangular building has a granite base, a limestone exterior, and a Corinthian colonnade on each of its four sides. It contains four research rooms: a Central Research Room for scholarly research, the National Archives Library, the Legislative Research Room, and the Microfilm Research Room for genealogical research. The National Archives administers a second site in College Park, Maryland, and the separate presidential libraries located in various parts of the country. The most treasured possessions of the National Archives, displayed in its half-domed rotunda, are the Charters of Freedom: the Declaration of Independence, the Constitution (two pages are displayed), and the Bill of Rights. Other important documents held by the National Archives include the papers of the Continental Congress, records related to American Indians, the **Civil War** photographs of **Mathew Brady**, Commodore Matthew Perry's journals from his trip to Japan, and President Richard Nixon's resignation letter.

NATIONAL ASSOCIATION FOR THE ADVANCEMENT OF COLORED PEOPLE (NAACP), WASHINGTON CHAPTER. Local affiliate of the country's oldest civil rights organization. The Washington chapter was organized in 1912, three years after W. E. B. DuBois founded the national organization. Beginning with 143 members, by 1916, the local group had grown to 1,164, making it the largest chapter in the United States. Under the leadership of **Archibald Grimké**, the chapter challenged the legal basis for the racial policies of the Wilson administration, organized a speakers bureau that visited local African American churches and voluntary organizations, and put the city at the heart of the national struggle for racial equality and civil rights. During the **Red Summer of 1919**, the chapter played a crucial role in easing racial tensions. In the 1930s, the group organized two of the city's earliest civil rights protests, against segregated toilet facilities at the Hecht Company **department store** and against Peoples Drug Store, which served black customers on paper plates and whites on china at its lunch counters. In the 1950s, the chapter campaigned against racial discrimination and brutality in the D.C. police department and against the discriminatory hiring practices of downtown department stores and merchants.

NATIONAL ASSOCIATION OF COLORED WOMEN. *See* TERRELL, MARY CHURCH.

NATIONAL BUILDING MUSEUM. A museum and research center of architecture, design, engineering, construction, and urban planning. Created by an act of Congress, the museum houses approximately 68,000 architectural prints and drawings, 40,000 photographs, 100 linear feet of documents, and 2,100 objects. The museum is housed in the immense Pension Building designed in 1881 by **Montgomery C. Meigs** and completed in 1887. Located on F Street between 4th and 5th Streets NW, the red brick building was patterned after the Italian Renaissance-style Palazzo Farnese in Rome, but doubled in size to a dimension of 400 feet long and 200 feet wide. Its interior Great Hall, measuring 316 feet long by 116 feet wide and approximately 15 stories high, is one of the great spaces in Washington and the site of many presidential inaugural balls. The building is constructed of 15.5 million bricks and adorned with an exterior terracotta frieze, three feet high and 1,200 feet long, which wraps around the entire building. Designed by Caspar Buberl (1834–1899), the frieze depicts a parade of Union soldiers and is symbolic of both the strength of the Union Army and the great number of those who lost their lives during the **Civil War**.

NATIONAL CAPITAL PARK AND PLANNING COMMISSION. Established by Congress in 1926, the commission's purpose was to "develop a comprehensive, consistent, and coordinated plan for the national capital and its environs in the states of Maryland and Virginia." The commission was directed to make recommendations to local authorities "as to traffic and transportation; plats and subdivisions; highways, parks, and parkways; schools and library sites; playgrounds; drainage, sewerage, and water supply; housing, building, and zoning regulations; public and private buildings; bridges and water fronts; commerce and industry; and other proper elements of city and regional planning." Each of the commission's 12 members, including the director of the National Park Service, the chief of engineers of the Army, and four citizens appointed by the president, serve six-year terms. The commission has played an important role in improving the infrastructure and quality of life in city. *See also* REDEVELOPMENT ACT OF 1945.

NATIONAL CATHEDRAL. *See* WASHINGTON NATIONAL CATHEDRAL.

NATIONAL CITY CHRISTIAN CHURCH. *See* POPE, JOHN RUSSELL.

NATIONAL COUNCIL OF NEGRO WOMEN. *See* BETHUNE, MARY McLEOD.

NATIONAL DEFENSE UNIVERSITY. *See* FORT LESLEY J. McNAIR.

NATIONAL ERA. Abolitionist weekly newspaper published in Washington before the **Civil War.** The *National Era* began publication in 1847 as a periodical of the American and Foreign Anti-Slavery Society and actively promoted the Republican party during its early years. Published in a building across from the U.S. Patent Office, the *Era* was sold for two dollars a year. Gamaliel Bailey (1807–1859), a doctor who left medicine to work for the abolition of **slavery,** was editor-in-chief of the newspaper throughout its publication. Poet John Greenleaf Whittier served as contributing editor, and the *Era* featured Whittier's poetry and prose. Other contributors included Nathaniel Hawthorne, Theodore Parker, and Harriet Beecher Stowe. Stowe's novel *Uncle Tom's Cabin* first appeared serialized in the *National Era* in 1851 and 1852. Bailey paid $300 for the work and published it in 40 installments over 10 months. In 1848 the *National Era* was at the center of rioting and controversy after the *Pearl* incident, when an angry mob stormed its publishing offices, blaming the slave escape on Bailey. A crowd of about 1,000 people demanded that Bailey shut down his presses and threatened to lynch him. Bailey refused, and law enforcement defused the situation after a three-day standoff. The *National Era* ceased publication when Bailey died in 1859.

NATIONAL GEOGRAPHIC SOCIETY. A private organization founded in 1888 by **Gardiner G. Hubbard** for the purpose of increasing geographic knowledge of the world. The society's headquarters are in a three-building complex at 17th and M Streets NW. Explorer's Hall, located on the ground floor of its 10-story glass and marble building designed by Edward Durrell Stone in 1964, introduces the work of the society. The hall features interactive exhibits about the earth, human evolution, and science. A 72-seat amphitheater simulates orbital space flight. The society has sponsored many expeditions, including the polar expeditions of Admirals Perry and Byrd and the undersea explorations of Jacques

Cousteau. It is well known as the publisher of the *National Geographic* magazine. Less well known is its research library and reading room that contains 50,000 books on geography, natural history, and travel.

NATIONAL INTELLIGENCER. National newspaper published in Washington in the 1800s. Samuel Harrison Smith, a publisher from Philadelphia, was encouraged by **Thomas Jefferson** to move to Washington and found a Republican newspaper based on Jeffersonian principles. Smith's paper, published triweekly and sold for five dollars per year, became the official voice of the Jefferson, Madison, and Monroe administrations. The *Intelligencer* was also a predecessor of the *Congressional Record*: The first session of Congress was closed to reporters, but by the second session Smith gained admission and the *Intelligencer* became the only printed record of early congressional proceedings. Smith sold the paper to Joseph Gales in 1810, and by 1812 William Winston Seaton joined Gales in the publishing venture. During the **War of 1812**, British troops burned the *Intelligencer* offices. Over the next 50 years the *Intelligencer* was circulated both locally and nationally. Gales died in 1860, and Seaton sold the newspaper in 1864. After the **Civil War** it was no longer viable to publish a newspaper from the point of view of one political party, and when public interest waned, the *Intelligencer* ceased publication.

NATIONAL JEWISH MUSEUM. *See* B'NAI B'RITH KLUTZNICK NATIONAL JEWISH MUSEUM.

NATIONAL MUSEUM OF AFRICAN ART. Smithsonian Institution museum devoted to African art. In 1964 Warren H. Robbins established a privately funded collection of African art that was exhibited in the **Frederick Douglass National Historic Site** in Washington. This Museum of African Art became part of the Smithsonian in 1979, and in 1981 it was renamed the National Museum of African Art. A museum building designed by architect Jean Paul Carlhian was constructed as part of the Quadrangle museum complex on the **Mall** and was opened to the public in 1987. The museum holds 8,000 works of sculpture, as well as artifacts of ancient and contemporary African history and culture, including textiles, musical instruments, jewelry, books, maps, and the extensive photography collection of Eliot Elisofon. The museum offers changing exhibitions and educational programs and houses a library of more than 25,000 volumes.

NATIONAL MUSEUM OF ASIAN ART. *See* ARTHUR M. SACK-LER GALLERY; FREER GALLERY.

NATIONAL MUSEUM OF HEALTH AND MEDICINE. *See* WALTER REED ARMY MEDICAL CENTER.

NATIONAL MUSEUM OF WOMEN IN THE ARTS. Museum near the **White House** that documents the contributions of women to art and art history. For more than 20 years founders Wallace and Wilhelmina Cole Holladay collected works by women artists. Their collection of some 500 pieces became the core of a museum, which they established in their home in 1981. In 1983 the museum purchased and began renovating a Masonic temple building constructed in 1907. The museum opened in 1987 and 10 years later added the Elizabeth A. Kasser wing. The museum's permanent collection contains over 2,700 pieces by more than 800 artists, displayed on four floors of exhibit space. The museum library holds 11,000 volumes, as well as files on some 17,000 women artists. It publishes a quarterly magazine about women's contributions to the arts and sponsors cultural events and educational programs.

NATIONAL POSTAL MUSEUM. **Capitol Hill** museum devoted to the postal history of the United States. Founded in 1990 by the **Smithsonian Institution** and the U.S. Postal Service, the museum opened in 1993. Its five galleries occupy the former City Post Office, a white Italian marble Beaux-Arts building designed by **Daniel H. Burnham** as a result of the **McMillan Report**. The design of the National Postal Museum complements nearby **Union Station**, which was also executed by Burnham. The City Post Office building was completed in 1914 and served as Washington's main post office until 1986. The building housed the most modern postal technology of the time, including conveyor belts, underground tunnels, and a miniature trolley system. In 1886 the Smithsonian began a postal collection with a sheet of 10-cent Confederate stamps. The postal museum collection, called the National Philatelic Collection, was housed in the **Arts and Industries Building** from 1908 until 1963. In 1964 it was moved to the National Museum of History and Technology and grew to 16 million items including stamps, stationery, postal vehicles, mailboxes, and letters. The National Postal Museum exhibits three airmail planes suspended from its 90-foot-high atrium and houses a research library of postal history, a stamp store, and a museum shop.

NATIONAL SOCIETY OF THE COLONIAL DAMES OF AMERICA. Patriotic membership organization. The group, founded in 1891, is comprised of women directly descended from persons resident in the American colonies by 1750 who engaged in public service before July 5, 1776. The society's national headquarters are in Dumbarton House on Q Street NW in **Georgetown.** Built between 1799 and 1805 for U.S. Treasury Department official Joseph Nourse, Dumbarton House went through a series of owners before 1915, when the D.C. government moved the entire house approximately 100 yards from its original location to construct an extension of Q Street to Rock Creek. The Colonial Dames purchased Dumbarton House in 1928 and extensively renovated the property, which now includes a house museum with period furnishings and a seminar series on colonial and federalist history, both of which are open to the public.

NATIONAL SYMPHONY ORCHESTRA. Washington orchestra that performs 175 classical and pops concerts each year. The National Symphony Orchestra (NSO) was incorporated in 1931 by Hans Kindler, who also served as the orchestra's first conductor. Under Kindler's direction the NSO grew to 90 musicians, giving 100 concerts a year. Howard Mitchell succeeded Kindler as conductor in 1949 and took the National Symphony on its first international tours. However, it was not until Antal Dorati took over in 1970 that the orchestra received real critical acclaim. Dorati expanded the repertoire and began to commission new works. When Mstislav Rostropovich became conductor in 1977, he commissioned six orchestral works, two of which won Pulitzer Prizes. In 1990 the NSO traveled with Rostropovitch to Russia. In 1996 Leonard Slatkin, a conductor known for his dedication to the performance of American music, succeeded Rostropovich. Originally based at Constitution Hall, in 1986 the NSO became formally affiliated with the **John F. Kennedy Center for the Performing Arts.**

NATIONAL THEATRE. America's oldest major touring playhouse. Six different versions of the National Theatre have occupied 1321 **Pennsylvania Avenue** NW since the theater's establishment in 1835. Four of those structures were destroyed by fire. The current building was constructed in 1922 and renovated in 1984. Many leading lights of the American and foreign stage have appeared at the National Theatre, including Sarah Bernhardt, Jenny Lind, John Wilkes Booth, **Helen Hayes**, John Barrymore, Laurence Olivier, **Pearl Bailey**, Spencer Tracy, and Katharine Hepburn. Every U.S. president since 1835 except Eisenhower has patronized the theater; Lincoln was a particularly enthusiastic customer. From 1873, when African Americans were first refused admittance, until its desegregation in 1952, the National Theatre's racist admissions policy drew repeated protests and boycotts from civil rights activists, organized labor, playwrights, and actors. A nonprofit organization, the theater is managed by the Shubert Organization.

NATIONAL TRAINING SCHOOL FOR WOMEN AND GIRLS. *See* BURROUGHS, NANNIE HELEN.

NATIONAL WOMEN'S PARTY. *See* SEWALL-BELMONT HOUSE.

NATIONAL ZOOLOGICAL PARK. The U.S. national zoo, part of the **Smithsonian Institution.** In the 1880s before the development of the National Zoo, the Smithsonian sometimes exhibited live animals behind the Castle building on the **Mall.** In 1889 Congress passed legislation founding the National Zoo, as envisioned by Smithsonian secretary Samuel P. Langley, to exhibit and breed endangered species. Land was purchased on Rock Creek, and architect **Frederick Law Olmsted** was consulted about the landscape and location of buildings. In the first half of the 20th century, several important expeditions added to the zoo's collection. The zoo has also received many exotic animals as gifts from foreign governments. During the New Deal, several zoo buildings were constructed by the Public Works Administration. The zoo now occupies about 187 acres and contains over 2,500 specimens. Zoo scientists conduct research on the breeding and protection of rare and endangered species.

NATIVE AMERICAN SETTLEMENTS. Washington's first habitation. Native Americans are thought to have entered the area some 12,000 years ago. By the 1600s, when Captain **John Smith** explored Washington, the Algonquin-speaking Nacotchtank people were well established. The Nacotchtanks were also known as Nacostins, from which the name "**Anacostia**" was given to the river and neighborhood of eastern Washington. Modern archaeological studies indicate the presence of three villages inside the current bounds of the District of Columbia. The largest of these villages was Nacochtanke, the tribe's capital district, located near the present site of **Bolling Air Force Base**. Other sites include the Nameroughquena settlement, probably located on the west bank of the **Potomac River** across from **Theodore Roosevelt Island**, and a site on a narrow bluff between the **Chesapeake and Ohio Canal** and MacArthur Boulevard, in Washington's westernmost precincts. The Nacostins were farmers, hunters, gatherers, and toolmakers. Several of their stone quarries and work camps have been discovered along the banks of Rock Creek. Caught between the Powhatan Confederation to the south and other Algonquin alliances to the north, the Nacostins welcomed English trade and alliances, but conflicts over property ownership led to bloody skirmishes and they eventually abandoned their settlements and retreated into the Maryland forests.

NAVAL OBSERVATORY. *See* U.S. NAVAL OBSERVATORY.

NAVY MEMORIAL MUSEUM. *See* NAVY YARD.

NAVY YARD. The oldest naval facility in the United States and now an administrative center and historic area. Located at 9th and M Streets SE, the Navy Yard was opened in 1799. The invading British destroyed its shipbuilding facilities in 1814, and although the yard was rebuilt, by the **Civil War** it had ceased shipbuilding and had become the Naval Gun Factory, producing the Navy's biggest guns. Today the grounds of the Navy Yard display the Willard Park outdoor collection of navy weapons, including old guns, military hardware, and the destroyer *John Barry* (1956–82). The grounds also contain two museums and an art gallery. The Navy Memorial Museum, opened in 1963, documents the naval history of the United States and attracts approximately 400,000 visitors each year. The smaller Marine Corps Museum houses the original flag depicted in the Iwo Jima Memorial and memorabilia belonging to **John Philip Sousa**. The upper two floors of the building house the Marine Corps Historical Center and a library of military history. The Combat Art Gallery displays a variety of naval art.

NEW NEGRO ALLIANCE. An African American grassroots organization, which employed economic pressure to achieve social change. In 1933 a group of young activists living in Washington's **Shaw** neighborhood picketed the Hamburger Grill—the patronage of which was all black—when its white owner summarily fired his African American employees and replaced them with whites. After three days the original employees were rehired and the New Negro Alliance was born. The activist group was encouraged to use organized protests as a means to achieve long-denied civil rights. During the years of the Great Depression, the alliance's picketing and boycotts persuaded several Washington businesses to employ African Americans, including the *Washington Star* newspaper, High's Ice Cream stores, and the A&P grocery chain. The Sanitary grocery chain, later Safeway, obtained an injunction against the alliance, but in 1938 the **U.S. Supreme Court** affirmed the right of consumers to use economic pressure against businesses that refused to employ African Americans. Some of the tactics used by the New Negro Alliance were later incorporated into the civil rights movement of the 1960s.

NEW YORK AVENUE PRESBYTERIAN CHURCH. Presbyterian church that grew out of the 1859 merger between F Street Presbyterian Church (organized 1803) and Second Presbyterian Church. Phineas D. Gurley (d. 1868), who became pastor of the F Street church in 1853, continued as the pastor of the New York Avenue church and was instrumental in the construction of its building. A friend of President Abraham Lincoln, Gurley delivered the eulogy for the slain president in the East Room of the **White House**. The church was the site of the famous Presbyterian General Assembly of 1893 that vetoed the election of Charles A. Briggs to the chair of biblical theology at Union Theological Seminary in New York. This led the seminary to withdraw from the denomination, an action that was part of a larger controversy over modernism and fundamentalism in American religious life. **Peter Marshall**, chaplain of the U.S. Senate (1947–49), was pastor of the church from 1937 to 1949. Many U.S. presidents and government officials have worshiped at the 800-member church.

NEWLANDS, FRANCIS G. *See* CHEVY CHASE.

NORTH PORTAL ESTATES. *See* SHEPHERD PARK.

NORTHERN LIBERTY MARKET. *See* PUBLIC MARKETS; WASHINGTON CONVENTION CENTER.

NORTON, ELEANOR HOLMES (b. 1937). Lawyer and D.C. delegate to Congress. Born in Washington, Norton attended Dunbar High School and went on to study at Antioch College in Ohio. She then earned degrees in law and American studies at Yale University. Norton worked as a lawyer for the American Civil Liberties Union in New York and then served as director of the New York City Commission on Civil Rights. She returned to Washington in 1977 when she was appointed by President Jimmy Carter to head the Equal Employment Opportunity Commission. In 1982 she became a law professor at **Georgetown University**. Her career in Congress began in 1990, when she was elected to succeed D.C. representative **Walter Fauntroy** as a nonvoting delegate to the U.S. House of Representatives. In 1993 Norton successfully lobbied for the right to vote on the House floor on behalf of D.C. residents, who are the only Americans to pay federal tax without full representation in Congress. She also lobbied Congress on the subject of D.C. statehood. The statehood vote did not pass, however, and two years later the vote of the D.C. delegate was taken away.

NOYES, THEODORE W. (1858–1946). Journalist and civic leader. Born in Washington, Noyes graduated from Columbia University and worked at the *Washington Evening Star*, where his father was editor. He studied law and moved to Sioux Falls, Dakota Territory, where he was admitted to bar in 1883. After four years of practicing law, he returned to Washington and resumed work at the *Star*. When his father died in 1908, Noyes became editor of the paper until 1946. He served on numerous boards and committees and supported congressional representation for the District of Columbia in testimony before the U.S. Senate. Noyes's publications include *The National Capital* (1873) and *The Fiscal Relations between the United States and the District of Columbia: The Argument of Theodore W. Noyes before the Joint Select Committee of the Congress of the United States* (1916).

NYE, BILL (b. 1955). Science educator. A native of Washington, Nye attended Lafayette Elementary and Sidwell Friends schools and graduated from Cornell University. He is known to school children and public television viewers as "Bill Nye the Science Guy," the name of his Emmy Award-winning science education program. Nye serves as spokesperson for several child advocacy groups and promotes numerous scientific and educational endeavors.

- O -

O STREET MARKET. *See* PUBLIC MARKETS.

OAK GROVE. *See* BRIGHTWOOD.

OAK HILL CEMETERY. A private cemetery located near R Street NW. In 1848 **William W. Corcoran** purchased a tract of land known as Parrott's Woods for more than $100,000 and the U.S. Congress chartered his Oak Hill Cemetery in 1849. Patterned after Mount Auburn Cemetery in Boston, it was developed as a Victorian garden with botanical garden-style plantings. Architect **James Renwick** designed the cemetery chapel. During the **Civil War**, Corcoran, a Southern sympathizer, fled to Europe and Unionists took over Oak Hill's board of directors. Upon his return, Corcoran regained control of the cemetery, which is still privately held. Notable figures buried at the cemetery include Secretary of War Edwin Stanton, evangelist Lorenzo Dow, and sportscaster Glenn Brenner.

OCTAGON HOUSE. A building of six sides meeting in eight angles, designed by William Thornton and built during 1799 to 1801 by Virginia planter John Tayloe. Located on New York Avenue NW, the structure served as the temporary residence of President James Madison after the **White House** was burned by the British during the **War of 1812**. The second-floor circular drawing room was used by Madison for the signing of the Treaty of Ghent ending the War of 1812. The building was probably a station on the Underground Railroad, and during the **Civil War** it housed a military hospital and Union Army records. The Sisters of Charity occupied the building in the late 19th century, and it was purchased by the American Institute of Architects in 1902 and preserved as a house museum.

OLD CAPITOL. The temporary home of the U.S. Congress from 1815 to 1819. After the British burned the **U.S. Capitol** building in 1814, a group of 38 Washingtonians formed the Capital Hotel Company to construct a new meeting place for Congress while the burned-out Capitol was being rebuilt. Located at 1st and A streets NE, the Old Capitol was a three-story Federal-style brick building. The Senate met on the first floor and the House of Representatives met on the second floor. When Congress could not agree on which floor to use for the inauguration of President James Monroe, the ceremony was moved outside, thus establishing a tradition of outdoor presidential inaugurals. The building was subsequently used as a private school, a boardinghouse for members of Congress, and a prison during the Civil War. In 1869 it was converted into three townhouses and during the 1930s it was demolished to make way for the **U.S. Supreme Court** building.

OLD DOWNTOWN. *See* SEVENTH STREET.

OLD GEORGETOWN ACT (1950). An act of Congress that created a historic district in **Georgetown** "to preserve and protect the places and areas of historic interest." The **mayor** of the District of Columbia was instructed to conduct a survey of "Old Georgetown" and transmit the results to the **Commission of Fine Arts**. The commission then drew up guidelines for the preservation of the town's architectural and historic sites. The act enabled Georgetown to preserve its cultural heritage.

OLD METHODIST BURYING GROUNDS. *See* MOUNT ZION CEMETERY.

OLD PENITENTIARY. *See* FORT LESLEY J. McNAIR; LINCOLN ASSASSINATION.

OLD PENSION BUILDING. *See* MEIGS, MONTGOMERY C.; NATIONAL BUILDING MUSEUM.

OLD POST OFFICE PAVILION AND CLOCK TOWER. Complex of businesses and federal offices in the former post office building on **Pennsylvania Avenue** NW. In the 1880s, Congress sought to improve the slum district of Murder Bay and authorized construction of a post office to encourage investment there. The 12-story Romanesque Revival building, completed in 1899, was the city's first steel-frame building and its first building with electric power. A new post office building, now the **National Postal Museum**, was constructed 15 years later. During the 1920s city planners slated the old post office for demolition, but it survived because of a lack of funds during the Great Depression. The building was then occupied by several government agencies and was again slated for demolition in the 1960s. However, lobbying by preservationists saved it from destruction and the building was adapted for commercial use. In 1984 the Old Post Office Pavilion opened, with an indoor courtyard of shops, restaurants, and a stage. The clock tower, operated by the National Park Service, offers a city view from a 270-foot-high observation deck. The tower houses the 10 Congress Bells, replicas of bells in Westminster Abbey, which are rung for the opening and closing of Congress and other state occasions.

OLD STONE HOUSE. The only surviving pre-Revolutionary War building in Washington. Located on M Street NW, the two-story structure, made of fieldstones, was constructed by cabinetmaker Christopher Layman around 1765. The furnishings of the six-room house reflect 18th-century life in the **Georgetown** seaport. The house is noted for its paneled dining room, simple furnishings, and large rear English-type garden containing fruit trees and perennials. In 1950 the U.S. Congress designated the house a historic site. It is now maintained as a museum by the National Park Service.

OLD U.S. PATENT OFFICE BUILDING. Greek Revival public building designed in 1836 by Ithiel Town and William Parker Elliot (the design was revised by **Robert Mills**, who supervised the building's construction), built to house the U.S. Patent Office after a Patent Office building on the same site was destroyed by fire. The white stone building, which took 30 years to construct, covers an entire city block and is composed of wings enclosing a rectangular courtyard. During the **Civil War** the building served as a Union hospital, visited often by **Walt Whitman**, and was the site of President Abraham Lincoln's second inaugural ball. In 1877 the third floor of the building was rebuilt after being badly damaged by fire. In the mid-20th century, the building was slated to be torn down to make way for a parking lot, but was instead turned over to the **Smithsonian Institution.** In 1968 after extensive renovations, it was opened to the public. Today the National Museum of American Art and the Archive of American Art share the building with the National Portrait Gallery. Currently under renovation, the building and its museums will reopen in 2003.

OLMSTED, FREDERICK LAW (1822–1903). Landscape architect. Born in Hartford, Connecticut, Olmsted worked as an apprentice topographic engineer and attended science and engineering lectures at Yale University (1842, 1847). Collaboration with British architect Calvert Vaux in the successful design of Central Park in New York City led to public landscape and park projects in Boston, Chicago, Detroit, and Philadelphia. In Washington, Olmsted improved the **U.S. Capitol** grounds (1874–95) by creating new lawns and walks, thinning plantings that were obstructing views of the building, planting outdoor areas with specimen trees, and constructing new stone terracing and retaining walls. In 1892 he was consulted about the design of the **National Zoological Park**, and beginning in 1894 he aided city officials who were extending Washington's **streets and avenues** past their original boundaries. He also designed the campuses of **Gallaudet University** and **American University**.

OPERA. *See* COLORED AMERICAN OPERA COMPANY; JOHN F. KENNEDY CENTER FOR THE PERFORMING ARTS.

ORGANIC ACT (1878). An act passed by Congress by which the residents of Washington lost self-government. The act vested governmental authority in three commissioners appointed by the president to three-year terms. Two of the commissioners were civilians and the third was appointed from the Army Corps of Engineers. This form of government continued until 1961, when municipal government was again returned to the city. *See also* HOME RULE.

ORPHANAGES. *See* VAN NESS, MARCIA BURNES; WASHINGTON CITY ORPHAN ASYLUM.

- P -

PACIFIC CIRCLE. *See* DUPONT CIRCLE.

PAINTER, URIAH H. *See* BELASCO THEATER.

PARENTS UNITED LAWSUIT. A lawsuit filed against the D.C. government in 1994 by Parents United for the D.C. Public Schools, an education advocacy group. The lawsuit charged that public school buildings had more than 10,000 life-threatening fire code violations and needed to be brought up to standard. The D.C. Superior Court ruled in favor of Parents United and ordered that school repairs be completed before the September 1994 school term. The judge's deadline was not met and public hearings were held every six months for three years to review the progress of school repairs. In 1996 the **District of Columbia Financial Responsibility and Management Assistance Authority** fired the school superintendent and, after further delays, the roofs on 90 schools were replaced. The suit was finally settled out of court in 1997.

PARROTT'S WOODS. *See* MONTROSE PARK; OAK HILL CEMETERY.

PATENT OFFICE BUILDING. *See* OLD U.S. PATENT OFFICE BUILDING.

PATOWMACK CANAL. An early attempt by **George Washington** to improve transportation on the **Potomac River** from western Maryland into the port of **Georgetown**. Under construction from 1785 until 1802, the canal consisted of five locks with a lift of 76 feet around Great Falls; some locks were carved from solid rock. Due to inconsistent river channels, low revenues, and erratic financial support, the Patowmack Canal Company was forced into bankruptcy in 1822 and its property conveyed to the **Chesapeake and Ohio Canal** Company in 1828.

PATTERSON, ELEANOR M. "CISSY" (1884–1948). Newspaper publisher. Born into a Chicago newspaper family, Patterson was educated in Boston and began her career in journalism in 1930, when she became editor of the *Washington Herald*. She later bought the paper from William Randolph Hearst and combined it with another of Hearst's newspapers, the *Washington Times*, creating the *Washington Times-Herald*. Her newspaper challenged the *Washington Post* for two decades, until the *Post* finally purchased its rival in 1954. Patterson was one of Washington's most powerful women and a flamboyant character. She firmly controlled the newspaper's editorial policies and put her energies into increasing its circulation and advertising. She hosted lavish parties for prospective advertisers and used her social connections to advance the newspaper. Her public feuds with socialite **Alice Roosevelt Longworth** and *Post* publisher Eugene Meyer became legendary.

PAUL, ALICE STOKES. *See* WOMEN'S SUFFRAGE PARADE.

PEARL. A small schooner used by a group of enslaved African Americans in April 1848 in their attempt to sail to freedom. The 77 slaves were owned by wealthy and prominent residents of Washington and **Georgetown**, including Dolley Madison. Sea captains

Daniel Drayton and Edmund Sayres planned the venture with Paul Jennings, a slave owned by Daniel Webster, but Jennings did not join the escape. The *Pearl* left the Washington wharf and anchored for 24 hours at Alexandria, Virginia. When the ship set sail from Alexandria, it was caught in a storm and sought shelter at Point Lookout, 140 miles south of Washington. By that time the escape had been reported and the *Pearl* was overtaken by a steamship belonging to an owner of some of the escapees. The recaptured slaves were sold to dealers in the South; Drayton and Sayres were convicted of kidnapping and jailed, but later received a presidential pardon. *See also* SLAVERY.

PENNSYLVANIA AVENUE. An avenue extending from **Georgetown** to the **Anacostia River**, along which are located the **White House**, **U.S. Capitol**, and numerous federal government agencies and landmarks. The city plan of **Pierre Charles L'Enfant** featured a grand avenue linking the Capitol and White House. Construction began in 1792, but it took four years to complete the 16-block section between the seats of power. Since the 1790s, when Center Market opened, Pennsylvania Avenue has been an important commercial district. The market was located at the junction of the Bladensburg Turnpike (on which Maryland farm produce was shipped) and the Washington waterfront (where Virginia hunters and fishermen brought their goods for sale). Taverns, hotels, restaurants, and boarding houses were constructed nearby. During the **Civil War**, Union troops marched along the avenue. Murder Bay, a notorious den of thievery and prostitution grew up on the avenue's south side. From 1880 to 1935, Chinese immigrants settled around Pennsylvania Avenue and 4th Street.

As Washington's "main street," Pennsylvania Avenue has been the site of national parades and has served as a major transportation artery. Every presidential inaugural since 1805 has featured a parade along Pennsylvania Avenue. Some of the most famous parades include the two-day Grand Review of the Union Army in 1865, the 1913 **women's suffrage parade**, the 1919 parade of 25,000 World War I soldiers led by General John Pershing, the notorious 1925 **Ku Klux Klan demonstration**, and the 1932 **Bonus Army march**. The funeral processions of Abraham Lincoln, Franklin D. Roosevelt, and John F. Kennedy also made their way along Pennsylvania Avenue.

From 1851 until 1903, several major railroad depots and stations were located on the avenue. In 1903 the railroads were removed by an act of Congress, and their operations were centralized at **Union Station** on Massachusetts Avenue. Between 1892 and 1962, the Washington and Georgetown streetcar line ran along Pennsylvania Avenue, first drawn by horses and later by underground cables.

With the exception of the construction of Union Station and removal of the railroad lines, the **McMillan Report** and City Beautiful movement of the early 20th century had little effect on Pennsylvania Avenue. The neighborhood had deteriorated into a mélange of tattoo parlors, brothels, and rooming houses. In 1928 the federal government purchased 70 acres along the avenue for construction of the **Federal Triangle** in an attempt to consolidate government offices and employees. **Chinatown**, Emergency Hospital, Southern Railway, Poli's Theater, and Center Market were all demolished and replaced by the **National Archives**, Federal Trade Commission, Post Office Department, and Internal Revenue Service. However, much of Pennsylvania Avenue continued to deteriorate. By the late 1960s the avenue was home to a burlesque house, pornography shops, liquor stores, and more than 90 vacant buildings. In 1972 Congress established the Pennsylvania Avenue Development Corporation to guide a renewal of the historic street. More than $100 million of public funds were spent on parks, lights, sidewalks, and paving, attracting more than $1.3 billion of private construction. Improvement included the construction of the Canadian Embassy, new and renovated office buildings, luxury condominiums, and the creation of an arts district and restaurant and retail trade.

PENSION BUILDING. *See* MEIGS, MONTGOMERY C.; NATIONAL BUILDING MUSEUM.

PEPCO. *See* POTOMAC ELECTRIC POWER COMPANY.

PERSHING PARK. A sunken garden honoring John Pershing, U.S. army general and military commander of the American Expeditionary Forces during World War I. Located one block from the **White House**, the park contains a statue of the general along with an engraved granite wall that tells the story of Pershing's campaigns. In 1919 a triumphant Pershing paraded his 25,000 troops along **Pennsylvania Avenue** while a crowd of 400,000 cheered his return.

Pershing Park contains a small outdoor ice rink and offers views of the **Washington Monument**. The park was once the site of the Washington Light Infantry Corps, a cavernous red brick building constructed in 1884. The upper floors of the building were occupied by the 2,000-seat auditorium of the Grand Opera House, later called Chase's Opera House (1901) and Poli's Theater (1913). The building was demolished in 1930 as part of the **Federal Triangle** project.

PETER, ROBERT (1726–1806). **Georgetown** tobacco merchant, landowner, and **mayor**. Born in Crossbasket, Scotland, Peter came to Georgetown in the early 1750s. In 1752 he opened Rock Creek Store, and began importing goods from Great Britain and exporting tobacco. His business flourished and he built a house on Wisconsin Avenue, becoming an influential citizen. In 1757 he was elected to the Georgetown Board of Commissioners. When the town was incorporated in 1790, Peter, who served on the town board for 32 years, was elected first mayor of Georgetown. In 1791, at the request of **George Washington**, he surrendered half of his lands within the proposed federal city to the U.S. government. These lands included properties around Washington Circle, an area west of 23rd Street to the **Potomac River**, and property north of T Street and along 14th Street. His extensive Maryland lands were later divided among his widow and eight children.

PETWORTH. An area bounded by Spring Road, Rock Creek Church Road, 16th Street, Colorado Avenue, and Ingraham Street in Northwest Washington. The area first appeared on Washington maps as the estate of James White (1715–1801), who built a mansion at present-day 13th and Longfellow Streets. By 1803 the property was in the hands of Colonel John Tayloe, owner of the **Octagon House**. Tayloe called the estate "Petworth" and farmed its 536 acres using slave labor. Petworth was quite isolated until 1819, when the 7th Street Turnpike (now Georgia Avenue; the neighborhood's commercial district) was built.

The area served as the regimental headquarters for a Massachusetts unit during the **Civil War** Battle of Fort Stevens. Between 1887 and 1892, Tayloe's heirs sold the property to real estate developers, who created a streetcar suburb. The trolley ride to downtown Washington took only eight minutes, and a mix of ethnic groups, including Italians, Irish, Germans, Jews, and Asians, settled in the neighborhood. Most of Petworth's red brick row houses, semidetached residences, and apartment buildings were constructed during the 1910s and 1920s.

During the 1950s African Americans moved into the Petworth neighborhood. Petworth declined in the 1960s and 1970s, but by the mid-1980s the centrally located neighborhood and its Victorian and Arts and Crafts style residences became attractive to professionals, and the area underwent some gentrification. During the 1990s, a substantial number of Hispanics have become residents of the community, adding to its diversity.

PHILLIPS COLLECTION. Museum founded by Duncan Phillips (1886–1966), heir to a Pittsburgh steel fortune. The Phillips family came to Washington and in 1897 built a Georgian Revival brownstone house on **Dupont Circle**, designed by the architectural firm of Hornblower and Marshall. Phillips began collecting art in 1916, and two years later, after the deaths of his father and brother, founded a museum in their memory. In 1921 Phillips opened his house to the public; it was the first museum of modern art in the country. In 1923 he bought Renoir's "Luncheon of the Boating Party" and made it the center of his collection. In 1930 the family moved so the entire house could be used by the museum. Duncan Phillips and his wife Marjorie Phillips added more than 2,000 works to the collection during a period of 50 years. Following his death, the directorship of the museum passed from Phillips to his wife, and then to their son Laughlin Phillips, who managed the museum until 1992. The Phillips Collection comprises 50,000 square feet of gallery space and operates on an annual budget of $5 million. The collection features impressionist works by European and American painters of the modern and postmodern periods, including works by Manet, Monet, Renoir, Van Gogh, Hopper, Rothko, O'Keeffe, de Kooning, Dove, and Klee.

PIERCE MILL. *See* ROCK CREEK PARK.

PLANNING COMMISSION. *See* NATIONAL CAPITAL PARK AND PLANNING COMMISSION.

POLLIN, ABE (b. 1923). Real estate developer who built the first houses in Washington sold under the favorable provisions of the GI Bill at the end of World War II. For many years Pollin owned two professional sports franchises, the Washington Wizards basketball team and the **Washington Capitals** ice hockey team; he sold the Capitals in 1999. When Pollin purchased the basketball team, it was known as the Bullets. His concern about high crime rates in the early 1990s led him to change the team's name to the Washington Wizards. He built a new home for his teams, the **MCI Center** on F Street NW, which opened in 1997, and expressed the hope that it would be a catalyst for downtown redevelopment. Pollin is as well known for his philanthropy as for his sports management. Among the charities he supports are the "I Have a Dream" Foundation, N Street Village, Salvation Army, and international hunger relief.

POOR PEOPLE'S CAMPAIGN. Civil rights protest and encampment during May and June of 1968. The Poor People's Campaign was an attempt to force the U.S. Congress to address issues of poverty, unemployment, and underemployment, especially among the nation's minority groups. It was planned by Martin Luther King, Jr., before his assassination and led by his successor, Ralph David Abernathy of the Southern Christian Leadership Conference (SCLC). The National Park Service allowed nearly 3,000 protesters to camp on 15 acres around the Reflecting Pool on the **Mall** beginning May 6. Known as Resurrection City, the settlement included 600 plywood and canvas structures organized into neighborhoods and blocks around two principal streets, King and Abernathy. A local committee, led by officials of **Giant Food**, mobilized churches, charitable organizations, and residents to provide meals for the predominantly African American group. When it rained for 28 of the encampment's 42 days, Resurrection City became a muddy mess. A Solidarity Day rally was held on June 19, drawing 50,000 protesters, far fewer than expected. On June 24, the D.C. police expelled the remaining campers 16 hours after their permit expired. The campaign dramatized the plight of America's poor, but left its organizers disappointed.

POPE, JOHN RUSSELL (1874–1937). Architect. Born in New York City, Pope studied architecture at the Columbia School of Mines (1894), the American Academy in Rome (1895), and the École des Beaux Arts in Paris (1898–1900). He worked as an architect in New York City and opened his own firm in 1903. Initially a residential architect, Pope later specialized in monuments and monumental buildings. His residential designs in Washington include houses for John R. McLean (1911), Mrs. Robert R. Hitt (1909), and Irwin Laughlin (1920s), called Meridian House. His monumental buildings, characterized by their classical forms, include Constitution Hall (1929); the American Pharmaceutical Institute (1933); the **National Archives** building (1935); the National Gallery of Art (1939), now known as the West Building; and the **Jefferson Memorial**, a controversial design (1941). He also designed the National City Christian Church on Thomas Circle and the Masonic **Scottish Rite Temple** on 16th Street NW. Pope's work is known for its unadorned surfaces, domes, and interior staircases. A member of the **Commission of Fine Arts** from 1917 to 1922, Pope contributed a commitment to classical architectural design that left an indelible mark on the city of Washington.

POST OFFICE. *See* NATIONAL POSTAL MUSEUM; OLD POST OFFICE PAVILION AND CLOCK TOWER.

POSTAL MUSEUM. *See* NATIONAL POSTAL MUSEUM.

POTOMAC ELECTRIC POWER COMPANY. Publicly held electric company that serves the District of Columbia and parts of suburban Maryland. Founded by O. T. Crosby in 1896, the company maintained its headquarters at **Pennsylvania Avenue** and 15th Street NW. Its first generating station was located in **Georgetown**. By 1902 it had 2,900 customers. It added Station B at 14th and B Streets when it acquired the United States Electric Company and moved the company headquarters there. The Benning plant was constructed in 1906 and the Buzzard Point plant was added by mid-century. Today the company serves over 690,000 customers in a 640-mile area. In addition to electricity, the company sells natural gas and provides telephone, Internet, and cable TV services.

POTOMAC PARK. A 724-acre recreation area lying along the **Potomac River** near the **Tidal Basin** and Washington Channel. The park is divided into two areas connected by Ohio Drive. Reclaimed from marshland in the 1890s, the 328-acre East Potomac Park contains an 18-hole golf course, two nine-hole courses, a driving range, and a miniature golf course. The park also has an indoor swimming pool and 16 outdoor tennis courts. "The Awakening," a large outdoor sculpture depicting a metal figure struggling up from the earth, is located at Hains Point. West Potomac Park is primarily used as a picnic and recreation area.

POTOMAC RIVER. A 383-mile river that drains 14,000 square miles of land in four states and the District of Columbia. The river begins in the Allegheny Mountains of West Virginia and flows across the Atlantic Piedmont until it meanders past Washington on its way to the Chesapeake Bay. Along the way it is fed by dozens of tributaries and descends from cloud level to sea level in a series of rapids and waterfalls, including the 35-foot-high Great Falls. Explored by Captain **John Smith** in 1608, upriver ports were later established at Alexandria and **Georgetown.** In 1800 the city of Washington rose out of swampy waters on the river's left (east) bank. The river plays an important role in the economic life of the region, supplies drinking water to the city of Washington, and provides a habitat for an abundance of wildlife. Ecological problems include pollution from more than 50 abandoned coal mines, sedimentation from construction and erosion of agricultural land, and wastes from Washington. Conservation groups, including the Alliance for the Chesapeake Bay, are working to address these problems.

PRESIDENT'S PARK. *See* LAFAYETTE SQUARE.

PROHIBITION. A period of 14 years (1919–33) during which the sale and consumption of alcoholic beverages was outlawed in the United States. Washington's period of alcohol prohibition began in 1917, two years before national Prohibition, when Congress passed the Sheppard Law. Sponsored by Texas senator Morris Sheppard, the intention of the law was to make the capital city a model of alcohol prohibition for the rest of the country. The Sheppard Law shut down some 100 local wholesalers of liquor and 300 retailers. Prohibition was strictly enforced in Washington, but illegal consumption of alcohol continued among all strata of Washington society and even among those in the **White House** and the **U.S. Capitol.** As many as 5,000 bootleggers operated within the city limits, and gun battles were fought among rival bootleggers and between bootleggers and police. The presence of foreign embassies in Washington created a unique problem for the enforcement of Prohibition: embassy employees had immunity from the law, and many became suppliers of imported liquor for Washington residents. In 1932 the Democratic party platform included the repeal of Prohibition, and under democratic President Franklin D. Roosevelt the 18th Amendment was repealed and liquor consumption again became legal in the United States. Shortly thereafter Congress also repealed the Sheppard Law.

PROSPECT HOUSE. Federal-style building on Prospect Street in **Georgetown**, built between 1788 and 1793. The first owner of Prospect House was James Maccubbin Lingan, a tobacco merchant and civic leader, whom **George Washington** appointed customs collector for the port of Georgetown. In 1793 Lingan sold the house to John Templeton, a banker and civic leader, who supervised construction of the Georgetown Bridge over the **Potomac River**. Templeton's family owned the building for more than 50 years. During the **Civil War**, military officers boarded at Prospect House; among them was Daniel Craig McCallum, the Union Army's director of military railroads. The building's owner at that time was William Whiton, who sold the house in 1868 to Franklin Steele, a merchant. Steele's daughter inherited the house and lived there with her husband, George Upham Morris, a U.S. Navy commodore. In the 1930s Prospect House underwent extensive restoration. Later, when President Harry Truman occupied **Blair House** during a **White House** renovation, Prospect House served as the U.S. presidential guest house.

PUBLIC ART LEAGUE OF WASHINGTON. *See* COMMISSION OF FINE ARTS.

PUBLIC EDUCATION. Washington City opened two publicly funded schools in 1806. However, Congress didn't mandate schooling for D.C. children under age 14 until 1862, and earlier attempts to establish public schools—aside from Georgetown's **Lancasterian School** (1811)—were unsatisfying and short-lived. Schools for African American students did not receive public funds until the 1874 merger of the district's four separate school boards, serving Washington City whites, **Georgetown** whites, Washington County residents, and African Americans.

For 80 years the consolidated board maintained two separate systems, one for white students and one for black; both school systems were chronically overcrowded and underfunded. Between 1880 and 1900, 81 public schools were built in Washington, including the first secondary school, the all-white Central High School. An African American school begun in 1870 in the basement of Fifteenth Street Presbyterian Church was taken over by the city in 1891, becoming the M Street High School, later renamed

Dunbar High School. Innovative curricula and instructional methods were instituted between 1885 and 1900, when Washington schools were reputed to be among the nation's best.

In 1925 Congress appropriated $20 million for a five-year building program that resulted in the construction of 23 new schools and the expansion or renovation of 33 additional schools. Another 13 schools were added in 1931. **School desegregation** was accomplished during the 1950s. In 1968 D.C. residents elected their own Board of Education, the first local suffrage in 94 years and the first time in D.C. history that the school board was publicly elected. However, throughout its 30-year existence the elected board has been marked by controversy. During the 1980s, reductions in the public education budget led to a deterioration of school plants. Protesting unsafe conditions, the education advocacy group, **Parents United** for the Public Schools, initiated a successful lawsuit, which led to school improvements. *See also* HOBSON v. HANSEN.

PUBLIC LIBRARIES. *See* CARNEGIE LIBRARY; MARTIN LUTHER KING, JR., MEMORIAL LIBRARY.

PUBLIC MARKETS. Commercial buildings and areas where grocers, farmers, merchants, and others sold their goods. Before the days of **department stores** and supermarkets, residents of Washington relied on several public markets to supply their daily necessities. Center Market was established in 1801 in the **Federal Triangle** area on **Pennsylvania Avenue**. The original 100-vendor market was destroyed by fire in 1870 and replaced by a 1,000-vendor market covering two city blocks on **Seventh Street**. Designed by **Adolph Cluss**, the red brick market was demolished in 1931 to make way for the **National Archives**. The Marsh Market was so named because of its location on fields that were regularly flooded by Tiber Creek. The market was one of the largest and most diverse in Washington before it closed in 1929. The historic **Georgetown** Market on M Street NW dates from the early 1790s and ceased operations in 1935; it was later reopened between 1980 and 1984 as the Market Place. Eastern Market, founded in 1802, still operates on **Capitol Hill**, although on a smaller scale. It is now housed in a red brick building designed by **Adolph Cluss** in 1873 and features everything from produce to jewelry in its vending booths. The Northern Liberties Market was begun in the early

19th century and was demolished in 1872 to make way for a public library. The O Street Market was built in 1886 and destroyed in the **riots of 1968**; it was designated a historic landmark and restored in 1980. The Western Market served the community from 1822 to 1872, when it was replaced by a structure at 21st and K Streets; the one-acre site was sold to the city in 1960.

PUBLIC SCHOOLS. *See* PUBLIC EDUCATION.

- R -

RADIO. One of the earliest pioneers of Washington radio was Arthur Godfrey, who began a popular morning show on WTOP-AM in the 1930s and then went on to TV stardom as host of a variety show. Few who heard it will ever forget Marian Anderson's 1939 Easter broadcast of "My Country 'Tis of Thee," carried live by NBC Radio in front of the **Lincoln Memorial**. Anderson was forced to move outside after she was turned away by the discriminatory practices of Constitution Hall. During the 1960s WOL was a popular soul station, playing Motown hits. African American businesswoman Cathy Hughes began her career in Washington radio in 1971, and her company, Radio One, eventually bought WOL, along with more than 20 other stations, becoming the largest U.S. radio group owned by an African American. In 1970 National Public Radio began its Washington broadcast of "All Things Considered," an evening news program that became a runaway hit. During the Cold War, Radio Free Europe and Voice of America broadcasts from Washington beamed American music and news to millions in the Soviet Union and Eastern Europe. With a variety of broadcasts and radio personalities, Washington became an important center of radio programming.

RANDLE HIGHLANDS. *See* ANACOSTIA.

REAGAN ASSASSINATION ATTEMPT. The 1981 shooting of President Ronald Reagan by John Hinckley, Jr., the 25-year-old son of an oil executive. Apparently inspired by a Hollywood film, Hinckley came to Washington for the purpose of killing the president. On March 30 he waited with a revolver on the sidewalk of T Street outside the Washington Hilton Hotel, where the president was talking to reporters. As Reagan left the hotel,

Hinckley, hidden in a crowd, fired a bullet into Reagan's chest. The president was taken to **George Washington University** Hospital, where he underwent surgery to remove the bullet lodged in his lung. The incident happened early in first term of the 70-year-old president; he returned to the **White House** 12 days after the shooting and gradually recovered from his wounds. Hinckley stood trial for the shooting and when a jury found him not guilty by reason of insanity, he was confined to **St. Elizabeths Hospital.**

RED CROSS. *See* CLARA BARTON.

RED SUMMER of 1919. Four days of racially motivated violence by white World War I veterans, aggravated by high unemployment and changing social conditions, that left 40 people dead and 150 wounded. Despite the distinguished service of Washington's African American soldiers during World War I, they returned home to deteriorating race relations—inflamed by local journalists and renewed Ku Klux Klan activity—including public lynchings of black war veterans wearing their army uniforms. In July 1919, a series of sex crimes allegedly committed by one black man, with sensational press coverage by Washington's four white newspapers, dramatically increased tensions. On Saturday evening, July 19, a mob of 400 white veterans left the saloons of **Pennsylvania Avenue** for an African American neighborhood in Southwest Washington, where they killed one man and badly injured another. When it became clear that D.C. police would not or could not protect them, African Americans armed themselves in self-defense and resisted the mob. President Woodrow Wilson's mobilization of 2,000 troops was ineffective in halting the riots, but a heavy rainstorm throughout the night of July 22 finally ended the fighting.

REDEVELOPMENT ACT OF 1945. An act passed by Congress that authorized the **National Capital Park and Planning Commission** to rebuild "substandard dwellings" and the "inhabited alleys and blighted areas" of the city. In addition to urban renewal, the act directed the commission to plan a new highway system, to purchase land for new parks and playgrounds, and to select sites for new public buildings.

REDEVELOPMENT LAND AGENCY. *See* SOUTHWEST.

District of Columbia boundary stone. *Courtesy of Prints and Photographs Division, Library of Congress.*

St. John's Church with the White House showing damage from British soldiers in the War of 1812. Watercolor by Benjamin Henry Latrobe. *Courtesy of Washingtoniana Division, D.C. Public Library.*

Ward K, Armory Square Hospital, circa 1862. By Mathew Brady. *Courtesy of the Washingtoniana Division, D.C. Public Library.*

Fort Totten's 100-pound gun, August 1865. By Mathew Brady. *Courtesy of the Washingtoniana Division, D.C. Public Library.*

Frederick Douglass. *Courtesy of Prints and Photographs Division, Library of Congress.*

Alexander "Boss" Shepherd. *Courtesy of Prints and Photographs Division, Library of Congress.*

C&O Canal at M Street and Key Bridge. Underwood & Underwood. *Courtesy of Prints and Photographs Division, Library of Congress.*

Pennsylvania Avenue, circa 1893. *Courtesy of Prints and Photographs Division, Library of Congress.*

Coxey's "Army of the Unemployed," 1894. *Courtesy of Prints and Photographs Division, Library of Congress.*

F Street commercial district looking toward the Treasury Department. Mathew Brady–Bert Hardy, circa 1900. *Courtesy of Prints and Photographs Division, Library of Congress.*

Walter Perry Johnson, while playing for the Washington Americans, 1911. *Courtesy of Prints and Photographs Division, Library of Congress.*

Center Market produce stands. Willard R. Ross, circa 1910. *Courtesy of Prints and Photographs Division, Library of Congress.*

Archibald Henry Grimké. By Addison Scurlock. *Courtesy of Moorland-Spingarn Research Center, Howard University.*

Washington Monument, as seen from the Lincoln Memorial during its first public ceremonies. Underwood & Underwood, 1922. *Courtesy of Prints and Photographs Division, Library of Congress.*

John Philip Sousa in the uniform of his civilian band. Defense Department photo, circa 1921. *Courtesy of Washingtoniana Division, D.C. Public Library.*

Knickerbocker Theater after the roof collapse of 1922. *Courtesy of Washingtoniana Division, D.C. Public Library.*

Alexander Graham Bell. *Courtesy of Washingtoniana Division, D.C. Public Library.*

Bonus Army demonstrators, 1932. *Courtesy of Prints and Photographs Division, Library of Congress.*

The White House in the hours following the December 7, 1941 attack on Pearl Harbor. World Wide Photos. *Courtesy of Prints and Photographs Division, Library of Congress.*

Marian Anderson at the dedication of a mural commemorating her public concert at the Lincoln Memorial in 1939, U.S. Department of Interior, 1943. OWI photo by Roger Smith. *Courtesy of Prints and Photographs Division, Library of Congress.*

Mary Church Terrell as depicted in a poster announcing one of her lectures. *Courtesy of Prints and Photographs Division, Library of Congress.*

View of Washington from the dome of the Library of Congress, 1944.
Courtesy of Prints and Photographs Division, Library of Congress.

Seventh and T Streets NW, following the riots of 1968. *Courtesy of the Historical Society of Washington, D.C.*

Duke Ellington. *Courtesy of Prints and Photographs Division, Library of Congress.*

The first two metro cars are delivered to the Brentwood yard. Paul M. Schmick, 1974. *Copyright* Washington Post, *Courtesy of the D.C. Public Library.*

REDSKINS. *See* WASHINGTON REDSKINS.

REEVES MUNICIPAL CENTER. D.C. government office building. Formally the Franklin D. Reeves Center for Municipal Affairs, named after the city's first African American commissioner and Democratic party committeeman, the eight-story stone and glass structure opened in 1986. The building is located at the corner of 14th and U Streets NW, in an area of the city that lay waste for nearly two decades after the **riots of 1968**. The $38 million center has 533,000 square feet of office space for its 1,000 city employees. With its street-level retail shops and a day care center, the building has been an important symbol of inner-city Washington renewal.

REFLECTING POOL. *See* LINCOLN MEMORIAL; POOR PEOPLE'S CAMPAIGN.

RENO CITY. *See* TENLEYTOWN.

RENWICK, JAMES (1818–1895). Architect of the **Smithsonian Institution** and **Renwick Gallery.** Born in New York City, Renwick graduated from Columbia University (1836) and worked on the engineering staff of the Erie Railroad. His design of Grace Church in New York City (1843) propelled him into an architectural career of national prominence. The self-taught architect primarily worked in Gothic and Romanesque styles. His signature building in Washington is the Gothic Revival Smithsonian "Castle," completed in 1855. It was the first of the Smithsonian buildings and serves as the headquarters of the Smithsonian museums. The Renwick Gallery was begun in 1859, but construction was delayed by the **Civil War** and the building was finally opened to the public in 1872. The building originally housed the **Corcoran Gallery of Art,** but the gallery outgrew the building and was relocated. The building was saved from demolition in 1965, has been restored, and is now part of the National Museum of American Art, housing American crafts and decorative arts. Renwick also designed two Washington churches: he carried out the enlargement and renovation of **St. John's Episcopal Church** (1883) and was commissioned to construct **St. Mary's Episcopal Church** (1887). The small chapel at **Oak Hill Cemetery** (1850) is also a Renwick design.

RESIDENCE ACT (1790). An act passed by Congress authorizing President **George Washington** to select a site along the eastern bank of the **Potomac River** for the "permanent seat of government of the United States." Congress specified that the site was not to exceed 10 miles square and authorized the construction of "suitable buildings for the accommodation of Congress, and of the president, and for the public offices of the government of the United States" by December 1800. The act, amended in 1791 to enlarge the boundaries of the site and to prohibit construction of buildings on the Virginia side of the river, established Washington as the capital of the United States.

RESURRECTION CITY. *See* GIANT FOOD; POOR PEOPLE'S CAMPAIGN.

RETROCESSION OF ALEXANDRIA (1846). An act passed by Congress, on the request of the state of Virginia, that returned to that state the county of Alexandria. At the time Congress passed the act, it was believed that "no more territory ought to be held under the exclusive legislation given to Congress over the District . . . than may be necessary and proper" for the seat of government and that "the portion of the District of Columbia ceded to the United States by the state of Virginia has not been, nor is ever likely to be, necessary for that purpose." Passage of the act reduced the size of the District of Columbia by one third.

RFK MEMORIAL STADIUM. The current home of the D.C. United professional soccer team, and the former home of the **Washington Redskins** (1961–96), the **Washington Senators** (1962–71), and the Washington Federals (1983–84). Located by the **Anacostia River**, a mile from the **U.S. Capitol**, the stadium also hosts concerts and special events. Originally called D.C. Stadium, the 56,000-seat open-air structure, built in 1961, was renamed in memory of Robert F. Kennedy, slain presidential candidate and brother of President John F. Kennedy. When used for football, RFK Stadium was known for its end zone seating near the playing field and for its crowd noise, which gave the Redskins an advantage over visiting teams.

RHODES TAVERN. Three-story Federal-style brick tavern that stood at 15th and F Streets NW. William Rhodes erected the building in 1799 as a tavern, but it served many other purposes in early Washington history. It was used as the city's first town hall, and in 1801 it was the polling place for the first **City Council** election. In

1814 the invading British used the building as an officers' headquarters. They oversaw the burning of Washington's public buildings from the tavern and, according to legend, ordered its candles to be put out at night, so they could dine by the light of the burning **White House**. The tavern building also served as the original home of the firm that became **Riggs National Bank**, and in the 1880s it housed the city's stock exchange. During the 20th century the tavern fell into disrepair, and a struggle ensued between preservationists and a Washington developer who wanted to demolish it to build an office and shopping complex. The public approved a 1983 city referendum calling for the tavern's preservation, but the city government permitted its demolition in 1984. All that remains of Rhodes Tavern is a commemorative bronze tablet, which was placed on a newly constructed building in 1999.

RIGGS NATIONAL BANK. The oldest continuously operating bank in Washington. **William Wilson Corcoran** opened a note brokerage house in **Georgetown** in 1836. In 1840 he entered into partnership with George Washington Riggs, Jr., son of a prominent New York banker. Corcoran & Riggs Bank became an official depository of the U.S. treasury, began overseas transactions, and helped finance the Mexican War (1846–48). Corcoran retired in 1854 and the firm became Riggs & Company. George Riggs led the 1867 syndicate that raised $7.2 million in gold bullion for the Alaska Purchase. In the 1920s, Riggs National Bank introduced savings accounts, opened a trust department, and purchased two other local banks, creating a branch banking network. In 1930 the firm acquired the Farmers and Mechanics Bank of Georgetown, a congressionally chartered bank established in February 1814 which helped finance the **War of 1812**. Communications executive Joe L. Allbritton purchased a controlling share in Riggs in 1981 and created Riggs National Corporation, expanding banking operations into Virginia and Maryland. Several of Riggs's branch banks are architecturally significant, including the Georgetown branch, designed by Marsh and Peter at Wisconsin Avenue and M Streets NW, which features a dramatic gold-leafed dome.

RIOTS OF 1968. Violent insurgence that occurred over a period of four days after the assassination of Martin Luther King, Jr., on April 4, 1968. Within a few hours of King's murder, cities across the United States erupted in violence over the death of the civil rights leader and in frustration at decades of racial and economic discrimination. Washington was particularly hard hit by the riots: 12 people were killed, 1,000 injured, and 3,000 arrested. More than 500 fires sent smoke billowing across the D.C. skyline. Nearly 12,000 federal troops joined D.C. police to enforce a 4:00 p.m. curfew and halt property damage, estimated in the millions of dollars. Rioting was most intense on H Street NE, and around the intersection of 14th and U Streets NW. Several areas of the city were devastated and many businesses moved out of the inner city or closed permanently. During the late 1990s, historic preservation efforts, real estate development, and city government incentives have led to the revitalization of some areas left blighted by the riots.

ROCK CREEK CEMETERY. The oldest cemetery in Washington. Located at Rock Creek Church Road and Webster Street NW, the 86-acre cemetery was founded in 1719 on the glebe lands of **St. Paul's Episcopal Church**. The grounds contain more than 75,000 interments, including those of cabinet officers, **U.S. Supreme Court** justices, and local political and business leaders. The cemetery was privately operated until 1871, when it was chartered as a nonprofit, public burial ground by act of Congress. Several important sculptures, mostly created between 1875 and 1925, distinguish the property. The most famous is Augustus Saint-Gaudens's untitled bronze statue, popularly known as "Grief," commissioned in 1886 by **Henry Adams**. Other notable artworks include "The Seven Ages of Man," sculpted by William Ordway Partridge for the grave of journalist Samuel Kauffman; and "Rabboni," created by Mount Rushmore sculptor Gutzon Borglum for banker Charles Ffoulke.

ROCK CREEK HUNDRED. A 1715 division of Maryland land on which the Federal City, later named Washington City, was established in 1791. Rock Creek Hundred was contained in the royal charter granted by British monarch Charles I to George Calvert, Lord Baltimore, in 1632. Although the Baltimore family began to grant land patents in this area in 1664, settlers did not arrive until about 1714. Rock Creek Hundred was originally part of Charles County, and later, Prince George's County, Maryland. By the time the District of Columbia was drawn onto the map, the Rock Creek Hundred had been divided into 30 individual tracts of land owned by the "original proprietors" of the new capital city.

ROCK CREEK PARK. A 2,800-acre wooded park located in the middle of urban Washington only five miles from the **White House**. Established in 1890, Rock Creek Park is one of the oldest in the national parks system. Its original 1,754 acres still form the center of the park. Recreational facilities include 30 picnic areas, playing fields, tennis courts, a golf course, and trails for hiking, jogging, cycling, and horseback riding. Other park attractions include the 4,000-seat Carter Barron Amphitheater, an outdoor theater for the performing arts; the Rock Creek Nature Center and Planetarium; and Pierce Mill, a water-driven flour mill constructed in the 1820s and last used in 1897. The mill is operated as a museum by the National Park Service.

ROOSEVELT, FRANKLIN DELANO. *See* FRANKLIN DELANO ROOSEVELT MEMORIAL.

ROOSEVELT, THEODORE. *See* THEODORE ROOSEVELT ISLAND.

ROSARIO, CARLOS. *See* ADAMS MORGAN.

- S -

SACKLER GALLERY. *See* ARTHUR M. SACKLER GALLERY.

SAINT-GAUDENS, AUGUSTUS. *See* ADAMS, HENRY BROOKS; McMILLAN REPORT; ROCK CREEK CEMETERY.

SAKS AND COMPANY. *See* DEPARTMENT STORES.

SCHOOL DESEGREGATION. The efforts after World War II to end racial segregation of the public schools in Washington and improve educational opportunities for African American students. In 1948 the highly critical **Strayer Report**, prepared by Columbia University professor George Strayer, recommended spending 75 percent of Washington's **public education** budget on buildings and equipment for African American students, but only eight schools were constructed. Two years later, 11 African American students were denied enrollment in Sousa Junior High School, a modern, all-white school in Southeast Washington. In response, the students sued the school board and the case (*Bolling v. Sharpe*) was appealed to the **U.S. Supreme Court**. It was consolidated with a Kansas case (*Brown v. Board of Education*), which resulted in the 1954 unanimous Supreme Court ruling that public school segregation was unconstitutional. In September 1954, 73 percent of D.C. schools were integrated for the first time, without violence. However, within three years many white families had moved to the Maryland and Virginia suburbs, and others enrolled their children in private schools. African Americans became the majority group in the city schools, but still suffered economic discrimination until 1966, when civil rights activist Julius Hobson won a court order requiring equalization of per-pupil expenditures citywide (***Hobson v. Hansen***).

SCHOOLS. *See* PUBLIC EDUCATION.

SCIDMORE, ELIZA. *See* CHERRY BLOSSOMS.

SCOTTISH RITE TEMPLE. Masonic temple located on 16th Street NW, also known as House of the Temple. One of Washington's most dramatic structures, the Scottish Rite Temple was designed by **John Russell Pope**, modeled after the 1862 restoration of the Mausoleum at Halikarnassos, Egypt—one of the Seven Wonders of the Ancient World—and completed in 1915. Built of Indiana limestone with finely carved Greek and Egyptian details, the building is organized around the arcane mathematical symbolism of freemasonry, such as 33-foot-high Ionic columns, representing the 33 degrees of membership. A pair of sphinxes by sculptor Adolph A. Weinman, symbolizing wisdom and power, guard the entrance. Poet and adventurer Albert Pike was disinterred from his grave in **Oak Hill Cemetery** and buried in the temple in 1944, 53 years after his death.

SCURLOCK, ROBERT (1917–1994). Photographer. Born in Washington, Scurlock graduated from Dunbar High School and **Howard University** (1937). After serving in World War II with the famed Tuskegee Airmen, he joined Scurlock Studio, founded by his father, Addison Scurlock. He opened one of the city's first custom color photo laboratories, and during the late 1940s and 1950s he operated the Capital School of Photography. Scurlock specialized in commercial and portrait photography and during the 1960s and 1970s his work appeared in *Fortune*, *Look*, and *Ebony* magazines. Perhaps his most famous photographs, depicting the Washington **riots of 1968**, appeared in a two-page spread in *Life* magazine.

SEATON, WILLIAM WINSTON. *See NATIONAL INTELLIGENCER.*

SECOND PRESBYTERIAN CHURCH. *See* NEW YORK AVENUE PRESBYTERIAN CHURCH.

SEPTEMBER 11 ATTACKS. Terrorist attacks that demolished the World Trade Center twin towers in New York City and destroyed part of the Pentagon near Washington, D.C. The attacks, which took place on September 11, 2001, were planned by al Qaeda, an organization led by a radical Islamist, Osama bin Laden. Using four hijacked airplanes, 19 terrorists piloted two planes into the World Trade Center buildings and one into the Pentagon building. The fourth plane, apparently headed for an attack on Washington, D.C., crashed in Pennsylvania when passengers resisted the hijackers.

In response to the attacks, the United States conducted a military campaign in Afghanistan, assisted by the Afghan resistance groups, that succeeded in destroying al Qaeda's base of operations, killing or capturing many al Qaeda fighters, and toppling Afghanistan's government, which had sheltered the group.

The Pentagon attack destroyed the newly renovated southwestern side of the Defense Department building, which housed offices of the army, navy, and Marine Corps. Killed in the attack were 125 Pentagon employees and 64 people on board the aircraft. The attack led to an immediate evacuation of the **White House, U.S. Capitol, U.S. Supreme Court**, and other federal buildings, and temporary closure of the city's museums, monuments, and nearby Reagan National Airport.

The September 11 attacks were followed in mid-September by anonymous mailings of anthrax-laced letters to media outlets in New York and Florida, and the Washington offices of senators Patrick Leahy of Vermont and Tom Daschle of South Dakota. The letters contaminated Washington's Brentwood mail facility, resulting in the deaths of two postal workers. Twenty-eight cases of anthrax exposure were confirmed in the Capitol building, and parts of the complex underwent an extensive cleanup, as did the central mailrooms of the House, Senate, and Supreme Court.

The terrorist attacks left short- and long-term marks on Washington. The immediate economic consequences included a sharp drop in city tourism, and the loss of about 40 percent of jobs in that industry. In the long term, the city's new security measures at airports, train stations, federal buildings, and the city's cultural arts attractions will likely become permanent. Other security measures designed to prevent sabotage will no doubt follow, as Washington remains a target for terrorist violence.

SEVENTH STREET (Old Downtown). An area north of **Pennsylvania Avenue** between the **U.S. Capitol** and the **White House**, roughly bounded by E, I, 7th, and 11th Streets in Northwest Washington. The neighborhood has long been Washington's major commercial thoroughfare; it was the route by which agricultural produce of old Washington County was transported to the merchants of 7th and 9th Streets and to the **Washington Canal**. Center Market was built on 7th Street in 1801; it was a major commercial enterprise and one of several **public markets** in Washington. Many of Washington's oldest surviving commercial structures are clustered along 7th Street. The majority of these buildings are modest low-rise structures of the late 1800s and early 1900s, but a few are major public and private buildings, such as the old Patent Office (now the Museum of American Art and National Portrait Gallery) and the U.S. General Post Office, constructed in the 1830s. Seventh Street was also a place of boarding houses that catered to members of Congress. The most famous boarding house belonged to **Mary Surratt**, whose establishment was used by conspirators who plotted the **Lincoln assassination**.

The first horsecar lines opened in 1862, and many Washington families moved to the newer suburbs. These families were replaced by German immigrants, many of whom were Jews. German culture was preserved in the neighborhood, and at St. Mary's Catholic Church confessions were heard in the German language until 1961. The downtown Jewish community grew from fewer than 200 residents in 1860 to more than 5,000 by 1910, establishing the city's earliest synagogues, **Washington Hebrew Congregation** (1852) and **Adas Israel** (1869). Some of these Jewish residents were merchants and retailers who developed Washington's finest **department stores**, including Lansburgh's, Saks, Kann's, and the Hecht Company. Italians, Russians, and Eastern European Jews arrived between 1880 and 1920. In 1931 the **Federal Triangle** development project pushed Washington's Chinese community to relocate en masse to 7th and H Streets. African Americans developed a shopping area on the northern periphery of Old Downtown, on upper 7th Street between Massachusetts and Florida Avenues. By 1923 the only places in the neighborhood not racially segregated were **Griffith Stadium** and the **Carnegie Library** on Mount Vernon Square.

After World War II, downtown businesses were desegregated beginning with the Hecht Company, which opened its lunchroom to all customers in 1951. Public **school desegregation** followed soon thereafter, and most white residents left the neighborhood. The synagogues were purchased by Black Baptist and African Methodist Episcopal churches, and after the **riots of 1968**, the Hecht Company was the only department store to remain open, moving to 12th and G Streets in 1985. During the 1990s, construction of the **MCI Center** helped to revitalize Old Downtown. An arts and entertainment district developed along 7th Street; the two **Smithsonian Institution** museums and **Ford's Theatre** were joined by the **Shakespeare Theatre** and several art galleries; and many restaurants, movie theaters, apartments, and office buildings were added to the neighborhood.

SEWALL-BELMONT HOUSE. A Georgian-style house on Constitution Avenue NE. Robert Sewall built a house on a lot that was purchased from **Daniel Carroll** in 1799. The house incorporated an earlier brick structure dating back to 1750, possibly the oldest building on **Capitol Hill**. Sewall rented the house to Albert Gallatin, secretary of the treasury during the administrations of Presidents James Madison and **Thomas Jefferson**. During the **War of 1812**, shots fired from the direction of the house killed the horse of a British officer and the building was burned by British troops. After the war the house was rebuilt and renovated several times before it was acquired in 1929 by Alva Belmont, a prominent women's rights activist. Belmont established it as headquarters for the National Women's Party. Today the building houses offices, a small museum, and a gift shop.

SHAKESPEARE THEATRE. America's leading Shakespeare company. Established in 1970, the Shakespeare Theatre performed for 22 years in the **Folger Shakespeare Library**'s replica of the Globe Theatre. In 1992 the company moved to a 441-seat auditorium in the Lansburgh Building on **7th Street** NW in Washington's developing arts district. During the tenure of artistic director Michael Kahn, appointed in 1986, the Shakespeare Theatre has gained a national and international reputation. A locally based group of classical actors, frequently joined by guest artists such as Kelly McGillis, Stacy Keach, Avery Brooks, Jean Stapleton, and Elizabeth Ashley, performs six plays each season, five at the Lansburgh and one, free to the public, at Carter Barron Amphitheater in **Rock Creek Park**, which has attracted more than 300,000 attendees since 1991. In June 2000 the Shakespeare Theatre and **George Washington University** instituted a Master of Fine Arts degree program in classical acting, the first of its kind in the United States.

SHARON, WILLIAM. *See* CHEVY CHASE.

SHAW, WALTER B. *See* KENILWORTH PARK AND AQUATIC GARDENS.

SHAW/U STREET. An area bordered by North Capitol Street on the east, 15th Street on the west, Florida Avenue on the north, and M Street on the south (including Logan Circle, Bloomingdale, and Strivers' Section) in Northwest Washington. When the District of Columbia was established in 1791, the Shaw neighborhood was a forested area, and the only road consisted of a dirt track (now **7th Street**) to Rockville, Maryland. Little changed until the **Civil War**, when streetcars began to run on 7th and 14th Streets. Camp Barker, a tent city holding as many as 5,000 runaway slaves, was located in the area bounded by modern 12th, 13th, Q, and R Streets. During the 1870s, infrastructure improvements made the Shaw neighborhood a prime site for new house construction. The first residents were a racially mixed group from outside the District, particularly from the rural South, who came to Washington seeking employment. The neighborhood's brick row houses, built during the last quarter of the 19th century, especially around Logan Circle, are today Washington's most complete collection of Victorian architecture.

Around the turn of the 20th century, many white residents relocated to new suburbs north and west of the Shaw neighborhood. Middle- and upper-middle-income African Americans moved into the neighborhood and, during the next few decades, established a remarkable community within the city. Building associations were organized by civic leaders to help new residents purchase or build houses. African American churches became the center of community life, and their pastors provided important leadership. Education was highly prized, and Dunbar High School became the premier African American college preparatory institution. Many Dunbar students went on to attend nearby **Howard University**, which, during the first half of the 20th century, educated 96 percent of the nation's African American lawyers and nearly half of the country's African American doctors, dentists, architects, and engineers.

From the 1920s to the mid-1960s, the Shaw/U Street neighborhood was a place of African American intellectualism, artistic creativity, and entrepreneurial success. The community's social and artistic life was developed at the **Howard Theatre, Lincoln Theater**, the **Whitelaw Hotel, True Reformers Hall**, and the nation's first black YMCA, later named **Anthony Bowen YMCA**. U Street was dubbed America's "Black Broadway," and local talent such as **Duke Ellington, Pearl Bailey**, and Billy Eckstine performed at theaters and nightclubs. Cab Calloway and other out-of-towners also vied for space on U Street marquees. African American-owned restaurants, movie theaters, jazz clubs, offices, and commercial establishments dotted the neighborhood, and its Victorian row houses were occupied by attorneys, scientists, educators, and artists.

During the 1950s, the desegregation of Washington prompted many of the neighborhood's more affluent residents to move to elegant residences on upper 16th Street in Northwest Washington or to newer suburbs. The once-glamorous neighborhood gradually deteriorated, and the **riots of 1968** decimated its theaters and businesses. Nearly 90 local businesses were destroyed or abandoned, and commerce in the 7th and 14th Street corridors dropped from more than $75 million to less than $4 million annually. Economic and social conditions remained bleak until the mid-1980s, when a small theater district sprang up at 14th and P Streets, featuring the **Source Theatre, Studio Theatre**, and Woolly Mammoth Theatre companies. The **Reeves Municipal Center**, a major city government office complex, opened in 1986, and in 1991 a U Street stop was added to the **Washington Metrorail System**, aiding neighborhood revitalization.

SHEPHERD, ALEXANDER ROBEY "BOSS" (1835–1902). Real estate developer and civic leader. Born in Southwest Washington, Shepherd was apprenticed at age 17 to J. W. Thompson, owner of Washington's largest plumbing and gas fitting company, and seven years later he became a partner in the firm. During the late 1860s he served as president of the Washington **City Council** while building nearly 1,500 houses around the city. When Washington's city charter expired in 1870, Shepherd strongly advocated the merger of Washington, **Georgetown**, and Washington County into one jurisdiction, administered by the federal government; it was not until 1968 that Washingtonians regained any voting rights over local affairs. Shepherd was appointed to—and dominated—the five-member Board of Public Works that ran the city. Under his controversial leadership, a three-year construction project employed thousands of workers who paved streets and built sidewalks, sewers, and water lines. The capital was transformed from a muddy backwater to a modern metropolis, but Shepherd's contracting practices were reckless, much of the work was shoddy, and poorer neighborhoods received few improvements. Cost overruns totaled more than $20 million. Shepherd was appointed territorial governor in 1873, but served only nine months before he declared bankruptcy. Six years later he moved to Mexico, where he made another fortune in the mining industry. He died there and was buried in Washington's **Rock Creek Cemetery** with grand ceremony. A bronze statue of Shepherd, erected in front of the District Building in 1909, was removed and placed in storage in 1979; by the mid-1980s it was relocated to Shepherd Avenue in Anacostia. *See also* SHEPHERD PARK.

SHEPHERD PARK. An area in the northern tip of Washington bounded by Eastern Avenue, **Rock Creek Park**, Georgia Avenue NW, and **Walter Reed Army Medical Center**. Until the early 20th century, Shepherd Park was virtually uninhabited, except for a few large farms and summer estates of wealthy Washingtonians. One of these estates was Bleak House, an ornate summer palace at modern 14th and Geranium Streets belonging to Territorial Governor **Alexander "Boss" Shepherd**. The 1909 construction of Walter Reed Medical Center at 16th Street and Alaska Avenue was a catalyst for growth, and real estate development began soon thereafter. In 1911 most of the Shepherd property was sold to an investment company, and streets were platted and given botanical names. The original deeds included restrictive covenants intended to bar African Americans, Jews, and other minority groups from the largely white Protestant community.

Before the mid-20th century, two well-defined enclaves were

added to the Shepherd Park community: Colonial Village and North Portal Estates. The 80 residences of Colonial Village were constructed in 1931 as reproductions of famous Colonial American buildings, such as **George Washington**'s boyhood home and the Yorktown, Virginia, house where Cornwallis surrendered. While Colonial Village was a mostly Protestant community, the 220-house North Portal Estates was developed by and for Jews in the aftermath of the 1948 **U.S. Supreme Court** decision that ruled as legally unenforceable racially restrictive real estate covenants. Many businesses catering to the Jewish community opened on Georgia Avenue. Between 1948 and 1964 the Jewish proportion of the population of Shepherd Park grew to nearly 80 percent. In 1959 Shepherd Park was a target of "race-baiting" real estate speculators who used "block-busting" tactics to cause white flight and price instability in other Washington neighborhoods. In response, residents organized an integrated civic association and conducted a number of community events that brought cohesion to the neighborhood.

Between 1960 and 1980, Shepherd Park gradually became an upper-income African American community; the black population grew from less than 2 percent to about 66 percent. Sections of upper 16th Street became known as the "Gold Coast" and the "Platinum Coast." During this period, several large houses were acquired by religious and educational institutions, including a **Hanafi Muslim** group, which in 1972 moved into an imposing stone structure on 16th Street. The following year, a rivalry with a Black Muslim group led to two outbursts of violence that left eight people dead and several wounded. In recent years the **Shaw/U Street** residents have opposed development along Georgia Avenue and in nearby downtown Silver Spring, Maryland. Shepherd Park remains an integrated, cohesive neighborhood.

SHEPPARD LAW. *See* PROHIBITION.

SHERIDAN CIRCLE. *See* KALORAMA; LETELIER-MOFFITT ASSASSINATION.

SHILOH BAPTIST CHURCH. Historic African American congregation. Before its 1862 attack on Fredericksburg, Virginia, the Union Army offered free transportation and protection to all African Americans who wished to evacuate the area before the **Civil War** battle commenced. An entire congregation, 300 members of Fredericksburg's Shiloh Baptist Church, accepted the military's offer and moved to Washington. After worshipping in private homes for a time, the group converted an L Street stable into a church. Their current building, on 9th Street NW, was purchased in 1924 but was seriously damaged by arson the following year. During its renovation, the congregation worshipped in the **Howard Theatre**. In 1982 Shiloh constructed a $5.5 million Family Life Center, designed by **Howard University** professor Robert Nash. The nonprofit recreational center in Washington's inner city includes restaurants, bowling alleys, and racquetball courts.

SHOEMAKER, LOUIS P. *See* BRIGHTWOOD.

SLASHES, THE. *See* DUPONT CIRCLE.

SLAVERY. Slaves were imported into Colonial America to provide manual labor for a primarily agrarian economy. Tobacco cultivation in the mid-Atlantic region generated a high demand for slaves to work the plantations. By 1745, when the first tobacco inspection house was built in **Georgetown**, nearly one-third of Maryland's population was African or African American. By the 1760s, at least one slave dealer, John Beattie, operated in Georgetown. Edward Burrows was probably the first to sell slaves in Washington City, in 1794. After the importation of African slaves was banned in 1808, Washington became a leading center for the domestic slave trade. A major slave auction center was located near Center Market, and several slave pens sprang up in Southwest Washington.

When the federal government moved to Washington City in 1800, local farmers had created a surplus of slave labor by abandoning tobacco for wheat, a less labor-intensive crop. The local economy was otherwise experiencing a labor shortage, and to meet the needs of the growing city, slaves were hired out for work on various city projects. These projects included construction of the **U.S. Capitol**, the **White House**, and other federal buildings and the creation and repair of city streets. These workers were permitted to keep a portion of their wages, and many slaves were eventually able to purchase their freedom. District law permitted manumission, allowed free blacks to remain in the city, and included legal procedures by which wrongfully enslaved persons could recover their freedom. These laws created safer, less oppressive living conditions than were experienced further south, although the city did maintain **Black Codes**, and during the late 1820s less-fortunate slaves spent days in Washington's federal prisons while awaiting transit to the plantations of southern purchasers. Still, by 1830 free blacks outnumbered slaves in the District of Columbia.

During the early 1830s and 1840s, Washington became the focus of the national abolitionist movement. In 1831 Benjamin Lundy, a Quaker from New Jersey, founded the city's first anti-slavery newspaper, the *Genius of Universal Emancipation*. Around 1840 a group of abolitionist Congressmen began holding strategy meetings with former president, then-Congressman, John Quincy Adams. A second abolitionist newspaper, the ***National Era***, was launched in 1847. The abolitionist-led Underground Railroad also became active in the District, hiding escaped slaves and providing shelter, disguises, and guides to help them reach the Northeast or Canada. Several Underground Railroad "stations" were located in Washington, including **Mount Zion United Methodist Church** and the Methodist Cemetery in Georgetown, several downtown churches, and Anthony Bowen's house at 9th and E Streets SW, near the Potomac wharf. The Compromise of 1850 abolished the slave trade, but not slavery, in the District. After the **Civil War** broke out, thousands of escaping slaves, known as "**contrabands**," arrived in Washington, with many settling near Union military encampments. In 1862, several months before the Emancipation Proclamation, President Abraham Lincoln freed D.C. slaves in the country's only **compensated emancipation.**

SMITH, JOHN (ca. 1580–1631). English soldier and adventurer. After leaving home at age 15, Smith fought for the Dutch against the Spanish and in a European campaign against the Turks. He was captured by Turkish forces in 1601 and sold into slavery, but escaped to Russia and returned to England. In 1606 Smith joined in the effort to establish an English colony in Virginia. He was leader of the Jamestown Colony and between 1608 and 1609 he established order and discipline in the community and traded with various **Native American settlements.** In one of his periodic forays searching for food and trade, Smith and a small party were the first Europeans to sail up the **Potomac River** as far as present-day Washington. Smith fished in the river, traded with the Nacostin people, and left the first written description of the area that later became the District of Columbia. Smith also explored the Massachusetts Bay area in 1614 and is responsible for many New England place names. A relentless pragmatist, he wrote several books promoting American colonization and urging careful screening of potential settlers.

SMITH, MARGARET BAYARD (1778–1844). Socialite and author. In 1800, 22-year-old Margaret Bayard married Samuel H. Smith, who became employed in the administration of President **Thomas Jefferson**. Because of her husband's position, Smith was thrust into the role of society hostess. She presided at parties and balls and received a variety of guests from diplomats to philosophers. In addition to her social activities, Smith wrote two novels, including the two-volume work *A Winter in Washington; or, Memoirs of the Seymour Family* (1824). Her correspondence was edited by Gaillard Hunt and published as *The First Forty Years of Washington Society* (1906). Both her novels and letters provide important descriptions of Washington life from 1801 to 1840.

SMITHSONIAN INSTITUTION. One of the world's largest research and educational centers. The Smithsonian comprises 16 museums, four research centers, the **National Zoological Park**, the Smithsonian library system, and a publishing house and magazine. Its museums house 140 million artifacts and the U.S. national collections in history, science, and the arts. The Smithsonian was founded through the bequest of a wealthy Englishman, James Smithson. Born in 1765, Smithson was educated at Oxford and went on to conduct research in chemistry, geology, and mineralogy; a chemical compound, smithsonite, was named in his honor. Smithson's wealth was inherited; his will specified that his fortune, as well as his scientific collections, should be given to the United States to found an institution in Washington devoted to the increase and diffusion of knowledge. Smithson never visited the United States, nor did he explain why he left his fortune to the new nation. The Smithsonian was established by a congressional act, signed into law by President James K. Polk in 1846. Physicist Joseph Henry was named the Smithsonian's first chief executive. Nine Smithsonian museums are located on the **Mall**, including the main Smithsonian Building (now known as the Castle), which was designed in the medieval revival style by **James Renwick**, and built of red sandstone in 1855. A board of regents oversees the Smithsonian; the board's members include the U.S. vice president, the chief justice of the **U.S. Supreme Court**, three U.S. Senators, and three U.S. Representatives. *See also* ANACOSTIA MUSEUM AND CENTER FOR AFRICAN AMERICAN HISTORY AND CULTURE; ARTHUR M. SACKLER GALLERY; ARTS AND INDUSTRIES BUILDING; FREER GALLERY; HIRSHHORN MUSEUM AND SCULPTURE GARDEN; NATIONAL AIR AND SPACE MUSEUM; NATIONAL MUSEUM OF AFRICAN ART; NATIONAL POSTAL MUSEUM.

SNOW RIOTS (1835). Racially motivated mob violence that took place in the wake of the Nat Turner Rebellion, a slave revolt in Virginia. The events that led to the Snow Riots included the assault of the widow of **William Thornton** by one of her slaves. Soon after, the physician Reuben Crandall was jailed for possession of abolitionist literature, and rumors that he would incite a slave revolt propelled an angry mob to try to lynch him. When police prevented that attack, the mob went after Beverly Snow, a successful restaurateur and free black who had allegedly criticized some white women. Snow's saloon and several other black-owned businesses and churches were vandalized, and a school was burned. Police and U.S. Marines restored order one week after the riots began. The riots led the Washington **City Council** to institute policies that restricted black commercial activities and toughened the city's **Black Codes**.

SOCIAL BETTERMENT MOVEMENT. *See* EDSON, JOHN JOY.

SOCIETY OF THE CINCINNATI. Patriotic fraternal organization. The society was founded in 1783 by a group of officers who served under **George Washington** in the American Revolution. They named the club for Roman General Lucius Quinctius Cincinnatus, with whom Washington was frequently and favorably compared. Membership in the society is limited to the direct male descendants of its founders. In 1937 the society acquired Anderson House, an English Baroque mansion built for diplomat Lars Anderson and his wife, writer Isabel Weld Perkins. Completed in 1905, the tan limestone building is the masterpiece of Boston architects Arthur Little and Herbert W. C. Browne. The interior of the house is decorated with vintage furnishings and with portraits of society members by artists such as John Trumbull and Gilbert Stuart. The public is welcome to use its reference library and to view its collection of Revolutionary War artifacts.

SOLDIERS' AND AIRMEN'S HOME. *See* U.S. SOLDIERS' AND AIRMEN'S HOME.

SOURCE THEATRE COMPANY. Professional theater company, specializing in contemporary drama and classic plays staged in modern and unorthodox settings. Founded in 1977 by Bart Whiteman, then a graduate student at **American University**, the company began by performing in various venues around downtown and **Capitol Hill.** In 1980 the company located in a 60-seat theater at 14th and P Streets NW, and in 1982 moved one block north on 14th Street to the Warehouse. In 1999 this facility underwent a $650,000 remodeling, creating a flexible seating configuration for 150 patrons. Since 1981, Source Theatre has produced the Washington Theatre Festival, which annually stages more than 40 new plays. In addition to its regular five productions each year, the theater directs a commercial casting service, student internships, and the "Plays Alive!" outreach program for school children.

SOUSA, JOHN PHILIP (1854–1932). Composer, conductor, and writer. Born in Washington, Sousa was educated in local schools and at the Esputa Conservatory of Music. From age 13 to 20 he served as an apprentice in the U.S. Marine Band. In 1876 Sousa moved to Philadelphia, where he was a theater violinist and conductor. His successful conducting in Philadelphia led to his appointment as the 14th conductor of the U.S. Marine Band (1880), a position he held for 12 years. He then organized his own band, Sousa's Band, which he led for the next 39 years. Sousa composed 136 marches, including "Semper Fidelis" (1888), "The *Washington Post* March" (1889), "El Capitan" (1895), "Stars and Stripes Forever" (1897), and "Hands across the Sea" (1899). His music reflects an era of American patriotism when the United States was becoming a world power. Sousa wrote three novels and an autobiography.

SOUTHARD REPORT (1835). Congressional report on Washington's financial condition, which recommended federal assistance for the city. When the city fell into debt during the early part of the 19th century, a congressional investigation was launched. Headed by Senator Samuel Southard of New Jersey, the committee concluded that the city's debts stemmed from congressionally imposed financial burdens and restrictions, including city maintenance of oversized **streets and avenues** and federal restrictions that prevented the city from developing an adequate tax base. The report recommended that street maintenance be a shared expense between the city and the federal government, but it found no long-term solution to the fiscal woes that plagued the city. A formula of federal funding was established decades later, but many of the same financial issues involved in the city's operation of Washington have resurfaced during later periods of economic distress.

SOUTHWEST. A neighborhood bounded by South Capitol Street, the **Anacostia River**, Washington Channel, and Independence Avenue in Southwest Washington. When Captain **John Smith** of Jamestown sailed up the **Potomac River** in 1608, he met Native American traders who had resided in this area for hundreds of years. During the late 1600s, English immigrants planted tobacco in the area, and after the District of Columbia was formed in 1790, a small town grew up around Greenleaf's Point, a tip of land jutting into the confluence of the Potomac and Anacostia Rivers. Named for James Greenleaf, a fortune-hunting real estate speculator who was soon bankrupt, the point was a strategic site for protection of the new capital city. By 1794 a fort, military arsenal, and federal prison were built; the site now houses **Fort Lesley J. McNair** and the National Defense University. After the **Washington Canal** was built in 1815, the area became known as "The Island," describing its physical and psychological distance from the rest of the city. The Southwest neighborhood had wharves and warehouses, not government buildings, and its residents were tradesmen and laborers, not politicians and clerks.

During the antebellum period, the area was home to a community of free African Americans, including Anthony Bowen, director of a mission and day school for neighborhood youth and a "conductor" on the Underground Railroad. Bowen met escapees at the 6th Street wharf and assisted them on a journey north toward Philadelphia. During the **Civil War**, the docks were used to transport arms, supplies, and troops for the Union Army. A gun and powder factory was also built at the Greenleaf's Point armory. After the war, thousands of emancipated slaves moved to the area, and by 1870 nearly 40 percent of residents were black. That same year, the Washington Canal was filled and replaced by a railway line; new streetcars provided some help in reducing the community's isolation. The area developed into a segregated community, with blacks living mostly east and whites mostly west of 4½ Street. During the 1880s German and Eastern European Jews immigrated to the area. They worked as tailors, butchers, bakers, merchants, and grocers, mostly along 4½ and 7th Streets. Talmud Torah Synagogue was built in 1906 and was led by cantor and rabbi Moses Yoelson; his son became film star **Al Jolson**.

The ominous future of the Southwest neighborhood was foreshadowed around 1900, when federal office buildings and private commercial warehouses, markets, and freight yards began to replace its housing. Noise and pollution increased, while the housing of its absentee landlords deteriorated. The area became blighted and crime-ridden. In 1946 the U.S. Congress chartered the Redevelopment Land Agency (RLA) and provided it with funds for slum clearance, redevelopment, and housing construction. In the spring of 1954, RLA began purchasing Southwest residences and businesses, making no distinction between hovels and well-kept Victorian row houses, without the consent of the dispossessed. Nearly 20,000 residents were displaced, about two-thirds of whom were African Americans. One merchant sued the RLA, charging that the condemnation of his property was unfair and arbitrary. The **U.S. Supreme Court** ruled that the government could legally acquire well-maintained property in a slum clearance area. Many residents received considerably less than the market value of their houses. The Southwest neighborhood was demolished by 1960. Over the next decade, government office buildings, luxury high-rise apartments, and many blocks of public housing projects were built. The 4th and 7th Street shops were replaced by the still half-empty Waterside Mall on 10th Street. Few Washingtonians consider the urban renewal experiment a success.

SOUTHWORTH, E. D. E. N. (1819–1899). Novelist. Emma Dorothy Eliza Nevitte Southworth was Washington's most prolific novelist and one of the most successful female writers of 19th century America. Her father, an Alexandria merchant, was bankrupted during the **War of 1812** and died soon after the birth of his daughter, who grew up in abject poverty in a **Capitol Hill** apartment. In 1840, Southworth married an inventor with whom she moved to a log cabin on the Wisconsin frontier. After their second child was born, he abandoned the family. She returned to Washington, where she taught in the public schools and supplemented her income by

writing. Southworth's 73 novels were "models of Victorian senti-
mentality." Several sold more than one million copies and some
were in print until the 1930s. Her *Retribution* (1849) was the first
American novel to be serialized, in the *National Era*, Washington's only abolitionist newspaper.

SPOFFORD, AINSWORTH RAND. *See* LIBRARY OF CON-
GRESS; MURRAY, DANIEL ALEXANDER PAYNE.

ST. ALOYSIUS ROMAN CATHOLIC CHURCH. *See* SWAMPOO-
DLE.

ST. ANDREW'S EPISCOPAL CHURCH. *See* JOHN WESLEY
AFRICAN METHODIST EPISCOPAL ZION CHURCH.

STATEHOOD. *See* HOME RULE; NORTON, ELEANOR HOLMES.

ST. CHARLES HOTEL. Federal-style hotel located at 3rd Street and
Pennsylvania Avenue NW. Constructed in 1820, the hotel entrance was noted for its four stone columns, originally designed by
Benjamin Latrobe for the **U.S. Capitol** and salvaged from the
building after it was gutted by the British in 1814. The basement of
the hotel served as a holding area for slaves purchased in Washington. During the 1840s and 1850s it was a popular place of residence for U.S. Senators and other government officials. The hotel
gradually declined and closed in 1924.

ST. ELIZABETHS HOSPITAL. Hospital for the mentally ill on
Martin Luther King, Jr., Avenue. formerly Asylum Avenue. The
hospital was founded as a result of the lobbying efforts of Dorothea Dix and other advocates for humane care of the mentally ill. It
opened as the Government Hospital for the Insane in 1855; before
that, mental patients in Washington were sent to a facility in Baltimore. The hospital was built on "St. Elizabeths Tract," a 415-acre
parcel overlooking the **Anacostia River.** The main Gothic Re-
vival-style building, now a historic landmark, was designed by
Thomas U. Walter. During the **Civil War** the hospital took on war
wounded temporarily, and gradually acquired the name "St. Elizabeths Hospital" because some soldiers did not want to tell their
families that they were being treated at the Government Hospital
for the Insane. Congress formalized the name in 1916. The hospital
housed Ezra Pound after his treasonous conduct during World War
II and currently houses John Hinckley, Jr., perpetrator of the
Reagan assassination attempt in 1981. In 1987 the administration

of St. Elizabeths Hospital was transferred from the federal government to the District of Columbia.

STEVENS, ROGER L. (1910–1998). Performing arts executive. Born in Michigan, Stevens dropped out of college during the Great Depression and worked for five years on an automobile assembly line at Ford Motor Company. After naval service in World War II, Stevens earned a fortune in real estate, including urban renewal projects in Southwest Washington and other cities. His financial success permitted a second career in theatrical production. He produced more than 250 plays and musicals, including seminal American works of the 20th century: "West Side Story," "Cat on a Hot Tin Roof," "A Man for All Seasons," and "Death of a Salesman." In 1961 President John F. Kennedy appointed Stevens chair of what was then known as the National Cultural Center. As the center's founding director, he was responsible for transforming a congressional authorization and local dreams into one of the nation's finest performance venues. Over the next 27 years he raised more than $150 million and guided the center's design, construction, maintenance, and programming. He refused to accept compensation for his work and suggested that the center be renamed the **John F. Kennedy Center for the Performing Arts**. Stevens served as President Lyndon Johnson's special assistant for the arts and as the first chair of the National Endowment for the Arts. He received a Kennedy Center Honor and the U.S. Medal of Freedom for his service to the performing arts.

ST. JOHN'S EPISCOPAL CHURCH. One of Washington's most historic buildings and one of its most socially prominent congregations. The church was designed by **Benjamin Henry Latrobe** and constructed in 1816 on the north side of **Lafayette Square** near the **White House**. Of classical design and shaped in the form of a Greek cross, the building featured a gold-colored dome and white interior. In order to accommodate more worshipers, the church was expanded in 1822, changing its shape from a Greek to a Latin cross. Latrobe originally designed the church with a south entrance on H Street, but the new shape of the building required a west entrance, which was fitted with a Doric portico. A wooden bell tower was also added; the bell is cast from a cannon captured from the British in the **War of 1812**. Latrobe not only designed the church, but remained there as its organist and choirmaster. Additional renovations were carried out in 1883 by **James Renwick,** including an extension of the chancel. Many U.S. presidents have been church members and many others have periodically worshipped here. Near the center of the church is pew 54, reserved for presidential visits. The church has more than 900 members. *See also* GREEN, CONSTANCE McLAUGHLIN.

ST. JOHN'S EPISCOPAL CHURCH, GEORGETOWN PARISH. The first Episcopal services were held in **Georgetown** in 1794. Construction of St. John's began on O Street NW in 1796 and the Federal-style stucco building, designed by **U.S. Capitol** architect **William Thornton,** was completed in 1809. **Francis Scott Key** was a member of the church vestry. By 1831 the declining tobacco economy of Georgetown devastated the congregation. The church was put up for sale for unpaid real estate taxes. Banker **William Wilson Corcoran** purchased the church in 1837 and rented it as an artist's studio for $25 a month. As the Georgetown economy recovered, a group of young parish women raised $50 toward the purchase price of the church; Corcoran forgave the rest of the amount and restored the building to the congregation. The church has more than 450 members.

ST. LUKE'S EPISCOPAL CHURCH. One of the oldest African American churches in Washington. Located on 15th Street NW, the origin of St. Luke's Church goes back to 1865, when **St. John's Episcopal Church** helped to organize the predominantly African American **St. Mary's Episcopal Church.** When a group of families from St. Mary's formed a separate congregation in 1873, Alexander Crummell (d. 1898) was hired to be the rector of what is now St. Luke's Church. Crummell proved to be a gifted intellectual who not only led St. Luke's for 23 years but also helped to shape the life of the African American community in Washington. Under his leadership the congregation raised funds to construct a building on 15th Street in 1879. Designed by Calvin T. S. Brent, an African American architect, the church was constructed of bluestone. By 1880 many of the African American members of St. Mary's had transferred to the independent St. Luke's Church. By the end of the century the church had grown to 300 members and during the 1930s membership climbed to over 1,000. In 1960 the church building was razed to make way for a new structure on the same site. Today the church has over 650 members.

ST. MARY'S EPISCOPAL CHURCH. An African American church located on 23rd Street NW. The original members of St. Mary's Church had attended **St. John's Episcopal Church** and the Church of the Epiphany on **Lafayette Square.** An influx of African Americans into the capital, along with an unwillingness to fully integrate city churches, led the two congregations to organize a separate church for African Americans in 1865. A lot was obtained in **Foggy Bottom** on 23rd Street near G Street, and a chapel, originally built for soldiers at Kalorama Hospital, was moved to the site and used for church services. In the early 1870s several families from St. Mary's left the church to begin **St. Luke's Episcopal Church** as a fully independent congregation. In 1886 **James Renwick** was hired by St. John's and the Church of the Epiphany to design the Victorian Gothic building that now occupies the site in Foggy Bottom. Completed in 1887, the church interior features a vaulted wood ceiling, red tile floor, and stenciled walls.

ST. MATTHEW'S CATHEDRAL. Cathedral of the Roman Catholic Archdiocese of Washington. The first St. Matthew's Church was a Greek Revival structure built in 1838 near **Lafayette Square** and named to honor Father William Matthews, pastor of **St. Patrick's Roman Catholic Church,** who was instrumental in developing the new parish. The current building, on Rhode Island Avenue NW, was designed in a neo-Byzantine style by C. Grant LaFarge, architect of the Cathedral of St. John the Divine in New York City, and built between 1893 and 1913. The red brick and sandstone cathedral features five chapels, a red mosaic portrait of St. Matthew by John deRosen, and a 190-foot-high green copper dome topped by a St. Matthew's cross. In 1939 Pope Pius XII established the Archdiocese of Washington and named St. Matthew's as its cathedral. The congregation helped found the Catholic Temperance Union of America, two convents, several social services organizations, and several schools, including St. John's College High School. President John F. Kennedy's funeral was held at St. Matthew's in November 1963.

ST. NICHOLAS CATHEDRAL. Washington's Russian Orthodox parish church. The Russian Orthodox Church of St. Nicholas was founded in 1930 on Riggs Place NW, moving to Church Street NW in 1935. Services were conducted in Russian until 1938. In 1951 the parish purchased a site on Massachusetts Avenue at Edmunds Street NW, where the cathedral was completed in 1962. It was dedicated as a National War Memorial Shrine the following year. From 1991 to 1994, a group of iconographers led by Alexander Moskalionov developed a series of icons for the St. Nicholas narthex, creating works that commemorate the arrival of Russian Orthodoxy in America and several 20th-century Russian tragedies. Since the collapse of the Soviet Union (1989–91), St. Nicholas's membership has included an increasing number of Georgian immigrants.

STODDERT, BENJAMIN (1751–1813). Merchant and first secretary of the navy. Born in Charles County, Maryland, Stoddert was a captain in the Revolutionary War (1777–79), was elected secretary to the Board of War (1779–81), and then went into business with the **Georgetown** firm of Forrest, Stoddert, & Murdock. The company was heavily involved in shipping and trade on the **Potomac River**, and Stoddert acquired vast parcels of land in the District of Columbia. When the site for the new federal city was being planned, **George Washington** asked Stoddert to privately purchase land there for the government. To carry out these transactions, Stoddert organized the **Bank of Columbia** in 1793. He bought land at a lower price than the government would have paid and subsequently transferred the tracts to federal ownership. Although he had a successful tenure as the first secretary of the navy (1798–1801), Stoddert's business took a downward turn and the **War of 1812** left him heavily in debt.

STOKES, THOMAS H. *See* DEANWOOD.

STOWE, HARRIET BEECHER. *See* FREDERICK DOUGLASS NATIONAL HISTORIC SITE; MINER, MYRTILLA; *NATIONAL ERA*.

ST. PATRICK'S ROMAN CATHOLIC CHURCH. First Roman Catholic parish in the Federal City. In January 1794, Archbishop John Carroll appointed Father Anthony Caffry to organize a parish for the Irish artisans and laborers who were constructing the federal government buildings and city streets. Until 1798, when its first chapel was completed at 10th and F Streets NW, the congregation met on the second floor of a brick house a block away. In

1809 **James Hoban**, a parishioner and architect of the **U.S. Capitol**, designed a larger church that faced 10th Street. That church was torn down in 1870, and the congregation worshipped in the parish hall until their Gothic Revival building, designed by Laurence J. O'Connor, was dedicated in 1884. St. Patrick's has pursued a special ministry in education for nearly two centuries. The parish helped establish a Jesuit school for boys in 1815 that still operates as Gonzaga High School; a girls' school in 1825 that, after merging with the Academy of the Visitation, still operates as Georgetown Visitation; St. Patrick's Academy; and the Paul VI Institute for the Arts.

ST. PAUL'S EPISCOPAL CHURCH, ROCK CREEK PARISH. The oldest church in the District of Columbia. The first service was held on the church grounds in 1712. Of Flemish design, the ivy-covered brick structure on Creek Church Road NW dates from 1775. Only one brick wall remains from the original structure. The church's stained-glass windows depict the history of the Eucharist from its sacrificial beginnings in the Old Testament, to the Last Supper of Christ, to the first celebration by the Jamestown, Virginia, settlers in 1607. The adjoining **Rock Creek Cemetery** is the oldest cemetery in the city. The church has about 200 members.

STRAYER REPORT. A 1948 study of the D.C. Public School System authorized by the U.S. Senate Appropriations Subcommittee and conducted by Columbia University professor George Strayer. The report was the first serious attack on the inadequate **public education** staffing and facilities provided for African American students attending segregated D.C. public schools. It recommended spending at least 75 percent of the total school system budget on buildings and equipment for black schools in order to equalize opportunities and instruction for black students. Congress responded with an appropriation to build eight new schools for African Americans, but these schools did not resolve the disparities. Two years later, 11 black students attempted to enroll at the all-white Sousa Junior High School in Southeast Washington, but were turned away; they filed a lawsuit (*Bolling v. Sharpe*), which resulted in court-ordered **school desegregation** in D.C.

STREETS AND AVENUES. In the original city plan of **Pierre Charles L'Enfant**, the streets of Washington were laid out in a grid pattern, overlapped by wide diagonal avenues. When the city was built, north-south streets were assigned numbers and east-west streets letters. **Thomas Jefferson** named the diagonal avenues after the 13 original states. However, as the city expanded, new streets were added and named in such a haphazard fashion that mail delivery became a problem. The street system physically deteriorated during the **Civil War**. Post-Civil War improvements, including new grading, paving, and lighting, were finally made during the 1870s. In 1880 **Georgetown** became part of Washington and its streets were incorporated into the city plan. However, confusion was still evident and in 1899 Congress formulated rules for the naming of streets. These rules, still followed today, specify, in part, that all "north-south streets are numbered consecutively in each direction, commencing at the meridian of the [**U.S. Capitol**]"; "east-west streets are lettered, then given one-, two-, and three-syllable names in alphabetical order . . . of distinguished Americans. . . . The streets that follow should be named for members of the plant kingdom in alphabetical order"; "diagonals are named for states and territories of the United States"; "streets not part of the rectangular plan are designated roads, drives, places, courts, etc."; and "circles are named after individuals who have been prominent in their service to the country." The large task of renaming the streets and avenues of the city was completed in 1904, with the result that very few of the original street names remained.

STRIVERS' SECTION. *See* DUPONT CIRCLE; SHAW/U STREET.

ST. SOPHIA CATHEDRAL. Washington's oldest Greek Orthodox congregation. The first Greek Orthodox worship service was held in 1904 by a small group of Greek immigrants, who named their church after the renowned Hagia Sophia of Istanbul, Turkey. Land was purchased at 8th and L Streets NW in 1913, but eight years elapsed before a small church was built on the site. In 1943 the congregation purchased its present site at 36th Street and Massachusetts Avenue NW, but did not break ground for its cathedral until 1951. President Dwight D. Eisenhower helped lay the cathedral's cornerstone in September 1956. Scholars from Harvard University's Center for Byzantine Studies at **Dumbarton Oaks** planned and created the church's iconography, primarily executed in mosaic, and patterned after art of the 10th-century Macedonian Dynasty. In 1990 Archbishop Demetrios I, spiritual leader of the Eastern Orthodox Church, conducted the first patriarchal worship service in North America at the cathedral.

STUART, GILBERT. *See* SOCIETY OF THE CINCINNATI; WAR OF 1812.

STUDIO THEATRE. Midsize live theater company. The theater was founded in 1987 by director Joy Zinoman and designer Russell Metheny as an outgrowth of Zinoman's drama school, the Acting Conservatory, originally located in an old hot dog warehouse. In 1987 Studio leased the historic Peerless Motor Company building, a 1919 Italian Renaissance Revival automotive showroom at 14th and P Streets NW. With assistance from the Meyer Foundation, Studio Theatre purchased the building in 1991 and completed an extensive remodeling of the property in 1997. The facility includes two 200-seat auditoriums, the Milton Theatre and the Mead Theatre, scenery and costume construction shops, rehearsal studios, and classrooms for the Acting Conservatory. Studio produces five to six plays each season, ranging from classic drama to contemporary works to performance art. The Arts Motivating Youth project offers free student matinee performances, ticket discounts, and scholarships to the Acting Conservatory to at-risk youth in the Washington area.

SUBURBAN GARDENS AMUSEMENT PARK. *See* DEANWOOD.

SUBWAY. *See* WASHINGTON METRORAIL SYSTEM.

SUFFRAGE. *See* WOMEN'S SUFFRAGE PARADE.

SULGRAVE CLUB. Social club. Located on **Dupont Circle** at the corner of Massachusetts Avenue, the building was originally a private residence built by Martha and Herbert Wadsworth in 1901. The Red Cross occupied the house during World War I and in 1932 it was purchased by a group of Washington socialites who named it after **George Washington's** ancestral home, Sulgrave Manor, in England. The private club welcomes guests from Washington's social and political elite. Its second floor oval drawing room has a commanding view of Dupont Circle.

SUMNER SCHOOL MUSEUM AND ARCHIVES. The first public high school for African American students in the United States. Designed by architect **Adolph Cluss** and opened at 17th and M Streets NW in 1872, Sumner School also housed an elementary school and the offices of the superintendent and trustees of the Colored Public School Systems of Washington City and **Georgetown**. The school was named for Senator Charles Sumner of Massachusetts, who advocated integrated **public education**, abolition of **slavery** in the District of Columbia, repudiation of fugitive slave laws, and establishment of the Freedmen's Bureau. The adjacent Magruder School was built in 1887 to relieve Sumner's overcrowding. In 1979 a portion of the Sumner School roof collapsed and school officials expected to demolish the building. Instead, it was beautifully restored between 1980 and 1986 and reopened as a museum, archive, and cultural center.

SUNDERLAND, BYRON (1819–1900). Presbyterian minister and U.S. Senate chaplain. Born in Shoreham, Vermont, Sunderland graduated from Middlebury College (1838) and Union Theological Seminary in New York (1843). He served a Presbyterian church in Batavia (1843–51) and Park Presbyterian Church in Syracuse (1851–53), New York, and then moved to Washington to become the pastor of First Presbyterian Church (1853–98). He remained in Washington during the **Civil War** and served as chaplain of the Senate from 1861 to 1864. He was a confidant of President Abraham Lincoln and later formed close friendships with Presidents James Garfield and Grover Cleveland and other government officials. From 1873 to 1879 Sunderland again served as Senate chaplain. He was president of the board of directors of **Howard University**, served on the first board of **Gallaudet University**, and was a board member of several hospitals and charitable organizations.

SURRATT, MARY ELIZABETH JENKINS (1823–1865). Born in Clinton, Maryland, in 1840 Surratt moved with her husband to a farm in Washington. In 1852 the Surratt family inherited a large sum of money and bought a 278-acre tract of land in Prince George's County, Maryland, where they opened a general store and saloon, which also served as the community's post office and polling place. After the death of her husband, Surratt leased the property to John M. Lloyd and moved to Washington in 1864, where she operated a boarding house on H Street. It was here that John Wilkes Booth met with other conspirators to plan the **Lincoln assassination**. Three days after the assassination, Surratt was arrested, and then tried, convicted, and executed. Surratt may have had sympathies toward the South, and her boarding house may have become a place of refuge for alienated Confederates, but her guilt in the plot is still in question. The prosecution's principal witness was Lloyd, there were flaws in the proceedings of the trial, and some have wondered if Surratt's Catholic religion influenced the outcome.

SUTER'S TAVERN. **Georgetown** tavern; site of key events in the founding of Washington. The single-story frame building, originally called the Fountain Inn, was built in the late 1700s by **Robert Peter**, first **mayor** of Georgetown. The tavern was commonly known by the name of its proprietor, John Suter, who operated the business until 1800. In March 1791 **George Washington** and city commissioners met there with local landowners. Washington had chosen a site for the federal capital city, and he successfully persuaded these landowners to sell parcels of land to the government for $66.67 per acre. In September 1791 city commissioners **Daniel Carroll**, David Stuart, and Thomas Johnson met at the tavern and named the new federal city Washington. Suter's Tavern also served as headquarters for **Pierre Charles L'Enfant** and **Andrew Ellicott**, who worked on the city plan. In 1792 John Lockwood opened Georgetown's first lending library in the tavern building. The controversial election of 1801 was settled at the tavern in the favor of **Thomas Jefferson**. The building was razed in the mid-19th century, and today historians dispute its exact location.

SWAMPOODLE. A 19th-century neighborhood along North Capitol Street, between F and K Streets. Although it began as a working-class neighborhood for the mostly Irish employees of the U.S. Government Printing Office (built in 1856) and parishioners of St. Aloysius Roman Catholic Church (built in 1859), Swampoodle is remembered as a disreputable, crime-ridden shantytown on the swampy banks of Tiber Creek. It was once called "the ideal place to turn a dishonest dollar." Swampoodle's residents were vociferously loyal to the Union during the **Civil War**, although a few made wartime fortunes fencing stolen government property. During the 1870s, notorious Irish gangs led by Matt Roch and Doggie McGraw were headquartered in Swampoodle. When the area was absorbed into the more proper and upstanding **Capitol Hill** neighborhood, Swampoodle's petty criminals moved to Murder Bay, along **Pennsylvania Avenue**. **Union Station**, office buildings, and more substantial housing are now located on the site of the once-infamous neighborhood.

SYLVAN THEATRE. Outdoor amphitheatre on the grounds of the Washington Monument. In 1916, **Alice Pike Barney**, a wealthy patroness and practitioner of the arts, approached W. W. Hartz, superintendent of public buildings and grounds for the National Park Service, with a proposal for an outdoor theater. Barney envisioned a performance venue for Shakespearean and classical dramas. The skeptical Hartz doubted Congress's willingness to appropriate $600 for such a venture, but Barney was eventually successful. More than 15,000 people attended the Sylvan's opening performance in 1917. The original theater was a grassy knoll bordered with evergreens. Several years after the opening, a stage with a proscenium was constructed. In recent years, the Sylvan has presented mostly military, big band, and pop music concerts.

- T -

TAFT, WILLIAM HOWARD (1857–1930). Twenty-seventh president of the United States. A graduate of Yale University (1878), Taft practiced law in Ohio, served as a judge on the Ohio superior court, and held several federal judicial posts. After the Spanish-American War (1898), President William McKinley appointed him to the Second Philippine Commission (1900) and Taft became a popular governor of the Philippines (1901–04). President Theodore Roosevelt named him secretary of war, and in 1908 he was elected president. During his one-term presidency (1909–13), Taft tried to reorganized the federal government and reduce the size of its budget and its Washington work force. Although Congress largely rejected Taft's proposals, the president did succeed in carrying out some reforms through executive order and through his Commission on Economy and Efficiency. He cut 400 jobs in the Treasury Department and reduced military appropriations. He left his mark on Washington by supporting redevelopment plans along the **Mall**, the purchase of new parklands, and the establishment of the **Commission of Fine Arts**. His wife Helen supported efforts to bring **cherry blossoms** to the **Tidal Basin**. Taft later taught at Yale Law School and served as chief justice of **U.S. Supreme Court** (1921–30).

TAKOMA PARK. An area of the District located along Eastern Avenue in Northwest Washington, adjacent to Takoma Park, Maryland. In 1862 Benjamin Franklin Gilbert arrived in Washington from New York State. A real estate developer and opportunist, Gilbert took advantage of the city's post-**Civil War** population growth and federal government expansion. In 1883, a decade after construction of the Metropolitan Branch of the Baltimore and Ohio Railroad from downtown Washington to Point of Rocks, Maryland, Gilbert bought 90 acres of land along the boundary between D.C. and Montgomery County, Maryland. Gilbert called the subdivision "Takoma Park," choosing an alternate spelling of the Native American word "tacoma," (meaning "high up, near heaven") in order to distinguish his town from Tacoma, Washington.

Uninterested in jurisdictional boundaries, the developer placed the subdivision on both sides of the state line. By 1888 Gilbert had purchased, subdivided, and developed 1,000 acres. Most residences were build for middle-class families—he extensively marketed to federal workers—although Takoma Park included grand houses, a business district, and a resort hotel. The residences featured a range of architectural styles, including Queen Anne, Stick, Shingle, Colonial Revival, and Victorian Eclectic. A cohort of scientists from the Department of Agriculture located in the neighborhood and conducted extensive azalea-breeding experiments, beautifying their neighborhood in pursuit of their research.

Gilbert persuaded Boston physician R. C. Flower to buy land above Sligo Creek for a sanitarium, which was never built. In 1903 the Seventh Day Adventist Church purchased the Flower land and relocated their national headquarters from Battle Creek, Michigan, to Takoma Park, constructing a headquarters building, publishing house, Washington Training College, and Washington Sanitarium, which was later named Washington Adventist Hospital.

During the 1890s, the trains of the Metropolitan Branch were joined with the **Brightwood** Railway streetcar line from Georgia Avenue and the line of Capital Traction from 14th Street. The Panic of 1893 dramatically affected the neighborhood, and the overextended, cash-poor Gilbert was forced to sell his mansion and move into the North Takoma Hotel. No single developer followed in Gilbert's footsteps, but several businessmen created smaller subdivisions, ranging from modest properties to large residences for the wealthy. Between 1920 and 1940, the population of Takoma Park nearly tripled as the availability of automobiles and new highway construction made the suburbs more desirable.

In the postwar period, Takoma Park's business district declined as residents drove to newly built shopping centers on Georgia and New Hampshire Avenues. African Americans began moving to Takoma Park in the early 1960s. Local residents joined with those in Manor Park and **Shepherd Park** to form Neighbors, Inc., an advocacy group that worked to establish an integrated community and to oppose the block-busting techniques of exploitative real estate agents. In 1964 black and white neighbors joined to block construction of the North Central Freeway, and 10 years later they defeated plans to rezone the Maryland side for more dense land use. The community's tradition of liberal activism, including recycling, preservation of green space, and antinuclear advocacy has resulted in the nickname, "People's Republic of Takoma Park." In the early 1980s, a subway stop was opened in the community, and Gilbert's earliest subdivisions were listed on the National Register of Historic Places.

TALMUD TORAH SYNAGOGUE. *See* SOUTHWEST.

TELEVISION. *See* W3XK.

TEMPERANCE FOUNTAIN. Dry fountain at Indiana Plaza, at the corner of 7th Street and **Pennsylvania Avenue** NW. Once offering drinking water, the Temperance Fountain was a gift of Henry Daniel Cogswell, a dentist who grew wealthy in the California Gold Rush and spent some of his fortune designing water fountains, which he offered to cities across the United States. Cogswell hoped that by providing free drinking water he could keep people out of taverns. The Washington Temperance Fountain, one of a number of Cogswell fountains installed around the country, of which very few now remain, was accepted by joint resolution of Congress in 1882. Erected in 1884, the design features two entwined dolphins under a canopy, and a water crane on top of the canopy, symbolizing the purity of water over liquor. The fountain's Greek columns are inscribed with the words Faith, Hope, Charity, and Temperance.

TEMPLE OF FREEDOM UNDER GOD, CHURCH OF GOD. Nondenominational church founded by Elder Lightfoot Solomon Michaux (1885–1968) in a Georgia Avenue NW storefront in

1928. Michaux conducted mass baptisms, marriages, healing ceremonies, and religious pageants on boats sailing down the **Potomac
River** and later in **Griffith Stadium**. By the mid-1960s, he was
one of the best-known African Americans in the United States, due
to his national Saturday morning "Happy Am I" CBS radio broadcast. At the height of the Great Depression, the Temple of Freedom
opened the Happy News Cafe, selling lunches for a penny a plate;
in 1934 they served more than 250,000 meals at a significant financial loss to the congregation. In 1942 the church bought the 34-
acre Benning Race Track on Kenilworth Avenue NE and built
Mayfair Gardens on the Parkway, now known as Mayfair Mansions, the nation's first federally subsidized housing for African
Americans, most of whom had been evicted from houses demolished for construction of federal office buildings. Mayfair was designed by Albert I. Cassell, founder of the **Howard University**
School of Architecture, and includes 17 three-story Colonial Revival garden apartment buildings overlooking the **Anacostia
River**. At the time of its construction in 1958, the $335,000 temple
on Georgia Avenue NW was the most expensive African American
church building in the United States.

TENLEYTOWN. An area in Northwest Washington that has as its
center the junction of Wisconsin Avenue and River Road. The history of Tenleytown is inextricably linked to regional transportation
history. Wisconsin Avenue, the neighborhood's main artery, was
once a Native American trail and later a westward passage for
early European settlers. By the mid-18th century, the ancient path
was the main road from Frederick, Maryland, to **Georgetown**, the
route down which tobacco farmers rolled barrels of their crops to
waiting schooners headed for London and Amsterdam. In 1755 the
soldiers of British General Edward Braddock widened the road on
their way to Fort Duquesne (now Pittsburgh) and their ill-fated ex-
pedition against the French.

Although Charles Calvert, Lord Baltimore, had granted the
3,000-acre "Friendship" to Thomas Addison and James Stoddert in
1713, the first homestead in the area was built by Addison's grandson, John Murdock, around 1760. A generation later, Jacob Funk,
the developer of Hamburgh (**Foggy Bottom**), improved River
Road and extended it, parallel with the **Potomac River**, to Harpers
Ferry. In 1791, when the area was included in the newly formed

District of Columbia, John Tennally's crossroads tavern was thriving, and Tennallytown was a regular stop for travelers to and from Georgetown and the new capital city. In 1818 Tennallytown Road became the southeastern link in the Great National Road, from Washington to Wheeling on the Ohio River. By 1827 travelers had become annoyed by the road's poor quality and fear of stagecoach accidents led them to form the Washington Turnpike Company, which paved the road to Frederick.

Tenleytown was a crucial site during the **Civil War** because Washington's highest hill is located there, rising 430 feet above sea level. In 1861 the land was part of the Dyer farm, and on their hill the U.S. government built Fort Pennsylvania, later renamed Fort Reno. The Union soldiers stationed there provided backup support during the Confederate attack on the **7th Street** turnpike in 1864. After the war, the Dyer family subdivided and sold their property, mostly to African Americans who had been released from **slavery**. The 60 houses that comprised Reno City were built on the site of the fort. At the end of the 19th century, Victorian frame cottages were built by the working-class farmers, butchers, stonemasons, police officers, and streetcar drivers who began traversing Wisconsin Avenue in 1890. A few of these houses still stand along Grant Road and 41st Street.

A century of disagreement about the correct spelling of the town's name (Tenallytown, Tenley Town, Tennelleytown, or Tennallytown) was resolved by the U.S. Post Office in 1920 in favor of Tenleytown. The town's real estate developers filled the area with new middle-class housing to meet the needs of Washington's expanding post-World War I population. As construction proceeded, the long-residing African American families of Reno City were displaced from their homes. In 1928 federal and local agencies took additional black properties to construct a water reservoir and tower. Two years later, Congress acquired what remained of the fort site as a recreation area for inclusion in Washington's Civil War fort parks. In 1935 the last residents were forced out for construction of Alice Deal Junior High and Woodrow Wilson High School. Reno City had vanished without a trace.

After World War II, transportation improvements further altered Tenleytown. In 1936 the intersection of Nebraska and Wisconsin Avenues—Tenley Circle—became a crowded bus and streetcar terminus. During the 1940s, chain stores such as Sears

Roebuck, **Giant Food**, and Peoples Drug forced neighborhood shops to close. During the 1960s Wisconsin Avenue became a shopping and entertainment corridor, with movie theaters, restaurants, bars, and the accompanying automotive traffic. When the Tenleytown subway stop opened in 1984, housing prices escalated dramatically, and there was a boom in office and commercial construction in the now-urban community.

TERRA COTTA STATION. *See* TRAIN WRECK OF 1906.

TERRELL, MARY CHURCH (1863–1954). Civil rights leader and an advocate of women's suffrage. After completing a master's degree at Oberlin College, Mary Church taught Latin at M Street High School in Washington, and in 1891 she married her supervisor, Robert Terrell. He later became the city's first African American judge. The Terrells went through a lengthy and humiliating battle to buy a house. They finally moved to **LeDroit Park**, near **Howard University**, when the white employer of a black friend purchased a house and then sold it to the couple. Terrell, known as "Lady Mollie," served 24 years on the D.C. School Board and was a 30-year participant in the Women's Suffrage Movement. She was founding president of the National Association of Colored Women, helped establish the **National Association for the Advancement of Colored People** (NAACP), and provided leadership in several other civil rights organizations. In 1953, she sued Thompson's Restaurant for refusing her service, winning a landmark **U.S. Supreme Court** decision that prohibited segregation in public places in the nation's capital.

TERRITORIAL ACT. *See* DISTRICT TERRITORIAL ACT.

TERRITORIAL GOVERNMENT. *See* SHEPHERD, ALEXANDER ROBEY "BOSS."

TEXTILE MUSEUM. A museum devoted to the preservation, study, and display of handmade textile art. Located on S Street NW, the Textile Museum was founded in 1925 by George Hewitt Myers. Beginning with Myers's private collection of 335 textile works, the museum now holds more than 16,000 objects spanning 5,000 years. The museum's holdings emphasize the textile traditions of non-Western cultures: East Asian, Southeast Asian, and Middle Eastern, as well as African and Central American. In addition, the museum holds temporary exhibitions of such materials as American quilts and it houses a nonlending library of more than 15,000 books and 100 journal titles on the subject of textile arts. The museum occupies two adjacent buildings in the **Kalorama** neighborhood: a house designed in 1913 by **John Russell Pope**, which had been the home of George Hewitt Myers; and an adjacent building, designed in 1908 by Washington architect Waddy B. Wood.

THEATER DISTRICT. *See* SHAW/U STREET.

THEODORE ROOSEVELT ISLAND. An 88-acre island in the **Potomac River.** Before the founding of Washington, Native Americans called the island Analostan. When King Charles patented the land to Lord Baltimore, it was called "My Lord's Island." For more than a century the island was known as Mason's Island, after the Mason family, who used it for raising sheep and built a summer house and gardens there. During the **Civil War** the Union Army used the island for troop encampment, for the First U.S. Colored Troops, among others. After the war it became a popular picnic spot. In 1931 the island was acquired by the Theodore Roosevelt Memorial Association, with the intention of honoring Roosevelt's accomplishments with an outdoor memorial and nature preserve. The memorial, dedicated in 1967, features a 17-foot bronze statue of Roosevelt, sculpted by Paul Manship, standing in the center of a moated granite plaza, designed by Eric Gugler. The rest of the island is untouched except for several miles of hiking trails. The National Park Service manages the island, which is accessible from Virginia by a footbridge.

THOMAS JEFFERSON BUILDING. *See* LIBRARY OF CONGRESS.

THOMPSON BUILDING. *See* DISTRICT OF COLUMBIA v. THOMPSON COMPANY.

THORNTON, WILLIAM (1759–1828). First architect of the **U.S. Capitol**. Thornton was born in the West Indies and studied medicine in Scotland. A British subject who became a U.S. citizen, Thornton rarely practiced medicine, but was a self-taught architect. In 1792 he entered a contest for the design for the U.S. Capitol, and although his plan was submitted after the contest had closed, it was judged the winner by **George Washington**. Thornton's prize for the winning design was $500 and one Washington City lot. In 1794 Thornton was appointed one of three Washington city commissioners, charged with overseeing the layout of the new city and the construction of government buildings, including the Capitol. He worked on the project until 1802, when he quarreled with other architects who had more training. Although the Capitol design was modified many times, important aspects of the finished building reflect Thornton's original plan. In 1802 Thornton accepted an appointment as the first superintendent of the Patent Office, a post he held in Washington until his death. Thornton designed other Washington buildings, including the **Octagon House** and **Tudor Place**. *See also* SNOW RIOTS.

TIDAL BASIN. Reservoir dredged in 1897 by the Army Corps of Engineers to manage the waters of the **Potomac River**. The flood of 1881 came close to the **White House** and the **U.S. Capitol**, and some action by Congress was needed to correct the problem. Also, when the estuary waters of the Potomac receded, boats were sometimes stranded and sewage and malarial mosquitoes would collect. The Tidal Basin was dredged to provide water that could be channeled into the harbor. During the 1890s army engineer Peter C. Hains supervised the creation of the Tidal Basin, **Potomac Park**, and the site of the **Lincoln Memorial**. From 1917 to 1925 the Tidal Basin was a popular recreational area, with imported sand and a bathhouse; the beach was located on the site of the **Jefferson Memorial**. The Tidal Basin today is famous for the Japanese cherry trees along its banks that bloom each spring as Washington celebrates its **Cherry Blossom** Festival.

TOBACCO. *See* GEORGETOWN.

TOWERS, JOHN. *See* KNOW-NOTHING RIOTS.

TRAIN WRECK OF 1906. Train disaster at Terra Cotta Station in Northwest Washington. On December 30 a B&O Railroad locomotive smashed into the back of a local train, which had been en route to Washington from Frederick, Maryland. The locomotive was going more than 60 miles per hour and pulling six empty coach cars. The local train was crowded with holiday passengers, who were standing in the aisles. The rear coach cars of the passenger train burst into splinters on impact, and 46 people were killed and 79 injured. The accident, which was blamed on a signal error, created a terrible scene of bloody wreckage strewn over a quarter mile of track.

TRANSPORTATION. *See* AIR FLORIDA PLANE CRASH; CHESA-

PEAKE AND OHIO CANAL NATIONAL HISTORIC PARK; McMILLAN REPORT; PATOWMACK CANAL; TRAIN WRECK OF 1906; UNION STATION; WASHINGTON METRORAIL SYSTEM.

TRUE REFORMERS HALL. National historic landmark, constructed in 1903 on U Street NW for the United Order of True Reformers, a nonsecret fraternal benevolent society founded in 1881 to provide life insurance for African Americans. Designed by architect John A. Lankford, the five-story brick and limestone building attracted more than 100,000 persons to its dedication, proud of the complete African American control and creativity behind the project. In its early years, the hall housed a variety of retail, entertainment, and vocational establishments, including a room where **Duke Ellington**'s early performances were held and a drill room and armory for Washington's black national guard unit, the first Americans mustered into the defense of Washington as the United States entered World War I. The True Reformers declared bankruptcy in 1910 and the building passed through a series of owners. It was a popular dance hall for several years, and after 1937 housed the Metropolitan Police Boys Club #2, the city's only such venue for black children. In recent years, the building fell into disrepair, but in 1999 it was purchased by the Public Welfare Foundation, which is undertaking a full restoration of the property for use as its headquarters. *See also* SHAW/U STREET.

TRUMAN ASSASSINATION ATTEMPT. Incident on November 1, 1950, at **Blair House**, in which Puerto Rican nationalists tried to kill President Harry Truman. The conspirators, Oscar Collazo and Griselio Torresola, sought Puerto Rican independence, and hoped that if they assassinated the U.S. president, the ensuing political disorder would help their cause. Collazo and Torresola came to Washington and checked into a hotel near Blair House, where Truman was living while the **White House** was under renovation. The following day they approached Blair House when the president was inside and started firing in an attempt to get past the guards and into the building. In the shootout that followed, one member of the president's security detail was killed and two others were wounded, and Torresola was killed. Truman was not hurt, nor was his schedule interrupted by the incident. Collazo was sentenced to life in prison, but was released almost 30 years later by President Jimmy Carter.

TUCKER, ROSINA HARVEY (1882–1987). Union organizer and civil rights leader. Born in Washington, Tucker was raised on 4th Street NW. During the early 1920s she joined the **Fifteenth Street Presbyterian Church** and remained a member for 65 years. In the 1930s she helped to organize the Brotherhood of Sleeping Car Porters, the first black union in the United States. Tucker traveled to railroad stations across the country to recruit members for the union, and in 1937 the first contract was signed between the union and the Pullman Company. Thereafter, she became deeply involved in the civil rights movement, picketing businesses and stores that discriminated against African Americans and helping to organize the 1968 **March on Washington for Jobs and Freedom**.

TUDOR PLACE. Neoclassical mansion on 31st Street in **Georgetown**. The building features two wings constructed in 1794 by Francis Loundes, who intended to add a main house between them. In 1805 Loundes sold the unfinished structure to Thomas and Martha Custis Peter (granddaughter of Martha Washington), who commissioned **William Thornton** to design a main house and redesign the wing buildings. The stucco-covered brick mansion, completed in 1816, features a two-story circular portico with four Tuscan columns. During the **Civil War**, Tudor Place was owned by Britannia Peter Kennon, who was sympathetic to the Confederacy. In an effort to prevent Tudor Place from being commandeered as a Union hospital, she offered it as a boarding house for Union officers. The Peter family still owns Tudor Place, but the house is operated as a private museum, displaying a collection of family artifacts, including many items that belonged to Martha and **George Washington**.

- U -

U STREET. *See* SHAW/U STREET.

UNDERGROUND RAILROAD. *See* GRIFFING, JOSEPHINE SOPHIE WHITE; MOUNT ZION CEMETERY; MOUNT ZION UNITED METHODIST CHURCH; OCTAGON HOUSE; SLAVERY; SOUTHWEST.

UNIFICATION CHURCH. Washington temple of the religious sect founded by Sun Myung Moon (b. 1920). Located on 16th Street NW, the church building was the former Washington Chapel of the

Church of Jesus Christ of Latter Day Saints (Mormon) built in 1932. Architect Don C. Young, Jr., a grandson of Mormon leader Brigham Young, based his design on the Mormon Temple in Salt Lake City, and it was constructed of bird's eye marble quarried in Utah. The sect is controversial not only for its teachings, but also for its far-reaching business empire. Washington holdings include the *Washington Times* newspaper and the Kirov Ballet Academy.

UNION STATION. Train station that for more than five decades served as the main point of arrival in Washington. Constructed in 1907 at the intersection of Massachusetts and Delaware Avenues NE, the huge granite building united its predecessor Baltimore & Potomac and Baltimore & Ohio stations into a single passenger terminal. The $25 million terminal was one of the first fruits of the **McMillan Report** of 1902. With its immense size, a triple-arched entrance inspired by Rome's Arch of Constantine, an interior modeled after the Baths of Diocletian, and a main concourse featuring a 96-foot-high barrel-vaulted ceiling, the station is a masterpiece of the Beaux-Arts style of architecture championed by its designer, **Daniel H. Burnham.** An increase in automobile and air travel during the 1950s and 1960s caused a reduction in the demand for rail service, and the station declined. In the 1970s, as part of the U.S. bicentennial celebration, the station was made into a national visitors center; this center remained open for only two years (1976–78) and proved to be a costly failure. In 1981 Congress acted to restore the station to its original splendor and make it financially self-sufficient by incorporating 200,000 square feet of retail space (shops and restaurants), 100,000 square feet of office space, and 200,000 square feet of Amtrak passenger facilities and a **Washington Metrorail** subway connection. The $160 million restoration was completed in 1988.

UNIONTOWN. *See* ANACOSTIA.

UNITED HOUSE OF PRAYER FOR ALL PEOPLE. An independent church and religious denomination. Located on M Street NW, the church was founded by Charles M. "Sweet Daddy" Grace (1882–1960), who built his denomination into a three-million-member church. Members tithe, abstain from tobacco and alcohol, and marry only within the church membership. Grace—who maintained long red, white, and blue fingernails and a leonine mane of hair—preached spontaneously, "by appointment with God," and once baptized some 200 converts with a fire hose in the middle of M Street before 15,000 observers. Under the leadership of his successor, Bishop Walter "Sweet Daddy" McCullough, United House of Prayer has constructed several day care centers and retirement homes and now has affiliate congregations in 24 states. Each Christmas season since 1968, the episcopal residence on North Portal Drive NW is transformed into a spectacular holiday display featuring more than a million individual lights, moving reindeer, and a life-size nativity scene.

UNITED STATES THEATRE. First legitimate theater built in the District of Columbia. Designed by **James Hoban** and built at E and **7th Street**s NW, adjacent to **Blodgett's Hotel**, the theater opened in 1800 and was demolished by fire in 1836. The United States Theatre was the only public building in Washington not destroyed by the British during the invasion in the **War of 1812**.

UNIVERSAL FRANCHISE ASSOCIATION OF THE DISTRICT OF COLUMBIA. *See* GRIFFING, JOSEPHINE SOPHIE WHITE.

U.S. BOTANIC GARDEN. The national garden of the United States. Located across from the **U.S. Capitol** on First Street SW, the U.S. Botanic Garden was established by Congress in 1820 and its collection was developed by the Columbian Institute for the Promotion of Arts and Sciences in Washington, D.C. The garden now consists of the Conservatory, Bartholdi Park, and the National Garden. Completed in 1933, the Conservatory is a 40,000-square-foot Victorian facility that joins an iron-and-glass greenhouse and stone orangeries. A $33 million renovation of the Conservatory was begun in 1997. Bartholdi Park is famous for its colorful displays of annuals and for its cast-iron fountain (installed in 1932) designed by Frédéric-Auguste Bartholdi, the sculptor of the Statue of Liberty. The National Garden is a new, three-acre garden being developed adjacent to the Conservatory. Construction began in 1998 on a site that will include an Environmental Learning Center, Water Garden, Rose Garden, Showcase Garden, Butterfly Garden, and Lawn Terrace.

U.S. CAPITOL. The central building of the U.S. Congress. The 19th-century neoclassical Capitol building has been used for two centuries by the Senate and the House of Representatives. The building is composed of five levels and more than 540 rooms and is surrounded by 50 acres of grounds. Since it was first built, the Capitol has been burned, rebuilt, extended, and restored. The site of the Capitol was chosen in 1791 by **Pierre Charles L'Enfant** and **George Washington**, as part of the original plan for the federal city. They chose a spot on the east end of the **Mall**, on a plateau called Jenkins Hill, which L'Enfant called "a pedestal awaiting a monument." Washington initiated a contest for an architectural plan, and in 1793 **William Thornton** won with a design for a building with three parts: a domed main building and two wings, one for the Senate and one for the House of Representatives. The project was undertaken using stones that were cut and transported by slave labor from a sandstone quarry in Virginia.

In 1800, when the seat of government moved from Philadelphia to Washington, the Capitol building was still almost 30 years from completion, but the Congress, the **Library of Congress**, and the **U.S. Supreme Court** moved into the unfinished structure. In 1803 President **Thomas Jefferson** appointed **Benjamin Henry Latrobe** to be successor to Thornton as Capitol architect. During the **War of 1812**, British troops tried to burn down this symbol of American democracy, but weather intervened, and a downpour prevented the Capitol's destruction. Still, the building suffered damage, and for several years the Congress had to meet elsewhere, including in the **Old Brick Capitol**. Restoration after the fire was directed by Latrobe until he was succeeded in 1818 by **Charles Bulfinch**; by 1819 the building was ready to be used again, and in 1829 it was finished. As the country grew over the next 20 years, the Capitol building became too small to house the Congress, so in 1850 another Capitol design contest was initiated, this time for the building's expansion. A plan by Thomas U. Walter for House and Senate wings was chosen, and Walter was appointed Capitol architect. Walter's job was complicated in 1851, when the Library of Congress section of the building was destroyed by fire. It would be almost 50 years before the Library of Congress moved out of the Capitol to occupy its own buildings.

In 1855 the copper dome was replaced by a cast-iron dome, and in 1863 Thomas Crawford's bronze statue of Freedom was placed at the top. The function of the Capitol building shifted during the **Civil War**, as did that of many buildings in the city; it served the U.S. military as a barracks, a hospital, and a bakery. The building's interior beauty was still a priority even in wartime; Italian-born artist Constantino Brumidi painted Renaissance-inspired frescos and murals throughout the Capitol building from 1855 to 1880. During the 1880s, marble terraces designed by landscape architect **Frederick Law Olmsted** were added to the exterior. Before the end of the 19th century, the building was outfitted with electric lighting and modern plumbing. In 1935 Supreme Court moved out to occupy a separate building. In the second half of the 20th century, much of the Capitol was restored to its original appearance, and the sandstone front was redone in limestone.

U.S. ELECTRIC COMPANY. *See* POTOMAC ELECTRIC POWER COMPANY.

U.S. HOLOCAUST MEMORIAL MUSEUM. The national institution for the study and interpretation of the Holocaust, and a memorial to the 11 million Jews and other ethnic and political prisoners killed by the Nazis between 1933 and 1945. With the help of author and concentration camp survivor Elie Wiesel, planning for the museum began in 1979. Designed by James Ingo Freed and built on donated federal land near the **Mall**, the three-story museum was opened in 1993. Visitors walk through a Hall of Witness to view a permanent exhibition that includes thousands of photographs, films, video- and audio-taped oral histories, artifacts, and documents. An upper floor contains a railroad boxcar that had been used to transport Jews from Warsaw, Poland, to the Treblinka death camp. A Hall of Remembrance provides a place for visitors to engage in moral and spiritual reflection.

U.S. NATIONAL ARBORETUM. A 444-acre garden and forest preserve. Located two miles from the **U.S. Capitol** on New York Avenue NE, the arboretum conducts research and educational programs and displays trees, shrubs, and plants from around the world. The site was purchased by the government in 1927 as a forest preserve and is now operated by the Department of Agriculture. Its collections include flowering azaleas and dogwoods (late April and May), boxwood shrubs, bonsai and herb gardens, native plants, and other gardens. Nine miles of roads are used for walking, bicycling, and driving through the preserve.

U.S. NAVAL OBSERVATORY. The official distributor of information for accurate navigation and fundamental astronomy in the United States, and the source of U.S. standard time. Located on

Massachusetts Avenue NW, the observatory was established in 1830 to care for the Navy's charts, chronometers, and other navigational equipment. The Depot of Charts and Instruments, as it was then called, moved to **Foggy Bottom** in 1844. Reorganized as the Naval Observatory, the agency expanded its mission to include scientific observation of the heavenly bodies and measurements related to the speed of light. In 1855 the agency began publishing almanacs for astronomers and navigators. It was here in 1877 that Asaph Hall discovered the two moons of Mars. In order to improve the quality of its observations, the agency moved to its present location in 1893. Its main buildings were designed by Richard Mossis Hunt. Among these buildings is a Victorian superintendent's house that has served since 1974 as the official residence of the vice president of the United States.

U.S. SOLDIERS' AND AIRMEN'S HOME. Residential home for some 1,150 veterans. Located on 320 acres at Rock Creek Church Road and Upshur Street NW, the home was established by Congress as the Military Asylum in 1851, after years of lobbying by Major Robert Anderson, General Winfield Scott, and Jefferson Davis. It was renamed the U.S. Soldiers' Home in 1859. The site originally belonged to George W. Riggs of **Riggs National Bank,** who constructed an Early Gothic Revival cottage there in 1843. The cottage was used by Abraham Lincoln as a summer home during his presidency. It was there that he composed the last draft of the Emancipation Proclamation. The building is now named the Anderson Cottage, after Robert Anderson, who commanded the Union forces at Fort Sumter. Since the early 20th century, the home has accommodated airmen; women were first admitted in 1954. In 1972 it was renamed the U.S. Soldiers' and Airmen's Home.

U.S. SUPREME COURT. The judicial branch of the U.S. government, located on First Street NE, on the site of the **Old Brick Capitol**. The Supreme Court works coequally and independently of Congress, which meets in the **U.S. Capitol,** and the president, who resides in the **White House**. The court was first convened in 1790 and moved to Washington with the federal government in 1801. It was located in the basement of the Capitol until 1860, when the building was expanded and the court moved to the Old Senate Chamber. In 1934 it moved into its own neoclassical structure designed by Cass Gilbert, where it resides today. Originally considered the lowliest branch of government, the court has profoundly shaped American life by its judicial review of cases involving **slavery** and civil rights, the power of the federal government and that of the states, antitrust laws, reproductive rights, and other nationally important cases of federal law and public policy where a final interpretation of the Constitution is required.

USS *PRINCETON* EXPLOSION. Gun explosion on a navy ship in the **Potomac River** on February 28, 1844. The USS *Princeton*, a new steamship, was outfitted with wrought-iron guns, which at the time were the largest ever installed on a warship. President John Tyler, with several members of his Cabinet, boarded the *Princeton* for a festive day trip and demonstration of the guns. One of the giant guns, known as the "Peacemaker," exploded on firing, killing several passengers, including Secretary of State Abel Upshur and Secretary of the Navy Thomas Gilmer. The president was unhurt, but several other passengers died and many others were injured.

U.S. THEATRE. *See* UNITED STATES THEATRE.

- V -

VAN HOOK, JOHN. *See* FREDERICK DOUGLASS NATIONAL HISTORIC SITE.

VAN NESS, MARCIA BURNES (1782–1832). Child welfare advocate. Van Ness was the sole heir to the substantial fortune of **David Burnes**, who in 1791 sold land to the U.S. government for the establishment of the federal city. Concerned about the numerous children left orphaned and homeless by the **War of 1812**, Van Ness founded the Washington Female Orphan Asylum in 1815 and directed its operations until 1831. Only the third children's welfare institution to be established in the United States, and since 1926 known as Hillcrest Children's Center, it still provides mental health services to local children. Together with her husband, General John Peter Van Ness, she helped found many of Washington's social, cultural, and religious organizations, including the Columbian Institute (a precursor to the **Smithsonian Institution**), and donated parcels of land for the construction of three churches. When Van Ness died in the 1832 cholera epidemic, Congress adjourned for her public funeral, the first such service for an American woman.

VIDAL, GORE (b. 1925). American novelist and playwright. Vidal grew up in the Broad Branch Road NW home of his grandfather, Senator Thomas Pryor Gore of Oklahoma, and attended St. Alban's School. Senator Gore was blind, and Vidal's education was supplemented by reading congressional documents to his grandfather. Vidal has written 24 novels, five plays, several Hollywood screenplays, one memoir, and nine collections of essays. His essay collection, *United States*, won the 1993 National Book Award. Among his best-known works are the American Chronicle novels: *Burr, Lincoln, 1876, Empire, Hollywood, Washington, D.C.*, and *The Golden Age.*

VIETNAM VETERANS MEMORIAL. A memorial to the veterans of the Vietnam War (1955–75). Located on the **Mall** on two acres of **Constitution Gardens,** the Vietnam Veterans Memorial was authorized by Congress in 1980. The memorial is composed of three parts: the Wall (1982), the Statue of the Three Soldiers (1984), and the Women's Memorial (1993). Designed by architectural student Maya Ying Lin, the Wall is made of black granite, quarried in India and polished to a mirror-like surface. It bears the names of more than 58,000 American fatalities of the Vietnam War, arranged chronologically by date of death. The Statue of the Three Soldiers, a sculpture in bronze by Frederick Hart, depicts three men in uniforms representing the American military branches that fought in Vietnam. The statue stands in a grove of trees, positioned so that the three soldiers look toward the Wall. The Women's Memorial, a sculpture in bronze by Glenna Goodacre, depicts three women, one of whom is caring for a wounded soldier. Around the statue stand eight trees planted in honor of each of the American women who died in the Vietnam War.

VIETNAM WAR PROTESTS (1965–71). Demonstrations in Washington against U.S. involvement in the Vietnam War. During the first major protest in 1965, more than 16,000 people demonstrated at the **U.S. Capitol** and the **White House**, and a few people were arrested. Two years later in October 1967, after the war had begun to escalate and 13,000 American soldiers had died, the antiwar movement also began to escalate. More than 100,000 protestors came from all over the country, targeting Washington for its status as headquarters of the war. The protests included a rally at the **Lincoln Memorial** and a march on the Pentagon. This time, police in riot gear used tear gas and arrested more than 600 people. An event two years later, in November 1969, was the largest antiwar demonstration in U.S. history. There were as many as 500,000 protestors in the city. More than 3,000 police officers patrolled the event, and Army troops were readied in reserve. With a few exceptions, the 1969 demonstrations were peaceful, and only 135 people were arrested. In the spring of 1971, antiwar organizers planned a May Day shutdown of Washington by blocking bridges and other access routes to Maryland and Virginia. The city police, however, were aware of the plan and prevented the shutdown by driving many demonstrators out of town using tear gas and arresting 7,000 people. More than 150 people were injured in the 1971 protests. In 1972 President Richard Nixon withdrew the troops from Vietnam; historians later recognized the important impact of these protests on U.S. policy.

VINEGAR HILL. *See* BRIGHTWOOD.

- W -

W3XK. The earliest television station in Washington and one of the first in the world. In 1921 Charles Francis Jenkins (1867–1934), an American television pioneer, set up a research lab in Washington to experiment with "radiomovies." In 1925 Jenkins gave a public demonstration, transmitting a short film from the Naval Laboratory at **Anacostia** to a receiver in Washington. In 1928 the FRC (Federal Radio Commission, precursor to the Federal Communications Commission) issued the very first television license, assigning the call letters W3XK, to Jenkins Laboratories, which had a transmitter on Connecticut Avenue NW. Jenkins made silhouette films in a studio and then transformed the lights and shadows into electrical impulses, which were broadcast on the shortwave band. At the receiving end, the electrical impulses were reconstituted, producing a cloudy silhouette image on a small mirror, accompanied by audio narration. The "radiomovies" were transmitted across the eastern United States every night at 8:00 p.m. to an audience of as many as 20,000 people. Listeners were encouraged to add picture receivers to their radios and asked to report on their reception. In 1929 the transmitter was moved to Wheaton, Maryland, and in 1932 the station ceased broadcasting.

WALKER, JOHN THOMAS (1925–1989). Episcopal bishop of Washington, dean of the **Washington National Cathedral**, and vice president of the House of Bishops of the Episcopal Church. Born in Barnesville, Georgia, Walker graduated from Wayne State University (1951) and Virginia Theological Seminary (1954). Ordained a priest in 1955, he was rector of St. Mary's Church in Detroit and taught at St. Paul's School in Concord, New Hampshire (1957–66). In 1966 Walker became canon of the National Cathedral, where he was responsible for urban ministry. In 1977 he was appointed bishop of Washington. An African American in a predominantly white church, Walker helped to integrate the parishes of Washington, reached out to the city's poor, and was active in ecumenical affairs through the Interfaith Conference of Metropolitan Washington. His work was influential beyond the Washington area, affecting the life of his denomination. In addition to serving on ecumenical committees, Walker traveled throughout Africa and taught at the Bishop Tucker Theological College in Uganda.

WALKER, MARY (1832–1919). Physician. A graduate of Syracuse Medical College, Walker traveled to Washington at the beginning of the **Civil War** hoping for an appointment as a U.S. Army surgeon. She was denied a commission because of her gender but volunteered in the city's military hospitals. While treating wounded rebel soldiers behind Confederate lines, she overheard southern officers discussing military maneuvers. Returning to Washington, she relayed the information to General W. T. Sherman, who arranged her commission as an assistant surgeon with a rank of first lieutenant. Congress passed special legislation permitting her to wear trousers. After her 1864 capture and imprisonment, Walker was the first woman prisoner of war exchanged for a male officer of equal rank. In November 1865, she became the first woman awarded the Congressional Medal of Honor, America's highest military honor. In 1917 qualifications for the honor were changed, and her medal was revoked. She refused to return the medal and wore it until she died. Congress restored Walker's Medal of Honor in 1977.

WALTER REED ARMY MEDICAL CENTER. One of America's leading military hospitals and medical research centers, named for Major Walter Reed (1851–1902), the Army physician who discovered that yellow fever is transmitted by infected mosquitoes rather than by contact with sufferers. Walter Reed General Hospital was established by Congress and opened in 1909 with 10 patients; 14 years later General John Pershing authorized its expansion to a teaching and research center. The complex, located on Georgia Avenue NW, includes more than 100 rose-brick Georgian buildings. Its centerpiece, a 425-bed hospital built in 1977, stands 10 stories tall, covers 28 acres of floor space, and admits more than 16,000 patients each year. In addition to the medical center, Walter Reed's campus houses the Army Institute of Research, Army Physical Disability Agency, Armed Forces Institute of Pathology, and National Museum of Health and Medicine. The museum, first known as the Army Medical Museum, opened in 1862, and in 1887 moved to a Victorian structure designed by **Adolph Cluss** and Paul Schulze, at Independence Avenue and **7th Street** SW, before locating at Walter Reed. It holds America's largest collection of anatomical specimens and medical artifacts.

WAR OF 1812. A war between the United States and Great Britain that took place between 1812 and 1815, during which Washington was sacked by British troops. On August 19, 1814, more than 4,000 British veterans of the Napoleonic Wars landed at Benedict, Maryland, and marched to Bladensburg where, in a brief engagement on August 24, they routed nearly 7,000 inexperienced Americans, most of whom were untrained local militia. While the battle raged, D.C. residents fled their homes, and government clerks ferried important documents out of the city. First Lady Dolley Madison cut Gilbert Stuart's portrait of **George Washington** from its frame and carried it from the city. British troops arrived in the evening and set fire to the **U.S. Capitol**, burning the 3,000-volume **Library of Congress**. The British soldiers consumed an elaborate dinner prepared for President James Madison in anticipation of a battlefield victory and then burned the **White House**. Americans torched the **Navy Yard**, including the nearly completed frigate *Columbia*, to keep it from enemy hands. An evening rainstorm temporarily brought the inferno under control. The next morning, August 25, the State, War, and Treasury Departments were burned, and the printing presses of the anti-British newspaper, the ***National Intelligencer***, were destroyed. Local residents looted the Navy Yard, White House, and abandoned houses. A severe afternoon storm swept through the city. The British silently marched out that evening, leaving their wounded behind and their dead unburied. They re-embarked at Benedict August 30 and headed north to lay siege to Baltimore, where their defeat inspired **Francis Scott Key** to write "The Star-Spangled Banner." It was not until 1819 that Congress and the **U.S. Supreme Court** returned to the rebuilt U.S. Capitol. Although neither side won the war, the conflict solidified U.S. independence and ushered in a period of American confidence and expansion.

WARDMAN, HARRY (1872–1938). Real estate developer. Born in Bradford, England, Wardman came to Washington and began a construction company in 1897. Located on K Street NW, his business grew into the largest residential building firm in the city, constructing more than 5,000 houses. Wardman also built more than 400 apartment buildings and several hotels, including the 1,200-room Wardman Park Hotel (1918, later redeveloped by Sheraton and then under Marriott ownership), the 250-room Carlton (1926), and the **Hay-Adams Hotel** (1927). His real estate empire was worth about $30 million in 1929, but as a result of the Great Depression, he was forced to turn over his properties to a banking syndicate in 1930. Broke, Wardman resumed the construction business and during the next eight years he recovered some of his personal fortune. His buildings significantly eased the housing shortage in Washington and made the city a modern urban center.

WARNER THEATRE. Historic movie palace and vaudeville house. In 1924 the Stanley Company of Philadelphia built the elaborate Louis XIV-style theater, then known as the Earle Theatre, at 13th and E Streets NW, at a cost of $2 million. Designed by theater architect C. Howard Crane, it featured a long, three-story entrance lobby, a rooftop garden, restaurants, and a radio studio. The Earle presented such acts as George Burns and Gracie Allen, Tommy and Jimmy Dorsey's orchestra, and first-run films. In 1928 the Warner Brothers film studio purchased the Stanley Company and renamed the theater, which played all of the studio's films. After the **riots of 1968**, the theater declined, along with much of downtown Washington. The Warner Theatre was declared a historic landmark in 1979, and during the 1970s and 1980s it featured concerts, films, and live performances. In 1989 the Kaempfer Company undertook a major renovation of the theater building. Construction uncovered the remains of an **alley dwelling** site dating to the 1850s. Artifacts from the archaeological study of "Slate Alley" are now displayed in the theater lobby. With 1,850 seats, the Warner is the largest auditorium in downtown Washington and hosts touring musical and dramatic productions.

WASHINGTON, GEORGE (1732–1799). Commander of the Continental Army during the Revolutionary War and first president of the United States. Washington's influence on the nation's capital was pivotal during his first term in office from 1789 to 1792. In 1790 he signed congressional bills establishing a "temporary and permanent seat" of government for the United States. The federal capital was then moved from New York to a temporary site in Philadelphia, with the intention of developing a permanent site on the **Potomac River**. Washington knew the Potomac area well and believed that the river site would become a great center of communication and commercial activity for the new nation. He deftly thwarted Philadelphia interests that sought to retain the capital by proposing to build a federal hall and a house for the president. Washington refused to move into the presidential house. In contrast to **Thomas Jefferson**'s proposal of a 1,500-acre federal city, Washington approved plans for a city of more than 6,000 acres. In 1791 he ordered a survey of a 10-mile-square area on both sides of the Potomac, carried out by **Andrew Ellicott** and **Benjamin Banneker**. He appointed commissioners Thomas Johnson, **Daniel Carroll**, and David Stuart to direct the survey and to purchase land using funds appropriated by the states of Maryland and Virginia. He hired architect **Pierre Charles L'Enfant**, who prepared a monumental city plan. When several of the original landholders refused to sell, Washington met with them at **Suter's Tavern**. Through meetings and correspondence he finally reached an agreement, and a site for nation's capital was secured.

WASHINGTON, WALTER (b. 1915). **Mayor** of Washington. Walter Washington came to the District of Columbia from Jamestown, New York, and attended **Howard University**. He graduated in 1938 and received a law degree from Howard in 1948. Washington worked for the National Capital Housing Authority for 25 years, and in 1961 was appointed by President John F. Kennedy to direct that agency. He then served as chair of the New York City Public

Housing Authority until 1967, when President Lyndon Johnson appointed him commissioner of Washington, D.C. During the **riots of 1968**, Washington resisted pressure from **J. Edgar Hoover** and others to deal harshly with the rioters. In 1975 he became the first elected mayor of the city in more than a century. In 1978 he lost the mayoral election to **Marion Barry**, joined a private law practice, and has since worked for various city causes, particularly improvement of the **LeDroit Park** neighborhood.

WASHINGTON ARSENAL EXPLOSION. An accidental explosion and fire at a munitions manufacturing plant. Because of a labor shortage during the **Civil War**, women and girls were recruited to work in the manufacturing of munitions. During the summer of 1864, a group of these workers were assembling rifle cartridges at the Washington Arsenal when fireworks, stored outside in the hot sun, ignited. A piece of burning fuse was propelled through an open window and landed among the workers in loose powder, causing a giant explosion, fire, and secondary explosions. Twenty-one of the workers died. A memorial honoring those killed in the explosion was placed in the **Congressional Cemetery**.

WASHINGTON BALLET. The city's only professional ballet company. Washington Ballet was founded by internationally known instructor Mary Day in 1976, soon after the failure of the National Ballet. The 22-member dance company has made extensive overseas tours and presents a varied repertoire of neoclassical and contemporary ballets by such artists as George Balanchine, John Cranko, and Choo-San Goh, who served as resident choreographer and associate artistic director for 11 years until his death in 1987. Day resigned as artistic director in 1998 and was succeeded by choreographer Septime Weber.

WASHINGTON BEE. Weekly newspaper published in Washington from 1882 until 1922. The *Bee* documented the African American side of Washington life, which was underreported in other local newspapers. Publication of the *Bee* took place largely through the efforts of William Calvin Chase (1854–1922), who founded the newspaper in an office on I Street NW and served as its only editor and publisher until his death. Chase did not profit financially from the *Bee*, but earned his living as a lawyer. The *Bee* served as a voice of journalistic protest against racial discrimination and violence; it championed racial justice, solidarity, and economic cooperation among minorities in the district. The paper's front page carried the slogan "Honey for our friends—Stings for our enemies."

WASHINGTON BLADE. Gay and lesbian weekly newspaper. With publishing offices on U Street NW, the *Blade* is the oldest continuously published paper of its kind in the United States. The newspaper began publication in 1969 on single mimeographed sheets. The small group of founders distributed these copies by hand, "underground," in places where gays and lesbians gathered. By 1982 the *Blade* had grown to 24 pages and was circulated openly in libraries and stores throughout the Washington area. Today the *Washington Blade* covers gay and lesbian issues in local, national, and international news in more than 100 pages weekly, and its readers number more than 40,000.

WASHINGTON CANAL. A canal project to improve the commercial prospects of the capital city. In 1802 Congress granted a charter to Thomas Law to build a canal from Tiber Creek inlet, along the northern edge of the **Mall**, and south to the **Anacostia River**. A canal had been included the original city plan of **Pierre Charles L'Enfant**, but was never built. The purpose of the canal was to move grain and cargo across the city to vessels docked on the Anacostia River and to bring imported cargo into the city. A large section of the canal, running along the Mall and then south toward the river, was completed in 1815. The city bought the canal in 1831 and linked it to the **Chesapeake and Ohio Canal** at **Georgetown**. However, rather than bringing economic prosperity to the city, the canal proved to be of limited commercial value and gradually deteriorated so that it became a public health concern. During the 1870s, city sewer lines were run through the canal and it was filled over.

WASHINGTON CAPITALS. The professional ice hockey team of Washington. Organized in 1974, the team took 10 years to develop into a contender. The Capitals fielded strong teams during the 1980s and advanced to the Stanley Cup finals in 1998. Star players include Rod Langway, who was twice selected as the league's best defense player, and Mike Gartner, the all-time team leader in goals scored. The Capitals play at the **MCI Center** in downtown Washington.

WASHINGTON CENTENNIAL. A celebration held on December 12, 1900, to commemorate the moving of the capital from Philadelphia to Washington. The celebration was attended by President William McKinley, members of Congress, the **U.S. Supreme Court**, governors of the states and territories, and ambassadors and representatives of many foreign countries. Congress authorized the event and delegated its planning to a citizens committee from the District of Columbia. The event began with a reception at the **White House** for U.S. governors, which included the display of a model and drawings of a proposed enlargement of the East Room. This was followed by three addresses on the history of the White House, the District of Columbia, and the states. In the afternoon the assembled guests were escorted by military parade from the White House to the **U.S. Capitol**, where five additional addresses on the history of Washington and the future of the United States were given before a joint session of Congress. In the evening a reception for the governors was held at the **Corcoran Gallery of Art**. As part of the celebration, Congress authorized a Senate commission to prepare plans to improve the park system in the District of Columbia. This commission's **McMillan Report** not only suggested improvements in the city's parks but also recommended sweeping changes to the city plan and to the architectural direction of Washington.

WASHINGTON CHANNEL. *See* FORT LESLEY J. MCNAIR; POTOMAC PARK; SOUTHWEST.

WASHINGTON CIRCLE. *See* PETER, ROBERT.

WASHINGTON CITY JOCKEY CLUB. *See* HORSERACING; MOUNT PLEASANT.

WASHINGTON CITY ORPHAN ASYLUM. First orphanage in Washington. Founded in 1815 by a charitable group of wealthy Washingtonians, the Washington City Orphan Asylum began as a Protestant organization to take care of children of soldiers who had died in the **War of 1812**. It was one of only 10 orphanages in the United States, and Dolley Madison was its first president. A building was constructed at 14th and S Streets NW, and received a federal charter in 1828. The building was replaced when **William Wilson Corcoran** donated land for a new building to serve 150 children, which was opened in 1876.

WASHINGTON CONSERVATORY OF MUSIC. *See* MAR-SHALL, HARRIET GIBBS.

WASHINGTON CONVENTION CENTER. The District's primary facility for hosting large meetings, fairs, shows, and sporting events. Washington's first convention center, called the Northern Liberty Market, was constructed in 1874 on 5th Street NW between K and L Streets. A second floor was added to the structure in 1893, creating a 5,000-seat auditorium. During the 1930s, **Federal Triangle** construction forced vendors from Center Market to relocate to the convention center building, which was then renamed New Center Market. A 1946 fire caused the roof of the center to collapse and almost destroyed the building. It was rebuilt as a single-story structure, with a flat roof replacing its original curved steel roof. During the 1960s the building was used by the National Historical Wax Museum, and it was demolished by the mid-1980s. Plans for a new 800,000-square-foot Washington Convention Center were developed during the late 1970s, and the facility was completed in 1983. The need for even larger spaces to accommodate national conventions prompted city officials in 1993 to begin planning for a new Washington Convention Center at Mount Vernon Square. The new center will attract an estimated one million visitors per year.

WASHINGTON FEMALE ORPHAN ASYLUM. *See* VAN NESS, MARCIA BURNES.

WASHINGTON HEBREW CONGREGATION. First Jewish congregation in Washington. Organized in 1852 by 25 German immigrants, the congregation held services in several downtown locations before purchasing a Methodist church on 8th Street NW in 1863. When 35 members withdrew in 1869 to found **Adas Israel**, the congregation became a Reform synagogue. In 1946 local philanthropist Morris Cafritz deeded land at Massachusetts Avenue and Macomb Street NW to the congregation. This land was exchanged for an adjacent tract, which became the site of a new synagogue in 1952. The members of Washington Hebrew Congregation organized Washington's first Jewish religious school (1861) and have played important roles in the founding of nearly all local Jewish charities and historical and social agencies, including B'nai B'rith International, the Jewish Historical Society of Greater Washington, Jewish Social Service Agency, and the National

Council of Jewish Women.

WASHINGTON HEIGHTS. *See* ADAMS MORGAN.

WASHINGTON LOAN AND TRUST COMPANY. *See* EDSON, JOHN JOY.

WASHINGTON METRORAIL SYSTEM. The rapid-transit system for Washington and the surrounding area. The Metrorail system covers 92 miles of track, both under and above the ground, and uses more than 700 rail cars to provide service to 75 stations in the District, Virginia, and Maryland. Plans for the Metrorail were initiated in 1966, when President Lyndon Johnson created the Washington Metropolitan Area Transit Authority (WMATA), a compact of local governments in the three jurisdictions, to design and implement a rail and bus system for the area. In March 1968 WMATA approved a plan for a regional Metro system; six months later, construction began at Judiciary Square. In 1976 Metrorail opened to the public. The design of the Metro system was guided by the **Commission of Fine Arts**, whose members were determined that the architecture reflect a single, unified design. They worked closely with architect Harry Weese and a team of engineers to produce a system that became internationally known for its architectural beauty and simplicity. Metro stations feature high arched ceilings of white concrete coffers inspired by the Pantheon in Rome. Because the construction lacks columns, the resulting clean sight lines contribute to the security of the system, reducing the risk of crime and accident. Passengers exit to the street on steep escalators, which are among the longest in the world. As the subway doors close, warning chimes sound the first two notes of the folk melody "Swing Low, Sweet Chariot."

WASHINGTON MONUMENT. A 555-foot marble obelisk erected in honor of **George Washington**. Located on the national **Mall**, the monument was authorized by Congress in 1833, commissioned by the privately funded Washington National Monument Society, and designed by architect **Robert Mills**. Begun in 1848, the monument's construction was halted for lack of funding in 1854, but later resumed under the auspices of the U.S. Army Corps of Engineers after Congress voted to fund the project in 1876. In 1885 President Chester A. Arthur dedicated the monument, and in 1888 it was opened to the public. The Washington Monument houses a replica of a Jean-Antoine Houdon statue of George Washington, as well as 192 memorial stones, which are gifts from various public and private organizations. The monument is now administered by the National Park Service.

WASHINGTON NATIONAL CATHEDRAL. A cathedral church for national celebrations, addresses, prayers, and memorial services. Officially named the Cathedral of Saint Peter and Saint Paul, the complex is administered by the Episcopal Church USA. The cathedral is located on Mount St. Alban at Massachusetts and Wisconsin Avenues NW, where its 57-acre site overlooks Washington. City designer **Pierre Charles L'Enfant** had proposed the construction of a "great church for national purposes," but it wasn't until 1893 that Congress authorized the building of the cathedral. The site was purchased at the turn of the century and the foundation stone was laid in 1907. The construction of the cathedral, which was funded by private donations, was completed in 1990. Philip Hubert Frohman was the chief architect of the project from 1912 to 1971. The sixth-largest cathedral in the world, National Cathedral is 514 feet long, and its center tower rises 301 feet, making it the highest point in Washington. The building's 14th-century English gothic architecture, 200 stained-glass windows, Indiana limestone walls, and detailed craftsmanship make it an artistic masterpiece.

WASHINGTON OPERA. *See* JOHN F. KENNEDY CENTER FOR THE PERFORMING ARTS.

WASHINGTON POST. A morning daily newspaper published in Washington, D.C. One of the most important newspapers in the United States, the *Washington Post* was founded in 1877 by Stilson Hutchins, who set out to publish a four-page Democratic party paper concentrating on national and international news; local news was to be secondary. The first edition, which cost three cents, was typeset by hand at an office on Pennsylvania Avenue NW. Ten thousand copies were printed. In 1878 the *Post* acquired one of its competitors, the *National Union*, and moved to its offices, also on Pennsylvania Avenue NW. Two years later the *Post* became first paper in the city to publish seven days a week. In 1888 Hutchins purchased another *Post* rival, the *National Republican*, and began to publish the *Evening Post*. Eager to benefit from new technology and replace hand typesetting with machine, Hutchins purchased an early linotype machine, but typographical workers were not receptive to the new technology, so it was another five years before the *Post* was typeset by machine.

In 1889 Hutchins sold the *Post* to Frank Hatton, a former U.S. postmaster general, and Beriah Wilkins, a former congressman from Ohio. The new owners dropped the Democratic party allegiance, and the *Post* came to be known as a conservative newspaper. When Hatton died, Wilkins became sole owner. After Wilkins died, his family sold the paper in 1905 to John R. McLean, owner of *Cincinnati Enquirer*. In the early 20th century, under McLean's direction, the *Post* featured society reporting and sensationalism, and as a result lost credibility and influence. McLean's son **Edward B. ("Ned") McLean** succeeded his father as publisher in 1916. Over the next two decades, *Post* circulation dropped below 50,000, and the company went bankrupt.

In 1933 financier Eugene Meyer purchased the *Washington Post* at public auction and, declaring his intent to restore its editorial integrity, tripled its circulation over the next 10 years. Under Meyer's leadership the *Post* won a Pulitzer Prize in 1935, the first of many. Over the 20th century, leadership passed through Meyer's family to his son-in-law Philip L. Graham (1946), to Meyer's daughter Katharine Meyer Graham (1963), and to her son Donald E. Graham (1979). In 1954 the *Post* purchased another local rival, the *Washington Times-Herald*, and became only morning paper in city. In 1961, when the company acquired *Newsweek* magazine, Ben Bradlee moved from *Newsweek* to become a prominent editor of the *Post*. In the early 1970s, Katharine Graham and *Post* editors encouraged their reporters' aggressive investigation of the President Richard Nixon's complicity in the **Watergate scandal**. Today the *Post* offices are located in the city at 15th Street NW, but the *Post* is now printed at printing plants in Virginia and Maryland. The *Washington Post* offers its daily content on the Worldwide Web and has a weekday print circulation of more than 750,000.

WASHINGTON REDSKINS. The professional football team of Washington, D.C. The franchise began in Boston, where the team was called the Braves (1932) and the Redskins (1933–36). The club moved to Washington in 1937 and under coach Ray Flaherty (1936–42) won four Eastern Division titles and two National Football League championships. During the next three decades the team won the division title only twice, in 1943 and 1945. In 1972, under owner **Jack Kent Cooke** and coach George Allen, the club won another Eastern Division title, and under Joe Gibbs (1981–92) it became a regular contender, winning six division titles and three Super Bowls. Star players from the early years include Sammy Baugh, Cliff Battles, and Bill Dudley. The team's recent Hall of Fame players include Sonny Jurgensen, Bobby Mitchell, John Riggins, and Charlie Taylor.

WASHINGTON SCHOOL OF BALLET. One of America's leading ballet schools. The Washington School of Ballet was founded in 1944 by Lisa Gardiner, a former ballerina with Anna Pavlova's company, and Mary Day, a teacher and coach who serves as the school's director. From 1962 to 1976, Washington School of Ballet operated the country's first residential ballet academy, combining a high school education with rigorous, preprofessional dance training. Its roster of graduates includes Virginia Johnson, Kevin McKenzie, Marianna Tcherkassky, and Amanda McKerrow, the first American to win the Moscow International Ballet Competition (1981).

WASHINGTON SCHOOL OF PSYCHIATRY. A professional school for practitioners in various fields of mental health. Established in 1936, the school's founders, led by Harry Stack Sullivan and William Alanson White, developed interdisciplinary training programs based on psychodynamic theory. Today the school sponsors seminars and conferences, the most prominent of which is the annual Forum on Psychiatry and the Humanities. For more than 50 years the Washington School has published the professional journal *Psychiatry*. It operates the Meyer Treatment Center, a mental health facility that offers services to D.C. area residents. In 1998 the school moved from **Dupont Circle** to Wisconsin Avenue NW.

WASHINGTON SENATORS. The American League professional baseball team of Washington from 1901 to 1971. A charter member of the American League, the team was a mediocre performer for most of its history. The Senators' glory days were in the mid-1920s, when pitcher Walter Johnson led them to their only pennant (1924). The Senators played at **Griffith Stadium** until 1961, when they moved to Minnesota and became the Twins. The following year Washington began an American League expansion team that was also called the Senators. The new team played for one season at Griffith Stadium and for the next 10 years (1962–71) at **RFK Memorial Stadium**, before moving to Texas to become the Texas Rangers.

WASHINGTON THEATER FESTIVAL. *See* SOURCE THEATRE COMPANY.

WASHINGTON WIZARDS. *See* MCI CENTER; POLLIN, ABE.

WATERGATE SCANDAL. Political scandal and constitutional crisis that began in 1972 with a break-in at the Democratic party headquarters in Washington and ended with the resignation of President Richard Nixon. Five burglars were caught in the act of installing electronic surveillance equipment on the sixth floor of the Watergate office building on Virginia Avenue NW in Washington. They were paid by Republicans to steal strategy secrets to gain an advantage in the upcoming presidential election. The **White House** staff staged an unsuccessful cover-up of the fact that members of the Nixon administration, including the president himself, were involved in the conspiracy from the beginning. Over the next two years, investigators, including *Washington Post* reporters, independent counsel, and the Senate Watergate Committee, uncovered a network of illegal activity that included political spying and sabotage, conspiracy to obstruct justice, and abuse of presidential power. The discoveries resulted in the indictments of more than 40 government officials and the resignation of President Nixon in August 1974. Gerald Ford took over as president and pardoned Nixon for his part in the scandal.

WATTERSTON, GEORGE (1783–1854). Lawyer, newspaper editor, librarian of Congress, and author. Raised in Washington from the age of eight, Watterston practiced law in Hagerstown, Maryland. In his early years he wrote novels, poetry, and a comedy. A first novel, *The Lawyer; or, Man as He Ought Not to Be* (1908), was followed by *Glencarn; or, the Disappointments of Youth* (1810). His published poetry includes *The Wanderer in Jamaica* (1810). Watterston served as editor of the *Washington City Weekly Gazette* (1813–15) and as head of the **Library of Congress** (1815–29). In 1830 he became editor of the *Daily National Journal*. He is best known as the leader of efforts to build the **Washington Monument** and as the author of *A New Guide to Washington* (1842).

WESLEY HEIGHTS. *See* GLOVER-ARCHBOLD PARK.

WESLEY THEOLOGICAL SEMINARY. United Methodist theological school, which grants master's degrees in divinity and theological studies, and doctor of ministry degrees. The seminary traces its roots to Westminster Theological Seminary, founded in 1882 on the grounds of Western Maryland College in Westminster, Maryland. When the three major Methodist denominations united in 1939, efforts were made to strengthen Westminster Seminary, but a 1947 study commissioned by the Association of Methodist Theological Schools deemed the school academically and physically inadequate, as well as geographically undesirable. Under Bishop G. Bromley Oxnam, a new campus was constructed adjacent to Methodist-affiliated **American University** on Massachusetts Avenue NW, and the school was renamed in memory of Methodist founder John Wesley. Philadelphia architect A. Hensel Fink designed the school's five buildings, constructed between 1957 and 1966. In addition to its degree programs, the seminary's Center for the Arts and Religion develops Christian art and artists.

WEST POTOMAC PARK. *See* POTOMAC PARK.

WESTERN MARKET. *See* PUBLIC MARKETS.

WHITE HOUSE. The U.S. executive mansion at 1600 Pennsylvania Avenue NW. The establishment of a president's house in Washington was authorized by Congress with the **Residence Act** of 1790, and the site was chosen by **Pierre Charles L'Enfant** and **George Washington** as part of the original plan for the federal city. The building's architectural plan was chosen by competition; the winning design, submitted by Irish-born architect **James Hoban**, was modeled after a neoclassical Georgian mansion near Dublin. The sandstone building stones were quarried and transported by slave labor from Virginia and then cut by stonemasons recruited from Scotland, so the stone carving is said to resemble that of medieval Scottish churches. The exterior was painted with whitewash to protect it from the elements, and the resulting color inspired the nickname "White House" from the beginning. In 1902 Congress formalized the name.

The White House was completed in 1800, and John Adams was the first president to occupy it. The second was **Thomas Jefferson**. The building was only a quarter of the size originally planned by Washington and L'Enfant, but Jefferson considered it large and pompous. Nevertheless, during his administration Jefferson added terraces to the east and west wings. During the **War of 1812**, British troops set fire to the White House and gutted it. Hoban was called back to oversee the reconstruction. **Benjamin Henry Latrobe** designed the portico, which was completed in 1824.

Besides being a presidential residence, the White House serves as a public building—so public, in fact, that by 1900 the president could no longer use the first floor as a home. Except during times of war and national emergency, the White House is open for free public tours. It has long been a popular Washington attraction.

The interior of the White House underwent great change during the 20th century. President Theodore Roosevelt had it remodeled by Charles McKim of the McMillan Commission; the first White House rose garden was added by Ellen Wilson, wife of President Woodrow Wilson. President Franklin Roosevelt's changes included the addition of the Oval Office, the East Wing, and a bomb shelter. During Harry Truman's time in office, the building was judged to be structurally unsound, so from 1948 to 1952, it was gutted and completely reconstructed with steel and concrete, retaining the original stone walls and generally following the original plan. There are now 132 rooms in the White House. Its buildings and grounds are overseen by National Park Service.

WHITELAW HOTEL. The first Washington hotel and apartment building financed, designed, built, and managed exclusively by and for African Americans. The hotel was located at 13th and T Streets NW, one block from Washington's celebrated "Black Broadway" (U Street). John Whitelaw Lewis, founder of the **Industrial Bank of Washington**, built the Whitelaw in 1919 to house black celebrities, entertainers, and business travelers who were turned away by segregated downtown hotels. Isaiah T. Hatton designed the Italianate exterior and Beaux-Arts interiors, including an elaborate art glass ceiling in the spacious ballroom. After the **riots of 1968**, the Whitelaw Hotel and surrounding **Shaw** neighborhood deteriorated. The building became a haven for drug addicts and prostitutes, and in 1977 it was closed for building code violations. Community activists negotiated the 1991 sale of the Whitelaw to Manna, Inc., one of the city's leading nonprofit housing developers, who undertook a $4 million historic renovation. The Whitelaw now holds 35 apartments for low-income residents and is listed on the Historic American Buildings Survey.

WHITMAN, WALT (1819–1892). Poet. Whitman was born in New York and attended elementary school; he was thereafter self-educated. He taught school, worked in publishing in New York and New Orleans, and began to write poetry. In 1855 he published his first collection of poems, *Leaves of Grass*. In 1862, during the **Civil War**, Whitman went to Washington to find his brother, who had been wounded at the battle of Fredericksburg. He remained in the city for 11 years, visiting wounded soldiers at nearly all of Washington's Civil War hospitals, especially Campbell and Armory Square Hospitals. Whitman worked in the army paymaster's office until 1865, was employed by the Department of the Interior and dismissed after his superiors learned of the controversial content of his writings, and then became a clerk at the Justice Department. Whitman's time in Washington had a profound influence on his poetry. He often saw President Abraham Lincoln in the streets of the city, and after the **Lincoln assassination**, wrote "When Lilacs Last in the Dooryard Bloom'd" in Lincoln's memory. Whitman suffered a paralytic stroke in 1873 and left Washington to stay with his family in Camden, New Jersey, where he died.

WHITTINGHAM SUBDIVISION. *See* DEANWOOD.

WILLARD HOTEL. A 341-room hotel located at 14th Street and **Pennsylvania Avenue** NW, just two blocks from the **White House**. Henry Willard bought the property in 1850 and his hotel became famous as a center of Washington social and political activity. Abraham Lincoln held staff meetings in front of the lobby fireplace in 1861. The hotel was regularly visited by President Ulysses S. Grant, who was assailed in the lobby by so many personal requests that he called those who approached him "lobbyists." In 1901 the original hotel was replaced by a new 12-story Beaux-Arts building designed by Henry Janeway Hardenbergh, architect of the original Waldorf-Astoria Hotel in New York City. The new building was the site of many important meetings and presidential visits. In 1946 the Willard family sold their interest in the hotel, which gradually declined. In 1963 Martin Luther King, Jr., wrote his "I Have a Dream" speech at the Willard, but in 1968 the hotel closed. After a prolonged legal battle by various development interests, the hotel was restored in all its Beaux-Arts splendor and reopened in 1986.

WILLIAMS, EDWARD BENNETT (1920–1988). Washington lawyer and sports executive. Williams was born in Hartford, Connecticut, and graduated from Holy Cross College in Worcester, Massachusetts. He earned a law degree from **Georgetown University** and eventually opened his own firm specializing in civil liberties cases. Williams took on many prominent and notorious clients such as Teamster boss Jimmy Hoffa, Wisconsin Senator Joseph McCarthy, and Mafia boss Frank Costello. He represented the *Washington Post* when it broke the Watergate story and was thought to have been a source for the book *All the President's Men*, which documented the **Watergate scandal**. For 20 years (1965–85), Williams was part-owner of the **Washington Redskins**, and in 1979 he bought the Baltimore Orioles baseball team. Williams sought unsuccessfully to acquire a baseball franchise for Washington.

WILSON, JOHN A. (1943–1993). **City Council** member and chairman. A native of Maryland's Eastern Shore, Wilson became involved in the civil rights movement through the Student Non-Violent Coordinating Committee. He moved to Washington in the late 1960s, entered local politics, and was elected to the City Council in 1974. Wilson was a political rival of Mayor **Marion Barry** and was known for his work on budget and finance issues. He was for many years Washington's financial and political conscience. Wilson had a large following, and in 1990 won a citywide election as chair of the City Council. He considered running for **mayor**, but dropped out of the race and committed suicide in 1993.

WILSON, WOODROW. *See* WOODROW WILSON HOUSE.

WILSON BUILDING. *See* JOHN A. WILSON BUILDING.

WOLLEN, C. RUSSELL (1922–1994). Composer and musician. Born in Hartford, Connecticut, Wollen was educated at St. Mary's Seminary and University in Baltimore, **Catholic University of America**, and Harvard University. Wollen was a Catholic priest from 1947 to 1964 and then joined the faculty of Catholic University, where he taught language (1946–47) and music (1948–52). From 1956 to 1980 he was a keyboard artist with the **National Symphony Orchestra**, playing celeste, harpsichord, organ, and piano. He also served as organist at the Unitarian Church of Arlington and **Adas Israel** synagogue. Wollen wrote more than 100 musical works, including "In Martyrum Memoriam," first performed by the Chicago Symphony, and two operas, "The Decorator" and "The Birthday of the Infanta," performed at the **John F. Kennedy Center for the Performing Arts**.

WOMEN'S SUFFRAGE PARADE (1913). A march down **Pennsylvania Avenue** by 8,000 supporters of women's voting rights. Organized by the Congressional Union for Woman Suffrage, founded by Alice Stokes Paul, the event was scheduled for March 3, the day before President Woodrow Wilson's presidential inauguration. Two weeks earlier, 16 suffrage demonstrators began a walk from New York City to Washington; other people joined along the way. The parade through Washington was led by Inez Milholland Boissevain, a lawyer, who wore a white cape and rode a white horse. She was followed by suffrage movement pioneers, working women in uniform, college women in academic gowns, state delegations, and a separate section of men who supported women's suffrage. On the steps of the Treasury Building, demonstrators presented an allegorical pageant. During the march, some bystanders became violent and abusive, harassing and beating the marchers, resulting in the hospitalization of more than 100 injured people. Instead of protecting the marchers from physical attack, police officers in some cases participated in the jeers and insults. Cavalry troops from Fort Myer were used to control the crowd, but the violence that ensued embarrassed the city and prompted congressional hearings the following week. The city's superintendent of police was fired for failing to provide adequate police protection for the event.

WOODROW WILSON HOUSE. The Washington home of Woodrow Wilson, now a house museum honoring the legacy of Wilson's presidency. The Georgian-style red brick townhouse near **Embassy Row** was designed in 1915 by architect Waddy B. Wood. Wilson bought the house in 1920 and lived there for the last three years of his life, becoming the first former president to stay in Washington after his terms of office expired. Now owned by the National Trust for Historic Preservation, the house is authentically furnished and holds memorabilia from Wilson's presidency and from American life in the 1920s. It offers public educational programs, exhibits, and tours.

WOODWARD AND LOTHROP. *See* DEPARTMENT STORES.

WORMLEY HOTEL. One of the most elegant hotels of late-19th-century Washington and the site of many social events and government functions. Located at 15th and H Streets NW, the hotel was opened in 1871 by African American businessman James Wormley (1819–1884). Wormley had been steward of the elite Metropolitan Club since its founding in 1863. The Wormley Hotel was the most expensive establishment in Washington and the level of service at the hotel became legendary, far exceeding that of other hotels of the post-**Civil War** era. Wormley purchased the hotel's dinner service in Paris and lent cooking equipment to the **White House**. After Wormley's death, the hotel was operated by his eldest son, James T. Wormley, until 1893, when a poor economy forced its sale to Charles E. Gibbs. In 1897 the hotel became the Colonial Hotel and in 1906 the building was demolished for construction of the Union Trust Bank building.

- Y -

YMCA. *See* ANTHONY BOWEN YMCA.

- Z -

ZERO MILESTONE. *See* ELLIPSE.

ZOO. *See* NATIONAL ZOOLOGICAL PARK.

Bibliography

CONTENTS

I. INTRODUCTION   252

II. GENERAL WORKS   257
    A. Bibliographies   257
    B. Biographies and Autobiographies   257
    C. History of Washington   261
        1. Building the Federal City
        2. General History
            a. Nineteenth-Century Histories
            b. Early to Mid-Twentieth-Century Histories
            c. Mid- to Late Twentieth-Century Histories
        3. Historic Buildings
    D. General Directories and Guidebooks   265
        1. Directories
        2. Guidebooks
            a. Nineteenth Century
            b. Early to Mid-Twentieth Century
            c. Late Twentieth Century
    E. Newspapers and Journals   267
    F. Photographs and Views   267
    G. Statistics, Demographics, and Genealogy   268

III. SUBJECTS   268
    A. Amusements and Recreation   268
    B. Architecture   269
        1. General Works
        2. Architects
        3. Buildings and Sites

C. Art   272
    1. General Works
    2. Guidebooks
D. Business and Economic Life   272
    1. General Works
    2. Banking and Finance
    3. Retail Businesses
E. Civil Rights and Race Relations   275
F. Diplomatic Washington   276
G. Education   276
    1. Private Schools
    2. Public Schools
    3. Higher Education
H. Housing and Employment   279
I. Literary Society   279
J. Local Government   280
    1. General Works
    2. Courts
    3. Government
    4. Public Works and Utilities
K. Medical and Social Services   281
L. Memorials and Monuments   282
M. Museums, Libraries, and Research Institutions   282
    1. Museums and Galleries
    2. Libraries and Archives
N. Neighborhoods   284
    1. General Works
    2. Adams Morgan
    3. Anacostia
    4. Brightwood
    5. Brookland
    6. Capitol Hill
    7. Chevy Chase
    8. Cleveland Park
    9. Columbia Heights
    10. Deanwood
    11. Dupont Circle

    12.   Foggy Bottom

    13.   Georgetown

    14.   Kalorama

    15.   LeDroit Park

    16.   Mount Pleasant

    17.   Pennsylvania Avenue

    18.   Petworth

    19.   Shaw

O. Parks, Gardens, and Cemeteries   289

P. Performing Arts   290

    1.   General Works

    2.   Theaters

Q. Racial and Ethnic Groups   291

    1.   African Americans

    2.   Hispanic Americans

    3.   Other Ethnic Groups

R. Religious life   293

    1.   General Works

    2.   Congregation Histories

S. Society in Washington   296

T. Slavery   297

U. Transportation   297

V. War Years in Washington   298

    1.   War of 1812

    2.   Civil War

    3.   World War II

W. Women   300

I. INTRODUCTION

This selected bibliography presents some of the more important books, dissertations, newspaper and journal articles, and electronic resources that document the history of Washington, D.C. The materials listed herein represent only a small fraction of the available material housed in Washington libraries and the Historical Society of Washington, D.C. (see appendix 2 for a list of repositories). Also worth consulting are hundreds of specialized studies, reports, surveys, and documents issued by Congress and the District connected with municipal operations and with fiscal, environmental, transportation, and legal matters.

Of the various types of literature sought by the researcher, biographical reference works seem most difficult to locate. There are directories and scattered volumes of "Who's Who in Washington," but researchers interested in biography must turn to newspaper obituaries and full-scale biographies in place of reference works. The bibliography lists many individual biographies and autobiographies.

There are some excellent histories and historical studies of Washington. For the full sweep of Washington history, see Constance McLaughlin Green's *Washington: Village and Capital, 1800–1878* (1962) and *Washington: Capital City, 1879–1950* (1963) and the survey by Keith Melder, *City of Magnificent Intentions*, 2d ed. (1997). Some recent studies include Letitia Woods Brown, *Washington in the New Era, 1870–1970* (1972); Howard Gillette, Jr., et al., *Southern City, National Ambition: The Growth of Early Washington, D.C., 1800–1860* (1995); and Gillette, *Between Justice and Beauty: Race, Planning, and the Failure of Urban Policy in Washington, D.C.* (1998). There are also many historical works written during the 19th century; this literature varies in quality, but is often worth consulting. A recent photographic history is Fredric M. Miller and Howard Gillette, *Washington Seen: A Photographic History, 1875–1965* (1995).

Several guidebooks dating from the 19th century cover many aspects of city life. The well-publicized Federal Writers' Project, *Washington: City and Capital* (1937), published in the American Guide Series and reprinted in 1992, contains a massive amount of information, but is marred by inaccuracy. Four recent guides that successfully cover their subject from different angles are E. J. Applewhite's architectural-historical *Washington Itself* (1983); Sandra Fitzpatrick and Maria R. Goodwin, *The Guide to Black Washington* (1999); Stephen

M. Forman, *A Guide to Civil War Washington* (1995); and Candyce H. Stapen's exhaustive *Blue Guide Washington, D.C.* (2000).

Particularly important as sources of information are many of the articles that appear in *Records of the Columbia Historical Society* and *Washington History*, journals published by the Columbia Historical Society and its successor the Historical Society of Washington, D.C. While some of the early articles in the *Records* are amateurish, overall the series provides valuable information not easily available elsewhere. Also of primary importance are the Washington newspapers, including the *National Intelligencer, Washington Advertiser, Washington Evening Star*, and *Washington Post*.

The city's architectural treasures are amply covered in a number of works. Full treatment is given in Pamela Scott and Antoinette J. Lee, *Buildings of the District of Columbia* (1993), and in Christopher Weeks and Francis D. Lethbridge, *The AIA Guide to the Architecture of Washington, D.C.* (1994). These works are supplemented by James M. Goode's *Capital Losses: A Cultural History of Washington's Destroyed Buildings* (1979). The more specialized studies include Kenneth R. Bowling, *Creating the Federal City, 1774–1800* (1988); William C. Allen, *The United States Capitol: A Brief Architectural History* (2000); John Young Cole, *The Library of Congress: The Art and Architecture of the Thomas Jefferson Building* (1998); and Sally Kress Tompkins, et al., *A Quest for Grandeur: Charles Moore and the Federal Triangle* (1993). Another book worth noting is Sue A. Kohler's history of the commission that has shaped much of modern Washington, *The Commission of Fine Arts: A Brief History, 1910–1995* (1995).

For business and economic life, a good place to begin is Julie Abell's, *A Guide to Business History in Washington* (1998). A helpful survey is Walter F. McArdle, "The Development of the Business Sector in Washington, D.C., 1800–1973," *Records of the Columbia Historical Society* 1973–74 (1976). Several Washington hotels, banks, department stores, and other business have published histories.

Race relations have always been important in Washington. Constance McLaughlin Green's *The Secret City: A History of Race Relations in the Nation's Capital* (1967) laments missed opportunities. The racial divide has often been played out in Washington's neighborhoods, according to Nelson F. Kofie's, *Race, Class, and the Struggle for Neighborhoods in Washington, D.C.* (1999). Washington experienced several riots during its history; contemporary accounts of two pivotal ones are Edgar M. Gray, *The Washington Race Riot: Its Causes and Effects* (1919), and Ben W. Gilbert, *Ten Blocks from the White House: Anatomy of the Washington Race Riots of 1968* (1968). Some of the credit for the national civil rights movement of the 1960s goes to Washington's New Negro Alliance, a foundational movement, according to Michele F. Pacifico, "History of the New Negro Alliance of Washington, D.C., 1933–1941" (1983).

The city's housing ills of different eras are documented in James Alan Borchert, *Alley Life in Washington* (1980), and Daniel Thurz, *Where Are They Now? A Study of the Impact of Relocation of Former Residents of Southwest Washington* (1973).

Many of the issues connected with the political control of Washington are reviewed in Charles Wesley Harris, *Congress and the Governance of the Nation's Capital: The Conflict of Federal and Local Interests* (1995). Still useful for historical study is Laurence Schmeckebier, *The District of Columbia: Its Government and Administration* (1928). For legal issues, the multivolume *District of Columbia Code* (1981, 1994) is fundamental.

The number of Washington memorials and monuments grows each year, so it is difficult for the literature to keep up with the pace of construction. Still useful is James M. Goode, *The Outdoor Sculpture of Washington, D.C.* (1974). Recent works include Kathryn Allamong Jacob, *Testament to Union: Civil War Monuments in Washington, D.C.* (1998), and Jack Meyer, *Washington, D.C., Monuments in Architectural and Historical Review* (1993).

Washington has outstanding museums and libraries. A general guide to its museums is Betty Ross, *Washington, D.C., Museums: A Ross Guide* (3d ed. 1999). Also helpful for background and context is Mark Bello, *The Smithsonian Institution: A World of Discovery: An Exploration of Behind-the-Scenes Research in the Arts, Sciences, and Humanities* (1993); David Edward Finley, *A Standard of Excellence: Andrew W. Mellon Founds the National Gallery of Art at Washington* (1973); and Richard I. Kurin and Michael Heyman, *Reflections of a Culture Broker: A View from the Smithsonian* (1997). Carol M. Highsmith and Ted Landphair tell the story of *The Library of Congress: America's Memory* (1994), and Kathryn Schneider Smith tells us about "Today's Historical Society: The Promise of the Past and Future," *Washington History* (1994–95).

The literature is of uneven quality when it comes to the history of Washington's neighborhoods. Some of the best work has been written or edited by Kathryn Schneider Smith, including *Washington at Home: An Illustrated History of Neighborhoods in the Nation's Capital* (1988), and *Port Town to Urban Neighborhood: The Georgetown Waterfront of Washington, D.C., 1880–1920* (1989). Our bibliography contains several articles and theses, which add to Schneider's work on the various neighborhoods.

Several works document the rise of Washington's performing arts community and its venues. Among these are Ted Libbey, *The National Symphony Orchestra* (1995); Laurence Maslon, *The Arena Adventure: The First Forty Years* (1990); and Roger Meersman and Robert Boyer, "The National Theatre in Washington: Buildings and Audiences, 1835–1972," *Records of the Columbia Historical Society* (1971–72).

There are a number of studies relating to ethnic and social history. African American studies include Letitia Woods Brown, *Free Negroes in the District of Columbia, 1790–1846* (1972); James Oliver Horton, *Free People of Color* (1993); and Kathleen M. Lesko, Valerie Babb, and Carroll R. Gibbs, *Black Georgetown Remembered: A History of Its Black Community* (1991). See also Olivia Cadaval, *Creating a Latino Identity in the Nation's Capital: The Latino Festival* (1998); Terry A. Repak, *Waiting on Washington: Central American Workers in the Nation's Capital* (1995); and Young Chang Chae, ed., *History of Korean-Americans in the Washington Metropolitan Area* (1995).

Also of uneven quality are the studies of Washington's religious life, largely comprised of the histories of its houses of worship. Among the best congregational histories are Constance McLaughlin Green, *The Church on Lafayette Square: A History of St. John's Church, Washington, D.C., 1815–1970* (1970); Robert E. Kendig, *The Washington National Cathedral: This Bible in Stone* (1995); Jane Donovan, ed., *Many Witnesses: A History of Dumbarton United Methodist Church, 1772–1990* (1998); Frank E. Edgington, *A History of the New York Avenue Presbyterian Church: One Hundred and Fifty-Seven Years, 1803–1961* (1961); Stanley Rabinowitz, *The Assembly: A Century in the Life of Adas Israel Hebrew Congregation of Washington, D.C.* (1993); and Morris J. MacGregor, *A Parish for the Federal City: St. Patrick's in Washington, 1794–1994* (1994) and *The Emergence of a Black Catholic Community: St. Augustine's in Washington* (1999).

Washington's high society is the subject of Kathryn Allamong

Jacob, *Capital Elites: High Society in Washington, D.C., after the Civil War* (1995).

Transportation history is covered in several studies, including Thomas F. Hahn, *The Chesapeake & Ohio Canal: Pathway to the Nation's Capital* (1984); Mike High, *The C&O Canal Companion* (1997); James D. Dilts, *The Great Road: The Building of the Baltimore & Ohio, the Nation's First Railroad, 1828–1853* (1993); LeRoy O. King, *One Hundred Years of Capital Traction: The Story of Streetcars in the Nation's Capital* (1972); and Amy L. Alotta, *George Washington Never Slept Here: The History of Street Names in Washington, D.C.* (1993). Articles in the *Washington Post* document the history of the Washington Metro subway system.

For war years in Washington, see Anthony S. Pitch, *The Burning of Washington: The British Invasion of 1814* (1998); Benjamin Franklin Cooling, *Mr. Lincoln's Forts: A Guide to the Civil War Defenses of Washington* (1988); and Frank Everson Vandiver, *Jubal's Raid: General Early's Famous Attack on Washington in 1864* (1992). On the World War II era, see David Brinkley, *Washington Goes to War* (1988).

Among the many Internet sites devoted to Washington, the following are of special importance: the District government and the mayor's office (www.dc.gov); the *Washington Post* (www.washingtonpost.com); the Smithsonian Institution (www.si.edu); the U.S. Capitol (www.aoc.gov); the White House (www.whitehouse.gov); the Washington Metrorail System (www.wmata.com). Also, see the internet addresses for Washington area history collections in appendix 2.

II. GENERAL WORKS

A. Bibliographies

Adams, Cheryl, and Art Emerson. *Religion Collections in Libraries and Archives: A Guide to Resources in Maryland, Virginia, and the District of Columbia.* Washington, D.C.: Library of Congress, 1998.

Calvan, Rita A. *Selected Theses and Dissertations on the Washington, D.C., Region.* Washington, D.C.: George Washington Center for Washington Area Studies, 1982.

Fisher, Perry G. "Materials for the Study of Washington: A Selected Annotated Bibliography." *George Washington Studies*, no. 1 (1974): 3–63.

Hanford, Sally. *Architectural Research Materials in the District of Columbia.* Washington, D.C.: American Institute of Architects Foundation, 1982.

Meglis, Anne Llewellyn. *A Bibliographic Tour of Washington, D.C.* Washington, D.C.: D.C. Redevelopment Land Agency, 1974.

Morales, Leslie Anderson. *District of Columbia's Battle for Home Rule: A Bibliography.* Monticello, Ill.: Vance Bibliographies, 1988.

National Capital Planning Commission. *Bibliography of Studies and Reports on the District of Columbia and the Washington Metropolitan Area.* Washington, D.C.: National Capital Planning Commission, 1967.

B. Biographies and Autobiographies

Agronsky, Jonathan I. Z. *Marion Barry: The Politics of Race.* Latham, N.Y.: British American Publications, 1991.

Alexander, Sally K. "A Sketch of the Life of Major Andrew Ellicott." *Records of the Columbia Historical Society* 2 (1899): 168–69.

American Biographical Directories: District of Columbia, 1908–1909. Washington, D.C.: Potomac Press, 1908.

Barnes, Bart. "Philanthropist Paul Mellon Dies." *Washington Post*, 3 February 1999, A1, 6–7.

———. "Roger Stevens Dies at 87; Founding Chairman of Kennedy Center." *Washington Post*, 4 February 1998, A1.

Barras, Jonetta Rose. *The Last of the Black Emperors: The Hollow Comeback of Marion Barry in a New Age of Black Leaders.* Baltimore, Md.: Bancroft Press, 1998.

Bedini, Silvio A. *The Life of Benjamin Banneker: The First African-American Man of Science.* New York: Charles Scribner's Sons, 1972.

Brownlow, Louis. *A Passion for Anonymity: The Autobiography of Louis Brownlow.* 2 vols. Chicago: University of Chicago Press, 1958.

Bruce, Robert V. *Alexander Graham Bell and the Conquest of Solitude.* Boston: Little, Brown and Company, 1973.

Bryan, Wilhelmus Bogart. "Something about L'Enfant and his Personal Affairs." *Records of the Columbia Historical Society* 2 (1899): 111–17.

Caemmerer, Hans Paul. *The Life of Pierre Charles L'Enfant.* Washington, D.C.: National Republic Publishing Company, 1950.

Clark, Allen C. "Rev. Stephen Bloomer Balch, a Pioneer Preacher of Georgetown." *Records of the Columbia Historical Society* 15 (1912): 73–95.

Coletta, Paolo E. *The Presidency of William Howard Taft.* Lawrence: University Press of Kansas, 1973.

Conroy, Sarah Booth. "Going to Georgetown to Take a Gander: The Glory of 'Friendship' and the Spirit of Evalyn Walsh McLean." *Washington Post*, 26 April 1981, L1.

Cooper, Anna J. *Anna J. Cooper: A Voice from the South.* Washington, D.C.: Smithsonian Institution Press, 1981.

Coulson, Thomas. *Joseph Henry: His Life and Work.* Princeton, N.J.: Princeton University Press, 1950.

Dance, Stanley. *The World of Duke Ellington.* New York: Charles Scribner's Sons, 1970.

Darrah, William C. *Powell of the Colorado.* Princeton, N.J.: Princeton University Press, 1951.

Dickson, D. Bruce, Jr. *Archibald Grimké: Portrait of a Black Independent.* Baton Rouge: Louisiana State University Press, 1993.

Douglass, Frederick. *Life and Times of Frederick Douglass.* Boston: De Wolfe, Fiske and Company, 1892.

Ellington, Edward Kennedy. *Music Is My Mistress.* New York: Da Capo Press, 1973.

French, Roderick S. "Letitia Woods Brown, 1915–1976." *Records of the Columbia Historical Society* 50 (1980): 522–24.

Gallagher, H. M. Pierce. *Robert Mills: Architect of the Washington Monument, 1781–1855.* New York: Columbia University Press, 1935.

Goggin, Jacqueline. *Carter G. Woodson: A Life in Black History.* Baton Rouge: Louisiana State University, 1993.

Golovin, Anne Castrodale. "William King, Jr., Georgetown Furniture

Maker." *Antiques* 109, no. 5 (May 1977): 1034.

Hagedorn, Hermann. *Brookings: A Biography*. New York: Macmillan, 1936.

Halasa, Malu. *Mary McLeod Bethune*. New York: Chelsea House Publishers, 1989.

Hamlin, Talbot. *Benjamin Henry Latrobe*. New York: Oxford University Press, 1955.

Hines, Thomas S. *Burnham of Chicago, Architect and Planner*. New York: Oxford University Press, 1974.

Huger, Lucie Furstenberg. "Dr. Mary Edwards Walker: The Little Lady in Pants." *Daughters of the American Revolution*, December 1989, 813–14, 846, 848.

Jewel, Derek. *Duke: A Portrait of Duke Ellington*. New York: W. W. Norton & Company, 1977.

Keck, Andrew S. "'Uncle Henry's Mind': Henry Adams and His 'Bronze Figure.'" *Records of the Columbia Historical Society* 52 (1989): 183–205.

Kelly, Joseph Thomas. "Rev. John C. Smith, D.D., and Other Pioneer Presbyterian Ministers of Washington." *Records of the Columbia Historical Society* 24 (1922): 118–35.

Klaus, Susan L. "'Some of the Smartest Folks Here': The Van Nesses and Community Building in Early Washington." *Washington History* 3, no. 2 (1991–92): 22–45.

Kling, Jean L. *Alice Pike Barney: Her Life and Art*. Washington, D.C.: Smithsonian Institution Press, 1994.

Love, Spencie. "'Noted Physician Fatally Injured': Charles Drew and the Legend That Will Not Die." *Washington History* 4, no. 2 (Fall/Winter 1992–93): 4–19.

Lowry, Edward G. *Washington Close-Ups: Intimate Views of Some Public Figures*. 1921. Reprint. Freeport, N.Y.: Books for Libraries Press, 1971.

Marlin, William. "Washington Architect, Arthur Cotton Moore." *Architectural Record* 162 (December 1977): 84–95.

McFeely, William S. *Frederick Douglass*. New York: Simon & Schuster, 1992.

"The Measure of a Man: James Wormley, a Nineteenth-Century African American Entrepreneur." Exhibition catalog, Washington Historical Society, 1993.

Moore, Charles. *Daniel H. Burnham: Architect, Planner of Cities*. 2 vols. New York: Houghton Mifflin, 1921.

———. *The Life and Times of Charles Follen McKim*. New York: Houghton Mifflin, 1929.

Morgan, James Dudley. "Robert Brent, First Mayor of Washington City." *Records of the Columbia Historical Society* 1 (1894–97): 235–46.

Mott, R. A. *Henry Cort: The Great Finer*. London: The Metals Society, 1983.

Oberholtzer, Ellis Paxson. *Robert Morris: Patriot and Financier*. New York: Burt Franklin, 1903.

O'Connor, Ellen M. *Myrtilla Miner: A Memoir*. New York: Houghton Mifflin, 1885.

Odgers, M. M. *Alexander Dallas Bache, Scientist and Educator, 1806–1867*. Philadelphia: University of Pennsylvania Press, 1947.

Osman, Mary E. "Arthur Cotton Moore Associates of Washington: Practice Profile." *AIA Journal* (May 1974): 58–61.

O'Toole, Patricia. *The Five of Hearts: An Intimate Portrait of Henry Adams and His Friends, 1880–1918*. New York: Clarkson Potter, 1990.

Place, Charles A. *Charles Bulfinch: Architect and Citizen*. New York: Da Capo Press, 1968.

Pollin, Abe. "Abe Pollin Reminisces." *Metro History News* 6, no. 2 (Winter 1998): 1–2.

Prominent Personages of the Nation's Capital. Washington, D.C.: Washington Times Company, 1924.

Remini, Robert V. *Daniel Webster: The Man and His Time*. New York W. W. Norton & Company, 1997.

———. *Henry Clay: Statesman for the Union*. New York: W. W. Norton & Company, 1991.

Richard, Paul. "Paul Mellon's Final Gifts." *Washington Post*, 11 February 1999, A1, 30.

Seaton, Josephine. *William Winston Seaton of the* National Intelligencer. Boston: J. R. Osgood & Company, 1871.

Serwer, Jacquelyn Days. *Gene Davis: A Memorial Exhibition*. Washington, D.C.: Smithsonian Institution Press, 1987.

Teichmann, Howard. *Alice: The Life and Times of Alice Roosevelt Longworth*. Englewood Cliffs, N.J.: Prentice-Hall, 1979.

Trindal, Elizabeth Steger. *Mary Surratt: An American Tragedy*. Gretna, La.: Pelican Publishing Company, 1996.

Tucker, Mark. *Ellington: The Early Years*. Urbana: University of Illinois Press, 1991.

Van Horne, John C., ed. *The Correspondence and Miscellaneous Papers of Benjamin Henry Latrobe.* 3 vols., ser. 4. New Haven, Conn.: Yale University Press, for the Maryland Historical Society, 1984–88.

Vidal, Gore. *Palimpsest: A Memoir.* New York: Random House, 1995.

Wall, Donald, ed. *Gene Davis.* New York: Praeger Publishers, 1975.

Wheeler, Douglas H. "Patrick Hayes, 1909–1998." *Washington History* 10, no. 2 (1998–99): 64–65.

Who's Who in the Nation's Capital, 1923–1938/39 (published sporadically). Washington, D.C.

Who's Who in Washington. Bethesda, Md.: Tiber Reference Press, 1984.

Williams, Roger M. "The Monument Meister." *Capital Style,* May 1999, 36–41.

C. History of Washington

1. Building the Federal City

Arnebeck, Bob. *Through a Fiery Trial: Building Washington, 1790–1800.* Lanham, Md.: Madison Books, 1991.

Bedini, Silvio A. "Benjamin Banneker and the Survey of the District of Columbia, 1791." *Records of the Columbia Historical Society* 47 (1970): 7–30.

———. "The Survey of the Federal Territory: Andrew Ellicott and Benjamin Banneker." *Washington History* 3, no. 1 (1991): 76–79.

Bowling, Kenneth R. *Creating the Federal City, 1744–1800: Potomac Fever.* Washington, D.C.: American Institute of Architects Press, 1988.

———. *The Creation of Washington, D.C.: The Idea and Location of the American Capital.* Fairfax, Va.: George Mason University Press, 1991.

———. "'A Place to Which Tribute Is Brought': The Contest for the Federal Capital in 1783." *Prologue* 8 (Fall 1976): 129–39.

Boyd, Julian P. "Fixing the Seat of Government." In *The Papers of Thomas Jefferson,* ed. Julian P. Boyd, 20:3–72. Princeton, N.J.: Princeton University Press, 1982.

Chaffee, Kevin, ed. *Fifty Maps of Washington, D.C.* New York: Gousha, 1991.

Ellicott, Andrew. *Maps of the District of Columbia and the City of Washington and Plats of the City of Washington.* Washington, D.C.: A. Boyd Hamilton, 1852.

First Maps of Washington. Washington, D.C.: U.S. Department of Commerce, 1968.

Goff, Frederick R. "Early Printing in Georgetown, 1789–1800, and the Engraving of L'Enfant's Plan of Washington, 1792." *Records of the Columbia Historical Society* 1951–52 (1955): 103–19.

Kite, Elizabeth S. *L'Enfant and Washington, 1791–1792*. 1929. Reprint. New York: Arno Press, 1970.

National Capital Planning Commission. *Boundary Markers of the Nation's Capital*. Washington, D.C.: Government Printing Office, 1967.

Padover, Saul K., ed. *Thomas Jefferson and the National Capital*. Washington, D.C.: Government Printing Office, 1946.

Schmidt, Lorraine H. *Washington: The Design of the Federal City*. Washington, D.C.: National Archives, 1972.

Shuster, Ernest A. *The Original Boundary Stones of the District of Columbia*. Washington, D.C.: National Geographic Society, 1909.

Smith, Richard Norton. *Patriarch: George Washington and the New American Nation*. New York: Houghton Mifflin, 1993.

Thatcher, Erastus. *Founding of Washington City*. Washington, D.C.: Law Reporter Company, 1891.

Todaro, Richard M. "The Four Cornerstones of the Original D.C." *Washington Post*, 7 June 1998, C8.

Woodward, Fred E. "A Ramble along the Boundary Stones of the District of Columbia with a Camera." *Records of the Columbia Historical Society* 10 (1907): 63–87.

2. General History

a. Nineteenth-Century Histories

Brooks, Noah. *Washington in Lincoln's Time*. New York: Century Company, 1895.

Crew, H. W., ed. *Centennial History of the City of Washington, D.C.* Dayton, Ohio: United Brethren Publishing House, 1892.

Elliot, Jonathan. *Historical Sketches of the Ten Miles Square Forming the District of Columbia*. Washington, D.C.: J. Elliot, Jr., 1830.

Hines, Christian. *Early Recollections of Washington City*. 1866. Reprint. Washington, D.C.: Junior League of Washington, 1981.

MacFarland, Henry B. B. *The Development of the District of Columbia*. Washington: National Capital Centennial Committee, 1900.

Mackall, Sally Somervell. *Early Days of Washington*. 1899. Reprint. Sterling, Ill.: G. E. Bishop Publishing Company, 1934.

b. Early to Mid-Twentieth-Century Histories

Baldwin, Elbert F. "Washington Fifty Years Hence." *Outlook* 14 (5 April 1902): 817–29.

Bigler, Philip. *Memories.* Washington, D.C.: W. F. Roberts Company, 1931.

Brown, Glenn. *History of the United States Capitol.* 2 vols. 1900–1903. Reprint. New York: Da Capo Press, 1970.

Bryan, Wilhelmus Bogart. "The Central Section of the City." *Records of the Columbia Historical Society* 7 (1904): 135–45.

———. *A History of the National Capital.* 2 vols. New York: Macmillan, 1914.

Cox, William V., comp. *Celebration of the One Hundredth Anniversary of the Establishment of the Seat of Government in the District of Columbia.* Washington, D.C.: Government Printing Office, 1901.

Moore, Charles. *Washington, Past and Present.* New York: Century Company, 1929.

Nicolay, Helen. *Our Capital on the Potomac.* New York: Century Company, 1924.

Proctor, John Clagett. *Washington Past and Present: A History.* 5 vols. New York: Lewis Historical Publishing Company, 1930.

Slauson, Allan B., ed. *A History of the City of Washington by the* Washington Post. Washington, D.C.: Washington Post Company, 1903.

Tindall, William. *Standard History of the City of Washington.* Knoxville, Tenn.: H. W. Crew, 1914.

c. Mid- to Late Twentieth-Century Histories

Bergheim, Laura. *The Washington Historical Atlas.* Washington, D.C.: Woodbine House, 1992.

Bigler, Philip. *Washington in Focus.* Arlington, Va.: Vandamere Press, 1988.

Brown, Letitia. *Washington in the New Era, 1870–1970.* Washington, D.C.: National Portrait Gallery, 1972.

Bustard, Bruce I. *Washington behind the Monuments.* Washington, D.C.: National Archives, 1990.

Cary, Francine Curro, ed. *Urban Odyssey: A Multicultural History of Washington, D.C.* Washington, D.C.: Smithsonian Institution Press, 1996.

Evelyn, Douglas E., and Paul Dickson. *On This Spot: Pinpointing the Past in Washington, D.C.* Washington, D.C.: Farragut Publishing, 1992.

Furer, Howard B., ed. *Washington: A Chronological and Documentary History.* Dobbs Ferry, N.Y.: Oceana Publications, 1975.

Gillette, Howard, Jr. *Between Justice and Beauty: Race, Planning, and the Failure of Urban Policy in Washington, D.C.* Baltimore, Md.: Johns Hopkins University Press, 1998.

Gillette, Howard, Jr., et al. *Southern City, National Ambition: The Growth of Early Washington, D.C., 1800–1860.* Washington, D.C.: George Washington Center for Washington Area Studies, 1995.

Green, Constance McLaughlin. *The Secret City.* Princeton, N.J.: Princeton University Press, 1967.

———. *Washington: Capital City, 1879–1950.* Princeton, N.J.: Princeton University Press, 1963.

———. *Washington: Village and Capital, 1800–1878.* Princeton, N.J.: Princeton University Press, 1962.

Junior League of Washington. *The City of Washington: An Illustrated History.* New York: Alfred A. Knopf, 1985.

Karp, Melvin. *Washington, D.C.: City of Many Dreams.* New York: Crescent Books, 1983.

Lessoff, Alan. *The Nature and Its City: Politics, Corruption, and Progress in Washington, D.C., 1861–1902.* Baltimore, Md.: Johns Hopkins University Press, 1994.

Lewis, David L. *District of Columbia: A Bicentennial History.* New York: W. W. Norton & Company, 1976.

Melder, Keith. *City of Magnificent Intentions.* 2d ed. Washington, D.C.: Intac, 1997.

Novins, Harriet. *Lisner-Louise-Dickson Home: A Brief History.* Washington, D.C.: Lisner-Louise-Dickson Home, 1993.

Ogilvie, Philip. "Chronology of Events in the History of the District of Columbia." Historical Society of Washington, D.C.

Penczer, Peter R. *Washington, D.C., Past and Present.* Arlington, Va.: Oneonta Press, 1988.

Reps, John W. *Washington on View: The Nation's Capital since 1790.* Chapel Hill: University of North Carolina Press, 1991.

Tobin, William Anthony. "In the Shadow of the Capitol: The Transformation of Washington, D.C., and the Elaboration of the Modern U.S. Nation State." Ph.D. dissertation, Stanford University, 1993.

Young, James Sterling. *The Washington Community, 1800–1828.* New York: Columbia University Press, 1986.

3. Historic Buildings

Beale, Marie. *Decatur House and Its Inhabitants*. Washington, D.C.: National Trust for Historic Preservation, 1954.

Crane, Katherine E. *Blair House, Past and Present*. Washington, D.C.: U.S. Department of State, 1945.

Goode, James M. *Capital Losses: A Cultural History of Washington's Destroyed Buildings*. Washington, D.C.: Smithsonian Press, 1979.

National Trust for Historic Preservation. *Decatur House*. Washington, D.C.: National Trust for Historic Preservation, 1967.

U.S. Capitol Historical Society. *We the People: The Story of the United States Capitol*. Washington, D.C.: U.S. Capitol Historical Society, 1985.

White House Historical Association. *The White House: An Historic Guide*. Washington, D.C.: White House Historical Association, 1996.

Whitehill, Walter Muir. *Dumbarton Oaks: The History of a Georgetown House and Garden, 1800–1966*. Cambridge, Mass.: Belknap Press, 1967.

D. General Directories and Guidebooks

1. Directories

Boyd, W. Andrew, comp. *Boyd's Directory of the District of Columbia, 1895*. Washington, D.C.: William H. Boyd, 1895.

Delano, Judah. *The Washington Directory*. Washington, D.C.: William Duncan, 1822.

Elliot, S. A. *The Washington Directory*. Washington D.C.: S. A. Elliot, 1827.

Washington Information Directory. Annual. Washington, D.C.: Congressional Quarterly.

2. Guidebooks

a. Nineteenth Century

Barton, E. E., ed. *Historical and Commercial Sketches of Washington and Environs*. Washington, D.C.: E. E. Barton, 1884.

New Standard Guide of the City of Washington and Environs. Washington, D.C.: Arlington Publishing Company, 1886.

Pepper, Charles M. *Every-Day Life in Washington with Pen and Camera*.

New York: Christian Herald, 1900.

Warden, David Baillie. *A Chorographical and Statistical Description of the District of Columbia*. Paris: Smith, 1816.

Watterston George. *New Guide to Washington: Containing a History and General Description of the Metropolis, Its Public Buildings, Institutions, Etc.* Washington, D.C.: Robert Farnham, 1847–48.

b. Early to Mid-Twentieth Century

Federal Writers' Project. *Washington: City and Capital*. American Guide Series. Washington, D.C.: Government Printing Office, 1937. Later published in a condensed version as *The WPA Guide to Washington, D.C.* (Washington, D.C.: George Washington University Press, 1992).

Reynolds, Charles Bingham, ed. *The Standard Guide: Washington: A Handbook for Visitors*. New York: Foster and Reynolds Company, 1896–1919.

Rider, Fremont, ed. *Rider's Washington: A Guidebook for Travelers*. New York: Macmillan, 1924.

c. Late Twentieth Century

Applewhite, E. J. *Washington Itself*. New York: Alfred A. Knopf, 1983.

Brown, Joe, et al. *Travel and Leisure Washington, D.C.* New York: Macmillan, 1997.

Fodor's '98 Washington, D.C. New York: Fodor's Travel Publications, 1997.

Hogarth, Paul. *Walking Tours of Old Washington and Alexandria*. McLean, Va.: EPM Publications, 1985.

Kennon, Donald R., and Richard Striner. *Washington Past and Present: A Guide to the Nation's Capital*. Washington, D.C.: U.S. Capitol Historical Society, 1993.

Kessler, Pamela. *Undercover Washington: Touring the Sites Where Infamous Spies Lived, Worked, and Loved*. McLean, Va.: EMP Publications, 1992.

Michelin Washington, D.C. (Green Guide). 3d ed. Greenville, S.C.: Michelin Travel Publications, 1997.

Protopappas, John J., and Lin Brown, eds. *Washington on Foot*. Washington, D.C.: Smithsonian Institution Press, 1981.

Walker, John, and Katherine Walker. *The Washington Guidebook*. Washington, D.C.: Metro Publishers Representatives, 1969.

Wiencek, Henry. *Smithsonian Guide to Historic America: Virginia and the Capital Region*. New York: Stewart, Tabori, Chang, 1989.

E. Newspapers and Journals

Ames, William E. *A History of the* National Intelligencer. Chapel Hill: University of North Carolina Press, 1972.

Babb, Laura Longley. *Keeping Posted: One Hundred Years of News from the* Washington Post. Washington, D.C.: Washington Post Company, 1977.

Chase, Hal Scripps. "Honey for Friends, Stings for Enemies: William Calvin Chase and the *Washington Bee.*" Ph.D. dissertation, University of Pennsylvania, 1973.

———. "Shelling the Citadel of Race Prejudice: William Calvin Chase and the *Washington Bee*, 1882–1921." *Records of the Columbia Historical Society* 49 (1973–74): 371–91.

Chen, Sung Chiao. "The News and Editorial Performance of the *Washington Evening Star.*" M.A. thesis, American University, 1962.

Clark, Allen C. "Joseph Gales, Jr., Editor and Mayor." *Records of the Columbia Historical Society* 23 (1920): 86–146.

Davis, Deborah. *Katharine the Great: Katharine Graham and Her* Washington Post *Empire*. 3d ed. New York: Sheridan Square Press, 1991.

Dixon, Joan M., comp. National Intelligencer *and* Washington Advertiser *Newspaper Abstracts, 1800–1805*. Bowie, Md.: Heritage Books, 1996.

Felsenthal, Carol. *Power, Privilege, and the* Post*: The Katharine Graham Story*. New York: Putnam, 1992.

Fleming, Martin L. *Inside the* Washington Post. New York: Vantage Press, 1996.

Graham, Katharine. *Personal History*. New York: Alfred A. Knopf, 1997.

Johnson, David K. "'Homosexual Citizens': Washington's Gay Community Confronts the Civil Service." *Washington History* 6, no. 2 (Fall/Winter 1994–95).

Kaufmann, Samuel H. *The* Evening Star*, 1852–1952: A Century at the Nation's Capital*. Princeton, N.J.: Newcomer Publications, 1952.

Kelly, Tom. *The Imperial* Post. New York: William Morrow, 1983.

Marbut, F. B. *News from the Capital: The Story of Washington Reporting*. Carbondale: Southern Illinois University Press, 1971.

Seaton, Josephine. *William Winston Seaton of the* National Intelligencer. 1871. Reprint. New York: Arno Press, 1970.

F. Photographs and Views

Collins, Kathleen. *Washingtoniana Photographs*. Washington, D.C.: Library of Congress, 1989.

Frank, Judith Waldrop, and Volkmar Wentzel. *Washington by Night: Vintage*

Photographs from the Thirties. Washington, D.C.: Starwood, 1992.

Levey, Jane Freundel. "The Scurlock Studio." *Washington History* 1, no. 1 (1989): 41–58.

Miller, Fredric M., and Howard Gillette. *Washington Seen: A Photographic History, 1875–1965.* Baltimore, Md.: Johns Hopkins University Press, 1995.

Moore, Joseph West. *Picturesque Washington: Pen and Pencil Sketches.* Providence, R.I.: J. A. & R. A. Reid, 1886.

Phillips, P. Lee, and F. J. Manasek. *Maps and Views of Washington and the District of Columbia.* Norwich, Vt.: Terra Nova Press, 1996.

Reed, Robert C., and Stephen M. Reed. *Old Washington, D.C., in Early Photographs, 1846–1932.* New York: Dover Publications, 1980.

G. Statistics, Demographics, and Genealogy

Browne, Henry J. *Assessment and Taxation in the District of Columbia and the Fiscal Relation to the Federal Government.* Washington, D.C.: Carnahan Press, 1915.

Gahn, Bessie Wilmarath. *Original Patentees of Land at Washington Prior to 1700.* Silver Spring, Md.: Westland Press, 1936.

Gart, Jeanne Brooks. "The Association of Oldest Inhabitants of the District of Columbia." *National Genealogical Society Quarterly* 82, no. 4 (1994): 292–95.

Grier, Eunice. *Understanding Washington's Changing Population.* Washington, D.C.: Washington Center for Metropolitan Studies, 1961.

Metcalf, Frank J., and George H. Martin. *Marriages and Deaths 1800–1820 from the* National Intelligencer, *Washington, D.C.* Washington, D.C.: National Genealogical Society, 1968.

Proctor, John Clagett. "The Oldest Inhabitants." *Washington Star,* 6 December 1931, 7:6.

Ridgely, Helen W. *Historic Graves of Maryland and the District of Columbia.* 1908. Reprint. Westminster, Md.: Family Line Publications, 1992.

III. SUBJECTS

A. Amusements and Recreation

Bealle, Morris A. *The Washington Senators.* Washington, D.C.: Columbia Publishing Company, 1947.

Gibson, J. Timberlake. "They're Off at Benning! The Rise and Fall of Horse Racing in Washington." *Washingtonian,* 37–38, 57–58, n.d., clipping file, Historical Society of Washington, D.C.

Gomery, Douglas. "Movie-Going Capital: Washington, D.C., in the History of Movie Presentation." *Washington History* 9, no. 1 (1997): 4–23.

Headley, Robert K. *Motion Picture Exhibition in Washington, D.C.: An Illustrated History of Parlors, Palaces, and Multiplexes in the Metropolitan Area, 1894–1997.* Jefferson, N.C.: McFarland, 1999.

Jones, William H. *Recreation and Amusement among Negroes in Washington, D.C.: A Sociological Analysis of the Negro in an Urban Environment.* Washington, D.C.: Howard University Press, 1927.

Povich, Shirley. *The Washington Senators.* New York: G. P. Putnam's Sons, 1954.

Ribowsky, Mark. *A Complete History of the Negro Leagues, 1884–1955.* Secaucus, N.J.: Carol Publishing Group, 1995.

Wheeler, Linda. "Preserving a Century of Service in Shaw: A Historic YMCA Finds New Community Role." *Washington Post,* 24 September 1998, J01.

B. Architecture

1. General Works

Bowling, Kenneth R. *Creating the Federal City, 1774–1800: Potomac Fever.* Washington, D.C.: American Institute of Architects Press, 1988.

Cox, Warren J., et al. *A Guide to the Architecture of Washington, D.C.* New York: McGraw-Hill, 1974.

Evans, James Matthew. *The Landscape Architecture of Washington, D.C.* Washington, D.C.: Landscape Architecture Foundation, 1981.

Forgey, Benjamin. "How 1902's City of Tomorrow Became the Capital of Today." *Washington Post,* 4 January 1999, A1, 12.

Gutheim, Frederick. *The Federal City: Plans and Realities.* Washington, D.C.: Smithsonian Institution Press, 1976.

———. *Worthy of the Nation: A History of Planning for the National Capital.* Washington, D.C.: Smithsonian Institution Press, 1977.

Hoagland, Alison K. "Nineteenth-Century Building Regulations in Washington, D.C." *Records of the Columbia Historical Society* 52 (1989): 57–77.

Jacobsen, Hugh Newell, ed. *A Guide to the Architecture of Washington.* New York: Praeger, 1965.

Kousoulas, Claudia D., and George W. Kousoulas. *Contemporary Architecture of Washington, D.C.* Washington, D.C.: Preservation Press, 1994.

McLoud, Melissa. "Craftsmen and Entrepreneurs: Buildings in Late Nineteenth-Century Washington." Ph.D. dissertation, George Washington University, 1988.

Reed, Henry Hope. *The Golden City*. New York: W. W. Norton & Company, 1970.

Reps, John W. *Monumental Washington: The Planning and Development of the Capital Center*. Princeton, N.J.: Princeton University Press, 1967.

Rieff, Daniel D. *Washington Architecture, 1791–1861: Problems in Development*. Washington, D.C.: U.S. Commission of Fine Arts, 1971.

Schwartz, Nancy B., comp. *Historic American Buildings Survey: District of Columbia Catalog*. Charlottesville: University Press of Virginia, for the Columbia Historical Society, 1974.

Scott, Pamela, and Antoinette J. Lee. *Buildings of the District of Columbia*. New York: Oxford University Press, 1993.

Weeks, Christopher, and Francis D. Lethbridge. *The AIA Guide to the Architecture of Washington, D.C.* Baltimore, Md.: Johns Hopkins University Press, 1994.

2. Architects

Berk, Sally Lichtenstein. "The Richest Crop: The Rowhouses of Harry Wardman, 1872–1938, Washington, D.C., Developer." M.A. thesis, George Washington University, 1989.

Bryan, Gray MacWhorter, III. "Waddy Wood's Residential Structures in Washington, D.C." M.A. thesis, University of Virginia, 1980.

Bryan, John M., ed. *Robert Mills, Architect*. Washington, D.C.: American Institute of Architects Press, 1989.

Cantor, Jay. "The Public Architecture of James Renwick, Jr." M.A. thesis, University of Delaware, 1967.

Hitchcock, Henry-Russell. *The Architecture of H. H. Richardson and His Times*. Cambridge, Mass.: M.I.T. Press, 1966.

Kirker, Harold. *Architecture of Charles Bulfinch*. Cambridge: Harvard University Press, 1977.

Placzek, Adolf K., ed. *Encyclopedia of Architects*. New York: Macmillan, 1982.

Tompkins, Sally Kress, et al. *A Quest for Grandeur: Charles Moore and the Federal Triangle*. Washington, D.C.: Smithsonian Institution Press, 1993.

3. Buildings and Sites

Abbott, James A., and Elaine M. Rice. *Designing Camelot: The Kennedy White House Restoration*. New York: Van Nostrand Reinhold, 1997.

Adam Davidson Galleries. *I. M. Pei and Partners: Drawings for the East Building, National Gallery of Art*. Washington, D.C.: Adam Davidson Galleries, 1978.

Allen, William C. *The United States Capitol: A Brief Architectural History*. Washington, D.C.: Government Publishing Office, 2000.

Butler, Jeanne F. "Competition 1792: Designing a Nation's Capitol." *Capital Studies* 4 (1976): 10–96.

Cole, John Young. *The Library of Congress: The Art and Architecture of the Thomas Jefferson Building*. New York: W. W. Norton & Company, 1998.

Eberlein, Harold Donaldson, and Cortlandt VanDyke Hubbard. *Historic Houses of George-Town and Washington City*. Richmond, Va.: Dietz Press, 1958.

Georgetown Commercial Architecture: M Street. Historic American Buildings Survey Selections, no. 2. Washington, D.C.: Commission of Fine Arts and the Historic American Buildings Survey, 1967.

Georgetown Historic Waterfront: A Review of Canal and Riverside Architecture. Washington, D.C.: U.S. Commission of Fine Arts and Office of Archaeology and Historic Preservation, 1968.

Georgetown Residential Architecture: Northeast. Historic American Buildings Survey Selections, no. 5. Washington, D.C.: Commission of Fine Arts and the Historic American Buildings Survey, 1969.

Georgetown Residential Architecture: The Waterfront. Historic American Buildings Survey Selections, no. 4. Washington, D.C.: Commission of Fine Arts and the Historic American Buildings Survey, 1968.

Goode, James M. *Best Addresses: A Century of Washington's Distinguished Apartment Houses*. Washington, D.C.: Smithsonian Institution Press, 1988.

Hazelton, George C. *The National Capitol: Its Architecture, Art, and History*. New York: J. F. Taylor and Company, 1902.

Heine, Cornelius W. *The Old Stone House*. Washington, D.C.: U.S. Department of the Interior, 1955.

Ridout, Orlando. *Building the Octagon*. Washington, D.C.: American Institute of Architects Press, 1989.

Scott, Pamela. *Temple of Liberty: Building the Capitol for a New Nation*. New York: Oxford University Press, 1995.

Thomas, Christopher A. *Architecture of the West Building of the National Gallery of Art.* Washington, D.C.: National Gallery of Art, 1992.

Wright, William M. "White City to White Elephant: Washington Union Station since World War II." *Washington History* 10, no. 2 (1998–99): 24–43.

C. Art

1. General Works

Art in the United States Capital. Washington, D.C.: Government Printing Office, 1978.

Cosentino, Andrew J, and Henry H. Glassie. *The Capital Image: Painters in Washington, 1800–1915.* Washington, D.C.: Smithsonian Institution Press, 1983.

Fairman, Charles E. *Art and Artists of the Capital of the United States of America.* Washington, D.C.: Government Printing Office, 1927.

Goode, James M. *The Outdoor Sculpture of Washington, D.C.* Washington, D.C.: Smithsonian Institution Press, 1974.

Kohler, Sue A. *The Commission of Fine Arts: A Brief History, 1910–1995.* Washington, D.C.: Commission of Fine Arts, 1996.

Mechlin, Leila. *Works of Art in Washington.* Washington, D.C.: Washington Society of Fine Arts, 1914.

Richard, Paul. "Local Art Collections and Their Benefactors." *Washington Post*, 15 March 1999, A6.

2. Guidebooks

Arden, Lorraine, et al. *Washington Art: A Guide to Galleries, Art Consultants, and Museums.* Great Falls, Va.: Art Calendar, 1988.

Fairman, Charles E. *The Outdoor Sculpture of Washington, D.C.: A Comprehensive Historical Guide.* Washington, D.C.: Smithsonian Institution Press, 1974.

Ross, Betty. *A Museum Guide to Washington, D.C.* Washington, D.C.: Americana Press, 1989.

D. Business and Economic Life

1. General Works

Abell, Julie. *A Guide to Business History in Washington, D.C.* Fairfax,

Va.: George Mason University, 1998.

Allen, Roger W. "Summary of Twentieth-Century Economic Development of the District of Columbia and the Washington Metropolitan Area." *Records of the Columbia Historical Society* 1973–74 (1976): 532–55.

Brodix, Charles R., comp. *Brodix's Business Directory of the District of Columbia for the Year 1886–7.* Washington, D.C.: Charles R. Brodix Publisher, 1886.

Bryan, Wilhelmus Bogart. "Hotels of Washington prior to 1814." *Records of the Columbia Historical Society* 7 (1904): 71–106.

Clark, Allen C. "The Old Mills." *Records of the Columbia Historical Society* 31–32 (1930): 81–115.

Cohen, Judith R. *The Mayflower Hotel: Grande Dame of Washington, D.C.* New York: Balance House, 1987.

Cook, Patricia M. "'Like the Phoenix': The Rebirth of the Whitelaw Hotel.'" *Washington History* 7, no. 1 (1995): 4–23.

Elfenbein, Jessica. *Civics, Commerce, and Community: The History of the Greater Washington Board of Trade, 1889–1989.* Washington, D.C.: Dubuque, Iowa: Kendall/Hunt Publishing Company, 1989.

Holmes, Oliver W. "The City Tavern: A Century of Georgetown History, 1797–1898." *Records of the Columbia Historical Society* 50 (1980): 1–35.

———. "The Colonial Taverns of Georgetown." *Records of the Columbia Historical Society* 1951–52 (1955): 1–18.

———. "Suter's Tavern: Birthplace of the Federal City." *Records of the Columbia Historical Society 1973–74* (1976): 1–34.

Hurst, Harold W. "Business and Businessmen in Pre-Civil War Georgetown, 1840–1860." *Records of the Columbia Historical Society* 50 (1980): 161–71.

Kerr, K. Austin. *Local Businesses: Exploring Their History.* Nashville, Tenn.: American Association for State and Local History, 1990.

MacMaster, Richard K. "Georgetown and the Tobacco Trade, 1751–1783." *Records of the Columbia Historical Society* 1966–68 (1969): 1–33.

McArdle, Walter F. "The Development of the Business Sector in Washington, D.C., 1800–1973." *Records of the Columbia Historical Society* 1973–74 (1976): 556–94.

Miller, Elizabeth Jane. "Dreams of Being the Capital of Commerce." *Records of the Columbia Historical Society* 51 (1981): 71–82.

Montgomery, Dean R. "The Willard Hotel of Washington, 1847–1968."

Records of the Columbia Historical Society 1966–68 (1969): 277–93.

Moreno, Sylvia, and Ann O'Hanlon. "Regrets for a Lost Landmark." *Washington Post*, 10 September 1999, E1, 9.

Nolen, John, Jr. "Some Aspects of Washington's Nineteenth-Century Economic Development." *Records of the Columbia Historical Society* 1973–74 (1976): 524–31.

Rosenberger, Homer Tope. "The Economic Development of Washington: An Introduction." *Records of the Columbia Historical Society* 1973–74 (1976): 521–23.

Washington Board of Trade. *The Book of Washington.* Washington, D.C.: Cleland C. McDevitt, 1927.

2. Banking and Finance

Beatty, Mary Alexins. *Bank Failures in the District of Columbia in Twentieth-Century Washington.* Washington, D.C.: Catholic University of America Press, 1949.

Fleming, Walter L. *The Freedman's Savings Bank: A Chapter in the Economic History of the Negro Race.* Chapel Hill: University of North Carolina Press, 1927.

Miller, M. Sammye. "An Early Venture in Black Capitalism: The Capital Savings Bank in the District of Columbia, 1888–1902." *Records of the Columbia Historical Society* 50 (1980): 359–66.

National Metropolitan Bank, Washington, D.C.: Oldest National Bank in the District of Columbia. Washington, D.C.: Press of W. F. Roberts, 1913.

Walsh, John J. *Early Banks in the District of Columbia, 1792–1818.* Washington, D.C.: Catholic University of America Press, 1940.

Wright, Carroll D. *The Economic Development of the District of Columbia.* Washington, D.C.: The Academy, 1899.

Yowell, William, Jr. "Historical Highlights of Washington's Oldest Bank." *Records of the Columbia Historical Society* 1957–59 (1961): 58–68.

3. Retail Businesses

From Founders to Grandsons: The Story of Woodward and Lothrop. Washington, D.C.: Woodward & Lothrop, 1955.

Haggerty, Maryann, and Stephanie Stoughton. "A Last Stampede to Hechinger—for the Sites." *Washington Post*, 10 September 1999, E1, 9.

Heurich, Gary F. "The Christian Heurich Brewing Company." *Records of the Columbia Historical Society* 1973–74 (1976): 604–15.

Longstreth, Richard. *The Mixed Blessings of Success: The Hecht Company and Department Store Branch Development after World War II.* Washington, D.C.: George Washington University Center for Washington Area Studies, 1995.

Miller, Elizabeth Jane. *The Dry Goods Trade in Washington, D.C., 1880–1899.* Thesis, George Washington University, 1977.

Pyatt, Rudolph A., Jr. "Another Retail Institution Is Reduced to a Footnote." *Washington Business,* supplement to the *Washington Post,* 13 September 1999, 4.

Sedar, Scott, and Bari Sedar. *Fifty Years of Caring.* Landover, Md.: Giant Food, 1986.

Stoughton, Stephanie. "Giant Food's Share of the Market Up." *Washington Post,* 16 June 1999, E1–2.

———. "The Hechinger Presence." *Washington Post,* 11 September 1999, A20.

E. Civil Rights and Race Relations

Beyan, Amos J. *The American Colonization Society and the Creation of the Liberian State.* Lanham, Md.: University Press of America, 1991.

Campbell, Penelope. *Maryland in Africa: The Maryland State Colonization Society, 1831–1857.* Urbana: University of Illinois Press, 1971.

Clopton, Willard, Jr., and Robert G. Kaiser. "Washington in Flames." *Washington Post,* 7 April 1999, C16.

Gentile, Thomas. *March on Washington: August 28, 1963.* Washington, D.C.: New Day Publications, 1983.

Gilbert, Ben W. *Ten Blocks from the White House: Anatomy of the Washington Riots of 1968.* New York: F. A. Praeger, 1968.

Goldfield, David R. *Black, White, and Southern: Race Relations and Southern Culture, 1940 to the Present.* Baton Rouge: Louisiana State University Press, 1990.

Green, Constance M. *The Secret City: A History of Race Relations in the Nation's Capital.* Princeton, N.J.: Princeton University Press, 1967.

Johnson, Thomas R. *The City on the Hill: Race Relations in Washington, D.C., 1865–1885.* Ph.D. dissertation, University of Maryland, 1975.

———. "Reconstruction Politics in Washington: An Experimental Garden for Radical Plants." *Records of the Columbia Historical Society* 50 (1980): 180–90.

Kofie, Nelson F. *Race, Class, and the Struggle for Neighborhoods in*

Washington, D.C. New York: Garland, 1999.

Lipton, Eric. "District to Sell Houses along Path of '68 Riots." *Washington Post*, 30 June 1999, B1, 7.

Miller, Floyd J. *The Search for a Black Nationality: Black Emigration and Colonization, 1787–1863.* Urbana: University of Illinois Press, 1975.

Moore, Jacqueline. *Leading the Race: The Transformation of the Black Elite in the Nation's Capital, 1880–1920.* Charlottesville: University Press of Virginia, 1999.

Murray, Robert K. *Red Scare: A Study in National Hysteria, 1919–1920.* Minneapolis: University of Minnesota Press, 1955.

Pacifico, Michele F. "Don't Buy Where You Can't Work: The New Negro Alliance of Washington." *Washington History* 6, no. 1 (1994): 66–88.

———. "History of the New Negro Alliance of Washington, D.C., 1933–1941." Thesis, George Washington University, 1983.

Perl, Peter. "In the Race Riot of 1919, a Glimpse of Struggles to Come." *Washington Post*, 1 March 1999, A1, 6.

F. Diplomatic Washington

Bachrach, Judy. "The Dictator and the Dead." *Vanity Fair*, June 1999, 126–41.

Dilworth, Donald C. *Embassies of the World: Five Walking Tours and Directory.* Washington, D.C.: Communications Press, 1986.

Highsmith, Carol M., and Ted Landphair. *Embassies of Washington.* Washington, D.C.: Preservation Press, 1992.

Lynton, Stephen J., and Lawrence Meyer. "Blood in Sheridan Circle." *Washington Post*, 22 September 1999, C16.

Miller, Hope Ridings. *Embassy Row: The Life and Times of Diplomatic Washington.* New York: Holt, Rinehart, and Winston, 1969.

G. Education

1. Private Schools

Kayser, Elmer Louis. "Columbian Academy, 1821–1897: The Preparatory Department of Columbia College in the District of Columbia." *Records of the Columbia Historical Society* 48 (1971–72): 150–63.

Null, Druscilla J. "Myrtilla Miner's 'School for Colored Girls': A Mirror on Antebellum Washington." *Records of the Columbia Historical Society* 52 (1989): 254–68.

2. Public Schools

Atlee, Samuel Yorke. *History of the Public Schools of Washington City, D.C., from August, 1805 to August, 1875.* Washington: McGill and Witherow, 1876.

Collins, Carolyn B. "Mayor Sayles J. Bowen and the Beginnings of Negro Education." *Records of the Columbia Historical Society* 42 (1956): 293–308.

Dabney, Lillian Gertrude. *The History of Schools for Negroes in the District of Columbia, 1807–1947.* Washington, D.C.: Catholic University Press, 1949.

Diner, Steven J. *Crisis in Confidence: The Reputation of Washington's Public Schools in the Twentieth Century.* Washington, D.C.: Department of Urban Studies, University of the District of Columbia, 1982.

———. *The Governance of Education in the District of Columbia: An Historical Analysis of Current Issues.* Washington, D.C.: Department of Urban Studies, University of the District of Columbia, 1982.

Donovan, Jane, and Brian McClure. *Lafayette Life.* Washington, D.C.: Historic Chevy Chase, D.C., 1999.

Federal Schoolmen's Club. *Official History: Federal Schoolmen's Club, Washington, D.C.: 50th Anniversary.* Washington, D.C.: Federal Schoolmen's Club, 1957.

Feinberg, Lawrence. "Teacher Shift Hits Hardest in Northwest." *Washington Post*, 14 August 1971.

———. "Henley Cites Pupil Costs in Bias Case." *Washington Post*, 11 August 1970.

Kessler, Ann. *A History of Ben W. Murch Elementary School, 1930–1990.* Washington, D.C.: Ben W. Murch Elementary School, 1990.

Lofton, Williston. "The Development of Public Education for Negroes in Washington, D.C.: A Study of Separate but Equal Accommodations." Ph.D. dissertation, American University, 1944.

Proctor, John Clagett. "Joseph Lancaster and the Lancasterian Schools in the District of Columbia." *Records of the Columbia Historical Society* 25 (1923): 1–35.

Public Schools of the District of Columbia. *The Charles Sumner School: Rededication.* Washington, D.C.: D.C. Public Schools, 1986.

Richey, Alice Molyneux. "History of the Night Schools of the District of Columbia." M.A. thesis, George Washington University, 1944.

Robinson, Henry S. "The M Street High School, 1891–1916." *Records of the Columbia Historical Society* 51 (1984): 119–43.

Speicher, Anna. "Community Involvement in Public Education: Parents United for the D.C. Public Schools." Occasional Paper 11. Center for Washington Area Studies, George Washington University, 1992.

Strauss, Valerie, and Debbi Wilgoren. "The D.C. School Board, Troubled Still." *Washington Post*, 25 July 1999, C1, 5.

3. Higher Education

Alexis, Karain M. E. "The American University: Classical Visions of the National University." *Records of the Columbia Historical Society* 52 (1989): 163–82.

Atwood, Albert W. "Gallaudet in Washington: The World's Only College for the Deaf." *Records of the Columbia Historical Society* (1963–65): 432–47.

Chandler, Douglas R. *Pilgrimage of Faith: A Centennial History of Wesley Theological Seminary, 1882–1982.* Cabin John, Md.: Seven Locks Press, 1984.

Christiansen, John B., and Sharon N. Barnartt. *Deaf President Now! The 1988 Revolution at Gallaudet University.* Washington, D.C.: Gallaudet University Press, 1995.

Curran, Robert Emmett, and Leo J. O'Donovan. *The Bicentennial History of Georgetown University.* Vol. 1: *From Academy to University, 1789–1889.* Washington, D.C.: Georgetown University Press, 1993.

Daley, John M. *Georgetown University: Origin and Early Years.* Washington, D.C.: Georgetown University Press, 1957.

Durkin, Joseph T. *Georgetown University: First in the Nation's Capital.* Garden City, N.Y.: Doubleday, 1964.

———. *Georgetown University: The Middle Years, 1840–1900.* Washington, D.C.: Georgetown University Press, 1963.

Ellis, John Tracy. *The Formative Years of the Catholic University of America.* Washington, D.C.: American Catholic Historical Association, 1946.

George Washington University. *From Strength to Strength: A Pictorial History of the George Washington University, 1821–1996.* Washington, D.C.: George Washington University, 1996.

Kayser, Elmer Louis. *Bricks without Straw: The Evolution of George Washington University.* New York: Appleton-Century Crofts, 1970.

Logan, Rayford. *Howard University: The First Hundred Years, 1867–1967.* New York: New York University Press, 1969.

Nelson, Bernard Hamilton. *Miner Teacher's College: The First Century,*

1851–1951: Biography of a School. Washington, D.C.: District of Columbia Teacher's College, 1973.

Shea, John Gilmary. *Memorial of the First Centenary of Georgetown College, D.C., Comprising a History of Georgetown University.* New York: P. F. Collier, 1891.

H. Housing and Employment

Barnes, William R. "Battle for Washington: Ideology, Racism, and Self-Interest in the Controversy over Public Housing, 1943–1946." *Records of the Columbia Historical Society* 50 (1980): 452–83.

Borchert, James Alan. "Alley Life in Washington: An Analysis of 600 Photographs." *Records of the Columbia Historical Society* 49 (1973–74): 244–59.

———. *Alley Life in Washington.* Urbana: University of Illinois Press, 1980.

Hannold, Elizabeth. "'Comfort and Respectability': Washington's Philanthropic Housing Movement." *Washington History* 4, no. 2 (Fall/Winter 1992–93): 29–39.

Jones, William H. *The Housing of Negroes in Washington, D.C.: A Study in Human Ecology.* Washington, D.C.: Howard University Press, 1929.

Kaiser, Robert G. "Resurrection City." *Washington Post*, 25 June 1999, C12.

Kober, George M. *The History and Development of the Housing Movement in the District of Columbia.* Washington, D.C.: Washington Sanitary Housing Companies, 1927.

McMurray, Donald Le Crone. *Coxey's Army: A Study of the Industrial Army Movement of 1894.* Boston: Little, Brown and Company, 1929.

Thurz, Daniel. *Where Are They Now? A Study of the Impact of Relocation of Former Residents of Southwest Washington.* Washington, D.C.: Health and Welfare Council of the National Capital Area, 1973.

Turner, Margery Austin. *Housing Market Impacts of Rent Control: The Washington D.C. Experience.* Washington, D.C.: Urban Institute, 1990.

Waters, Walter W. *The Whole Story of the Bonus Army.* New York: John Day Company, 1933.

I. Literary Society

Alexander, John. *Ghosts: Washington's Most Famous Ghost Stories.*

Washington, D.C.: Washingtonian Books, 1975.

Cutler, David. *Literary Washington: A Complete Guide to the Literary Life in the Nation's Capital*. Lanham, Md.: Madison Books, 1992.

Dale, Alzina Stone. *Mystery Reader's Walking Guide, Washington, D.C.* Lincolnwood, Ill.: Passport Books, 1998.

Nicolay, Helen. *Sixty Years of the Literary Society*. Washington, D.C.: H. L. & J. B. McQueen, 1934.

Schafer, Edith Nalle. *Literary Circles of Washington*. Washington, D.C.: Starrhill Press, 1994.

J. Local Government

1. General Works

Alfers, Kenneth G. *Law and Order in the Capital City: A History of the Washington Police, 1800–1886*. Washington, D.C.: George Washington Center for Washington Area Studies, 1976.

O'Cleireacain, Carol. *Orphaned Capital: Adopting the Right Revenues for the District of Columbia*. Washington, D.C.: Brookings Institution Press, 1997.

Openchowski, Charles. *Guide to Environmental Law in Washington, D.C.* Washington, D.C.: Environmental Law Institute, 1990.

Williams, Vanessa. "D.C. Government Reclaims City Hall." *Washington Post*, 11 November 1999, B1, 9.

2. Courts

Kowalsky, Adrian D., et al., eds. *District of Columbia Court Rules*. Annotated 1991 edition, vol. 1. Charlottesville, Va.: Michie Company, 1991.

McGuire, Matthew F. *An Anecdotal History of the United States District Court for the District of Columbia, 1801–1976*. Washington, D.C.: n.p., 1976.

Voorhees, Theodore. "The District of Columbia Courts: A Judicial Anomaly." *Catholic University Law Review* 29, no. 4 (1980): 917–38.

3. Government

Acts of the Corporation of the City of Washington. Washington, D.C.: City Council, 1802–1818.

Arnold, Linda M. "Congressional Government of the District of Columbia, 1800–1846." Ph.D. dissertation, Georgetown University, 1974.

District of Columbia Code. Annotated 1981 edition. Charlottesville, Va.: Michie Company, 1994. Vol. 4A replacement. Charlottesville, Va.: LEXIS Law Publishing, 1999.

Fehr, Stephen C. "Davis Nearing End of D.C. Oversight." *Washington Post*, 21 January 2000, B1, 8.

———. "District Moves to Reclaim Self-Rule." *Washington Post*, 18 January 2000, B1, 4.

Harris, Charles Wesley. *Congress and the Governance of the Nation's Capital: The Conflict of Federal and Local Interests.* Washington, D.C.: Georgetown University Press, 1995.

Mathews, Jay, and LaBarbara Bowman. "Washington for Washington." *Washington Post*, 6 November 1999, C14.

Schmeckebier, Laurence. *The District of Columbia: Its Government and Administration.* Baltimore, Md.: Johns Hopkins University Press, 1928.

4. Public Works and Utilities

Cromwell, Joseph H. *The C&P Story: Service in Action.* Washington, D.C.: Chesapeake & Potomac Telephone Company, 1981.

Maury, William M. "Alexander R. Shepherd and the Board of Public Works." *Records of the Columbia Historical Society* (1971–72): 394–410.

Metzger, Philip C. *The Re-Invention of Water Management: Solving Water Supply Problems in the Washington, D.C., Metropolitan Area.* Washington, D.C.: Conservation Foundation, 1988.

Noreen, Sarah Pressey. *Public Street Illumination in Washington, D.C.: An Illustrated History.* Washington, D.C.: George Washington University, 1975.

Potomac Electric Company. *One Hundred Years of Matchless Service: An Illustrated History of Potomac Electric Power Company.* Laurel, Md.: PEPCO, 1996.

Washington Gas Light Company. *Growing with Washington: The Story of Our First Hundred Years.* Washington: n.p., 1948.

Ways, Harry C. *The Washington Aqueduct, 1852–1992.* Washington, D.C.: H. C. Ways, 1996.

K. Medical and Social Services

Council of Social Agencies. Records, 1938, 1940–48. Historical Society of Washington.

Holt, Thomas, Cassandra Smith-Parker, and Rosalyn Terborg-Penn. *A Special Mission: The Story of Freedmen's Hospital, 1862–1962.* Washington, D.C.: Howard University Academic Affairs Division, 1975.

Overholser, Winfred. "An Historical Sketch of St. Elizabeth's Hospital." In *Centennial Papers, St. Elizabeth's Hospital, Washington, D.C.*, 1–24. Baltimore, Md.: Waverly Press, 1956.

Washington, D.C., Board of Trade. *Public and Private Hospitals and Charities in the District of Columbia.* Washington, D.C.: n.p., 1912.

Weitzmann, Louis G. *One Hundred Years of Catholic Charities in the District of Columbia.* Ph.D. dissertation, Catholic University of America, 1931.

L. Memorials and Monuments

Coldwell, Thomas. *Granite Sea: Navigating the United States Navy Memorial and Visitor's Center.* Washington, D.C.: U.S. Navy Memorial Foundation, 1992.

Doherty, Craig A., and Katherine M. Doherty. *The Washington Monument.* Woodbridge, Conn.: Blackbirch Press, 1995.

Halprin, Lawrence. *The Franklin Delano Roosevelt Memorial.* San Francisco: Chronicle Books, 1997.

Jacob, Kathryn Allamong. *Testament to Union: Civil War Monuments in Washington, D.C.* Baltimore, Md.: Johns Hopkins University Press, 1998.

Meyer, Eugene L. "History Chiseled in Stone." *Washington Post*, 30 October 1998, Weekend section, 6–9.

Meyer, Jack. *Washington, D.C., Monuments in Architectural and Historical Review.* Green Bay, Wis.: CSU Publications, 1993.

M. Museums, Libraries, and Research Institutions

1. Museums and Galleries

Bello, Mark. *The Smithsonian Institution: A World of Discovery: An Exploration of Behind-the-Scenes Research in the Arts, Sciences, and Humanities.* Washington, D.C.: Smithsonian Institution Press, 1993.

Carmichael, Leonard, and J. C. Long. *James Smithson and the Smithsonian Story.* New York: Putnam, with the Smithsonian Institution, 1965.

Field, Cynthia R. *The Castle: An Illustrated History of the Smithsonian*

Building. Washington, D.C.: Smithsonian Institution Press, 1993.

Finley, David Edward. *A Standard of Excellence: Andrew W. Mellon Founds the National Gallery of Art at Washington*. Washington, D.C.: Smithsonian Institution Press, 1973.

Kurin, Richard I., and Michael Heyman. *Reflections of a Culture Broker: A View from the Smithsonian*. Washington, D.C.: Smithsonian Institution Press, 1997.

Linenthal, Edward T. *Preserving Memory: The Struggle to Create America's Holocaust Museum*. New York: Viking, 1995.

National Museum of American Art. *National Museum of American Art, Smithsonian Institution*. Washington, D.C.: The National Museum of American Art, 1995.

Oehser, Paul H. *Sons of Science: The Story of the Smithsonian Institution and Its Leaders*. New York: H. Schuman, 1949.

Ross, Betty. *Washington, D.C., Museums: A Ross Guide: Museums, Historic Houses, Art Galleries, Libraries, and Other Special Places*. 3d ed. Washington, D.C.: Americana Press, 1999.

Smithsonian Institution. Annual Reports of the Smithsonian Institution. Washington, D.C.: Smithsonian Institution, 1847–.

Weinberg, Jeshajahu, and Rina Elieli. *The Holocaust Museum in Washington*. New York: Rizzoli International, 1999.

Wheeler, Linda. "The District Takes Its Place in History: Library to Open as City Museum." *Washington Post*, 24 October 1998, C3.

2. Libraries and Archives

Cole, John Young. *Capital Libraries and Librarians: A Brief History of the District of Columbia Library Association, 1894–1994*. Washington, D.C.: Library of Congress, 1994.

Highsmith, Carol M., and Ted Landphair. *The Library of Congress: America's Memory*. Golden, Colo.: Fulcrum Publishers, 1994.

Jacob, Kathryn Allamong. "'To Gather and Preserve . . .': The Columbia Historical Society Is Founded, 1894." *Washington History* 6, no. 2 (Fall/Winter 1994–95): 4–23.

Phalen, Lane. *The Book Lover's Guide to Washington, D.C.* Hoffman Estates, Ill.: Brigadoon Bay Books, 1993.

Smith, Kathryn Schneider. "Today's Historical Society: The Promise of Past and Future." *Washington History* 6, no. 2 (Fall/Winter 1994–95): 24–43.

Sowerby, E. Millicent. *Catalogue of the Library of Thomas Jefferson*.

Charlottesville: University Press of Virginia, 1983.
Stille, Alexander. "Overload." *New Yorker*, 8 March 1999, 38–44.

N. Neighborhoods

1. General Works

Abell, Alicia. "Seventh Street Arts District." *Washingtonian* 34, no. 10 (July 1999): 25.
Cochran, Sheila Smith. *River Road: An Early History*. 2d ed. Washington, D.C.: Sheila Smith Cochran, 1990.
Commission of Fine Arts. *Massachusetts Avenue Architecture*. 2 vols. Washington, D.C.: Government Printing Office, 1973–75.
Helm, Judith Beck. *Tenleytown, D.C.: Country Village into City Neighborhood*. Washington, D.C.: Tennally Press, 1981.
McNeil, Priscilla W. "Rock Creek Hundred: Land Conveyed for the Federal City." *Washington History* 3, no. 1 (1991): 34–51.
Smith, Kathryn Schneider. "Remembering U Street." *Washington History* 9, no. 2 (1998): 28–53.
———, ed. *Washington at Home: An Illustrated History of Neighborhoods in the Nation's Capital*. Northridge, Calif.: Windsor Publications, 1988.
Wheeler, Linda. "Broken Ground, Broken Hearts." *Washington Post*, 21 June 1999, A1, 7.
Williams, Brett. *Upscaling Downtown: Stalled Gentrification in Washington, D.C.* Ithaca, N.Y.: Cornell University Press, 1988.

2. Adams Morgan

Henig, Jeffrey. *Gentrification in Adams Morgan: Political and Commercial Consequences of Neighborhood Change*. Washington, D.C.: George Washington University, 1982.
Kehne, W. Denver. *Adams Morgan: A New Concept in Community Planning and Social Progress*. Washington, D.C.: n.p., 1964.
West, Woody, and Earl Byrd. "This Is the Most Diverse Neighborhood in the City." *Washington Star*, 11 February 1975, B1, 3.

3. Anacostia

Cantwell, Thomas J. "Anacostia: Strength in Adversity." *Records of the Columbia Historical Society* 1973–74 (1976): 330–70.
Hutchinson, Louise Daniel. *The Anacostia Story, 1608–1930*. Washing-

ton, D.C.: Smithsonian Institution Press, 1977.

Martin-Felton, Zora. *A Different Drummer: John Kinard and the Anacostia Museum, 1967–1989.* Washington, D.C.: Smithsonian Institution Press, 1993.

4. Brightwood

Grandine, Katherine Elizabeth. "Brightwood: Its Development and Suburbanization, 1800–1915." Thesis, George Washington University, 1983.

5. Brookland

McDaniel, George W., ed. *Images of Brookland: The History and Architecture of a Washington Suburb.* Washington, D.C.: George Washington University, 1979.

Nichols, Joseph. "Brookland." Tourguide notes. Historical Society of Washington, D.C., 1986.

6. Capitol Hill

Downing, Margaret Brent. "The Earliest Proprietors of Capitol Hill." *Records of the Columbia Historical Society* 21 (1918): 1–23.

Herron, Paul. *The Story of Capitol Hill.* New York: Coward-McCann, 1963.

Myers, Susan H. "Capitol Hill, 1870–1900: The People and Their Homes." *Records of the Columbia Historical Society* 1973–74 (1976): 276–99.

Taylor, Frank A. "Growing Up on Capitol Hill." *Records of the Columbia Historical Society* 50 (1980): 508–21.

7. Chevy Chase

French, Roderick S. "Chevy Chase Village in the Context of the National Suburban Movement, 1870–1900." *Records of the Columbia Historical Society* 1973–74 (1976): 300–29.

Town History Committee. *The Town of Chevy Chase, 1909–1959.* Chevy Chase, Md: Chevy Chase, 1990.

8. Cleveland Park

Moore, David, and William A. Hill. *Cleveland Park.* Washington, D.C.: Colonial Historical Society, 1904.

Peter, Grace Dunlop, and Joyce D. Southwick. *Cleveland Park: An Early Residential Neighborhood of the Nation's Capital.* Washington, D.C.: Cleveland Park Community Library Committee, 1958.

9. Columbia Heights

Columbia Heights Citizens Association. *A Statement of Some of the Advantages of Beautiful Columbia Heights: A Neighborhood of Homes.* Washington, D.C.: Columbia Heights Citizens Association, 1904.

Lipton, Eric. "An Angry Reaction Wasn't Part of the Plan." *Washington Post,* 20 September 1999, B1, 5.

———. "A Case of Competing Desires." *Washington Post,* 13 May 1999, DC1, 4

———. "Columbia Heights Taking Flight." *Washington Post,* 1 April 1999, DC1, 3.

Montgomery, David. "Protest Gives Mayor a Taste of Disfavor." *Washington Post,* 13 September 1999, B3.

———. "Ready for Renewal." *Washington Post,* 10 September 1999, B1, 8.

Wax, Emily. "A Street Struggles for Peace: Columbia Heights Seeks End to Crime." *Washington Post,* 6 September 1999, B1, 4.

10. Deanwood

Henley, Laura, and Robert Verrey. "Final Report on Historical and Building Investigation of the Northeast Washington, D.C. Community of Deanwood, Phase I, Submitted by Far East Community Services, 30 September 1987." Historical Society of Washington, D.C., 1987.

Lynch, Rene M. "Deanwood: Close-Knit D.C. Community." *Washington Post,* 6 August 1988, E1, 5.

McGraw, Vincent. "Tradition Develops Deanwood's Charm." *Washington Times,* 19 June 1981, C1, 4.

11. Dupont Circle

Dan, Linda Cash. *Dupont Circle Revisited.* Edited by Laura Smith Auster. Washington, D.C.: L'Enfant Trust, 1984.

Olszewski, George. *Dupont Circle, Washington, D.C.* Washington, D.C.: Division of History, National Park Service, 1967.

Rubin, Courtney. "Sidewalks: Dupont Circle." *Washingtonian,* June 1999, p. 26.

12. Foggy Bottom

Conroy, Sarah Booth. "Foggy Bottom Brightens Up for a Celebration." *Washington Post*, 14 June 1999, C2.

Evans, Jessie Fant. *Hamburg: The Colonial Town That Became the Seat of George Washington University*. Washington, D.C.: George Washington University General Alumni Association, 1935.

Herman, Jan K. *A Hilltop in Foggy Bottom: Home of the Old Naval Observatory and the Navy Medical Department*. Washington, D.C.: Department of the Navy, 1984.

Parris, Albion Keith. "Recollections of Our Neighbors in the First Ward in the Early Sixties." *Records of the Columbia Historical Society* 29–30 (1928): 269–89.

13. Georgetown

Davis, Deering, Stephen P. Dorsey, and Ralph Cole Hall. *Georgetown Houses of the Federal Period*. New York: Architectural Book Publishing Company, 1944.

Davis, Donald, and Scott Hart. *Georgetown, 1751 to the Present*. Washington, D.C.: D. S. Davis, 1965.

Ecker, Grace Dunlop. *A Portrait of Old George Town*. Richmond, Va.: Dietz Press, 1951.

Evans, Henry Ridgely. *Old Georgetown on the Potomac*. Washington, D.C.: Georgetown News, 1933.

Holmes, Oliver W. "The City Tavern: A Century of Georgetown History, 1797–1898." *Records of the Columbia Historical Society* 50 (1980): 1–35.

———. "The Colonial Taverns of Georgetown." *Records of the Columbia Historical Society* 1951–52 (1955): 1–18.

———. "Suter's Tavern: Birthplace of the Federal City." *Records of the Columbia Historical Society* 1973–74 (1976): 1–34.

Hurst, Harold W. "Business and Businessmen in Pre-Civil War Georgetown, 1840–1860." *Records of the Columbia Historical Society* 50 (1980): 161–71.

Jackson, Cordella. "People and Places in Old Georgetown." *Records of the Columbia Historical Society* 33–34 (1932): 133–62.

Jackson, Richard P. *The Chronicles of Georgetown, D.C., from 1751 to 1878*. Washington, D.C.: R. O. Polkinhorn, 1878.

Kinney, William A. "Washington's Historic Georgetown." *National Geographic* 103, no. 4 (April 1953): 513–44.

Lapish, J. H. *Georgetown's Bicentenary*. Washington, D.C.: St. John's

Episcopal Church, 1951.

Leary, Josephine Davis. *Backward Glances at Georgetown*. Richmond, Va.: Dietz Press, 1947.

Maroon, Fred J. *Maroon on Georgetown*. Rev. ed. New York: Lickle Publishing Company, 1997.

Mitchell, Mary. *Chronicles of Georgetown Life, 1865–1900*. Cabin John, Md.: Seven Locks Press, 1986.

———. *Divided Town*. Barre, Mass.: Barre Publishers, 1968.

———. *Glimpses of Georgetown Past and Present*. Washington, D.C.: Road Street Press, 1983.

Palmer, John Williamson. *Old Georgetown: A Social Panorama*. New York: Century Company, 1897.

Smith, Kathryn Schneider. *Port Town to Urban Neighborhood: The Georgetown Waterfront of Washington, D.C., 1880–1920*. Dubuque, Iowa: Kendall/Hunt Publishing Company, 1989.

Taggart, Hugh T. *Old Georgetown*. Lancaster, Pa.: New Era Printing, 1908.

Watson, Carol Stuart. "Old Georgetown on the Potomac." Map, 1959. Peabody Collection, Georgetown Public Library.

Williams, Mathilde D. *Georgetown, 1621–1951: A. Brief Outline of Its History*. Washington, D.C.: Peabody Library Association, 1951.

14. Kalorama

Bacon-Foster, Corra. "The Story of Kalorama." *Records of the Columbia Historical Society* 13 (1910): 98–118.

Mitchell, Mary. "Kalorama: Country Estate to Washington Mayfair." *Records of the Columbia Historical Society* 1971–72 (1973): 164–89.

Wallace, John K. "The Growth and Development of a Late Nineteenth-Century High-Status Suburb: The Case of Kalorama, Washington, D.C." Thesis, University of Maryland, 1991.

15. LeDroit Park

Burwell, Lilian Thomas. "Reflections on LeDroit Park: Hilda Wilkinson Brown and Her Neighborhood." *Washington History* 3, no. 2 (1991–92): 46–61.

16. Mount Pleasant

Riggs National Bank. *The Story of Mount Pleasant and Milestones of Its Later Day Development*. Washington, D.C.: Riggs National Bank,

1923.

17. Pennsylvania Avenue

Highsmith, Carol M., and Ted Landphair. *Pennsylvania Avenue: America's Main Street*. Washington, D.C.: American Institute of Architects Press, 1988.

18. Petworth

Barras, Jonetta Rose. "Petworth Strives to Reclaim Its Old Serenity." *Washington Times*, 14 May 1990, B1, 4.
Brown, DeNeen L. "Petworth, Where Friendship Has Aged Well." *Washington Post*, 23 March 1996, E1, 12.
Fehr, Stephen C. "Grant Circle Warily Eyes Going Green." *Washington Post*, 7 March 1992, E1, 14.
Lazarus, Elizabeth. "Petworth Residents Take Pride in Area." *Washington Post*, 9 January 1988, E1.
Proctor, John Clagett. "City Growth as Reflected in Petworth Development." *Washington Star*, 16 April 1944, C4.
———. "Early Georgia Avenue." *Washington Star*, 7 April 1946, C4.

19. Shaw

Fitzpatrick, Michael A. "A Great Agitation for Business: Black Economic Development in Shaw." *Washington History* vol. 2, no. 2 (1990–91): 48–73.
———. "Shaw: Washington's Premier Black Neighborhood." Thesis, University of Virginia, 1989.

O. Parks, Gardens, and Cemeteries

Bushong, William. *Rock Creek Park District of Columbia*. Washington, D.C.: U.S. Department of Interior, 1990.
Greenwood, Ann, and Rae Haas. "Rock Creek Cemetery." Paper presented at the Historical Society of Washington, D.C., 9 November 1991.
Heine, Cornelius W. *A History of National Capital Parks*. Washington, D.C.: U.S. Department of the Interior, 1953.
Higgins, Adrian, and Mick Hales. *The Secret Gardens of Georgetown: Behind the Walls of Washington's Most Historic Neighborhood*. Boston: Little, Brown and Company, 1994.
McAtee, W. L. "A Sketch of the Natural History of the District of Columbia." *Bulletin of the Biological Society of Washington*, no. 1. Wash-

ington, D.C.: Biological Society of Washington, 1918.

P. Performing Arts

1. General Works

Battey, Jean. "With Passionate Clarity." *Dance Magazine* 37, no. 7 (July 1963): 44–48.

Elliott, Laura. "Dancing through Time." *Washingtonian* 30, no. 2 (November 1994): 86–91.

Goldstein, Laura. "The Best-Kept Secret in Washington." *Washington Post Magazine*, 5 December 1993, 16–20, 43.

Gomery, Douglas. "A Movie-Going Capital: Washington, D.C., in the History of Movie Presentation." *Washington History* 9, no. 1 (1997): 4–23.

Harrington, Richard. "Hitting the Historical High Notes." *Washington Post*, 18 February 2000, Weekend, 37–41.

Hunt, Marilyn. "Offstage View: Virginia Johnson as Herself." *Dance Magazine* 64, no. 10 (October 1990): 38–42.

Kliman, Todd. "Performance Anxiety." *Capital Style*, May 1999, 27–29.

Libbey, Ted. *The National Symphony Orchestra*. Washington, D.C.: NSO Book Project, 1995.

Milk, Leslie, and Chuck Conconi. "It's Show Time." *Washingtonian* 33, no. 11 (September 1998): 52–59.

Pressley, Nelson. "D.C. Theater's Uncast Role." *Washington Post*, 3 October 1999, G1, 4–5.

Preston, Katherine K. *Music for Hire: A Study of Professional Musicians in Washington, 1877–1900*. Stuyvesant, N.Y.: Pendragon Press, 1992.

Rosenfeld, Megan. "For Thespians, The Bard of Education." *Washington Post*, 20 January 1999, C1, 8.

2. Theaters

Hinson, Hal. "After Tonight, the Light That Was the Biograph Theatre Goes Dark." *Washington Post*, 29 June 1996, F1.

Horwitz, Jane. "Straining at the Lease." *Washington Post*, 27 April 1999, C5.

"Hundreds, Dead or Injured, Buried under Ruins as Roof of Knickerbocker Theater Collapses." *Washington Post*, 29 January 1922, A1.

Judge, Mark Gauvreau. "In a City of Monuments, No Room for the Howard?" *Washington Post*, 25 April 1999, B3.

Maslon, Laurence. *The Arena Adventure: The First Forty Years*. Washington, D.C.: Applause Theatre Book Publishers, 1990.

Meersman, Roger, and Robert Boyer. "The National Theatre in Washington: Buildings and Audiences, 1835–1972." *Records of the Columbia Historical Society* (1971–72): 190–242.

Proctor, John C. "Old Historic Theaters and Concert Halls." *Washington Star*, 20 December 1931, §7, pp. 6–7.

Wheeler, Linda. "True Reformer Building to Be Renovated." *Washington Post*, 18 October 1999, B2.

Q. Racial and Ethnic Groups

1. African Americans

American Society for Colonizing the Free People of Colour. *Seventh Annual Report of the American Society for Colonizing the Free People of Colour.* Washington, D.C.: Davis and Force, 1824.

Berlin, Ira. *Slaves without Masters: The Free Negro in the Antebellum South.* New York: Pantheon Books, 1974.

Beyan, Amos J. *The American Colonization Society and the Creation of the Liberian State.* Lanham, Md.: University Press of America, 1991.

Borchert, James. *Alley Life in Washington: Family, Community, Religion, and Folklife in the City, 1850–1970.* Urbana: University of Illinois Press, 1980.

Brown, Letitia Woods. *Free Negroes in the District of Columbia, 1790–1846.* New York: Oxford University Press, 1972.

Campbell, Penelope. *Maryland in Africa: The Maryland State Colonization Society, 1831–1857.* Urbana: University of Illinois Press, 1971.

Clark-Lewis, Elizabeth. *Living In, Living Out: African American Domestics in Washington, D.C., 1910–1940.* Washington, D.C.: Smithsonian Institution Press, 1994.

Fitzpatrick, Sandra, and Maria R. Goodwin. *The Guide to Black Washington.* Rev. ed. New York: Hippocrene Books, 1999.

Fox, Early Lee. *The American Colonization Society, 1817–1840.* Baltimore, Md.: Johns Hopkins University Press, 1919.

Fryd, Vivien G. *Art and Empire: The Politics of Ethnicity in the United States Capitol, 1815–1860.* New Haven, Conn.: Yale University Press, 1992.

Gatewood, Willard B. *Aristocrats of Color: The Black Elite, 1880–1920.* Bloomington: Indiana University Press, 1990.

Hayes, Laurence J. W. *The Negro Federal Government Worker: A Study of His Classification Status in the District of Columbia, 1883–1938.*

Washington, D.C.: Howard University, 1941.

Horton, James Oliver. *Free People of Color*. Washington, D.C.: Smithsonian Institution Press, 1993.

———. "Restricted Liberty: Free Blacks in Slaveholding Washington, D. C." Paper delivered at the Historical Society of Washington, D.C., 20 April 1993.

Ingle, Edward. "The Negro in the District of Columbia." In *Johns Hopkins University Studies in History and Political Science*. 11th Series, nos. 3 and 4. Baltimore, Md.: Johns Hopkins University Press, 1893.

Johnson, Ronald M. "Those Who Stayed: Washington Black Writers of the 1920s." *Records of the Columbia Historical Society* 50 (1980): 484–99.

Lemann, Nicholas. *The Promised Land: The Great Black Migration and How It Changed America*. New York: Alfred A. Knopf, 1991.

Lesko, Kathleen M., Valerie Babb, and Carroll R. Gibbs. *Black Georgetown Remembered: A History of Its Black Community*. Washington, D.C.: Georgetown University Press, 1991.

Mintz, Stephen. "Historical Ethnography of Black Washington, D.C." *Records of the Columbia Historical Society* 52 (1989): 235–53.

Provine, Dorothy S. *District of Columbia Free Negro Registers, 1821–1861*. Bowie, Md.: Heritage Books, 1996.

Williams, Melvin R. "Blueprint for Change: The Black Community in Washington, D.C., 1860–1870." *Records of the Columbia Historical Society* 48 (1972): 359–93.

———. "Statistical Study of Blacks in Washington, D.C., in 1860." *Records of the Columbia Historical Society* 50 (1980): 172–79.

2. Hispanic Americans

Boone, Margaret S. *Capital Cubans: Refugee Adaptation in Washington, D.C.* New York: AMS Press, 1989.

Cadaval, Olivia. *Creating a Latino Identity in the Nation's Capital: The Latino Festival*. New York: Garland Publications, 1998.

Constable, Pamela. "Latinos' Dream Changes a Neighborhood." *Washington Post*, 29 May 1995, C1, 9.

Repak, Terry A. *Waiting on Washington: Central American Workers in the Nation's Capital*. Philadelphia: Temple University Press, 1995.

3. Other Ethnic Groups

Altshuler, David, ed. *The Jews of Washington, D.C.: A Communal His-*

tory Anthology. New York: Rossel Books, 1985

Humphrey, Robert Lee. *Ancient Washington: American Indian Cultures of the Potomac Valley.* Washington, D.C.: George Washington University Center for Washington Area Studies, 1977.

Hyslop, Stephen G. "Life in America Four Hundred Years Ago: When Algonquin Culture Ruled Our Region." *Washington Post,* 14 June 1995, H1, 4–5.

Viola, Herman J. *Thomas L. McKenney: Architect of America's Early Indian Policy, 1816–1830.* Chicago: Swallow Press, 1974.

White, Josh. "A New Year's Parade for All." *Washington Post,* 22 February 1999, B3.

Young Chang Chae, ed. *History of Korean-Americans in the Washington Metropolitan Area, 1883–1993.* Washington, D.C.: Korean Association of Greater Washington, 1995.

R. Religious Life

1. General Works

Baker, Gordon Pratt, ed. *Those Incredible Methodists: A History of the Baltimore Conference of the United Methodist Church.* Nashville, Tenn.: Parthenon Press, 1972.

Broadway, Bill. "The District's Holy Land." *Washington Post,* 6 March 1999, B8.

Clarke, Nina Honemond. *History of the Nineteenth-Century Black Churches in Maryland and Washington, D.C.* New York: Vantage Press, 1983.

George, Carol V. R. *Segregated Sabbaths: Richard Allen and the Emergence of Independent Black Churches, 1760–1840.* New York: Oxford University Press, 1973.

Johnson, Lorenzo D. *The Churches and Pastors of Washington, D.C.* New York: M. W. Dodd, 1857.

Mintz, John. "Moon Empire Gets Bang for Its Buck." *Washington Post,* 10 March 1999, A1, 10.

Payton, Jacob Simpson. "Preachers in Politics." *Methodist History* 1, no. 4 (July 1963): 14–26.

Warner, William W. *At Peace with All Their Neighbors: Catholics and Catholicism in the National Capital, 1787–1860.* Washington, D.C.: Georgetown University Press, 1994.

Woodson, Carter G. *The History of the Negro Church.* Washington, D.C.:

Associated Publishers, 1945.

2. Congregation Histories

Abdul-Rauf, Muhammad. *History of the Islamic Center.* Washington, D. C.: Islamic Center, 1978.

Alldredge, Everett O. *Centennial History of First Congregational United Church of Christ, Washington, D.C.* Baltimore, Md.: Port City Press, 1965.

Bayless, John H. "History of the Washington Cathedral." *Records of the Columbia Historical Society* 1948–50 (1952): 181–88.

Calkin, Homer L. *Castings from the Foundry Mold: A History of Foundry Church, Washington, D.C., 1814–1946.* Nashville, Tenn.: Parthenon Press, 1968.

Christian Science in Washington, D.C.: An Historical Sketch. Washington, D.C.: Office of the Christian Science Committee on Publication, 1983.

Cobb, William B. *St. John's Episcopal Church, Georgetown Parish: A Short History.* Washington, D.C.: St. John's Episcopal Church Congregation, 1996.

Donovan, Jane, ed. *Many Witnesses: A History of Dumbarton United Methodist Church, 1772–1990.* Interlaken, N.Y: Heart of the Lakes Publishing, 1998.

Edgington, Frank E. *A History of the New York Avenue Presbyterian Church: One Hundred Fifty-Seven Years, 1803–1961.* Washington, D. C.: New York Avenue Presbyterian Church, 1961.

Endahl, Lowell. *Memorial Evangelical Lutheran Church: The First Century, 1873–1973.* Washington, D.C.: Luther Place Memorial Church, 1973.

Ennis, Robert Brooks. "Christ Church, Washington Parish." *Records of the Columbia Historical Society* 1969–70 (1971): 126–77.

Feller, Richard T. *Completing Washington Cathedral for Thy Great Glory.* Washington, D.C.: Washington Cathedral, 1989.

From Strength to Strength: A History of the Shiloh Baptist Church, 1863–1988. Washington, D.C.: Shiloh Baptist Church, 1989.

Frye, Virginia King. "St. Patrick's: First Catholic Church of the Federal City." *Records of the Columbia Historical Society* 23 (1920): 26–51.

Gatti, Lawrence. *Historic St. Stephen's: An Account of Its Eighty-Five Years, 1867–1952.* Washington, D.C.: n.p., 1952.

Green, Constance McLaughlin. *The Church on Lafayette Square: A His-*

tory of St. John's Church, Washington, D.C., 1815–1970. Washington, D.C.: Potomac Books, 1970.

Harper, John C. A Symbol of a Nation Praying: A Brief History of St. John's Episcopal Church, Lafayette Square, Washington, D.C., 1815–1965. Washington, D.C.: St. John's Episcopal Church, 1965.

Jones, Pauline J. "One Hundred Fortieth Anniversary of St. Augustine's." Washington History 10, no. 2 (1998–99): 66–67.

Kendig, Robert E. The Washington National Cathedral: This Bible in Stone. McLean, Va.: EPM Publications, 1995.

Lumbard, Frances Barbour. The Changing Face of St. John's: Two Hundred Years in Georgetown. Washington, D.C.: St. John's Episcopal Church, 1998.

MacGregor, Morris J. The Emergence of a Black Catholic Community: St. Augustine's in Washington. Washington, D.C.: Catholic University Press of America, 1999.

———. A Parish for the Federal City: St. Patrick's in Washington, 1794–1994. Washington, D.C.: Catholic University Press of America, 1994.

McCartney, Albert Joseph. "The National Presbyterian Church and Its Heritage in Washington." Records of the Columbia Historical Society 1960–62 (1963): 206–23.

Metzdorf, Glenn A. Without Wavering: A Short History of Christ Church, Georgetown. Washington, D.C.: Christ Episcopal Church, 1992.

Mitchell, Pauline Gaskins. "History of Mt. Zion United Methodist Church and Mt. Zion Cemetery." Records of the Columbia Historical Society 51 (1984): 103–18.

Mt. Zion United Methodist Church, Washington, D.C., 1816–1986. Washington, D.C.: Bryant & Bryant, 1986.

Nannes, Caspar Harold. The National Presbyterian Church and Center. Washington, D.C.: Vinmar Lithographing Company, 1970.

New York Avenue Presbyterian Church. The Centennial of the New York Avenue Presbyterian Church, Washington, D.C., 1803–1903. Washington, D.C.: New York Avenue Presbyterian Church, 1904.

Philibert, Helene, et al. Saint Matthew's of Washington, 1840–1940. Baltimore, Md.: A. Hoen, 1940.

Pinkett, Harold T. National Church of Zion Methodism: A History of John Wesley A.M.E. Zion Church, Washington, D.C. Baltimore, Md.: Gateway Press, 1989.

Rabinowitz, Stanley. The Assembly: A Century in the Life of the Adas Israel Hebrew Congregation of Washington, D.C. Hoboken, N.J.: Ktav

Publishing House, 1993.

Schaffter, Dorothy, *The Presbyterian Congregation in George Town, 1780–1970*. Washington, D.C.: Session of the Presbyterian Church in George Town, 1971.

Scrivener, Mary Allen. *History of the Georgetown Evangelical Lutheran Church*. Washington, D.C.: ABA Electric Typed Letters Co., 1955.

Sluby, Paul E., Sr., *Asbury: Our Legacy, Our Faith, 1836–1993*. Washington, D.C.: Asbury United Methodist Church, 1993.

———, ed. *History of Plymouth Congregational Church, United Church of Christ, Washington, D.C.* Washington, D.C.: Plymouth Congregational Church, 1997.

Spaulding, Dorothy W. *Saint Paul's Parish, Washington: One Hundred Years*. Washington, D.C.: St. Paul's Church, 1967.

St. Dominic's Church, Washington, D.C., 1875–1975. Washington, D.C.: St. Dominic's Church, 1975.

Theis, Nancy and Paul Theis. *"Blessed Are They Who Believe . . .": A History of the First Eighty-five Years of St. Thomas Apostle Parish, 1909–1994*. Washington, D.C.: St. Thomas Apostle Parish, 1994.

Trainor, Kathleen. "But the Choir Did Not Sing: How the Civil War Split First Unitarian Church." *Washington History* 7, no. 2 (1996): 54–71.

S. Society in Washington

Abell, George. *Let Them Eat Caviar*. New York: Dodge Publishing Co., 1936.

Andrews, Marietta Minnigerode. *My Studio Window: Sketches of the Pageant of Washington Life*. New York: Dutton, 1928.

Barry, David S. *Forty Years in Washington*. Boston: Little, Brown and Company, 1924.

Dunn, Arthur Wallace. *Gridiron Nights: Humorous and Satirical Views of Politics and Statesmen as Presented by the Famous Dining Club*. New York: Arno Press, 1974.

Hunt, Gaillard, ed. *The First Forty Years of Washington Society in the Family Letters of Margaret Bayard Smith*. New York: Charles Scribner's Sons, 1906.

Jacob, Kathryn Allamong. *Capital Elites: High Society in Washington, D.C., after the Civil War*. Washington, D.C.: Smithsonian Institution Press, 1995.

Keim, De Benneville Randolph. *Society in Washington, Its Noted Men, Accomplished Women, Established Customs, and Notable Events*.

Washington, D.C.: Harrisburg Publishing Company, 1887.

Sands, Francis P. B. *The Founders and Original Organizers of the Metropolitan Club, Washington, D.C.* Washington, D.C.: n.p., 1909.

Washburn, Wilcomb. *The Cosmos Club of Washington: A Centennial History, 1878–1978.* Washington, D.C.: Cosmos Club, 1978.

T. Slavery

Berlin, Ira, and Ronald Hoffman, eds. *Slavery and Freedom in the Age of the American Revolution.* Urbana: University of Illinois Press, for the U.S. Capitol Historical Society, 1986.

Clephane, Walter C. "The Local Aspect of Slavery in the District of Columbia." *Records of the Columbia Historical Society* 3 (1900): 224–56.

Harris, Alfred Garrett. *Slavery and Emancipation in the District of Columbia, 1801–1862.* Ph.D. dissertation, Ohio State University, 1946.

Harrold, Stanley C., Jr. "The *Pearl* Affair: The Washington Riot of 1848." *Records of the Columbia Historical Society* 50 (1980): 140–60.

Mitchell, Mary. "'I Held George Washington's Horse': Compensated Emancipation in the District of Columbia." *Records of the Columbia Historical Society* (1963–65): 221–29.

National Park Service. *Underground Railroad.* Washington, D.C.: National Park Service, 1998.

Wade, Richard C. *Slavery in the Cities: The South, 1820–1860.* New York: Oxford University Press, 1964.

U. Transportation

Alotta, Amy L. *George Washington Never Slept Here: The History of Street Names in Washington, D.C.* Chicago: Bonus Books, 1993.

Bisbort, Alan. "The Draw of Bridges." *Washington Post,* 10 April 1992, Weekend, N8.

Dilts, James D. *The Great Road: The Building of the Baltimore and Ohio, The Nation's First Railroad, 1828–1853.* Stanford, Calif.: Stanford University Press, 1993.

District of Columbia Engineers' Office. *Washington Bridges.* Washington, D.C.: Engineers' Office, 1945.

Emery, Fred A. "Washington's Historic Bridges." *Records of the Columbia Historical Society* (1938): 49–70.

Forgey, Benjamin. "Mover and Shaper; Harry Weese Helped Preserve the Past and Chart the Future." *Washington Post,* 7 November 1998, C1.

Green, Rodney D., and David M. James. *Rail Transit Station Area*

Development: Small Area Modeling in Washington, D.C. Armonk, N.Y.: M. E. Sharpe, 1992.

Hahn, Thomas F. *The Chesapeake and Ohio Canal: Pathway to the Nation's Capital.* Metuchen, N.J.: Scarecrow Press, 1984.

————. *The Chesapeake and Ohio Canal Lock-Houses and Lock-Keepers.* Morgantown, W.Va.: Institute for the History of Technology and Industrial Archaeology, 1996.

High, Mike. *The C&O Canal Companion.* Baltimore, Md.: Johns Hopkins University Press, 1997.

Hungerford, Edward. *The Story of the Baltimore and Ohio Railroad, 1827–1927.* 2 vols. New York: G. P. Putnam's Sons, 1928.

King, LeRoy O. *One Hundred Years of Capital Traction: The Story of Streetcars in the Nation's Capital.* College Park, Md.: Taylor Publishing Company, 1972.

Sanderlin, Walter S. *The Great National Project: A History of the Chesapeake and Ohio Canal.* Baltimore, Md.: Johns Hopkins University Press, 1946.

Spratt, Zack. "Rock Creek's Bridges." *Records of the Columbia Historical Society* (1953): 101–34.

V. War Years in Washington

1. War of 1812

Arnold, James Riehl. "The Battle of Bladensburg." *Records of the Columbia Historical Society* 37–38 (1937): 145–68.

Cassell, Frank A. "Slaves of the Chesapeake Bay Area and the War of 1812." *Journal of Negro History* 57, no. 2 (April 1972): 144–55.

Daily National Intelligencer, 22, 30, 31 August 1814.

Dudley, William. "The War of 1812: British Attacks on Washington and Alexandria in 1814." Paper delivered at Dumbarton House, Washington, D.C., 23 February 1994.

Ewell, James. "Unwelcome Visitors to Early Washington." *Records of the Columbia Historical Society* 1 (1895): 55–88.

Hickey, Donald R. *The War of 1812: A Forgotten Conflict.* Urbana: University of Illinois Press, 1989.

Lloyd, Alan. *The Scorching of Washington.* Washington, D.C.: Robert B. Luce Company, 1975.

Mahon, John K. *The War of 1812.* 1972. Reprint. New York: Da Capo Press, 1991.

Marine, William M. *The British Invasion of Maryland, 1812–1815.* 1913. Reprint. Baltimore, Md.: Genealogical Publishing Company, 1977.

Pitch, Anthony S. *The Burning of Washington: The British Invasion of 1814.* Annapolis, Md.: Naval Institute Press, 1998.

Tucker, Glenn. *Poltroons and Patriots: A Popular Account of the War of 1812.* 2 vols. Indianapolis, Ind.: Bobbs-Merrill, 1954.

Whitehorne, Joseph. *While Washington Burned.* Baltimore, Md.: Nautical & Aviation Publishing Company of America, 1992.

2. Civil War

Babington, Charles. "Early's Rebel Raid." *Washington Post,* 14 July 1992, B1, 5.

Billings, Eldon E. "Military Activities in Washington in 1861." *Records of the Columbia Historical Society* (1960–62): 123–33.

Brown, Clarence E. "Walt Whitman and Lincoln." *Journal of the Illinois State Historical Society* 47 (Summer 1954): 176–84.

Clark-Lewis, Elizabeth. *First Freed: Washington in the Emancipation Era.* Washington, D.C.: A.P. Foundation Press, 1998.

Conrad, Thomas Nelson. *A Confederate Spy.* New York: J. S. Ogilvie Publishing Company, 1892.

Cooling, Benjamin Franklin, III. "Defending Washington during the Civil War." *Records of the Columbia Historical Society* (1971–72): 314–37.

———. *Jubal Early's Raid on Washington in 1864.* Baltimore, Md.: Nautical and Aviation Publishing Company of America, 1989.

———. *Mr. Lincoln's Forts: A Guide to the Civil War Defenses of Washington.* Shippensburg, Pa.: White Mane Publishing Company, 1988.

Forman, Stephen M. *A Guide to Civil War Washington.* Washington, D.C.: Elliott & Clark, 1995.

Judge, Joseph, et al. *Season of Fire: The Confederate Strike on Washington.* Berryville, Va.: Rockbridge Publishing Company, 1997.

Kimmel, Stanley Preston. *Mr. Lincoln's Washington.* New York: Coward-McCann, 1957.

Lee, Richard M. *Mr. Lincoln's City: An Illustrated Guide to the Civil War Sites of Washington.* McLean, Va.: EPM Publications, 1984.

Leech, Margaret. *Reveille in Washington, 1860–1865.* Alexandria, Va.: Time-Life Books, 1991.

McClure, Stanley W. *The Defense of Washington, 1861–1865.* Washington, D.C.: U.S. Office of National Capital Parks, 1957.

Murray, Martin G. "Traveling with the Wounded: Walt Whitman and

Washington's Civil War Hospitals." *Washington History* 8, no. 2 (1996–97): 58–73.

Vandiver, Frank Everson. *Jubal's Raid: General Early's Famous Attack on Washington in 1864*. Lincoln: University of Nebraska Press, 1992.

Whitman, Walt. *The Wound Dresser: Letters Written to His Mother from the Hospitals in Washington during the Civil War*. Edited Richard M. Bucke. New York: Bodley Press, 1949.

Whyte, James H. "Divided Loyalties in Washington during the Civil War." *Records of the Columbia Historical Society* (1960–62): 103–21.

Wills, Mary Alice. *The Confederate Blockade of Washington, D.C., 1861–1862*. Shippensburg, Pa.: Burd Street Press, 1998.

3. World War II

Brinkley, David. *Washington Goes to War*. New York: Alfred A. Knopf, 1988.

W. Women

Duncan, Jacci, and Lynn Page Whittaker. *The Women's History Guide to Washington*. Alexandria, Va.: Charles River Press, 1998.

Graham, Sarah Hunter. *Woman Suffrage and the New Democracy*. New Haven, Conn.: Yale University Press, 1996.

History of the League of Women Voters of the District of Columbia. Washington, D.C.: n.p., 1960.

Moldow, Gloria. *Women Doctors in Gilded-Age Washington: Race, Gender, and Professionalization*. Urbana: University of Illinois Press, 1987.

U.S. Senate Committee on the District of Columbia. *Women's Suffrage and the Police: Three Senate Documents*. New York: Arno Press and the *New York Times*, 1971.

Walker, Anne. "Should the President of the United States and Congress Legally Restore the Medal of Honor to the Only Woman Recipient?" *Alert Science/Medical Weekly*, 16 June 1973, 1–7.

Washington League of Women Voters. *Washington D.C.: A Tale of Two Cities*. Washington, D.C.: Washington League of Women Voters, 1962.

Weatherford, Doris. *A History of the American Suffragist Movement*. Santa Barbara, Calif.: ABC/CLIO, 1998.

Appendix 1: Washington, D.C., at a Glance

Population

1999	519,000
1990	606,900
Change	-14.5%

Population by Race—1999

White	35.2%
Black	61.4%
American Indian	0.3%
Asian and Pacific Islander	3.1%
Hispanic	7.4%

Population by Age—1999

0–17 (Youth)	18.4%
18–44	44.2%
45–64	23.5%
65 and over (Seniors)	13.9%
Median Age	37.6

Income

Median Household Income —1998	$43,011
Poverty Rate (1997–1999 average)	19.7%

Education

High School or Higher	82.3%
Bachelor's Degree or Higher	37.4%

Housing

Housing Units—1998	264,831

Households—1998	224,548
Persons per Household—1998	2.15
Homeownership Rate (1997–1999 average)	40.9%
Median Value of Single-Family Unit—1998	$150,060
Sales (Single-family, Condos, Co-ops)—1999	13,800
Vacant for Rent (1997–1999 average)	12.6%
Vacant for Sale (1997–1999 average)	3.3%

Housing Units Authorized by Permit—1999

Single-Family	528
Units in Multi-unit Structures	335

Employment—August 2000

Wage and Salary Employees	623,000
Private Sector	393,700
Federal Government	183,800
Local Government	45,500
Residential Unemployment Rate	5.4%
High-Tech Jobs in Private Sector—1997	37,522
Rank among 114 Cities	15

Business Establishments—1998

Total	19,571
Utilities	36
Construction	316
Manufacturing	183
Wholesale Trade	372
Retail Trade	2,011
Transportation & Warehousing	218
Information	649
Finance & Insurance	937
Real Estate, Rental, & Leasing	937
Professional, Scientific, Technical Services	4,134
Educational Services	398
Health Care & Social Services	2,069
Arts, Entertainment, Recreation	243
Accommodation & Food Services	1,682

Other Services	5,028
Other	358

Commercial Construction Starts—1999 (sq ft)

Retail	150,242
Office	2,424,274
Educational & Medical	94,292
Research & Development	0
Mixed Use	1,100,000
Hotel/Motel	367,000
Other	134,681

Private Office Space—2nd Quarter 2000

Total Existing Space (sq ft)	95,587,124
Available Vacant (sq ft)	4,335,871
Vacancy Rate	4.5%
Rental Rate Range Class A	$40.71
Rental Rate Range Class B	$33.12

Conventions/Meetings at Convention Center and Area Hotels)—1999	1,411
Tourists/Visitors (Metro Area)—1999	20,900,000

Source: D.C. Office of Planning/State Data Center

Appendix 2: Washington History Collections

D.C. Archives
1300 Naylor Ct. NW
Washington, D.C. 20001
(202) 727-2054
http://os.dc.gov/archives/services/
index.shtm

George Washington University
Melvin Gelman Library
William Lloyd Wright Collection
2130 H St. NW
Washington, D.C. 20052
(202) 994-6455
http://www.gwu.edu/gelman/spec/
collections/

Georgetown Public Library
Peabody Room
Wisconsin Ave. and R St. NW
Washington, D.C. 20007
(202) 282-0220

Georgetown University
Lauinger Memorial Library
Special Collections
37th and O Sts. NW
Washington, D.C. 20057
(202) 687-7444

Historical Society of Washington, D.C.
1307 New Hampshire Ave. NW
Washington, D.C. 20036
(202) 785-2068
http://www.hswdc.org/

Howard University
Moorland-Spingarn Research
    Center Library
500 Howard Pl. NW
Washington, D.C. 20059
(202) 806-4237
http://www.founders.howard.edu/
    moorland-spingarn/

Library of Congress
10 First St. SE
Washington, D.C. 20540
(202) 707-5537
http://www.loc.gov/

Martin Luther King, Jr., Memorial
    Library
Washingtoniana Division
901 G St. NW
Washington, D.C. 20001
(202) 727-0321
http://www.dclibrary.org/
    washingtoniana/

Appendix 3: Calendar of Annual Events

January

Biennial Exhibition of Contemporary American Art, Corcoran Gallery
of Art (January or February every odd year)
Congress convenes, Capitol (first Tuesday)
Martin Luther King, Jr.'s Birthday (mid-January)
Chinese New Year Festival, Chinatown (late January)

February

Chinese New Year Festival, Chinatown (late January or early to mid-
February)
Abraham Lincoln's Birthday, Lincoln Memorial (February 12)
George Washington's Birthday, George Washington University campus

March

Georgetown Garden Tour
U.S. Army Band Anniversary Concert, Kennedy Center (early March)
St. Patrick's Day Parade, Constitution Avenue NW (mid-March)
U.S. Botanic Gardens Spring Flower Show (late March)
Easter Egg Roll, White House (Easter Monday)
Smithsonian Kite Festival, Mall (late March or early April)

April

Imagination Celebration, Kennedy Center
Cherry Blossom Festival, Tidal Basin (late March or early April)
Spring Flower Show, U.S. Botanic Garden
Thomas Jefferson's Birthday, Jefferson Memorial (April 13)
American College Theater Festival, Kennedy Center (mid-April)
Filmfest D.C., various theaters (mid-April)
Spring Garden Tours, White House (mid-April, two days only)
Duke Ellington Birthday Celebration (April 20)
Shakespeare's Birthday, Folger Shakespeare Library (April 23)

Georgetown House Tour, Georgetown (late April)

George Washington Parkway Classic, George Washington Memorial Parkway (late April)

Smithsonian Institution's Spring Celebration (late April)

Public tours of embassies and Georgetown houses (late April or early May)

May

Artists at work—mimes, musicians, and dancers perform along the Mall (Saturdays and Sundays all summer)

Folk and pop music concerts, C&O Canal at 30th and Jefferson Street NW (every other Sunday afternoon all summer)

Concerts and parades by the Army, Air Force, Navy, and Marine bands (mid-May through mid-August)

Asian Pacific American Heritage Festival (first weekend in May)

Washington Cathedral Flower Mart and Fair (first weekend in May)

Georgetown Garden Tour (early May)

Gross National Parade, Georgetown (early May)

Capitol Hill Restoration Society House Tour (Mother's Day)

Cherry Blossom Rugby Tournament, Mall (mid-May)

Goodwill Embassy Tour, Embassy Row (mid-May)

U.S. Marine Corps Sunset Parades, 8th and I Streets SW (mid-May)

Kemper Open Pro-Am Golf Tournament, area golf courses (late May)

Memorial Day Ceremony, Vietnam Veterans Memorial (Memorial Day)

Memorial Day Weekend Concert, Capitol West Lawn (late May)

June

Summer Terrace Show, U.S. Botanic Garden (June through August)

International Arts Fair, throughout city (first weekend in June)

Dupont-Kalorama Museum Walk Day, Dupont-Kalorama neighborhood (early June)

Gay and Lesbian Pride Festival, Freedom Plaza (early June)

Smithsonian Children's Day (mid-June)

Smithsonian Boomerang Festival, Washington Monument grounds (mid-June)

Caribbean Carnival Extravaganza, Georgia Avenue (late June)

Smithsonian Festival of American Folklife, Mall (late June and early July)

July

Twilight Tattoo Pageant, Army band, Ellipse (July and August)
D.C. Jazz Festival, Freedom Plaza (early July)
Independence Day Celebration, Downtown, Capitol, Mall (July 4)
Bastille Day Waiters' Race, 20th Street and Pennsylvania Avenue (July 14)
Legg Mason Tennis Classic, Rock Creek Tennis Stadium, 16th and Kennedy Street NW (mid-July)
Latin-American Festival, Adams Morgan and Mall (late July)

August

Redskins football exhibition season begins (early August)
U.S. Army Band, "1812 Overture," Ellipse (mid-August)
Georgia Avenue Day, Georgia and Eastern Avenues NW (late August)
Shakespeare Theatre Free for All, Carter Barron Amphitheatre in Rock Creek Park (mid-August through early September)

September

Labor Day Weekend Concert, Capitol West Lawn (first Sunday)
Black Family Reunion, Mall (early September)
D.C. Blues Festival, Carter Barron Amphitheatre in Rock Creek Park (early September, 3 days)
Kennedy Center Open House (early September, weekend)
National Frisbee Festival, Washington Monument (early September)
Adams Morgan Day, Adams Morgan, Columbia Road and 18th Street NW (mid-September)
Constitution Day Commemoration, National Archives (September 17)
Rock Creek Park Day, Rock Creek Park (late September)
Washington Cathedral Open House (late September)

October

Opening of Supreme Court (first Monday)
U.S. Navy Band Birthday Concert, Constitution Hall (early October)
Fall Garden Tours, White House (mid-October, 2 days)
Columbus Day Ceremonies, Columbus Memorial Plaza (mid-October)
Taste of D.C. Festival, Freedom Plaza
Theodore Roosevelt's Birthday Celebration, Theodore Roosevelt Island
Halloween Street Parade, Dupont Circle (high-heel "drag" race) 17th and P Streets NW (late October)

November

Marine Corps Marathon, through the city (early November)
Veterans Day Ceremony, Vietnam Veterans Memorial (November 11)
Christmas Craft Fairs, numerous locations around city (late November and December)

December

Christmas Poinsettia Show, U.S. Botanic Garden
Woodlawn Plantation Christmas (early December)
National Christmas Tree Lighting, Ellipse (early December)
Nutcracker ballet, Kennedy Center (early through mid-December)
Pageant of Peace, Ellipse and Mall (mid-December through January 1)
Washington National Cathedral Christmas Celebration (late December)
Christmas Candlelight Tours, White House (late December)

Appendix 4: Mayors, Governors, and Founding Commissioners

Georgetown Commissioners, 1751

Henry Wright Crabb
John Needham
John Cleggett
James Parris
Samuel Magruder III
Josias Beale
David Lynn

These were succeeded by:

John Murdock
Richard Thompson
William Deakins
Thomas Richardson
Charles Beatty

Mayors of Georgetown

Robert Peter	January 1790–January 1791
Thomas Beale	January 1791–January 1792
Uriah Forrest	January 1792–January 1793
John Threlkeld	January 1793–January 1794
Peter Casenave	January 1794–January 1795
Thomas Turner	January 1795–January 1796
Daniel Reintzel	January 1796–January 1797
Lloyd Beall	January 1797–October 1799
Daniel Reintzel	October 1799–January 1805
Thomas Corcoran	January 1805–January 1806
Daniel Reintzel	January 1806–January 1808
Thomas Corcoran	January 1808–January 1811
David Wiley	January 1811–January 1812
Thomas Corcoran	January 1812–January 1813

John Peter	January 1813–January 1819
Henry Foxall	January 1819–January 1821
John Peter	January 1821–January 1823
John Cox	January 1823–March 1845
Henry Addison	March 1845–March 1857
Richard R. Crawford	March 1857–March 1861
Henry Addison	March 1861–March 1867
Charles D. Welch	March 1867–March 1869
Henry M. Sweeney	March 1869–May 1871

Washington Commissioners, 1791–1802

Thomas Johnson	January 1791–August 1794
David Stuart	January 1791–September 1794
Daniel Carroll	March 1791–May 1795

These were succeeded by:

Gustavus Scott	August 1794–December 1800
William Thornton	September 1794–July 1802
Alexander White	May 1795–July 1802

These filled Scott's seat:

| William Cranch | January 1801–March 1801 |
| Tristram Dalton | March 1801– July 1802 |

Governors of D.C., 1871–1874

| Henry D. Cook | February 1871–September 1873 |
| Alexander R. Shepherd | September 1873–June 1874 |

(D.C. loses self–government; governed by federally appointed commissioners, 1874–1974)

Mayors of Washington

Robert Brent	June 1802–May 1812
Daniel Rapine	June 1812–June 1813
James H. Blake	June 1813–June 1817
Benjamin G. Orr	June 1817–June 1819
Samuel N. Smallwood	June 1819–June 1822
Thomas Carbery	June 1822–June 1824
Samuel N. Smallwood	June 1824–September 1824

Roger C. Weightman	October 1824–July 1827
Joseph Gales, Jr.	July 1827–June 1830
John P. Van Ness	June 1830–June 1834
William A. Bradley	June 1834–June 1836
Peter Force	June 1836–June 1840
William W. Seaton	June 1840–June 1850
Walter Lenox	June 1850–June 1852
John W. Maury	June 1852–June 1854
John Thomas Towers	June 1854–June 1856
William B. Magruder	June 1856–June 1858
James G. Berret	June 1858–August 1861
Richard Wallach	August 1861–June 1868
Sayles Jenks Bowen	June 1868–June 1870
Matthew Gault Emery	June 1870–June 1871
Walter Washington	1975–1979
Marion Barry	1979–1991
Sharon Pratt Kelly	1991–1995
Marion Barry	1995–1999
Anthony Williams	1999–

About the Authors

ROBERT BENEDETTO (B.A., San Francisco State University; M.A., Pittsburgh Theological Seminary; M.L.S., University of Hawaii) was until recently associate librarian and associate professor of bibliography at Union Theological Seminary and Presbyterian School of Christian Education in Virginia. He is a contributor to the multivolume *Virginia Dictionary of Biography* (1998–) published by the Library of Virginia, and has written on aspects of Virginia history and life. He is director of special collections at the library of Princeton Theological Seminary.

JANE DONOVAN (B.A., West Virginia University) is a freelance writer. She is the author of five books, and her articles and photography have appeared in the *Washington Post, Georgetown Courier, Virginia Heritage*, and other publications. Her book, *Many Witnesses* (1998), a history of Methodism in Georgetown, was funded by the D.C. Community Humanities Council and received the Council's Voice of the City Award. A longtime resident of Washington, D.C., she is the past president of the William Watters Foundation and serves on the board of directors of the United Methodist Commission on Archives and History.

KATHLEEN DUVALL (B.A., The College of William and Mary) is a writer and editor who currently works as a freelance copyeditor for several academic publishing houses. She lives in Richmond, Virginia.